Keywords for Children's Literature

 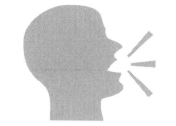

Keywords for Children's Literature

Edited by Philip Nel and Lissa Paul

NEW YORK UNIVERSITY PRESS
New York *and* London

NEW YORK UNIVERSITY PRESS
New York and London
www.nyupress.org

© 2011 by New York University
All rights reserved

Library of Congress Cataloging-in-Publication Data
Keywords for children's literature / edited by Philip Nel and Lissa Paul.
p. cm. Includes bibliographical references.
ISBN 978 – 0 – 8147 – 5854 – 0 (cloth : alk. paper)
ISBN 978 – 0 – 8147 – 5855 – 7 (pbk. : alk. paper)
ISBN 978 – 0 – 8147 – 5889 – 2 (e-book)
1. Children's literature — History and criticism — Terminology.
I. Nel, Philip, 1969 – II. Paul, Lissa.
PN1009.A1K48 2011
809'.89282014 — dc22   2010052514

New York University Press books are printed on acid-free paper,
and their binding materials are chosen for strength and durability.
We strive to use environmentally responsible suppliers and materials
to the greatest extent possible in publishing our books.

Manufactured in the United States of America

C 10 9 8 7 6 5 4 3 2 1
P 10 9 8 7 6 5 4 3 2 1

Contents

Acknowledgments

For their work on and advocacy for this book, our thanks to Eric Zinner, Ciara McLaughlin, and Despina P. Gimbel at New York University Press. For providing a model for *Keywords for Children's Literature*, thanks to Bruce Burgett and Glenn Hendler, editors of *Keywords for American Cultural Studies*, and Tony Bennett, Lawrence Grossberg, and Meaghan Morris, editors of *New Keywords*. Extra thanks are due to Hendler, whose presentation at the 2007 *Futures of American Studies Institute* inspired this project.

Thanks to our agent, George Nicholson, for his support and guidance, and to George's assistant, Erica Silverman, for hers.

We are grateful to Rachel Parkin for her meticulous work, tidying up formatting, compiling the Works Cited section, and assembling final queries for each contributor. Thanks to Jon Eben Field for indexing. For helping us evaluate cover designs, thanks to Stephen T. Johnson, Mark Newgarden, and Megan Montague Cash. We also thank the anonymous external readers for their thoughts and suggestions.

For lending a spouse to the cause, thanks to Karin and Geoff.

Last, but very definitely most, our thanks to the contributors for their expertise, insights, generosity, and willingness to attend to our editorial comments. Writing expository theory—which is what each of these essays represents—requires an agility of both mind and word. It is challenging to balance etymological and critical genealogies, literary and cultural histories, and representative examples from different countries and traditions, and to do all of this in a concise, clear essay.

Introduction   Philip Nel *and* Lissa Paul

Since about 1970, scholarship in children's literature has brought together people from the fields of literature, education, library and information science, cultural studies, and media studies. "Children's literature" itself has become a kind of umbrella term encompassing a wide range of disciplines, genres, and media. One of the challenges of children's literature studies is that scholars from disparate disciplines use the same terms in different ways. As a result, meanings can be blurred and cross-disciplinary conversations confused. Drawing on the expertise of scholars in many fields, *Keywords for Children's Literature* responds to the need for a shared vocabulary by mapping the history of key terms and explaining how they came to be used in conflicted ways.

As Beverly Lyon Clark points out in *Kiddie Lit: The Cultural Construction of Children's Literature in America* (2003), the (often male) "professoriate" in English literature departments treated librarians "more as handmaidens than as fellow scholars." Academics working in education and schoolteachers working with children were regarded with equal suspicion. Yet viable critical vocabularies—including words and phrases such as "postmodern," "censorship," "reading," "liminality," and "young adult"—were being put into use in several disciplines. Separate vocabularies were also developing in other fields that intersect with children's literature, including American studies (from the 1950s on), cultural studies (from the 1960s on), and African-American studies and women's studies (from the 1970s on). The canon-expanding efforts of both cultural studies and feminism were especially influential in bringing terms such as "modernism," "gender," "ideology," and "body" into scholarly conversations about children's literature and culture.

In *Keywords for Children's Literature,* we consciously sought scholars from many disciplines and encouraged them, all experts in their own fields, to move into often-unfamiliar territory and explore their words in other disciplinary contexts. As with all evolving things, individual keywords enter the lexicon and slip away, and we have encouraged authors to follow the growth patterns of their words. In the spirit of Raymond Williams's original *Keywords* (1976/1983a), our book is a snapshot of a vocabulary that is changing, expanding, and ever unfinished.

"Keywords" itself is a case in point. Its definition depends on the discipline. For librarians, a "keyword" is a search term that identifies the main content of a document. For educators, it means a high-frequency word. In 1964, Ladybird Books in England launched the "Key Words Reading Scheme" book series, based on the premise that just twelve words make up 25 percent of the words we speak. The books, say the editors, introduce children "to the most commonly used words in the English language (Key Words), plus additional words necessary to tell the story." (Forty years later, the Key Words reading series is still in print and

[1]

has sold over 90 million copies.) Raymond Williams, we suspect, might be horrified to learn that words are more important than story; on the other hand, he might be jealous of the sales figures. *Keywords for Children's Literature* follows in the spirit of Williams's influential *Keywords*, in offering "an exploration of the vocabulary of a crucial area of social and cultural discussion." Through an inspired adaptation of the term "keywords," Williams unlocked discussions of society and culture that have endured into the twenty-first century, even as the words and their definitions have shifted.

Bruce Burgett and Glenn Hendler tracked shifting interpretations in the context of a particular field in their edited collection *Keywords for American Cultural Studies* (2007), a volume in tune with our general ideas. We adapted their format to our purposes, inviting a range of scholars—all with disciplinary stakes in the field—to write about a particular keyword for the study of children's literature and culture. We asked them to address specific questions about the kinds of critical projects enabled by their keyword, the critical genealogies of the term, the ways of thinking that are occluded or obstructed by its use, and the ways other potential keywords constellate around it. We invited attention to the ways individual terms came into common use, the ways those uses vary over time and place, and the ways terms are contested and/or conflicted. The forty-nine entries in this book vary in their emphases, but each maps meanings vital for those who read, teach, and study literature for children.

We say "maps meanings" because the goal of *Keywords for Children's Literature* is not to fix meanings in place, but rather to delineate tentative boundaries of a shifting conversation. In this sense, our book's aims depart from those of Göte Klingberg, who in 1970 began an ultimately unfinished "Nomenklatur-Project" in order to develop a common vocabulary for children's literature scholars of different languages (Müller 2009). Although they are used as translations of one another, the German "Märchen" (little story), the English "fairy tale" (translation of the French "conte de fées," thus "a story told by the fairies"), the Danish "Eventyr" (adventure), and the Swedish "saga" (something told) are quite different: Klingberg hoped to "introduce genre concepts which can be strictly defined" (Klingberg 2008). This is not the aim of *Keywords for Children's Literature*—and it also explains why terms such as "nursery rhymes," "fairy tales," "chapter books," "alphabet books," and "poetry" are not included. Although some genre concepts are keywords, these have not fostered the necessary degree of critical debate. As Williams said of his project, we say of ours: it is "not a dictionary or glossary," nor is it "a series of footnotes to dictionary histories." Instead, it is "the record of an inquiry into a vocabulary"—in this case, a vocabulary about children and children's literature. As Burgett and Hendler say of their volume, our *Keywords for Children's Literature* is not intended to be the last word on the subject; rather, our hope is that the book will be generative, launching scholars (whether beginning or advanced) on to new fields of inquiry.

Although we have listed the words in alphabetical order, we encourage readers *not* to start at the first entry and read through to the last. Instead, each reader should follow the associations suggested by each keyword. "Innocence" might guide you to "Audience," a word that may steer you to "Young Adult," "Crossover Literature," or "Multicultural." "Home" may inspire a look at "Domestic," which might entice you to read "Girlhood," and on to "Tomboy." And so on. To read *Keywords for Children's Literature*, pick a word and follow the signifying chain wherever it leads you.

Many of the keywords come from disciplines unmarked as either "children's" or "literature." With the growth of children's literature scholarship beginning around the last quarter of the twentieth century, fields with particular vested interests—including education, literature, and library sciences—began to develop their own specialized vocabularies. As each discipline settled within its own comfort zone, it began to treat outsiders with suspicion. Classroom teachers regarded literary critics, with their focus on analysis and theory, as being disconnected from real children reading real books. Librarians, with interests broadly including access to books, classification systems, and bibliographic histories, were often critical of what they saw as the narrowly defined expectations of classroom teachers.

We have chosen words we think crucial to the study of children's literature and culture. Readers will likely have alternate lists of words that are important and that they have observed being used in, as Williams

says, "interesting or difficult ways." That last criterion is particularly important and explains, for example, why "Latino/a" is included but "Native American" is not. Both are vital identity categories that inform the production of and responses to literature for children and adolescents. However, in the field of children's literature, a richer and more complex critical discourse has developed around "Latino/a": as Phillip Serrato explains in his essay, there is debate about the term's meaning, and it gets used in conflicting ways. The degree and complexity of conversation enveloping the term "Latino/a" has not yet happened with "Native American." However, this is a relatively new and burgeoning field. Were we to undertake a revised *Keywords for Children's Literature*, the conversations may by that point have elevated the term to "keyword" status.

On a few rare occasions, a word we had hoped to include (notably, "Agency," "Family," and "Genre") either did not find someone willing to undertake it or the formerly willing volunteer found it necessary to withdraw from the project. All other choices reflect our judgment of which words were a vital part of the conversation. In a few cases, experts suggested words that we had not considered—Philip Pullman ("Intention") and Michelle Abate ("Tomboy"), to name two.

It is the nature of a book such as ours to engender further debate and conversation. As Williams was, we too are "exceptionally conscious of how much further work and thinking needs to be done," and we follow his lead in adding that much of it "can only be done through discussion," for which his book and ours are "in part specifically intended." We too welcome "amendment, correction, and additions." *Keywords for Children's Literature* strives not to resolve all critical questions about children's literature, but to draw a provisional map. We hope it will inspire you to continue the conversation.

I

Aesthetics

Joseph T. Thomas, Jr.

There is perhaps no more vexing, fraught, and neglected concept in the study of children's literature than *aesthetics*. No doubt the neglect of a serious, theoretical inquiry into the aesthetics of children's literature stems from our contemporary understandings of the discipline of children's literature itself. The study of children's literature has, historically, been the work of librarians and educators of children. Children's literature came to be seen as an appropriate site of purely literary study only after the rise and fall of mid-twentieth century New Critical and formalist modes of criticism, a state of affairs made possible by the inchoate canon-busting/expanding cultural studies movements of the late 1960s and 1970s. Thus, the discipline of children's literature was shaped in a theoretical milieu suspicious of objective claims of aesthetic value, suspicious even of the unproblematic category of "literature" itself. Occupying itself, therefore, with ideological criticism, the discipline has largely—but not entirely—elided the tricky issue of aesthetics and the ideological roots of the same.

The word "aesthetics" first appeared, in its Latinate form, in Alexander Baumgarten's *Aesthetica* (1750–58). Baumgarten, as Raymond Williams reminds us, uses the term to describe "beauty as a phenomenal perfection" (Williams 1983a). Immanuel Kant complicates and extends Baumgarten's insights in his *A Critique of Judgment* (*Kritik der Urteilskraft*; 1790), providing a role for the intellect in the apprehension of aesthetic value. Whereas Baumgarten suggests that the aesthetic affects us solely through the senses, in Kant's view, the beautiful encourages *intellectual* contemplation. Kant also famously links beauty to taste, a concatenation that marks the aesthetic as both subjective *and* universal. He writes, "*Taste* is the ability to judge an object, or a way of presenting it, by means of a liking or disliking *devoid of all interest*. The object of such a liking is called *beautiful*." He continues, "[I]f someone likes something and is conscious that he himself does so without any interest, then he cannot help judging that it must contain a basis for being liked [that holds] for everyone." Taste, then, is the ability to discern what is and what is not beautiful, and it rests, for Kant, on *common sense*, a sense that, curiously, is anything but common. *Common sense* in the Kantian formulation is reserved for the educated elite, for there is a correct and incorrect apprehension of beauty, a quality that, Kant maintains, inheres in objects themselves. Some artifacts are beautiful and some are not. To distinguish between what is "agreeable to *me*" and that which is *beautiful*, one must cultivate *taste*. Thus, according to Kant (1987), one with taste may rightly reproach those who "judge differently."

Following Jacques Derrida's deconstruction of Kantian aesthetics in *Truth and Painting* (*La Vérité en peinture*; 1978), Amelia Jones (2002) notes, "This dual gesture, which affirms universality even as it admits particularity, structures the aesthetic in its dominant forms of articulation within Western art discourse." Kant's logic is seductive, especially when applied to children, and it no doubt informs ideological commonplaces such as the teleological notion that children have not yet developed *taste*. This lack of developed taste explains why their tastes are often not in concert with those of cultured adults. Adults *know* that Chris Van Allsburg's intricate pencil drawings are beautiful, whereas children may similarly (but "wrongly") apprehend the new Dora the Explorer sticker book as beautiful (in Kantian terms, we might grant that the former is "beautiful," whereas the latter would simply be "agreeable" to some, i.e., children). As Terry Eagleton (1990) explains, Kant's conception of aesthetic judgment works like ideology, for it is "essentially a form of altruism," a way of bracketing one's "own contingent aversions and appetencies" and putting oneself in the place of everyone else, judging the artifact "from the standpoint of a universal subjectivity." This altruism, like ideology itself, "promotes an inward, unconstrained unity between citizens on the basis of their most intimate subjectivity." Yet this unity is not simply feigned or adopted in order to be altruistic; rather, the viewer *knows* what is beautiful and what is not, just as one *knows* what is right and what is wrong. As Eagleton writes, "[T]he essence of aesthetic judgments [is] that they cannot be compelled." However, they can, like ideology, be learned. Consider the child who responds positively to Randall Jarrell and Maurice Sendak's *The Bat-Poet* (1964), a work *designed* to look sophisticated,

with its delicate black-and-white illustrations, fairy tale beginning, subtle humor, and finely crafted poetry. It is crafted to appeal to youngsters attuned to the prevailing adult view of aesthetic value. *The Bat-Poet* asserts itself as an *objet d'art* standing in contrast with, say, Sheila Sweeny Higginson's early reader *Mickey Mouse Clubhouse: Are We There Yet?* (2007).

The construction of such aesthetic hierarchies generally runs contrary to the study of children's literature, which, as a discipline, tends to focus on the ideological, social, and thematic implications of childhood texts rather than their aesthetic value. For instance, in "Perspective, Memory, and Moral Authority: The Legacy of Jane Austen in J. K. Rowling's *Harry Potter*," Karin E. Westman (2007b) compares the Harry Potter novels favorably to Jane Austen's. While convincing, Westman's comparison is largely limited to *thematic* issues. Austen is well regarded for her beautiful and innovative prose, her elegance of expression, and yet Rowling's much-maligned prose style never emerges as a point of comparison in Westman's essay. Westman has little to say about the *Potter* novels as aesthetic works, and never explicitly makes aesthetic comparisons. Of course, such comparisons can be made; Philip Nel gestures toward them in "Is There a Text in This Advertising Campaign? Literature, Marketing, and Harry Potter" (2005). Nevertheless, this sort of aesthetic inquiry is still rather rare in the scholarly discourse surrounding children's literature, especially when one looks for sustained studies with aesthetic questions at their heart.

The tendency in the discipline of children's literature to avoid aesthetics can also be traced to traditional aesthetics' rather limited focus—its inclination to concern itself with "fine art" to the exclusion of the "popular," those agreeable arts designed to entertain. Children's literature, a popular art, is what philosophers call a "heteronomous" rather than "autonomous" endeavor. For Lambert Zuidervaart (1991), heteronomous art—unlike autonomous art—is not adequately "independent from other institutions of bourgeois society." Heteronomous art is, therefore, that which is "produced and received to accomplish purposes that are directly served by other institutions." As examples, he includes "everything from liturgical dance to tribal masks, from advertising jingles to commercial movies." To this list we might add children's literature.

Although *The Bat-Poet* appears to be an *objet d'art*, in the eyes of most aestheticians it would fall among the entertaining "agreeable arts," for it is a heteronomous text lashed to the publishing industry, just as it "accomplishes purposes . . . directly served by other institutions" by serving the educational sphere as a primer on poetical craft. Thus, while Jerry Griswold (2002) urges scholars of children's literature to keep in mind the distinction between "children's literature" and "children's reading," he is nonetheless aware that all children's literature is deeply enmeshed in the market. It is all a matter of degree, from the grossly commercial (texts shaped explicitly to appeal to a given market, such as *Are We There Yet?*); to the less commercial (texts shaped a bit more autonomously, like *The Bat-Poet*). In

Aesthetic Theory (*Asthetische Theorie*), Theodor Adorno (1970/1997) suggests that a work of art's placement on this continuum depends upon how free it is of distortion "by exchange, profit, and the false needs of a degraded humanity." He notes that the autonomous work is not the product of "socially useful labor," and, as a result, it resists "bourgeois functionalization." Since aesthetics has conventionally focused on fine, autonomous art, ignoring popular, heteronomous art, the gap between aesthetics and the discipline of children's literature widens on both ends: the latter tends toward cultural studies and a postmodern aesthetic, whereas the former focuses on the "fine arts."

Even within the discipline of children's literature, there is a privileging of work that suggests autonomous "fine art" or references canonical painting or literature, such as the aforementioned Jarrell-Sendak collaboration, but also work like Anthony Browne's intertextual *Willy the Dreamer* (1997), Nancy Willard's allusive *A Visit to William Blake's Inn: Poems for Innocent and Experienced Travelers* (1982), Chris Van Allsburg's surreal *The Mysteries of Harris Burdick* (1984), or David Macaulay's architecturally precise *Castle* (1977). This aesthetic insecurity complex is evident in a great deal of children's literature scholarship. In *When You've Made It Your Own . . . Teaching Poetry to Young People*, for example, Gregory Denman (1988) defends what he doubtlessly sees as the more autonomous poetry of Robert Frost by stressing "there is more to poetry than Shel Silverstein." He continues, "[Y]ou no more need to teach children the poetry of Shel Silverstein than to give them lessons in eating McDonald's hamburgers, fries, and a shake." One suspects that when Denman claims that "there is more" to children's poetry than Silverstein, this "more" involves aesthetic value, not merely thematic complexity or didactic "appropriateness." Denman suggests that Silverstein's work has the aesthetic value of fast food while insisting that Frost is a writer of nutritional (read: "aesthetically valuable") poetry. These dismissive attitudes derive from a reliance, in the words of Beverly Lyon Clark (1992), "on New Critical strategies for criticizing a work," the very same strategies whose abandonment created space for the literary study of children's literature in the first place. Clark notes that New Critical approaches "privilege complexity, so that it will be difficult to find anything to say about seemingly 'simple' works of literature." For Perry Nodelman (2000), however, this simplicity is the basis of children's literature's aesthetic appeal, "because [children's texts] seem so simple and yet allow for so much thought." He continues, "There's something magical about texts so apparently straightforward being so non-straightforward." Striking a blow against the West's tendency to canonize a priori texts of a more evident complexity, Nodelman explains, "I find more obviously complex texts much less magical."

Nodelman's *Pleasures of Children's Literature* (1992/1996), now revised with co-author Mavis Reimer, engages aesthetics by analyzing the pleasures produced by the contemplation of literature for children, while also exploring the pleasures inherent in the contemplation of the ideological underpinnings of our aesthetic value, especially when those values involve texts prepared for children, a class about which we hold a myriad of often contradictory assumptions. Nodelman does not engage directly the philosophy of aesthetics in *Pleasures*, nor does he purport to be an aesthetician. On the other hand, Maria Nikolajeva's *Aesthetic Approaches to Children's Literature: An Introduction* (2005) summons aesthetics in the title only to skirt it in the text. Despite its title, it is a textbook of critical approaches to children's literature, and one that largely sidesteps the aesthetic debates philosophers have been engaging with since Kant. As a result, the chapter on "The Aesthetic of the Author" concerns not how beautiful a given author might be, but "the relationships between the author and the text," while "The Aesthetic of the Reader" treats only "the various categories of readers, real and implied." She elides the fundamental questions of what art is and how it functions in society, thereby dispensing with the issue of whether there is a distinction between what Griswold calls "children's literature" and "children's reading."

In the end, the question of aesthetic value in children's literature is closely aligned to the politics and history of a discipline that is itself still negotiating a place in the academy. There are scholars who carefully make the distinction between children's literature (art) and children's reading (not art) precisely so that discussions about children's *literature*, and hence aesthetics in children's literature, can easily fit into the academy's preexisting debates about aesthetics. As Griswold (2002) writes, "[W]hen we are able to talk about Children's Literature as literature, we will be able to address others outside our discipline with genuine confidence and authority." Kenneth Kidd (2002) is sensitive to Griswold's desire for disciplinarity and authority, noting that "[f]or so long children's literature wasn't taken seriously, and just as it's being granted greater respect, the academy is turning to cultural and area studies, theory and 'everyday life.'" Kidd asks, "Will our emergent interest in children's culture be indulged at the expense of the literary tradition we have worked so hard to champion?" His answer is an excited maybe, but he is quick to insist upon his "enthusiasm about the shift away from a narrow vision of literature, criticism, and academic life"—and, we should add, a narrow view of what is aesthetically successful in children's literature. Kidd's response points to the productive tensions between literature and cultural studies. Any future conversations about aesthetics in children's literature will have to be mindful of such productive tensions.

2

African American
Michelle Martin

From the beginnings of African American children's literature around the turn of the twentieth century, the parameters of what should be included has been as much of a source of conflict as the terminology used to label this group of people. Commenting on the contested nature of this genre, Dianne Johnson (1990) asserts in *Telling Tales: the Pedagogy and Promise of African American Literature for Youth*:

> Like children's literature, as a broad category, African American children's literature is a label which refers to the intended audience. On the other hand, like Afro-American literature, Black children's literature refers to the ethnic and racial identities of the authors. When the two categories are combined into one, the parameters of the new category are much less clear. This confusion in definition is important, largely because of the deliberate uses to which the literature is put.

In this passage, Johnson highlights the shifting terminology associated with the people, and therefore with the genre—African American, Afro-American, Black—as well as the anomalous nature of the genre itself: unlike most literary genres, children's and young adult literature are defined by audience, not by authorship.

Furthermore, in stating that "Black children's literature refers to the ethnic and racial identities of the authors," Johnson articulates her position on one end of a significant continuum. African American children's literature can be defined inclusively or exclusively. Scholars who define the genre inclusively (e.g., MacCann 1998; Nikola-Lisa 1998; Martin 2004) consider texts written by African American authors and illustrators as belonging to the genre, but also include texts about the Black experience and/or the image of the Black child written by non–African Americans. Those who define the genre exclusively (e.g., Bishop 1982, 2007; Johnson 1990; McNair and Brooks 2008) include only those texts written by African Americans about African Americans. Clearly, how broadly the genre is defined will largely shape discussions of its history and evolution, and one cannot trace this history without some understanding of the changing terminology that has labeled the genre throughout the late nineteenth, twentieth, and twenty-first centuries.

Countee Cullen's poem "Heritage" (1947) articulates a salient question for contemporary African Americans:

One three centuries removed

From the scenes his fathers loved,

Spicy grove, cinnamon tree,

What is Africa to me?

Of what relevance is Africa to Blacks whose home is North America and whose ancestors came from Africa? And more to the point of this discussion, how did "African Americans" come to be called African Americans, and what, then, constitutes "African American children's literature"? Since children's literature is defined by audience, critics who define African American children's literature by the race or ethnicity of the author identify it differently from the mainstream of children's literature. The genre that is now called "African American children's literature" has, from the early twentieth century on, experienced a number of title shifts. In their 2003 study "Understanding of Race and the Construction of African-American Identity," Vetta L. Sanders Thompson and Maysa Akbar summarize these descriptors: "African, African American, Black American, Black, and person/people of color . . . Negro, and Colored." Likewise, this literature has been called Negro, Black, Afro-American and African American children's literature. A brief examination of the changes in these descriptors will illuminate some of the perennial problems with defining Black American children's literature.

In *Race, Rhetoric and Identity: The Architecton of Soul*, Molefi Kete Asante (2005) writes that from 1619 until 1817, most Black Americans felt a sense of pride about their connection with Africa. Black shipping merchant Captain Paul Cuffee even launched an expedition in 1815–16 through which thirty-eight colonists emigrated to Sierra Leone (Cuffee 1811); Cuffee believed this would "allow Africans and African Americans to realize their full potential" (Gaines 2007). In 1817, however, when a group of influential Whites formed the African Colonization Society, which also sought to resettle American Blacks in Africa, many Blacks, particularly freedmen, made a concerted effort to disprove their Africanness, offering reasons that ultimately illustrated their acceptance of racist, white suprema-cist ideology (Asante 2005). Hence, after 1817, the term "Negro" came to be preferred over "African American."

The *Oxford English Dictionary* (*OED*) defines a "Ne-gro" as a member of a dark-skinned group of peoples originally native to sub-Saharan Africa; a person of black African origin or descent." The term "remained the standard designation throughout the 17th to 19th centuries, and was still used as a standard designation, preferred by prominent black American campaigners such as W. E. B. Du Bois and Booker T. Washington, un-til the middle years of the 20th century" (*OED Online*, s.v. "Negro").

This linguistic history illuminates why Carter G. Woodson, widely known as the "Father of Black His-tory," labeled his contributions "Negro" rather than "African": the Association for the Study of Negro Life and History (1915), the *Journal of Negro History* (1916), Negro History Week (1926), and the *Negro History Bul-letin* (1938) (Smith 2004).

During the 1960s Black Power movement, "*black* was reclaimed as an expression of racial pride" and "Negro" fell out of favor, though still employed in names of im-portant organizations such as the United Negro Col-lege Fund (*OED Online*, s.v. "African-American"), and "Black children's literature" is still widely accepted as a label for the genre. According to the *OED*, an African American is "An American (esp. North American) of African origin; a black American." Although the *OED* identifies "Afro-American" as a synonym, because "afro" also recalls the hairstyle popularized during the 1960s, the connotations of this term are, perhaps, more politicized. The *OED* also notes:

> Although both *African* and *African-American* were widely used in the United States in the 19th century, the adoption of African-American as a preferred term among black Americans dates from the late 1960s and early 1970s (particularly after an April 1972 conference at which Ramona Edelin, president of the National Urban Coalition, proposed its use). The term gained widespread ac-ceptance following its endorsement by the Rever-end Jesse Jackson (b. 1941) during his presidential nomination campaign in 1988.

Because of the turbulent history of African Americans and the power dynamics that remain in place within the American education system and publishing in-dustry, the definition of this genre continues to be conflicted.

Although they were not specifically for Black chil-dren, early literary efforts to educate a rapidly growing literate Black population included pit schools, freed-men's schools, and antebellum newspapers. Particu-larly important were church-based papers such as the African Methodist Episcopal's *Christian Recorder*; estab-lished in 1852, which remains the oldest continuously published Black paper in the United States (Bishop 2007). In *Children's Literature of the Harlem Renaissance*, Katharine Capshaw Smith (2004) offers an extensive analysis of "cross-written" texts—those that spoke to Black children and adults simultaneously, often with an eye toward influencing adults ideologically through children who, during Reconstruction and the early twentieth century, were often more literate than the adults who cared for them. Ironically, the novel widely considered the first work of Negro children's literature, *Clarence and Corrine, or God's Way* by Mrs. Amelia E. Johnson (1890), though written by a Black woman, features no Black characters. This, according to some, excludes it from the genre.

Those who define the genre exclusively consider the 1920s and the Harlem Renaissance the beginning of African American children's literature because this was the first time that so many Black writers composed texts specifically for Black children. Prior to this time, Black children appeared primarily in children's books written by White authors for White children's entertainment—usually at the expense of the Black characters. Although abolitionist tracts such as *The Slave's Friend* (1836–38) had made some efforts to portray the humanity of Black people, more common were plantation sketches such as E. W. Kemble's *A Coon Alphabet* (1898) and the rhyming ditty *The Ten Little Niggers* (1875). These stories looked nostalgically at plantation life, depicted Black characters as idiotic and dispensable pickaninnies with wooly, unkempt hair and exaggerated facial features. Although it is about a South Indian boy, and not an African American child, Helen Bannerman's *The Story of Little Black Sambo* (1899), one of the most controversial picture books in the history of children's literature, is often considered within Black children's literature partly because of the proliferation of unauthorized versions reillustrated

by Americans in the minstrel tradition. While some readers appreciate Sambo because he was for a long time one of the few children of color in the "all-white world" of children's fiction (Larrick 1965), others see Bannerman's images as demeaning and resent her use of the term "Sambo." Because mainstream American publishers had no interest in positive representations of the Negro in the early twentieth century and argued that Negroes neither read nor bought books, positive portrayals of Black children were rare until the 1920s.

The *Brownies' Book Magazine*, though it survived for only two years (1920–21), established many important ideals that still undergird African American children's literature. When W. E. B. Du Bois, Augustus Granville Dill, and Jessie Fauset, leaders of the National Association for the Advancement of Colored People (NAACP), which published *Crisis* magazine, first envisioned a magazine specifically for "Children of the Sun," they articulated seven goals for the publication. Three of these remain basic tenets of the genre: "To make colored children realize that being 'colored' is a normal beautiful thing"; "to make them familiar with the history and achievements of the Negro race"; and "to point out the best amusements and joys and worthwhile things of life" (Harris 1986). Their magazine, called *Brownies' Book*, included works of fiction, histories of important African Americans, poems, songs, plays, photographs from subscribers, riddles, puzzles, games, and more. Some of the most important authors within the African American literary canon published pieces in the *Brownies' Book*. Langston Hughes and

Arna Bontemps, two such writers, collaborated on children's books from the 1930s through the 1970s. Bontemps contributed such a significant body of literature to the genre that Violet J. Harris (1990) characterizes him as the "father" of African American children's literature.

While the Harlem Renaissance saw the first proliferation of literature written specifically for Black American children, and also established the precedent for what this literature should seek to accomplish, the Black Arts movement of the 1960s—the "aesthetic and spiritual sister of the Black Power concept"—brought dedicated Black authors to the genre, and with them came some significant ideological shifts (Neal 1971). Larry Neal notes that texts of this era reject the White aesthetic and confront the historical realities of the painful past so that they are not forgotten or repeated, and so that this knowledge can empower Black people. Community connections are key to this movement, and within it, the Black artist's "primary duty is to speak to the spiritual and cultural needs of Black people" (Neal 1971). Both nationalism and separatism fueled this movement, but since authors of children's books must always be mindful of the child, the militancy of the Black Power movement rarely surfaces in these books. What the genre has taken from this 1960s movement is an intolerance of the unequal treatment of Black children and a confrontation with harsh historical realities in forms that children can understand. Since this era, Black children's books have spoken much more directly than before to the cultural and spiritual needs of African American children—not necessarily excluding other readers, but addressing "cultural insiders" as the primary audience. Among others, Tom Feelings, Nikki Grimes, Julius Lester, Jerry Pinkney, and Walter Dean Myers—whose careers as children's and young adult authors began in the 1960s and 1970s—have approached these themes directly.

Where the 1960s gave the genre a sense of reality, the 1990s brought an explosion of delight—both thematic and visual. The last decade of the twentieth century saw more African American children's books published than ever before, along with a proliferation of Black authors and second-generation Black children's writers and artists, as well as a new strand of literary themes that invites readers to explore elements of Black culture—such as call-response, signifying, and celebrating nappy hair—that had previously remained more within the domain of Black oral culture. While these texts validate the cultural heritage of African American children, this new level of openness invites all children to learn about, understand, and celebrate some of the common truths of Black American life.

3

Audience

Beverly Lyon Clark

The term "audience" has only relatively recently come to acquire its dominant modern meaning, referring to the viewers of an entertainment or readers of a book. The earliest such usage listed in the *Oxford English Dictionary* (*OED*) dates to 1855. Earlier meanings include "[t]he action of hearing" (dating from c. 1374) and a "[f]ormal hearing," often with royalty or with a judge (from 1377). Derived from the Latin *audire*, to hear, the term has a special resonance for children's literature, for the youngest children are not readers but rather auditors of literature, truly an audience. Indeed the broad term "audience" better captures the many ways in which children consume literature—and other aspects of culture—than does "reader," the generally preferred term in literary criticism.

Raymond Williams (1976/1983a) did not include "audience" in his *Keywords*. The term does receive an entry in *New Keywords*, edited by Tony Bennett, Lawrence Grossberg, and Meaghan Morris (2005), though David Morley's account focuses almost entirely on the audience for mass media, especially addressing the extent to which such an audience is passively susceptible or actively shapes the messages received. This question of agency has been central to examinations of children's culture, broadly considered. Given that most scholars condescend to children, assuming them to be passive and hence mere pawns, a popular approach in cultural criticism has been to castigate the media, arguing that our children must be protected from its effects. Since at least 1965, when the librarian Frances Clarke Sayers fired a salvo (Sayers and Weisenberg 1965)—and perhaps even from 1938, when Anne Carroll Moore expressed her concern—critics have deplored how reductive and saccharine Disney products are, for instance. Yet a few cultural critics, such as Ellen Seiter (1993) and Gerard Jones (2002), highlight some of the ways in which children respond actively, perhaps reshaping what they see on television and elsewhere or using comic books to mitigate anxieties. Similarly, an extensive literature attends to the numerous uses of Barbie, that icon of modern children's culture—even if the most radical uses (Barbie as dildo) are often associated with adults (Rand 1995).

My focus here, however, is on "audience" with respect not to popular culture but to literature. The concept has a special salience for children's literature, beyond the root associations with the auditory, for this literature is not by children, as the possessive might conceivably imply, but rather literature read by or to them: it is defined by its audience. Yet how exactly audience defines it is subject to debate. Scholars disagree, for instance, as to whether it is defined by being intended for children (e.g., Nodelman 2008b) or is simply literature that they read (e.g., Lerer 2008). Does a book appropriated by children, such as *Robinson Crusoe* (Defoe 1719), count? Do books that a publisher markets for children count, even if an author didn't have such an audience in mind while writing? Scholars also disagree whether to focus more on the "book" or the "child" in their judgments, but even the "book" people cannot altogether forget the target audience: "Naturally a knowledge of and sympathy with children is . . . vital," notes Brian Alderson in "The Irrelevance of Children to the Children's Book Reviewer" (quoted in Hunt 1991).

Beyond debates within the field, the study of children's literature raises intriguing theoretical questions of broader interest that are too often missed by mainstream literary theorists, who generally ignore children's literature. However well Stanley Fish's (1980) concept of an "interpretive community" might work for adult readers, how does one define such a community for children's literature? Where might one find an interpretive community purely of children? As Deborah Stevenson (1997) notes, "The best child readers rise longitudinally [to a different reading level] rather than exerting power latitudinally, which means that there are no child gatekeepers of the canon."

Children's literature also points to the multiplicity of address of literature—necessarily so, given that no other literature so thoroughly excludes the intended audience from the various aspects of production. Very few young people have written, edited, published, or sold books. And relatively few children directly buy them; even if a smaller proportion of children's book sales are now to libraries than was the case in the 1960s, librarians, teachers, and parents are still the primary buyers (Stevenson 1997). The result, as Zohar Shavit (1986) and others have noted, is that children's literature always has at least a double address: the children who are the ostensible audience and the adults whose decisions make it available. Given that the decision makers are not part of the ostensible audience, the nature of children's literature very much depends on how adults construct childhood and children. Indeed, Jacqueline Rose (1984) would argue that it is impossible for adults truly to know children—rather, they are always constructing them. If adults construct children as beings to be molded for the future, then children's literature may be conceived as an important part of this molding—and therefore as necessarily didactic and needing to be monitored or censored. Others, following a Romantic construction of childhood, feel that children's literature should provide wings for the imagination. Yet maybe we should not lose sight of the fact that children are not just passive; they can be active agents too, constructing what they read—and themselves.

For children are real, too. A focus on the duality of the audience may, in fact, occlude its multiplicities, masking the heterogeneity of children. Who exactly comprises the target audience for children's literature? Some scholars study the kinds of address created within a work, the narratee or the implied reader (Wall 1991/1994); others examine the reading processes of actual child readers (Benton 1995/2005). Children differ among themselves—by age, for example. When does childhood end? Is the audience made up only of those under the age of, say, twelve, or does it include adolescents? But children also differ by gender, race, class, nationality. Focus on "the child" as audience too often misses the real differences among children.

In any case, what we now consider to be children's literature arose through early market segmentation. Literature for children wasn't always separated from literature for adults. Early literature in the West—mystery plays, ballads, folk tales, sermons—embraced children as part of its audience. Even later, literature for children long overlapped with that for the laboring and later working classes: children often read chapbooks, evangelical tracts, and dime novels. What is often considered children's literature per se—an imaginative literature directly targeting children—is generally seen as arising in the eighteenth century, along with the middle class, whether or not one dates the first work of Anglophone children's literature precisely to 1744 with *A Little Pretty Pocket-Book*, published by John Newbery (Darton 1932/1982). For most of the nineteenth century, nevertheless, writers and their gatekeepers often assumed they should publish nothing "that could not be read aloud in the family circle," to quote an editor of *Harper's Monthly* in the 1890s (Mott 1938): they assumed that the young would be part of the general readership. And works that ostensibly targeted children, and which subsequent readers have classified as children's literature, were often read by adults as well—not just in the company of children, as now with a bedtime story, but independently.

In the United States, boy books—most of which we would now consider children's literature—were for young and old, and juvenile domestic stories were not clearly separated from ones for a more mature audience. *Little Women* (Alcott 1868–69) was enjoyed by "[g]rave merchants and lawyers," "clerks," "the civil engineer," "the boy in the elevator" (Stearns 1895). In the nineteenth century, *The Adventures of Tom Sawyer* (Twain 1876) and *Adventures of Huckleberry Finn* (Twain 1884) were seen as equivalent books, usually mentioned in the same breath; only in the twentieth century did *Tom Sawyer* devolve into a children's book and *Huckleberry Finn* ascend to hypercanonicity, to use Jonathan Arac's term (1997), as a prime candidate for the great American novel (Clark 2003).

I use "devolve" advisedly. Late in the nineteenth and especially early in the twentieth centuries the canons of taste changed. As the cultural gatekeepers shifted from the likes of magazine editors to the professoriate, and Herman Melville's star, for one, ascended, only works (especially those by white men) seen as targeting an adult audience came to be seen as worthy of the highest approbation. Children's literature came to be seen as inferior. If, in 1893, "The Best American Books," published in the literary journal *The Critic*, included *Little Women* and *Little Lord Fauntleroy* (Burnett 1886) among its top forty, twentieth-century lists of important books rarely included works we now classify as for children.

In the twentieth century, the academy did not provide a friendly audience for children's literature. Now, however, as academic departments devote courses and programs to children's literature, as books such as those in the Harry Potter series have reached a crossover audience, as publishers seem to welcome such crossovers (Beckett 2009)—and, indeed, as books such as *Keywords for Children's Literature* are published—change would seem to be afoot.

4

Body

Kelly Hager

The *Oxford English Dictionary*'s (*OED*) definition of "body"—"the material frame of man (and animals)"—immediately sets before us one of the term's principal controversies in children's literature. That is, what Peter Hunt (1984) would call the adultist, not to mention the sexist, nature of the *OED*'s language reminds us that the matter of the corporeal is often not deemed proper for the consideration of children and is frequently bound up with questions of gender and the adult body. But when we consider the *OED*'s elaboration on this definition—"the material body and its properties"—the physical nature of the human body becomes more clearly a matter of interest and importance to the study of children's literature and culture. David Macaulay's picture book *The Way We Work: Getting to Know the Amazing Human Body* (2008) describes the parts of the body and its functions. The American Girl Just Like You® doll comes made to order with "hair and eye color" and "skin tone" "to match" the girl who buys her. And the Cookie Monster describes his new healthy eating habits in his "Healthy Food" rap, part of *Sesame Street*'s new "Healthy Habits for Life" initiative. As just these few examples suggest, children's culture reveals an overwhelming interest in describing, depicting, and reproducing images of the body in order to educate, orient, and delight the child consumer.

The body is just as much a matter of literary concern as it is a preoccupation of media and commodity culture, and education about the corporeal is just as often directed at adolescents and young adults as it is to the audiences of *Ten Little Fingers and Ten Little Toes* (Fox and Oxenbury 2008) or *Everyone Poops* (Gomi 1977). Perhaps the most explicit site of children's literature's engagement with the body and its physical vulnerability is the genre of young adult (YA) fiction, with its focus on sexual maturation, orientation, body size, and physical abuse. Alice Childress's *A Hero Ain't Nothin' But a Sandwich* (1973) depicts the damage inflicted on the body by substance abuse, while Shelley Stoehr's *Crosses* (1991) depicts the self-abuse of bodily mutilation. Abuse by parents, predators, and peers in the form of domestic violence, sexual assault, and bullying, respectively, is at the heart of E. L. Konigsburg's *Silent to the Bone* (2000), Laurie Halse Anderson's *Speak* (1999), and Judy Blume's *Blubber* (1974).

In *Keywords for American Cultural Studies*, Eva Cherniavsky (2007) reminds us that it was not until the rise of "feminism, race and ethnic studies, and postcolonial studies" that "critical attention" was paid "to forms of material and abstract embodiment," and that "body" thus has "a relatively brief [career] as a focus of critical engagement in the study of culture." Studies of race and gender made possible, she argues, "a turn to those human subjects historically associated with the discredited life of the material body and so constituted as marginal to the arenas of cultural production and political representation: women, Africans and their New World descendants, indigenous peoples, mestizos, and Asians, among other categories of 'overembodied' ethnic, sexual, and classed identity." To that list of marginalized bodies we might add the body of the child. The history of children's literature and culture seems to follow the pattern Cherniavsky lays out: the political correctness of *Sesame Street* (first broadcast in 1969) and the rise of the YA novel in the 1960s and 1970s suggests that an interest in the "corporealized identity" of the child was also made possible by theories of race, class, gender, and orientation.

However, children's literature and culture has long been invested in constructions of and instructions about the body of the child—a fact suggested by this volume's number of related entries ("African American," "Boyhood," "Gender," "Girlhood," "Identity," "Latino/a," "Queer," "Race," "Tomboy," and "Young Adult"). Eighteenth- and nineteenth-century novels tell stories that embody children in markedly graphic and pronounced ways. Alice's adventures in Wonderland are punctuated by her constantly changing body, and the "repeated images of corporeal punishment" in Catherine Sinclair's *Holiday House* (1839) are, as Jackie Horne (2001) argues, "deeply intertwined with the 'new' aspects of the novel, in particular its construction of the Romantic child." Just as indicative of children's literature's fascination with the body is the teacher's "'mysterious' copy of 'Professor somebody's Anatomy'" in *The Adventures of Tom Sawyer* (1876), "about which the children's curiosity is at fever pitch," as Claudia Nelson (2004) reminds us. The detail with which Thomas Bailey Aldrich describes the fights in his *The Story of a Bad Boy* (1869), the homosocial world of *Tom Brown's Schooldays* (Hughes 1857), and the hungry bodies of the boys who work on the streets in Horatio Alger, Jr.'s *Ragged Dick* (1868) and *The Erie Train Boy* (1890) all reveal that children's literature concerns itself with the "the material frame" of the child as much as with that child's intellectual, spiritual, and moral coming-of-age.

Similarly, the history of sex education that Lissa Paul (2005) charts in "Sex and the Children's Book" underscores how long texts written for and about children have been concerned to depict the corporeal nature of their subject and their audience: her history begins with *Youths behaviour, or, Decencie in conversation amongst men* (Hawkins 1672) and ends with Robie Harris and Michael Emberley's *It's Perfectly Normal: A Book about Changing Bodies, Growing Up, Sex, and Sexual Health* (1994). Indeed, we might risk neologism and point to a genre of corporeal *bildungsroman*, to a set of novels that detail the child's physical growth and development, in terms of both sexual maturation and more quotidian concerns like potty training and basic hygiene. Judith Plotz (1994) alerts us to the "polymorphic physicality" of Frances Hodgson Burnett's *The Secret Garden* (1911); the novel, she argues, "offers a resurrection through touch, through taste, through smell, through the exercise of bodilyness." The exaggerated bodies of Struwwelpeter and Pinocchio belong, as Seth Lerer (2008) points out, to "little boys whose deceits distort their physical appearance."

The Dantean punishments inflicted on the greedy, selfish children in *Charlie and the Chocolate Factory* (Dahl 1964) are physical in nature, and *Ozma of Oz*'s (1907) Princess Langwidere, who has thirty different heads to match her every mood, reveals a similar and intense interest in the body of the child and the culture that shapes it. Just as clearly, Alice McKinley's examination of her vagina with a hand mirror in Phyllis Reynolds Naylor's *The Grooming of Alice* (2000) and what Roberta Seelinger Trites (2000) calls the "play-by-play description of how to have intercourse" in Judy Blume's *Forever* (1975) bespeak twentieth- and twenty-first-century culture's desire to instruct (and delight) the child by explaining, analyzing, and celebrating her bodily nature.

Whether implicitly or explicitly, bodies in children's literature have served as sites of both sex and sexuality from as early as the eighteenth up through the twenty-first century. Ruth Saxton (1998) finds that "contemporary literary investigations into the Girl continue to envision girlhood according to tropes and plots familiar since the dawn of novelistic fiction. . . . Physicality—the Girl's experience of her body, engagement in or denial of sex, her cultural 'value' as young female body—remains crucial." By the same token, Robert Louis Stevenson's, Rudyard Kipling's, and H. Rider Haggard's novels of empire and adventure, so popular in the nineteenth century, "are, in the end, tales of the body," as Lerer (2008) puts it. Aidan Chambers's (1978–2005) six-novel "dance sequence" also treats "issues of touch, desire, [and] masturbation," and does so in what Paul (2005) calls a "deliberate" fashion. Kenneth Kidd (1998) similarly draws our attention to the very physical nature of Mole and Rat's relationship in *The Wind in the Willows* (Grahame 1908) and "its custodial investment in and playful exploration of what I like to think of as male homo-economics." While Kidd is careful to acknowledge that *The Wind in the Willows* is "not a gay text per se," he makes clear that "it is certainly about (among many other things) gendered male-male interaction." He thus reminds us not only that animals have bodies too, and bodies that often function as stand-ins for human ones, but also that "while we should distinguish contemporary 'explicit' works from pre-Stonewall classics, we should not assume that such distinctions are easy or always useful. It is helpful to acknowledge such continuities as well as shifts." Drawing attention to these "continuities" makes it clear that the body of the child was a matter of significance long before feminism, queer theory, or postcolonialism brought the corporeal into the cultural conversation.

But that is not to say that all bodies have always been attended to, nor to deny a powerful strain of censorship and of silencing with respect to the body of the child. James Kincaid (1992) argues that we are invested in ignoring the existence of children's sexuality: "By insisting so loudly on the innocence, purity, and asexuality of the child, we have created a subversive echo: experience, corruption, eroticism." We see much the same kind of silencing at work in the American Library Association's yearly Top Ten Most Frequently Challenged Books list. The books on the 2008 list were challenged on the following grounds: anti-ethnic, anti-family, homosexuality, religious viewpoint, unsuited to age group, political viewpoint, violence, offensive language, sexually explicit, occult/Satanism, drugs, nudity, and suicide. Nine of those thirteen reasons are corporeal in nature, and the two most frequently cited were "sexually explicit" and "unsuited to age group," a pattern that bears out Kincaid's claim that we are invested in a construction of the asexual child. Trites (2000) finds that that construction even extends past puberty: "in many YA novels, teenage sexuality is defined in terms of deviancy—even when the message to the reader is a Judy Blume special: 'Your masturbating/wetdreams/desire to have sex/(fill-in-the-blank) is normal.'"

Another body often under- or misrepresented in children's literature is the fat body. Robert Lipsyte's *One Fat Summer* (1977) is a positive counterexample to this trend. But Beth Younger (2003) finds, in a diverse collection of YA novels from the 1970s, 1980s, and 1990s, "an unacknowledged weightism": although the novels by Judy Blume, Norma Klein, Judith Ortiz Cofer, Cherie Bennett, Susan Terris, Connie Porter, and Lois-Ann Yamanaka that she explores

> portray an ethnically diverse group of young girls and women, they also reveal the difficulty many Young Adult fiction authors have resisting the contemporary hyper-thin European ideal of beauty. In a revealing intersection of sexuality and body

image, heavy characters are all represented as sexually promiscuous, passive, and powerless, while thin characters appear responsible and powerful. Promiscuous sexual activity, criticized and vilified, is linked to a character's weight.

In a blog post on fat-positive children's books, Rebecca Rabinowitz (2008a, b) describes "fatpol-friendly children's books" as "rare" and discovers few "'supersize' characters, nor many queer characters or characters of color." She finds only six picture books, three middle-grade chapter books, and six YA novels with positive depictions of fat characters, even after she includes "some books that are artistically/literarily weaker than I would normally recommend."

The recent work of Younger and Rabinowitz brings us back full circle to Cookie Monster's new healthy eating habits and the ways in which the child's body is normed by literature and culture. It reminds us, as does Rabinowitz's use of the word "supersize" to refer to the size of a character's body rather than a portion size at McDonald's, that mass culture "circulates bodies promiscuously; its technologies and commercial logic ensure the production of desirable body images made available to the widest market" (Cherniavsky 2007).

5

Boyhood
Eric L. Tribunella

Along with childhood and girlhood, boyhood is central to the definition of children's literature. John Newbery's *A Little Pretty Pocket-Book* (1744), frequently credited with igniting the children's literature industry, addressed boys and girls separately as distinct audiences: The book was available for purchase with a ball for boys and a pincushion for girls. Filled with descriptions of games specifically for boys and referring to boy players, the 1787 edition published by Isaiah Thomas in the United States paid additional attention to boys by including a prefatory address to adults about how to raise a healthy, virtuous, and wise *son*, thereby connecting the "birth" of children's literature with lessons on how to be and have a good boy.

"Boys," wrote Philippe Ariès in his controversial *Centuries of Childhood* (1962), "were the first specialized children." Sixteenth-century Europeans used clothes as markers to distinguish boys from children. As infants and toddlers, boys were not differentiated from girls: both wore dresses and ribbons and were identified as children. At seven or so, a boy celebrated his growth out of childhood via a "breeching" ceremony in which he exchanged a gender-neutral childhood of gowns and smocks for breeches or pants—and began to take a more active role in household labor. Girls lacked a similar ritual to mark the transition from early childhood to girlhood (Mintz 2004).

The linguistic record confirms this history. The term "boyhood" is much older than "girlhood," which appeared about 170 years later. "Boyhood" dates to the 1570s, while the word "boy" is much older (*Oxford English Dictionary* [*OED*]). Although first used in the mid-fifteenth century to refer to a male child, "boy" had also been used 150 years earlier, in a pejorative sense, to refer to a male servant or slave of any age, or a male person of low or nonwhite status. The common use of "boy" in this sense persisted well into the twentieth century as an offensive way to refer to men of color, irrespective of age, and it continues, perhaps with regional variation, to be used to refer to men who are perceived as subordinate in terms of race *or* age. Manhood is often defined by the ability to dominate, care for, or exercise power over others, but such behaviors can be difficult or impossible for male youths, poor men, or men of color.

Boyhood has therefore always constituted a kind of problem. To be a boy means to be a flawed, inchoate, or incomplete man, and boyhood involves the fundamental paradox between the privileges of maleness and the subaltern status of youth, class, or race. We can read in children's literature the morally and socially subversive high jinks of boyhood, the sense of boyhood as a time of constraint and confinement, and the themes of escape and empowerment that often permeate books about boys. All of these themes invoke the association between male youth and social subordination recorded in the history of the words "boy" and "boyhood." Boys in children's literature frequently chafe against their inferior status, and the qualities and scenarios of boyhood are symptomatic of either resistance to that status or attempts to escape it. These fictional boys typically seek to transcend the limitations of boyhood or to claim the privileges of manhood. The conflict between bucking the system and banking on future payoffs leaves books about boyhood rife with conflict and contradiction.

Despite Newbery's innovative marketing to boys and girls as readers with distinct interests, in the decades that followed it remained conventional even for books that featured boy protagonists, such as Thomas Day's *The History of Sandford and Merton* (1783–89), to be advertised to children more generally. The *OED* notes that the term "boyhood" rarely appears in print before the late eighteenth century, when children's literature began to crystallize as an established enterprise. This usage suggests that a more elaborate vocabulary and practice of childhood, including increased sex/gender specificity, went hand in hand with the expansion of children's culture.

As the experience of childhood became more elaborate and varied, in part due to increased attention to childhood and child-rearing by scholars like Jean-Jacques Rousseau, a more gender-specific literature appeared. John R. Gillis (1974) notes that the concept of boyhood became more clearly articulated in the latter half of the nineteenth century, before that of girlhood, and that children's literature played a key role in its emergence as a distinct period of life. Gillis cites the founding of periodicals specifically for boys such as *Boys Own Magazine*, which began publication in 1855, and Lorinda B. Cohoon (2006) has demonstrated the important role played by periodicals and serialized children's fiction in the construction of American boyhood in the nineteenth century. Gail Murray (1998) and Sally Mitchell (1995) have concurred, noting that the bifurcation of child readers along sex/ gender lines became more pronounced in the nineteenth century.

In their child-rearing guide *Practical Education* (1798), Maria and Richard Lovell Edgeworth warned parents *not* to permit young boys to read adventure stories. They argued that exciting tales of courage and heroism would enflame the natural proclivities of boys to wander and explore and would ruin them for the duller work of middle-class professional life, which requires patience and the acceptance of drudgery. Despite, or because of, this concern, adventure remained popular with boys, and adventure novels such as R. M. Ballantyne's *The Coral Island* (1857), the robinsonade against which William Golding wrote *The Lord of the Flies* (1954), featured boy protagonists escaping home and parents, traveling the world, facing pirates or cannibals, rescuing damsels, or discovering treasures. Along with adventure novels, the boys' school story, such as Thomas Hughes's *Tom Brown's Schooldays* (1857), and books about the quintessential bad boy, such as Mark Twain's *The Adventures of Tom Sawyer* (1876), helped constitute what became known

as the "boys' book" or "boy book," a critical site for the construction of boyhood.

The different genres of boy books suggest the diversity of boyhood's possibilities. The boys' adventure story depicts the boy as defined by his escape from the domestic sphere. In *The Coral Island*, three boy sailors ranging in age from fourteen to eighteen are cast away in the Fijian islands and cannot be happier to be free of the constraints of civilization. They are able to participate in imperial ventures, indicating the frequent connections between boys' adventure and empire. While the imperial boy of British boys' books traveled to faraway countries for adventure, the American bad boy stayed closer to home. Thomas Bailey Aldrich's *The Story of a Bad Boy* (1869) and Twain's *Tom Sawyer* both depict mischievous boys named Tom being raised by unmarried aunts and getting into scrapes in their own neighborhoods and towns. Gillian Avery's (1994) argument that boys' books of England and America were "virtually unexportable" suggests the extent to which they are steeped in their respective national cultures.

In addition to the domestic bad boy and imperial adventurer, we also find feral boys, who survive outside of civilized institutions (Kidd 2004), and schoolboys, who live within them. Surviving in the wild and raised by animals, notable feral boys include Mowgli from Rudyard Kipling's Jungle Books (1894, 1895) and Tarzan from Edgar Rice Burroughs's *Tarzan of the Apes* (1914). In contrast with books about feral boys are boys' school stories, most of which are British in origin and are set in all-male boarding schools. School stories such as *Tom*

Brown's Schooldays typically focus on a gang of boys that includes a variety of different types: the plucky and virtuous everyboy who embodies the nation, the mean and vindictive bully, the eccentric loner, and the sensitive or effeminate saint. Many of these classic boy books valorize elements that have come to be associated with boys and boy culture, including sports and games, physical play and combat, exploration and discovery, and courage and bravado.

Traces of these classic types continue to recur in twentieth- and twenty-first-century children's literature. Echoing the imperial boy, Max of Maurice Sendak's iconic picture book *Where the Wild Things Are* (1963) leaves home after being scolded by his mother, travels to the land of the wild things, and becomes their king. Max's wolf suit and wolfish behavior led Kenneth Kidd (2004) to read Sendak's book in the tradition of the feral tale as well. Gary Paulsen's *Hatchet* (1987), about a thirteen-year-old boy who survives a plane crash in the Canadian wilderness, emphasizes the survival aspects of boys' adventure. Joey from Jack Gantos's *Joey Pigza Swallowed the Key* (1998) might be read as a contemporary version of the bad boy, though Joey's presumed diagnosis of Attention Deficit Hyperactivity Disorder medicalizes mischief that *Tom Sawyer* leaves mostly unproblematized.

Boyhood is not synonymous with masculinity, and the boy book also includes a tradition of more sensitive boys like those of Frederic Farrar's classic school story *Eric* (1858), with their passionately homoerotic friendships, or the compassionate and stylish Cedric Errol of Frances Hodgson Burnett's *Little Lord Fauntleroy* (1886). These boys find their contemporary expression in the more avowedly sissy and queer boys of fiction published after the 1960s, like the proudly gay Paul in David Levithan's *Boy Meets Boy* (2003) and the exuberantly effeminate Roger of Lesléa Newman and Peter Ferguson's picture book *The Boy Who Cried Fabulous* (2004).

However, not all boy books fall easily into these patterns—especially not works of contemporary realist fiction. The suburban setting of Edward Bloor's *Tangerine* (1997) and the model behavior of its legally blind protagonist make it difficult to place this novel in any of the conventional categories of boy books. The stakes of Walter Dean Myers's *Monster* (1999), which focuses on a sixteen-year-old African American boy being tried for murder, seem too high to describe it as a bad-boy book, which is usually more comedic. Sherman Alexie's *The Absolutely True Diary of a Part-Time Indian* (2007) depicts the life of a Spokane Indian boy living with his family on a reservation in Washington State, and while it includes school sports as a major component, its contemporary setting and attention to life outside of school distinguish it from any of the classic models. Departing further from these classics, Annette Wannamaker (2008) argues that the books that most appeal to contemporary boy readers tend to be of more popular or "lowbrow" varieties like comics and graphic novels, series books, manga, nonfiction, and magazines. These different kinds of boys and boy books lead to a consideration of how boyhood is depicted in a variety of textual forms and genres.

To assume that boys are the only consumers of boyhood in children's literature would be a mistake. The Edgeworths' (1798) assertion that while adventure might be too risky for boys, it was safe for girls, who would supposedly be immune to the seduction of exploration, implies that girls might indeed read books about boys and boyhood. Beverly Lyon Clark (2003) finds evidence in reviews of *Tom Sawyer* that critics imagined both boys *and* girls as consumers of boyhood fiction. Mitchell (1995) notes that such works were relished by girls who entertained fantasies of boyhood freedom, indicating that boyhood is by no means only for boys. While girls could enjoy the possibilities of boyhood by reading children's literature, Catherine Robson (2001) has argued that the real boyhood of the Victorian gentleman was actually more akin to girlhood in its feminine dependency and vulnerability, and that male authors invented girl protagonists as a way to recapture their lost girlhoods. Boyhood might be elusive even for boys, who, like girls, might read boy books to experience the boyhoods they, too, lack. Anchored mainly to the fictional worlds of children's literature, an empowered or successful boyhood appears to be an ideal that no real boy or girl ever fully experiences. Though boyhood might be defined by subordination and subjection, at least boys can be represented in boy books as striking out on their own or claiming power unavailable to living children. This fantasy might partially explain the popular appeal of the boy book's depiction of boyhood, and also why girls read boy books more frequently than boys read books about girls.

Cohoon, Kidd, and Wannamaker have each called attention to the current "boy crisis," the broad cultural concern with the state of boys and boyhood and with how contemporary culture might harm or fail boys. That these concerns emerged as early as the nineteenth century indicates that this most recent "boy crisis" is just another sign of the perpetual concern with what it means to be a boy. Boys are supposed to possess male privilege, and yet their youth complicates their ability to claim the rewards of maleness or manhood. The multiple and fragmentary nature of identity and status along the lines of race, class, nation, or region can further intensify the subordination of boys and undermine their claims to sex/gender privilege. Some boys simply fail or refuse to enact the expectations or ideals of boyhood and face punishment for not seizing fully the benefits of maleness or masculinity. Being a boy and enacting boyhood can be difficult and even traumatic. Children's literature can provide sources of comfort and pleasure, models for behavior and identity, reflections of self and reality, and visions of better or less painful possibilities.

6

Censorship

David Booth

The earliest reference to "censor" appears as "one of two magistrates of ancient Rome" (*Oxford English Dictionary* [*OED*]), who in addition to taking the census (that is, the registration of citizens, originally for tax purposes), supervised public morals and censured the population (*Columbia Encyclopedia* 2008). The English words "censor" and "census" are from the Latin *censere*, which means to appraise, value, judge, consider or assess; "censure" is from the Latin *censura*, meaning judgment. During the era in which these terms originated, Cato the Elder (234–149 B.C.E.) undertook a vigorous campaign to stem the infiltration of Greek culture (Knowles 2006).

According to the *OED*, the first modern use of "censor" applied to people whose job it was to ensure that "books, journals, plays, etc." were free from anything "immoral, heretical or offensive to the State," and arose in relation to the theater. That is when the "Lord of Misrule" or the "Abbott of Unreason" evolved into the Stage Censor (c. 1555–83). A related term, "bowdlerize," also arising out of censorship of theatrical productions, commemorates Thomas Bowdler (1754–1825), who published a book of Shakespeare's plays—with all sexual or vulgar references removed (McArthur 1998).

The earliest use of the word "censorship" in the context of children's literature developed in tandem with Jean-Jacques Rousseau's eighteenth-century concept of "the natural child" as innocent and in need of protection. The only book Rousseau allowed his hypothetical boy protégé in *Émile* (1762) was Daniel Defoe's *Robinson Crusoe* (1719); ironically, Sarah Trimmer, in her *Family Magazine* (1778–89), attacked bawdy passages in Defoe's novel, as well as those in Perrault's fairy tales, as inappropriate for children. Over the last two hundred years, children's books targeted for censure reflect changing ideas about childhood and notions of suitability. What constitutes "censorship," and whether limiting access to a book violates children's right to read or protects them from danger, has been a longstanding matter of debate.

In dealing with sensitive and complex issues, there is no simple resolution to the dynamic tension between the need to protect children and the willingness to trust the relationship between a writer and a reader. British psychologist Nicholas Tucker, in *The Child and the Book* (1990), notes that occasionally a child may respond adversely to a story, but, while "situations like this are bound to happen sometimes, they can best be modified by discussion afterwards rather than censorships before." Similarly, Kornei Chukovsky (1963), in his study of Russian children "protected" from myths and fairy tales, says censorship does not work because children create their own fantasy stories and worlds in place of literature.

Attempts to suppress dime novels in the United States in the 1860s or penny dreadfuls in Britain (which later evolved into series books) were unsuccessful despite claims that they would encourage children and working-class youth to engage in criminal behavior. Foster's Education Act of 1870 was also opposed by some on the grounds that encouraging mass literacy would lead to crime and madness (Mullin 2003). Dr. Fredric Wertham's *Seduction of the Innocent* (1954) attacked comic books as a negative influence.

Prior to the rise of "new realism" in the 1960s, the general consensus about children's literature was that difficult topics such as death, racial conflict, or sexual permissiveness were taboo and therefore simply did not appear (Postman 1994). Topics often censored include sexual content, language, violence, homosexuality, race, and religion (Whelan 2009). By the twentieth century, censorship of children's literature developed a specialized vocabulary of its own, including words such as "challenge," "quiet-censorship," "covert-censorship," and "self-censorship."

"Challenge" takes the form of an official written complaint to a school or library (Hopkins 1996), though the American Library Association (2009) estimates that the number of challenges reported represent only a quarter of the actual total number, and also reports that the Harry Potter series ranks as the most challenged book series of the twenty-first century.

"Quiet censorship" refers to publishers of children's literature who, in anticipation of negative reaction or unwanted pressure from the public, exercise censorship outside of the public eye (Hunt 1997). Publisher censorship can occur at any stage of the process: prior to acceptance, in the final negotiations prior to publication, when the book is re-released in paperback, when illustrations are changed, or when the book is translated. Twice Beatrix Potter was pressured to delete material: in *The Tailor of Gloucester* (1903), a rat drinks from a black bottle (it was censored), and in *The Tale of Tom Kitten* (1907), Tom's clothes come off (she refused the changes).

Other actors in the quiet censorship arena include individuals, groups, or communities, who, once a book is published, may pressure publishers, public institutions (such as libraries or schools), or even commercial enterprises (such as book and video stores) to suppress, remove, or limit access to material (Hopkins 1996). These unofficial censors may attempt to enforce certain values by purging schools and libraries of "controversial" books or circulating lists of "objectionable" books and authors. Many librarians attest to acts of rogue or "covert censorship" in which angry readers white out, black out, tear out, razor out, or ink out what they deem to be offensive portions—as in copies of Maurice Sendak's *In the Night Kitchen* (1970) where such readers cover up the young boy's genitals.

Authors also practice self-censorship, making decisions about what might be acceptable in a children's book—sometimes, as Craig Howes (2004) says, "working against free expression [and thus becoming] self-silencing." Three children's book writers—Lois Lowry, Gillian Rubinstein, and Erik Haugaard—confess to occasional self-censorship, sometimes out of economic concerns or fear of publisher's remarks or possible attacks from pubic censors. As Lowry put it, "I began to consider each bad word that appeared from my . . . word processor, and to question whether it needed to be there" (Nilsen and Bosmajian 1996).

Conversely, children's literature has historically provided a venue for resistance to censorship. During the McCarthy era in the United States, writing for children became a safe refuge for creative people on the left who were able to work under pseudonyms and evade censorship (Mickenberg 2006). In *The Day They Came to Arrest the Book* (1988), Nat Hentoff highlights censorship issues by examining *The Adventures of Huckleberry Finn* (1884), which he believes is a useful tool for educators (in part because of its language) in exploring racism, slavery, and the moral dilemmas of its era.

Since librarians or teachers can easily be fired for censorship reasons (Kantor 2007), often a single complaint can frighten them into removing an item immediately. In addition to the fear of receiving a complaint or of corrupting children, teachers censor material to avoid frightening or saddening children, or to avoid introducing controversy into their classroom, thus steering clear of Eve Bunting's *Fly Away Home* (1991) (dealing with homelessness), or Faith Ringgold's *Tar Beach* (1991) (a family struggles for financial security) (Wollman-Bonilla 1998). One of the most common objections to children's books is "inappropriate language," often labeled obscene or pornographic. On these grounds, John Steinbeck's *Of Mice and Men* (1937), J. D. Salinger's *Catcher in the Rye* (1951), and Katherine Paterson's *The Great Gilly Hopkins* (1978) have all faced censorship.

While censorship of a book based on its gender bias, sexism, or racism is more accepted by society, this approach has led to certain books being censored for embodying "outmoded" attitudes representative of the period in which they were written. For example, Helen Bannerman's *Little Black Sambo* (1899), Travers's *Mary Poppins* (1934), Hugh Lofting's *The Story of Dr Dolittle* (1920), and Hergé's *Tintin au Congo* (1931) have all been banned due to negative representations of Africans or African-Americans (MacLeod 1983). Books attacked for their political message include George Orwell's *Animal Farm* (1945; communism) and Michael J. Caduto and Joseph Bruchac's *Keepers of the Earth* (1988; environmentalism, native spirituality) (Karolides 1999; Zimmerman 2000). Stories like these are attacked because of perceptions that, even within a sociohistorical context, negative attitudes toward multiculturalism, the role of women, the physically challenged, racial, social, or sexual minorities, or religion are no longer acceptable.

Some have sought to ban children's literature on moral grounds. Books targeted for promoting antisocial behavior include Dav Pilkey's *Adventures of Captain Underpants* (1997; bad behavior, toilet humor), Louise Fitzhugh's *Harriet the Spy* (1964; lying and window-peeping), Paul Zindel's *The Pigman* (1968; lying, swearing, drinking, drug abuse, disrespect for authority and property), Robert Cormier's *The Chocolate War* (1974; mob rule, masturbation), S. E. Hinton's *The Outsiders* (1967a; gangs), Alice Childress's *A Hero Ain't Nothin' But a Sandwich* (1982; drug addiction, swearing, Black militancy), Trina Schart Hyman's Caldecott-winning *Little Red Riding Hood* (1983; there is a bottle of wine in Little Red Riding Hood's basket), and Isabelle Holland's *Heads You Win, Tails I Lose* (1973; drug abuse). Safety concerns have also resulted in objections to books depicting young children engaged in dangerous behaviors such as turning on a stove, climbing a ladder, or walking alone. Books that have been banned due to depictions of violence include Fitzhugh's *Bang, Bang You're Dead* (1986) and R. L. Stine's Wizards, Warriors and You series (1985). Those opposed to these works argue instead for the use of ethical heroes (see Chetwin in Lehr 1995).

In a 2009 survey of librarians (Whelan 2009), 87 percent said the main reason they avoid certain books is because they include sexuality or sex education. This content seldom appears in literature for young children but is constantly surfacing in works for young adults and includes controversial themes such as: masturbation and sexuality, as in Judy Blume's *Are You There God? It's Me, Margaret* (1970), *Deenie* (1973), and *Then Again, Maybe I Won't* (1971); teenage pregnancy, as in Josephine Kamm's *Young Mother* (1968); conception, as in Norma Klein's *Naomi in the Middle* (1974); non-marital sex, as in Klein's *Mom, the Wolf Man, and Me* (1972); infanticide, as in Lois Lowry's *The Giver* (1993); abortion, as in Klein's *It's Not What You Expect* (1973); contraception, as in Blume's *Forever* (1975); AIDS, as in Mary Kate Jordan, Abby Levine, and Judith Friedman's *Losing Uncle Tim* (1989); and, of course, premarital sex, as in Blume's *Deenie* and *Forever,* Klein's *It's Okay If You Don't Love Me* (1977), and Francesca Lia Block's Weetzie Bat series (1989–2005). Teachers and administrators are often pressured to remove these books from schools. In a related but less sensitive topic, nudity or body parts are sometimes labeled as "obscene"; recently, for example, there have been objections to Susan Patron's Newbery Medal winner *The Higher Power of Lucky* (2006), in which a rattlesnake bites the main character's dog's "scrotum."

Homosexuality, often a focus of censorship, was cited by 47 percent of censoring librarians in the aforementioned survey (Whelan 2009). Books cited for this reason include John Knowles's *A Separate Peace* (1959), Michael Willhoite's *Daddy's Roommate* (1990), Aaron Fricke's *Reflections of a Rock Lobster* (1981), A. J. Homes's *Jack* (1990), Deborah Hautzig's *Hey Dollface* (1978), and Anne Heron's *Two Teenagers in Twenty* (1993).

Some images or references in literature may inspire a hostile reaction from people with particular religious convictions. Pullman's *The Golden Compass* (1995) was pulled from Catholic schools when the popular film adaptation was released in theatres (Abley 2007). One of the most contested issues in educational circles today is the labeling of Wicca, native spirituality, and other earth-based approaches to spirituality as witchcraft, the occult, or satanic worship (Barry 1992; "Books Involving Witchcraft" 1994). Due to their "occult" themes, Paterson's *Bridge to Terabithia* (1977) was once the most frequently challenged, and J. K. Rowling's Harry Potter books quickly became the most protested ever with 472 complaints. Some groups believe that *any* teaching about non-Western religions (Buddhism, Taoism, etc.), or even yoga or meditation, equate to witchcraft, cultish activity, or attempts to convert children to a religion (Shariff and Manley-Casimir 1999). Others believe that devils and witches are a real force for evil in the world, and argue against any literature featuring them; stories that feature magic, fairies, and ghosts have been attacked for similar reasons. In recent decades, despite strong opposition (Blair 1996), groups of self-declared witches have begun to defend their right to expression and have criticized authors of stories where witches do not appear in a favorable light, including Roald Dahl's *The Witches* (1983) (Barry 1992).

Today, questions of who can write or speak for whom often lead to charges of censorship. Many censors on the left either are sympathetic to or come from embattled cultural or racial minorities who feel they are already threatened—sometimes physically, sometimes socially. Concern about negative stereotypes leads naturally to the question of "cultural appropriation": should a non-Chinese interpret Chinese folktales? Should Europeans or their descendants try to retell native legends? Lissa Paul (2000), for example, attacks books such as Jan Bourdeau Waboose's *Morning on the Lake* (1997) for "boutique multiculturalism" (to use Stanley Fish's [1997] term), to explain how ethnicity is watered down and designated as "too foreign" for children. The difficult questions in censorship come to the fore more forcefully when children are given books written for adults, with mature themes and difficult choices. For example, Margaret Mitchell's *Gone with the Wind* (1936) and David Guterson's *Snow Falling on Cedars* (1994) were both written with adult audiences and sensibilities in mind. Also, it is important to note that banned books often become even more attractive to readers. As Peter Hunt (1997), who gets the final word on the subject, notes: "The censorship of children's literature is a texture of paradoxes: between benevolent control and fearful repression; between common-sense attitudes to words and meanings and necessary freedom of interpretation; between a 'trivial' subject and a far-from-trivial reaction to it—and, as we have seen in contemporary Britain, between the overt and the covert."

7

Character

Jay Mechling

The concept of character has two uses in children's literature discourse. One use belongs to literary criticism, as the critic and reader observe the people in a story or novel as "characters," that is, as agents or actors (Burke 1973) whose actions move a story through time. The other use refers to the moral qualities of a person. These uses of "character" are related, as the root of the English word lies in a Greek word for a tool used to mark or engrave a material (*Oxford English Dictionary* [*OED*]).

By the seventeenth century, the English word came to mean both "the individuality impressed by nature and habit on man or nation; mental or moral constitution" and a "personality invested with distinctive attributes and qualities, by a novelist or dramatist" (*OED*). In his 1927 lectures later published as *Aspects of the Novel*, E. M. Forster distinguished "flat" from "round" characters, the former being relatively simple and predictable in their thoughts and actions, such as the Wolf in the Grimms' "Little Red Riding Hood" (1812) or the title character of *The History of Little Goody Two-Shoes* (1765). The latter kind, such as Anne in L. M. Montgomery's *Anne of Green Gables* (1908) or Jin in Gene Luen Yang's *American Born Chinese* (2006), are more complex, full of tensions, contradictions, and human unpredictability—in short, more like real people. The complexity of characters in children's literature has increased over time. As adults came to see children as more complex people, not just as "miniature adults," so the authors for children came to write more complex and "real" characters in the twentieth century.

The concept of character as a moral quality of the individual reflected bourgeois gender arrangements in the nineteenth century. Historians see this very masculine concept as a product of the changing nature of men's work in the Industrial Revolution, in the creation of "separate spheres" of life (men in the workplace, women at home to take care of the moral education of the children), and in the related "crisis in masculinity" in the waning decades of the century. The concept also weds religious—especially Protestant—ideas to work and manliness. The idea of "muscular Christianity" arose in this era. As exemplified by fiction such as Thomas Hughes's *Tom Brown's Schooldays* (1857), "muscular Christianity" saw physical fitness, sports, and outdoor recreation as good for the boy's mind and morals as well as his body. Related to the concept of character were the concepts of honor and duty. The ideal man of the era demonstrated "good character," which meant that he understood and met his responsibilities to family, work, and the nation.

Boys and young men received instruction in good character through a number of genres. Between 1870 and 1910, for example, there was a flood of new nonfiction "success manuals" offering advice to young men on the virtues of "honesty, frugality, industry, reliability, and loyalty" (Hilkey 1997). These manuals, along with novels of the period, proclaimed the central truth of Andrew Carnegie's (1889) famous essay "Wealth"—namely, that the man of good character, the man who practices the social and moral virtues, will enjoy tangible and intangible wealth.

The advice manuals were for young men, but the fiction reinforcing these messages reached down to even younger boys. Horatio Alger, Jr.'s stories of young men whose fortunes improve through hard work, moral virtue, and some luck, as told in novels beginning with *Ragged Dick* (1868), became so famous that the phrase "Horatio Alger story" has come to signify the formulaic "rags-to-riches" story popular in American culture. Edward Stratemeyer's syndicate mass-produced hundreds of formulaic novels, usually in series, written by a stable of authors who worked under pseudonyms (Billman 1986; Johnson 1993). Stratemeyer began in 1899 with his own Rover Boys novels, but the syndicate eventually produced some of the most famous younger reader series in American history, including the Hardy Boys, Tom Swift, and Nancy Drew (Greenwald 2004; Rehak 2005; Connelly 2008).

By the early twentieth century, some adults were worrying that the adventure and violence in these novels were having adverse affects on young male readers. A few decades earlier there had been a "moral panic" about sensational "dime novels," and by 1910 the new concern was about the sorts of novels that the Stratemeyer syndicate was producing. In 1914 the Boy Scouts of America (BSA) enlisted Grosset and Dunlap,

the publishers of juvenile series novels, in a project to create a series known as "Every Boys Library—Boy Scout Edition." The series bore the imprimatur of the BSA and published a range of wholesome fiction meant to demonstrate good, strong character, from reprints of novels by Jack London and Ernest Thompson Seton to new works (e.g., Dimock 1912).

The novels of Percy Keese Fitzhugh (1876–1950) stand out as more complex fictional accounts of moral dilemmas and how boys might try to employ virtue to act as men of character. Beginning with *Tom Slade, Boy Scout* (1915), over the next two decades Fitzhugh wrote dozens of series novels with Boy Scouts as the central characters. These novels, published with the approval of the BSA by Grosset and Dunlap, departed from the simplistic moral didacticism of some of the other juvenile fiction. Fitzhugh uses humor and seriousness to explore the difficulties of applying rules (such as the twelve points of the Scout Law) to real situations, where the rules might conflict (e.g., in Fitzhugh 1920). The Fitzhugh novels show the boy reader that a man of character can face moral or ethical dilemmas, can act according to his best judgment, and (most important) can accept the consequences of his decision "like a man."

Historians see that first decade of the twentieth century as a watershed era, when American society moved from a production-oriented economy to a consumer-based one, and the nineteenth-century concept of "character" gave way to the twentieth-century concept of "personality" (Susman 1984). Whereas "character" was attached to masculine social virtues, including honor and duty, "personality" invoked a "real self" apart from social roles and even from the restricting rules of society—and, unlike "character," "personality" included feminine selves, too. So "character" largely disappeared from children's literature from the 1920s through the 1970s. More precisely, while some authors of children's literature still promoted social and personal virtues, talk of "character" seemed old-fashioned and even oppressive. It took the "culture wars" of the 1980s to revive the concept.

The election of Ronald Reagan to the presidency in 1980 and the role of the Religious Right in that victory signaled to many that the United States was experiencing new culture wars pitting social and religious orthodoxy against progressivism (Hunter 1991). As happened nearly a century earlier, many adults perceived a "character crisis" in young people and vowed to restore moral education, "character education," to schools and other institutions socializing the young (Hunter 2000). At the center of these efforts are the "Character Counts!" movement and network, created by the Center for Youth Ethics, a project of the Josephson Institute of Ethics (founded 1987), and the Center for the Fourth and Fifth Rs (Respect and Responsibility) at the Cortland campus of the State University of New York.

Character Counts! and related organizations recommend fiction for children and youth on their websites.

On the Character Counts! website is a list of "children's books that build character," coded by reading level and by one of the six "Pillars of Character" (trustworthiness, respect, responsibility, fairness, caring, and citizenship) that the particular novel or storybook reinforces. Schools and public libraries put similar lists on their websites, often using the same "Pillars" to help parents or young readers select books. On these lists appear some familiar authors, such as Betsy Byars, Louis Sachar, Armstrong Perry, and Cynthia Voight. Sachar's *Marvin Redpost: Why Pick on Me?* (1993b), for example, receives praise for its attention to trust, while his *Marvin Redpost: Is He a Girl?* (1993a) teaches children about caring. Some lists include more controversial authors, such as S. E. Hinton and J. K. Rowling, both of whom have experienced attempts to remove their books from school libraries and curricula.

The periodical banning of books for children and youth signals the very political nature of reading fiction amid the culture wars. Few adults would argue against the six virtues touted by Character Counts!, nor would many object to children's literature that values the virtues. The politicizing of children's literature, dragging authors and books into the culture wars, harms this project of communicating virtues to children and young readers, especially when some of the recommended literature presents simplistic didacticism and some sites steer parents and teachers away from juvenile fiction that is more complex and morally conflicted.

The gender issue permeates the debates over character education and literature in the early twenty-first century. The sense of a character crisis and the response by juvenile fiction writers a century ago was distinctly male. The present-day adult moral panic about character includes girls, but the term "character," with all of its historical contexts, seems not quite right in talking about the qualities the society now desires in girls and young women. Juvenile fiction for girls dealing with bullying, sexual abuse, teen pregnancy, and drug use—unlikely to appear on Character Counts! and related lists of recommended reading—certainly addresses the qualities of "strong" girls.

The concept of good "character" is so tied to the culturally conservative position in the culture wars (Hunter 1991, 2000), and is so locked into a nineteenth-century masculine concept of moral behavior, that the term no longer seems useful in thinking about the role of literature in the moral education of both boys and girls in the twenty-first century. Fieldwork-based research on the everyday lives of children and adolescents that seeks to understand how youth experience and deal with moral dilemmas in their everyday lives (e.g., Goodwin 2006) now sees boys and girls as much more alike than previously thought in the ways they deal with problems. If, as this research suggests, girls are becoming more like boys in their friendship cultures, and if both boys and girls actually practice more nuanced moral reasoning than the rigid, absolutist positions advocated by most "character education" experts, then reader-response criticism needs to respect the "native" categories young people use in thinking and talking about negotiating challenges, conflicts, and moral dilemmas in their everyday lives. Whether or not the term "character" is a native category among young people, male or female, remains to be seen.

8

Childhood

Karen Sánchez-Eppler

"Childhood" is an ancient word in English, not a young one. The *Oxford English Dictionary* takes as its earliest example for "cildhad" an English gloss inserted during the tenth century between the lines of the Lindisfarne Gospels. The meaning expressed there appears consistent with the most literal strand of our contemporary usage: this passage from the Gospel of Mark ("soð he cuoeð from cildhad"; 9:21) employs childhood as a temporal marker: a father explains to Jesus that his son had been wracked by fits since the earliest years of his life. The miraculous cure Jesus performs stands as a test of belief and a compelling instance of the power of prayer. The gathered crowd, the disciples, and generations of interpreters since have voiced many questions about this scene and what it means, but no one questions the meaning of childhood. This apparent clarity—the confident unanimity over the implications and significance of "childhood"—is perhaps the most potent, and indeed dangerous, thing about this keyword. We have, it seems, a miraculous faith in childhood itself.

"The child, and stories about the child," Adam Phillips explains, "have become our most convincing essentialism" (1998). Ever since Philippe Ariès's (1962) provocative assertion that "in medieval society the idea of childhood did not exist," historians of childhood,

scholars of children's literature, even psychoanalysts like Phillips, have striven to dismantle the essentialism of childhood. These accounts stress the complicated relations, and often glaring contradictions, between any society's idea of childhood and the lived experience of actual children. They offer persuasive evidence both of how attitudes toward childhood have changed over time and place, and of how much the content and duration of this life stage has differed even for children in the same society but of different genders, races, or class positions. Such studies reveal that ideas about childhood frequently articulated differences of status: modes of schooling and play serve as prime markers of class identity, of differences between boys and girls even within the same family, of the transition from an agricultural to an urban/industrial economy, and of racial inequality. Changes in children's literature have not only reflected these various biases, but in many ways served to create and disseminate them. The different models of behavior and desire voiced in Louisa May Alcott's *Little Women* (1868–69) and Thomas Bailey Aldrich's *The Story of a Bad Boy* (1869) schooled their readers in gender norms, and in their realist detail these books have similarly informed historians' accounts of mid-nineteenth-century American girlhood and boyhood. The idea of the child is repeatedly made and remade in the stories told to children.

Yet despite such constructionist scholarship, the sense of childhood as a ubiquitous and fundamental category of human life has proved remarkably resilient. Belief in the universal and unchanging essence of childhood can make all sorts of cultural arrangements and power structures appear natural. The configuration of the family and of gender roles, the socializing institutions of education, class and racial formations, literary and other forms of cultural production, national security, religious and sexual virtue all tout the needs of the child. Seen this way, children appear less as the object of control than as a rationale for regulation in general. Worse, the concept of childhood dependency has frequently been used to naturalize a lack of autonomy, not only for the young, but for all sorts of subservient people. In cases of poverty, colonial status, and racial or gender oppression, analogies to childhood easily implement exclusion from civil rights. "If politics is ultimately about the distribution of power," Henry Jenkins argues, "then the power imbalance between children and adults remains at heart a profoundly political matter" (1998). The question persists: How and why do evocations of childhood succeed so often and so well in enforcing social norms and justifying social hierarchies?

I suspect the essentialism of childhood has proved this resilient and convincing because it rests, at least in part, upon biological fact. Unlike the months, or days, or even hours of dependency for most animals, human young require years of training and protection before they are capable of surviving on their own. The need for care is indeed a natural and essential aspect of children's lives, as is children's growing self-reliance. Young children everywhere must be fed, carried, taught to speak, and prepared to function appropriately within their particular social world (Stearns 2009). The complexities of the idea of childhood, and the conflicting ways this keyword has been wielded, all harken back to this sense of beginnings, to the general trajectory from dependency toward autonomy, but there consensus ends. Few areas of human life are at once so universally shared and so differently experienced and understood. Is the mewling infant darling or bestial, the roaming youth a crusader or a truant, the laboring child valued or abused, the child reader virtuous, imaginative, or indolent? Childhood may be widely recognized as a life stage that stretches from birth until the taking on of adult competence and responsibility, but its contours and meanings are deeply circumstantial, formed by the particulars of each historical and social situation, and the stories we tell about them. Perhaps it is because childhood simultaneously roots itself in both biological and ideological ground that it proves so potent a means of naturalizing cultural formations.

Changes in the status of children are notable for what they indicate about shifts in social priorities, that is, for what they reveal about alterations in the desires and behaviors of adults. Ideas of childhood, however, are not only an adult concern. Ethnographic projects with contemporary children and archival research on the diaries, letters, and school compositions that children produced in earlier periods have enabled scholars to measure the gap between children and childhood, not only interrogating how adults' ideas about childhood inform children's experiences, but also documenting children's participation in the discourses of childhood. The letters written to the Children's Aid Society by nineteenth-century street children skillfully manipulate the philanthropic rhetoric of vulnerable child waifs to serve their own, often oppositional, needs (Sánchez-Eppler 2005). Children's literature plays a powerful part in these dynamics, mediating between societal ideas and child actors. Charles Loring Brace's work with the Children's Aid Society inspired Horatio Alger, Jr.'s "rags-to-riches" tales, and the Society's lodging houses for newsboys happily stocked Alger's novels and used them to promote newsboy savings accounts and other improving habits such as reading. Ideas of childhood inform a broad array of practices, institutions, and ways of thinking about human identity; genre shifts within children's literature have both spurred and been spurred by such changes.

As the example of Alger suggests, books written for children remain one of the best gauges we have for a particular society's views of childhood, and one that we know children themselves engaged with directly. The books written for children instruct the young in how their particular culture understands their role. Literacy primers, school books, and conduct manuals were produced for young readers since at least the late Middle Ages, but until the eighteenth century most childhood reading was gleaned from books primarily intended for adults. The publication of literature explicitly for children burgeoned into a flourishing wing of the publishing business with John Newbery's line of "toy books" in the 1740s (Avery 1995). The success of Newbery's offerings depended upon a new conception of childhood, which presumed that children should be sufficiently literate and leisured to make use of such volumes, that children's skills and taste as readers would differ enough from that of adults to warrant such separate publications, and that enough parents would be interested in pleasing and instructing their children to make such a specialized line profitable. The collection of illustrated alphabet cards and other reading aids, including home-made story books, which Jane Johnson carefully created for her four children, predates Newbery's commercial publications by a few years and attests to the intense desire in such affluent households for materials that would make reading instruction pleasurable (Arizpe and Styles 2004). Thus the very notion that there should be books produced specifically for child readers in itself indicates a great deal about the evolution of the idea of childhood.

The gloss in the Lindisfarne Gospel treats childhood as an easy temporal marker, but the "when" of childhood has in fact proved remarkably variable. In medieval Europe the notion of the "ages of life" provided a familiar symbolic frame, neatly dividing the human life span into distinct periods with specific social roles and clearly defined expectations. Infancy and childhood inaugurated these iconic series, but such life stages were not understood as tightly correlated to chronological age (Ariès 1962). Gary Dickson (2009) argues that the twelfth-century "Children's Crusade" served as a means of marking the passage from *pueri* to adulthood in a social world in which merely growing older did not necessarily enable a shift of status, especially for the rural poor. Later bureaucratic and institutional structures would increasingly depend on the more precise divisions offered by years, flanking childhood with the question, "How old are you?" (Chudacoff 1989). Whether through the increasingly rigorous recording practices of parish and state registers of birth in the seventeenth and eighteenth centuries, the age groupings of graded classrooms that would become standard educational practice in the mid-nineteenth century, or the exacting calibrations of developmental psychology in the twentieth, chronological age—gauged in years, not skills or activities—has gradually become a bulwark of identity.

This attention to age has resulted in ever more normative claims about the temporal limits of childhood, although the slightest prodding reveals them to be shallow claims indeed. The child mill-workers and miners of the Industrial Revolution, whose small, dexterous fingers and capacity to squeeze down shafts too low or thin for adults turned these five and six year olds into arduous and cheap workers, labored during the very period when children in the middle and professional classes began taking on more years of schooling before employment (Tuttle 1999). Still, the conviction that childhood can be measured in years is one of the ways that assertions about the nature of childhood gain authority and the aura of universality. Anna Barbauld's *Lessons for Children from Two to Three Years Old* (1778) demonstrates that from the first decades of children's publishing a conception of childhood measured in years structured the market, even though it would

be nearly a century before schools generally divided students and their lessons by age rather than ability (Chudacoff 1989). By the nineteenth century not only child readers, but also child characters were increasingly described by age—thus we are told that Alice enters Wonderland on her seventh birthday, and A. A. Milne merges child reader and child character in the identity of years: "now we are six."

Ariès (1962) argues that during the Middle Ages and early modern period, children might have been loved and cared for, but their lives were largely undifferentiated from those of adults. His account of the "invention of childhood" as a distinct social category during the seventeenth and eighteenth centuries presents it as an idea constructed by historical forces in response to more general cultural needs; thus he shows the specific utility of the idea of the child as different from adults in sanctioning the learned classes now needed to train the young, and in privatizing the family now needed to protect the innocent. Although he tends to base his arguments on other evidence (how children are represented in paintings, the gradual creation of distinctive dress for the young, the way parents write about their offspring in letters and journals), clearly the rise of children's publishing near the end of this period confirms that such a transformation had indeed been achieved. In narrating how the concept of childhood was forged in early modern Europe, Ariès does not present a narrative of progress. The alternately "coddled" and "disciplined" childhoods that emerge have in their different ways lost much of the autonomy and latitude that he identified in the lives of premodern children. Thus the vulnerabilities associated with modern conceptions of childhood prove double-edged: they elicit tenderness and care, but they also disallow agency.

Most accounts of Euro-American conceptions of childhood note how the development of these ideas has followed a general trajectory from the stern and punitive to the doting and indulgent. Yet for individual theorists, and in the daily life of culture, any such tidy history of ideas has tended to mix and muddle in ambivalent practice. The concept of "infant depravity" expressed in John Wesley's insistent plea—"Do not give up your child to his own will, that is, to the devil. Though it be pain to yourself, yet . . . make them submit" (1784)—expresses an understanding of childhood as a period of innate and inevitably sinful desires, but also gives voice to a desperate concern for children's ultimate wellbeing. Thus, accounts of shifts in the history of childhood that simply veer from a cruel reliance on the "rod" to a doting array of gifts and endearments mishear the anguished cherishing in these injunctions.

John Locke's (1690) depiction of the child as a *tabula rasa*, not already tainted by sin but simply waiting to be inscribed by experience, presents childhood in a manner both more benign and more passive than that offered by evangelical accounts of devilish will. Victorian child-rearing manuals would make Locke's epistemological thesis into a paean of malleability and a justification of parental authority: "Like clay in hands of the potter, they are waiting only to be molded" (quoted in Kincaid 1992, 90). Jean-Jacques Rousseau inverted the assumptions of infant depravity, instead declaring adulthood corrupt and the social world a sad decline from natural innocence. In *Émile, or On Education* (1762), Rousseau urged parents to "leave childhood to ripen in your children" (1979), but this idealization of childhood as a period of freedom and natural goodness did not actually grant children much latitude. Émile's tutor, after all, trusts to the boy's capacity for observation and induction, but the goals of this training remain firmly in the tutor's hands.

These competing theories of childhood seeded quite different assumptions about the most appropriate stories to tell to children, ranging from didactic to playful. Locke's image of the child's mind as a "white paper void of all characters" conflates child and page in a way that seems particularly illuminating for a discussion of children's literature, since it presents ideas and identity as not only strongly marked but powerfully embodied by the pages we read as children. The ideas of childhood proffered by Locke and Rousseau melded to disrupt older strategies of child-rearing, resulting by the mid-nineteenth century in an explicitly new set of goals for children's literature: "[W]e have ceased to think it the part of wisdom to cross the first instincts of children, and to insist upon making of them little moralists, metaphysicians, and philosophers, when great nature determines that their first education shall be in the senses and muscles, the affections and fancies" (Osgood 1865). Such changes in the content and purpose of childhood reading prove formative not only for the individual but for the culture. As Gillian Brown (2001) details, Locke's pedagogical models did as much as or more than his political theories to inform American revolutionary conceptions of governmental authority and consent. Similarly, Andrew O'Malley (2003) explains the genre shifts of children's literature from didacticism to humor, adventure, and fantasy in terms of political economy, suggesting that the moralizing children's books of the eighteenth century not just reflected but actually fostered the development of industrial capitalism, training docile workers and frugal masters. Thus, he suggests, the burgeoning of imaginative children's literature can be read as a sign of the secure triumph of the middle class, finally confident enough to play.

Children themselves participate in the construction of these different ideas of childhood, and these different attitudes toward children's books. Scraps of writing left behind by two young girls in mid-nineteenth-century New England articulate the change Osgood described and demonstrate the fluidity with which conflicting ideas about childhood can coexist even for children from fairly similar backgrounds. Lilly St. Agnan Barrett, whose father owned a dye house in Malden, Massachusetts (just north of Boston), penciled this pledge on a small piece of torn card: "I will try this day to live a simple sincere serene life; repelling every thought of discordant self-seeking an [sic] anxiety; cultivating magninimity [sic] self-control and the habit of silence; practicing economy cheerfulness and helpfulness" (c. 1856). Her hesitant handwriting and a vocabulary somewhat in advance of her spelling suggest she was probably somewhat under ten years old. Lilly's pledge charts the process of socialization to a docile domesticity, as she strives to subdue any discordant aspects of her childhood self. Eliza Wadsworth, the ten-year-old daughter of a successful farmer in West Hartford, Connecticut, added sly phrases in a small penciled script after many of the lessons in her *Practical Spelling-Book* (1861): "Do you not love bread and milk?" concludes the lesson entitled "The Gristmill"; "No I'll bet I don't," writes Eliza. She inserts the simple words "no yes" beneath the book's printed question "Good boys and girls try to behave well at school because it makes their parents happy. *Do you* do so?" Eliza may not behave well at school, but she still makes her parents happy; splitting obedience from the notion of parental pleasure, she takes pride in willful rebellion and seems to suspect that her parents will too. The differences between these girls' understanding of their childhood role, and the divergent ways they deploy their fledgling literary skills, suggests the fluidity of cultural change and the function of reading and writing in the redefinition of childhood.

The mid-nineteenth-century flourishing of children's literature as a site for fantasy and play ultimately produced a sense of childhood less as a period of preparation for adult life than as a time magically and wonderfully separate from it—a period where, as Eliza seems to feel, the rules don't really apply. Childhood from this perspective appears so different from the rest of life that it becomes another place entirely.

Virginia Woolf's lovely phrase for it—"that great cathedral space which was childhood" (1939)—is loaded with awe and beauty but also (this is Woolf, after all) with ironic pieties. All the magical places of children's literature (Wonderland, Neverland, Narnia, Oz, where the wild things are) understand childhood in these topical terms as someplace else, asserting a distance ripe for nostalgia. There is obvious class bias in the luxurious abundance of these fantasies, and indeed a way in which they sentimentalize and absolve inequalities, since even Hans Christian Andersen's destitute "Little Match Girl" can feel warmed by the glow of her imagination.

The sense of childhood as a time and space of enchantment intriguingly mirrors the development of psychoanalysis (Blum 1995). Psychoanalytic theory gave a new primacy to childhood as the origin of the adult self and its inchoate desires. In particular, Sigmund Freud's account of infantile sexuality and the processes of its repression served to equate the unconscious with childhood. Carolyn Steedman (1995) goes so far as to credit the figure of the child with grounding the modern concept of the self with its personal history and individual interiority. Thus, by the late nineteenth century childhood had become a locus of memory and imagination, a "secret garden," whose characteristics are in many ways shared with those of fiction itself.

At the beginning of the twenty-first century such an idealized romance of childhood appears to many cultural critics as something lost, or on the verge of loss. The hectic pace of modern life, the stress of high-stakes testing, the juvenilization of poverty, and the commercialization of desire all seem to threaten the sacred pastoral of childhood. Television and video games besiege the golden citadel of children's literature (Postman 1994), and the ravaged figure of the child soldier explodes the myths both of childhood adventure and of childhood security (Briggs 2005). Resisting childhood's essentialism, recognizing the constructed nature of this idyll, puts the language of crises in historical perspective. Pub signs and other commercial interests infiltrated alphabet primers from as early as the seventeenth century (Crain 2000), and as William Blake's *Songs of Innocence and Experience* (1794) insists, romantic celebrations of childhood were always shadowed by grim alternatives. Anne Higonnet (1998) urges that we replace the investment in childhood innocence with the recognition of the "knowing child," a figure aware of the world's threats and desires but still deserving of adult protection. We would do better at tending to the real needs and situations of children if we were to forgo our miraculous faith in any essential and singular idea of childhood. The historical record reveals the broad array both of ideas of childhood and of children's ways of living it. Contemporary "American society is unique in its assumption that all young people should follow a single, unitary path to adulthood," Steven Mintz observes with disapproval (2004). The plural "childhoods" could prove a more honest and productive keyword, and children's literature may help inscribe this change by telling an ever wider array of new and different stories.

9

Children's Literature

Peter Hunt

"Children's literature" is a term used to describe both a set of texts and an academic discipline—and it is often regarded as an oxymoron. If "children" commonly connotes immaturity, and "literature" commonly connotes sophistication in texts and reading, then the two terms may seem to be incompatible. Henry James, in "The Future of the Novel" (1900b), observed that "the literature, as it may be called for convenience, of children, is an industry," but not one to be taken seriously: "the sort of taste that used to be called 'good' has nothing to do with the matter; we are demonstrably in [the] presence of millions for whom taste is but an obscure, confused, immediate instinct" (quoted in Hughes 1978). As recently as 1997, Roderick McGillis wrote: "[B]ooks for the young still carry a burden of perceived simplicity that sets them outside the complexities we associate with literature for adults." This view is held by many regardless of whether the possessive (children*'s*) is taken to indicate "for," "by," "of," or "belonging to." Both parts of the term are what Raymond Williams (1976/1983a) would have called "difficult" in that both cover a huge range of possible meanings, synchronically and diachronically, and together they have caused much confusion and influenced (often negatively) the development of the areas that they ostensibly name. The term has so many practical and theoretical disadvantages that "books for children" or "children's fiction" are often used as equivalents.

The earliest use of the term to describe texts has not been established, although it appeared as the title of an anonymous article in the *Quarterly Review* in January 1860 (469–500); otherwise, the term "juvenile literature" was well-established by the end of the nineteenth century (for example, *Juvenile Literature As It Is* [Salmon 1888]), while Charles Dickens referred to "the fairy literature of our childhood" in "Frauds on the Fairies" (1853). Its use as a title for academic courses probably dates from the 1960s in the United States and the 1980s in the United Kingdom.

All definitions rely on their purpose, and so the broadest definition of "children's literature"—any text read by any child—is of little practical value. Another distinction, popularized in the United States in the 1960s, largely for administrative purposes, is between "children's literature" and "young adult literature." However, it goes back at least as far as Sarah Trimmer's *Guardian of Education* (1802) in which she distinguishes between "'Books *for Children*' and 'Books *for Young Persons*,'" adding, "We shall take the liberty of . . . supposing all young gentlemen and ladies to be *children*, till they are *fourteen*, and *young persons* till they are at least *twenty-one*."

It is helpful to consider the elements of the term, *children's* and *literature*, separately and together. The *Shorter Oxford English Dictionary* (1987) unhelpfully defines children as "boys or girls," but there is some question as to whether "children" is too broad a term.

Matthew Grenby (2008) asks: "Is there such a thing as children's literature? Might it be more accurate to talk of a boys' literature and a girls' literature?" Perry Nodelman (2008b) concurs in part: "[A] defining characteristic of children's literature is that it intends to teach what it means for girls to be girls and boys to be boys."

The cultural concept of "children" (and "childhood") also changes radically with time, place, gender, and perceiver, and so the corpus of texts ("children's literature") is unstable. Childhood two hundred years ago (and consequently the books designed for it) may seem so remote from current childhood (and its texts) that a distinction might be made between "historical children's literature" (or books that *were* for children) and "contemporary children's literature," books that address or relate to recognizable current childhoods (see P. Hunt 1996; Flynn 1997). The body of texts, however constituted, can be seen as a symbiotic moveable feast: the book defines its audience (children), and that in turn affects how children are generally defined, as well as how they actually *are* in the future. In this context, the term "children" is increasingly being interpreted as "comparatively inexperienced/unskilled readers."

Because of the possessive, the element "children's" in "children's literature" does not have the same standing as the adjective in "Canadian" in "Canadian children's literature": "children's literature" is one of the relatively few categories of texts/literature defined by its audience (compare "women's literature"). A. A. Milne, writing about the verses in *When We Were Very Young*, observed to a friend that "they are a curious collection; some *for* children, some by, with or from children" (Thwaite 1990), thus pinpointing the essential power-relationships within "children's literature." Leaving aside the very few examples of books written *by* children (such as Daisy Ashford's *The Young Visiters* [1919]), and the very many books that are *about* childhood that are sometimes brought into the category (such as William Golding's *The Lord of the Flies* [1954]), difficulties hinge on books *for* children. The current Western concept of "children" connotes immaturity, inexperience, lack of responsibility—and, perhaps most importantly, *dependence*. Hence the presence of "the hidden adult" in (almost) all texts for children (Nodelman 2008b), and hence the denial of the possibility of "children's literature's" existence at all as something independent of adults, something that *belongs* to children. Jacqueline Rose, who, in *The Case of Peter Pan* (1984), carefully uses the term "children's fiction," suggests (negatively) that

> children's fiction is impossible, not in the sense
> that it cannot be written (that would be nonsense),
> but that it hangs on . . . the impossible relation
> between adult and child. . . . Children's fiction sets
> up a world in which the adult comes first (author,
> maker, giver) and the child comes after (reader,
> product, receiver), but where neither of them enter
> the space in between.

As Jack Zipes (2001) puts it, in "Why Children's Literature Does Not Exist," "[T]here has never been a literature conceived *by* children *for* children, a literature that belongs to children, and there never will be."

"Literature" has proved a particularly contentious term for those working in the field of "children's literature," because the latter is most frequently taken as a category that subsumes any texts (written, spoken, visual) intended for children. Most of these fall into Williams's "popular literature" category:

> At the same time many, even most poems and plays and novels are not seen as literature; they fall below its level, in a sense related to the old distinction of *polite learning*; they are not "substantial" or "important" enough to be called "works of literature." A new category of popular literature or the sub-literary has then to be instituted, to describe works which may be fiction but which are not *imaginative* or creative, and which are therefore devoid of aesthetic interest, and which are not art.
> (Williams 1976)

Initially, this grouping together of *all* texts for children was a negative, default adoption: "children's literature" is any text not for adults. There have been several consequences of this. The first is that *all* has been compared to *some*: that is, because the category of "adult literature" (as opposed to the "sub-literary") is comparatively clear, texts that are demonstrably "sub-literary" for children have come to characterize the whole of "children's literature"—which therefore equates with "popular literature." The second consequence is that those texts within "children's literature" that have stylistic or content characteristics normally associated with "adult literature" (or which are valorized by their age) are (with a very few notable, rule-proving exceptions, such as Milne's *Winnie-the-Pooh* [1926]) removed from the category of "children's literature" into a hybrid category of "the classic." They become, in effect, canonical, and cease to be "children's literature" in any significant sense. Some of these (which are often crossover texts), such as Frances Hodgson Burnett's *The Secret Garden* (1911) or Robert Louis Stevenson's *Treasure Island* (1883), are published both in series of "classics" for children and scholarly editions for adults, supported by academic textual apparatus. In short, the less a book looks like a "popular" book for children, the more likely it is to acquire the status of "children's literature" or "literature" and to be treated with critical tools not specifically designed for it. The third consequence is that many people concerned with mediating or teaching children's books to children are still in thrall to the nebulous idea that some texts are "literature"—*inherently better* than others—and they consequently denigrate the very books that are most likely to connect with children.

More recently, as the literary canon has been challenged in a way that would not have been recognized by Williams (see Nodelman and Reimer 2003), the grouping of diverse texts into the "children's literature" category has been seen as indicative of a liberated critical approach. The premise is that all texts are complex, and therefore all texts are worthy of serious critical and theoretical examination. Hence category and discipline boundaries come together (or are crossed) in a positive concept of "children's literature" whose strength is its very diversity.

However, if "literature" is consequently defined *not* as a set of textual characteristics, but as a *way of reading*, this may still suggest that "children's literature" is an oxymoron. This leads to other kinds of definition of "children's literature," resting on the characteristics of the texts and the intent of the authors. Nodelman (2008b) presents an exhaustive analysis of definitions—"an overview of how adults over the past century or so in Europe, North America, and elsewhere have generally tended to think about children and literature."

Historians have attempted to distinguish between books of instruction and books designed for entertainment. As Patricia Demers and Gordon Moyles (1982) have noted, "If by the term 'children's literature' we mean only those books written specifically for the entertainment of the young, we are forced to exclude . . . a great deal of material that, in the early centuries of English civilization, was the only kind of literature children ever knew." Historians have suggested that "there was no clear dividing line in the Middle Ages between adult and children's literature" (Cunningham 2006); meaningful distinctions between "adult literature" and "children's literature" only begin with the separate marketing strategies of booksellers in England, such as John Newbery in the eighteenth century (O'Malley 2003). However, as Gillian Adams (1998) points out, this is to define "children's literature" "in terms of its commodification . . . that its very existence as a separate entity is tied to commercial interests." Her own view, that early concepts of childhood "do not logically preclude the possibility of a literature for children," has led her to posit a considerable body of "children's literature" not merely in medieval times, but "works closely associated with children" in the Sumerian civilizations of the fourth century B.C.E. (Adams 1986).

More frequently, circular definitions are derived from describing a body of texts already "self-evidently" for children. One of the most-reprinted is by Miles MacDowell (1973):

> Children's books are generally shorter; they tend to favour an active rather than passive treatment, with dialogue and incident rather than description and introspection; child protagonists are the rule; conventions are much used; the story develops within a clear-cut moral schematisation which much adult fiction ignores; children's books tend to be optimistic rather than depressive; language is child-oriented; plots are of a distinctive order.

Since then, definitions of "children's literature" have been based on rather more subtle textual elements. Aidan Chambers, in his seminal paper "The Reader in the Book" (1985b), adopted Wolfgang Iser's concept of the "implied reader" as a defining feature; this has been developed, directly or indirectly, through Barbara Wall (1991) and her theory of address: "My conclusions are founded on the conviction that adults, whether or not they are speaking ironically, speak differently in fiction when they are aware that they are addressing children. Such subtleties of address define a children's book."

These approaches generally avoid the question of "intent" as a defining element in whether a text is "for children" or "children's literature." History is littered with authorial ambiguities—notably Mark Twain's indecision over character in *The Adventures of Tom Sawyer* (1876), Louisa May Alcott's misjudgment of the quality of *Little Women* (1868), or Arthur Ransome's assertion that he wrote only for himself. Similarly, crossover books from Richard Adams's *Watership Down* (1972) to Mark Haddon's *The Curious Incident of the Dog in the Night-Time* (2003) demonstrate commercial ambiguities, and invalidate one of the earliest attempts at a definition, by John Rowe Townsend (1971a):

> I know from conversations over a period of years that there are intelligent and even bookish people to whom children's literature, by definition, is a childish thing which adults have put away. . . . [T]hey . . . regard . . . interest [in it] as an oddity, an amiable weakness. . . . Yet children are part of mankind and children's books are part of literature, and any line which is drawn to confine children or their books to their own special corner is an artificial one. . . . Arguments about whether such-and-such a book is "really for children" are always cropping up, and are usually pointless in any but organisational terms. The only practical definition of a children's book today—absurd as it sounds—is "a book which appears on the children's list of a publisher."

Other writers, such as Peter Hollindale (1997), feel that "children's literature" partakes of a certain *jouissance*, and can be seen as an "event":

The definition of children's literature which I propose therefore involves the author, the text and the child, but with qualified meanings in each case. The author is a person with imaginative interests in constructing childhood (usually but not necessarily through creating child characters) and who on purpose or accidentally uses a narrative voice and language that are audible to children. The text of children's literature is one in which this construction is present. The reader is a child who is still in the business of constructing his or her own childhood, and aware of its presentness—aware that it is not yet over. Where these conditions coexist, the *event* of children's literature takes place. This definition recognises a doubleness that we have to live with, namely that children's literature is characterized both by textual status and by readership, and its uniqueness is evident at the point where they meet.

In other words, "[C]hildren's literature knowingly engages with the idea of power at the heart of the relationship between author and reader" (Thacker and Webb 2002).

This idea has been elaborated by David Rudd (2005), who observed that "it is not enough to declare that children's literature is just 'a boojum'—a meaningless construction—and leave it at that":

> Children's literature consists of texts that consciously or unconsciously address particular constructions of the child, or metaphorical

equivalents in terms of character or situation . . . the commonality being that such texts display an awareness of children's disempowered status (whether containing or controlling it, questioning or overturning it). Adults are as caught up in this discourse as children, engaging dialogically with it (writing/reading it) just as children themselves engage with many "adult" discourses. But it is how these texts are read and used that will determine their success as "children's literature"; how fruitfully they are seen to negotiate this hybrid, or border country.

This same question of the "border country" has applied to "children's literature" as an academic discipline. There are many thousands of undergraduate and graduate degrees called "children's literature" across the world, although in practice many have little in common. They range from primary education to abstract theory, and from aspects of childhood studies to the most arcane bibliography—and despite a common title, they do not present a coherent, or even mutually comprehensible core. The basic division is sometimes seen as one between "child people" and "book people" (a distinction first coined by Townsend [1971a]); the one sees "children" as central to the enterprise, the other not. At the literary end of the spectrum, as Beverly Lyon Clark (2003) has pointed out, the distortion of the term "children's literature" to "kiddie lit" indicates the condescension of some in the academic establishment. This may be a reaction to the predominance of women teachers in the field of children's literature, and its association with low-status (female-dominated) disciplines, notably education and librarianship. As Clark notes, "[A]ttitudes to children's literature are never simple; they're always complexly connected to attitudes associated with gender or class or . . . a particular profession." "Children's literature" is marginalized by being excluded from critical and theoretical discourses to which it could contribute vitally (Thacker 2000); this is the more surprising in that it is widely established as an exemplar of interdisciplinary studies.

The reaction by those working within the academic-literary field called "children's literature" to academic "marginalization" has variously been to adopt the critical and theoretical strategies of their peers in "adult literature," or to position "children's literature" as a valuable partner in the cross-disciplinary "childhood studies" or an essential concomitant to established academic areas such as "Victorian Studies."

"Children's literature" as a term carries with it complex emotional freight, which a more precise term ("texts intended for inexperienced readers," for example) might not—but there is little chance that, for all its shortcomings, it will be displaced. As Nodelman (2008b) has observed, "[C]hildren's literature . . . is always ambivalent."

10

Class

Elizabeth Bullen

The word "class" comes to English from the Latin *classis* via the French *classe*. It first appears in Thomas Blount's *Glossographia* (1656), where he defined it in the language of the times as "an order or distribution of people according to their several Degrees." Citing Blount, the *Oxford English Dictionary* (*OED*) traces the term's origins to its use by Servius Tullius who, seeking to raise funds for the Roman military, conducted a census for the purpose of taxing citizens according to their means. He created six categories or classes, based on property or net wealth (Kostick 2005). In spite of the strong resonance of its etymology with contemporary socioeconomic understandings of class, when it first entered the English language *classe* had greater purchase in reference to a division of scholars or students, and later as a natural history term. According to the *OED*, its use in regard to a social division or grouping does not reappear until 1772. Until then, "estate," "order," "rank," and "degree," terms that originated in medieval times, continued to be used to describe social positions. The use of word "class" is therefore historically associated with the Industrial Revolution and the rise of capitalism, making it somewhat anachronistic to apply it to earlier systems of class division that appear in children's fiction.

According to Raymond Williams (1983a), the trigger that led to "class" superseding earlier terms was the recognition that "social position is made rather than merely inherited," indeed, increasing consciousness that particular social systems "actually created social divisions." The notion that social position is made is particularly important in children's literature, which abounds in rags-to-riches and triumph-of-the-under-dog stories, from Joseph Jacob's 1890 version of "Jack and the Beanstalk," to Horatio Alger, Jr.'s *Ragged Dick* (1868), *Struggling Upward* (1890), and other books for boys, to Louis Sachar's *Holes* (1998). It informs modernized variants of the Cinderella story, including the feature film *A Cinderella Story* (Rosman 2004) and Shannon Hale's novel *Princess Academy* (2005). These tropes bear witness to a notion of class as a hierarchical system of social classification—or as E. P. Thompson (1963/1980) puts it, a relational category evident in the notions of upper, middle, lower, and under classes—that nevertheless offers the potential for social mobility that is usually upward in children's texts, although occasionally downward for privileged protagonists, as in Lauren Child's *Hubert Horatio Bartle Bobton-Trent* (2004).

Children's fiction is less straightforward in representing the unequal distribution of social and economic resources, or how power and privilege inheres in class structure and impedes social mobility. This may be because, as Williams (1983a) points out, "class" is a "difficult word" when it comes to the actual basis upon which social divisions are understood and thus represented. Its ambiguities are a product of the national and historical variations in usage, as well as the different empirical criteria and conceptual models used to measure and theorize it. These competing genealogies result in understandings of class that alternately overlap, occlude, and contradict each other.

Williams identifies the source of confusions about *class* in the late eighteenth century. In addition to referring to a system of ranking according to social status—implicit in Blount's glossing of the term—it begins to be used to differentiate "productive" and "unproductive classes." Coining "class" as a verb in *The Wealth of Nations* (1776), Adam Smith states, "'I have classed artificers, manufacturers, and merchants among the productive laborers'" (*OED*). Class thus begins to become an expression of an economic relationship, a model brought to fruition by Karl Marx as a relation to modes of production. Although clearly linked, status and economic models of class do not exactly coincide. The former is a hierarchical ranking based on social distinction; the latter is a fundamentally binary split based on the division between those who own the mode of production and those who sell their labor (Marx 1859). Historical and contemporary constructions of the middle class make this tension explicit: grouped with the working class according to the economic model—middle-class people work, after all—they are ranked more highly than the working class according to the status model.

The status model of social stratification reflects, but is not reducible to, economic inequality or material productive forces (Williams 1983a; Wright 1985), a fact made apparent in images of genteel poverty in Louisa May Alcott's *Little Women* (1868–69) and Ethel Turner's *Seven Little Australians* (1894). Marx's model is economically determinist, but it offers a mode of class analysis that *explains* class inequality and offers the potential for revolutionary change (Connell 1983). These two systems sit in an uneasy relation in children's literature and its scholarship, not only because in literary theory class is inextricably linked with Marxist criticism, but because of children's perceived relation to production.

At the same time as notions of productive and unproductive classes gained currency, children and their literature began to acquire special status. Didactic and utopian in sentiment, eighteenth- and nineteenth-century children's fiction came to reflect a belief in the myth of childhood as lying outside of the injustices of the social order and the world of work. The result, according to Fred Inglis (1981), is that in children's fiction the reading of class is "always and endlessly capable of being relocated in the classless paradise." Pointing to the likes of Arthur Ransome's *Swallows and Amazons* (1931), Kenneth Grahame's *The Wind in the Willows* (1908), and E. Nesbit's *The Railway Children* (1906) as "stabilizing fictions," Ian Wojcik-Andrews (1993) asks, "[W]hat better way to control and assuage class struggle and class conflict in reality than through classless utopias in fiction?" However, to the extent that class consciousness and struggle centers on a recognition of the exploitation of labor, this is problematic, since, as Maria Nikolajeva (2002a) points out, "children don't work." Although, as she acknowledges, this is not historically true, children cannot have an occupation as such. When labor is depicted in children's literature, it tends to be transformed into "play," "an evil," or "distanc[ed] to the historical past," as in Robert Cormier's *Fade* (1988). In contemporary fiction showing the exploitation of labor, such as Cynthia Kadohata's *Kira-Kira* (2004), or the effects of poverty, such as Sherman Alexie's *The Absolutely True Diary of a Part-Time Indian* (2007), issues of class are often overwritten by race or ethnicity. This does not mean that Marxist criticism is irrelevant to children's literature, but the project it enables may in fact occlude the pertinence of status models to the genre.

Certainly, Marx saw a direct correspondence between the economic base or mode of production and the social, intellectual, and political superstructure as an ideological vehicle of the class status quo. Refined by Louis Althusser (1971), class ideology is a system of representation, making literature a potential means for disseminating and normalizing values in the service of the interests of the dominant class—or resisting them. Thus, the Marxist critic of children's literature Jack Zipes (1983) shows how the folk tales of the common people were transformed into literary fairy tales that reflected and subverted the values of the aristocracy. Writing about English children's literature, Bob Dixon (1977) emphasizes the corollary, arguing that "until

very recent times, working class characters, if they appeared at all, appeared invariably in minor roles and in very few categories. They could be objects of charity (but only if loyal and obedient workers); repugnant characters, often criminals, who posed a menace to the social structure; or menials who were usually funny." However, here again the tension between productive and unproductive classes comes to the fore, since in spite of the persistence of inherited class positions in Britain, the opposition underpinning Dixon's analysis is between the working and middle classes. Children's literature has long been middle class in it consumption and production, and from this perspective, class division is necessarily informed by status.

If the opposition between productive and unproductive classes suggests an economic relationship, it also encodes value judgments, including those of moral and other worth such as Dixon's observations about the British working class suggest. In *The Making of the Modern Child: Children's Literature and Childhood in the Late Eighteenth Century*, Andrew O'Malley (2003) shows how the demonization of the rich and stigmatization of the poor in children's literature under the rise of industrial capitalism reflected a preoccupation with the construction of the middle-class subject. This subject embodies the values of individualism, such as "thrift, self-denial, industry . . . and education," and achieves social mobility through personal merit, virtue, and hard work. Thus, the child protagonists in the English-American author Frances Hodgson Burnett's *Little Lord Fauntleroy* (1886) and *A Little Princess*

(1905) are rewarded for their virtue by being rescued from their penury. Obscuring the structural inequality created by the mode of production, such tropes locate class positions and their transcendence as a function of individual dispositions, rather than the collective struggle associated with working-class consciousness in Marx's model.

Although Max Weber (1922) argued for an opposition between class and status, and Williams treats them as separate entries in *Keywords*, their connectedness is particularly important in relation to the representation of class in children's literature, especially in contemporary texts. Clearly, the two are intricately linked, as demonstrated by Pierre Bourdieu's (1986) theorization of the nexus between economic capital and the symbolic, social, and cultural capital that underpin the status model. Indeed, children's literature typically depicts class difference through symbols of status, rather than relations to labor. It also resolves class conflict through the status model: characters such as Charlie in Roald Dahl's *Charlie and the Chocolate Factory* (1964) or Ryan in the U.S. teen television series *The OC* (2003–7), who perform (or learn to perform) behaviors and express values appropriate to the middle class, are rewarded with social mobility (Bullen 2007). However, insofar as the "language of status" displaces the "language of class" in these texts, it dissipates the radical aspects of class consciousness by "appearing to cancel out class in the sense of formation or even broad group, and [by] providing a model of society which is not only hierarchical and individually competitive but

is essentially defined in terms of consumption and display" (Williams 1983a). To the extent that children's narratives reduce class to a status model, they serve the interests of capital.

This is even more acute in American children's literature, informed as it is by the myths of a classless society, the American Dream, and a descriptive model of socioeconomic status that identifies up to 70 percent of Americans as middle class (Gilbert 2002; Thompson and Hickey 2005) in spite of economic inequality. As Eric Lott (2007) points out, in the United States, class is "[c]losely related to such categories as 'station,' 'status,' 'group' and 'kind'" and "resonates with implications of value, quality, respectability, and religious virtue," and that it is thus "difficult to pry capital loose from rectitude." Similarly, middle-class values are difficult to "pry loose" from social mobility, as is social status from consumerism and display. The contemporary heroine of Meg Cabot's *The Princess Diaries* (2000), Mia, may be a modern-day Cinderella, but her political-activist sensibilities reflect the values of the contemporary middle class. She also performs its consumerist values—an ethos that is even more overt in mass-market young adult fiction series such as *Gossip Girl* (Von Ziegesar's 2002) and *The Insiders* (Minter 2004), which conflate class status with the conspicuous consumption of luxury goods, excluding those who fail as consumers of taste and distinction.

However, it is not only in America that class awareness is weak. Some argue that the late twentieth century witnessed the "death of class" (Pakulski and

Waters 1996). It also saw a decline in the use of class as a category of analysis in children's literature (Wojcik-Andrews 1993) and, with the shift towards identity politics, in cultural and literary studies more generally (Eagleton 1996). This does not mean that class is no longer relevant. In its continued promotion of middle-class values, children's literature seeks to socialize readers into values and ways of being that may facilitate social mobility. At the same time, in using the language of status, it obfuscates those structural inequalities in the capitalist class system that impede social mobility. The core conflict in children's literature analysis of class, then, is how the critic employing the concept understands its reference points in terms of Marxist class analysis, the Weberian status model, or a Bourdieuan synthesis of the economic and non-economic capital. The application of these approaches is also highly dependent on the historical period in which the narrative is written and/or set, given that class demarcations have changed dramatically with the rise of consumer capitalism, globalization, and expansion of the middle classes in the contemporary West. Current children's literature research and scholarship will need to be responsive to the changing class structures of the contemporary world.

II

Classic
Kenneth Kidd

In her study of comparative children's literature, Emer O'Sullivan (2001) notes that children's classics come from three sources: (1) appropriations of adult works; (2) adaptations from traditional (usually oral) narratives; and (3) works written specifically for children. A classic, then, could be a text adopted by children as well as a work written for them. But, as O'Sullivan's study also makes clear, things are not so simple. "Classic" is an overdetermined and elastic term, one encompassing very different ideas and attitudes. The notion of a children's classic amplifies the contradictions of the term, especially to the degree that children's literature has been devalued. The idea of the children's classic has helped legitimize children's literature and has thus proven useful; at the same time, "classic" continues to signify a traditional faith in aesthetics, provoking resistance alongside affirmation.

While it lacks a separate entry in *Keywords*, Raymond Williams (1983a) notes that "classic" shares its derivation with "class": both come from the Latin *classicus*, which "had social implications before it took on its general meaning of a standard authority and then its particular meaning of belonging to Greek and Roman antiquity." The first definition in the *Oxford English Dictionary* (*OED*) links "classic" securely to "class": "Of the first class, of the highest rank or importance;

approved as a model; standard, leading." Both adjective and noun, "classic" came to designate the literary works of antiquity, not only as literary but also as standard works, part of a shared culture. A closely related term is "canon," derived from biblical discourse. According to the *OED*, "canon" refers not only to sacred books but also to "those writings of a secular author accepted as authentic"; a 2002 draft addition equates it with "the classics." Classics comprise canon and derive authority from it. Both terms suggest a selective literary heritage, with "classic" still linked to classical culture and "canon" to religious tradition.

In its migration to modern narratives and contexts, the meaning of "classic" has been expanded as well as preserved. For Charles Augustin Sainte-Beuve in the 1850s and then T. S. Eliot in 1944, "classic" means the Roman literary classic and, in particular, Virgil's *The Aeneid.* Eliot favors "maturity" as the major criterion of literary and cultural excellence, but also makes the counterintuitive argument that classics tend not so much toward singularity but toward "a common style" and a "community of taste"—toward shared culture. Moreover, Eliot suggests that classics are culminating moments not only of mature civilizations but also of dead or dying ones. Although Frank Kermode (1975) concurs with Eliot's sense of "classic" as bearing (in Kermode's words) "the assumption that the ancient can be more or less immediately relevant and available, in a sense contemporaneous with the modern," he also points out that empire "is the paradigm of the classic: a perpetuity, a transcendent entity, however remote its

provinces, however extraordinary its temporal vicissitudes." Where Eliot finds a modern classic impossible to imagine (English being too "alive" and more mongrel than ancient languages), Kermode resists Eliot's imperialist conception and allows for the "modern classic," which is particularly open to accommodation and indeed refuses "to give a definitive account of itself." More critical still of Eliot's faith in the perpetuity of classic/empire, South African novelist J. M. Coetzee (2001) calls Eliot's lecture "an attempt to claim a cultural-historical unity for Western European Christendom including its provinces, within which the cultures of its constituent nations would belong only as parts of a greater whole." The debate goes on: is "classic" a neutral description of excellence, or a politicized and always problematic term?

For better and for worse, "classic" continues to suggest a "common culture," one both shared and accessible. In fact, the word entered commercial and middlebrow American culture in part through the children's classic, a preoccupation of the early twentieth century. Middlebrow culture and children's literature alike were envisioned as respectable as well as accessible. As Janice Radway (1997) notes, the first Book-of-the-Month Club selection was Sylvia Townsend Warner's *Lolly Willowes* (1926), often considered a children's book (Paul 1990). The first winner of the Newbery Medal (first awarded in 1922) was Hendrik Willem van Loon's *The Story of Mankind* (1921), one among many popular "outlines" designed to educate and uplift the reading public (another was Will Durant's *The Story of Philosophy* [1926]).

(On outlines and other middlebrow genres, see Rubin 1992.) Whatever skepticism we may have toward particular middlebrow projects—say, audiotape programs on "The World's 100 Greatest Books!"—we all share this sense of "classic" as not only immutable and grand but also portable and familiar. The classic is meant to circulate widely, even promiscuously. It tends, in short, toward seemingly contradictory things: time and temporality, exceptionality and the commonplace, the remote and the familiar, the organic and the manufactured. Moreover, it tends toward children's literature as much as away from it.

Another of the great mechanisms of middlebrow culture/children's literature, the brainchild of publishers and booksellers as well as librarians, has been the children's book award, beginning with Newbery Medal—only the second literary award to be established in the United States, after the Pulitzer Prizes in 1917 (Kidd 2007). Other such "medals" and awards eventually followed, some specific to national cultures (such as Britain's Carnegie Medal) and others ostensibly international in scope, such as the Hans Christian Andersen Medal, founded in 1956 to honor "a lasting contribution to children's literature." Coterminous with the early book awards were rhetorics of "gold," as in "golden" anthologies of children's literature ("golden treasuries") and the influential 1929 booklist *Realms of Gold*. This language of gold is at once naturalizing, suggesting that classics are found or mined, and associated with commerce—with coining, minting, and even alchemy—suggesting that classics are not

born but rather made (even forged). (At least one early Newbery title, Eric Philbrook Kelly's *The Trumpeter of Krakow* [1929], takes up the subject of alchemy and what we might call the problem of enduring value.) Thus, new or fast classics were manufactured according to modern demands and tempos. New classics joined a proto-canon of Anglo-European children's literature made up of fairy tales—especially those of Perrault, Grimm, and Andersen—and fantasies such as Lewis Carroll's Alice books (1865; 1871), J. M. Barrie's *Peter Pan* (1911), Kenneth Graham's *The Wind in the Willows* (1908), and L. Frank Baum's *The Wonderful Wizard of Oz* (1900), now collectively referred to as "Golden Age" literature.

Consider briefly the career of Louise Seaman Bechtel, the first woman head of a children's book division within a major publishing house. When Bechtel started at Macmillan in 1922, she inherited a book list of around 250 children's titles. She immediately repackaged those titles, launching two lines of children's classics, called, respectively, Children's Classics and the Little Library. Included in Children's Classics were Carroll's two Alice books and A. J. Church's *Iliad for Boys and Girls* and *The Odyssey for Boys and Girls*. The Little Library was a set of miniature books, roughly four by six inches, designed to be easily carried around. In both lines, Bechtel conjoined the old with the new, leveraging the classic status of existing titles into classic status for new ones. Bechtel understood very well the power of the market in inventing and/or maintaining the classic. In her unpublished memoir (Bechtel n.d.), she remarks, "I just needed to put [children's titles] in similar bindings, devise new jackets, and call them classics." She also understood that controversy was good for the business of classics and children's literature: "The more argument as to what *is* a children's classic *for* children, the better." In a speech, she called the classic simply "a book so widely loved that it lives on long in print and in people's hearts. It doesn't have to be great literature" (Bechtel 1953). Perhaps this is the "paraclassic," to adapt Catharine R. Stimpson's (1990) notion of the "paracanon" as a set of books that "some people have loved and do love." (For more on Bechtel, see Kidd 2006.)

Librarians were the first arbiters of taste on the scene of children's literature, functioning as book award judges, book reviewers, and general advisors to the reading public. Their lists of recommended books overlapped considerably with the sales lists of publishers. But even as they shared with publishers a desire to get new books quickly into print, they marshaled cultural authority and professional identity around already-established texts, like the literary critics after them. (For comparative attention to librarians and literary critics, see Clark 2003; Eddy 2006; Marcus 2008; and especially Lundin 2004.) Alice Jordan begins her 1947 booklist *Children's Classics* thus: "Perhaps no other book for children is so generally called a classic as *Alice's Adventures in Wonderland*. It delights us when we are young, it is cherished, reread and quoted for its philosophy when we are old." Jordan then turns to "the four great books, not written for them but adopted by

them and universally counted" among their books: Miguel de Cervantes's *Don Quixote* (1606/1615), John Bunyan's *Pilgrim's Progress* (1678), Daniel Defoe's *Robinson Crusoe* (1719), and Jonathan Swift's *Gulliver's Travels* (1726). A book cannot be considered a classic until it has "weathered at least one generation and is accepted in the next." Jordan also acknowledges the importance of series such as Children's Classics. Jordan's list of sixty classics gives priority to fairy tale and fantasy—*Arabian Nights* (1706), John Ruskin's *The King of the Golden River* (1841), George MacDonald's *At the Back of the North Wind* (1871), and Kenneth Grahame's *The Wind in the Willows*—but also anoints realistic works such as Mary Mapes Dodge's *Hans Brinker* (1866), Louisa May Alcott's *Little Women* (1868–69), and Johanna Spyri's *Heidi* (1880; English trans. 1884).

Jordan's list has been "updated" several times, and each edition reflects shifts in the collective attitude toward what constitutes a "classic." In his 1976 version of the list, Paul Heins takes issue with Jordan's test of time, writing, "[A] classic that has weathered two generations—or even more—is not necessarily guaranteed to endure. For historical or cultural reasons, such a book can be justifiably dropped from the company of the classics, and some comparative newcomers may appear to be qualified to join the honorable gathering." Dropped from his version of the list are Sir Walter Scott's *Ivanhoe* (1819–20), Richard Henry Dana's *Two Years Before the Mast* (1840), and Thomas Hughes's *Tom Brown's Schooldays* (1857); replacements include Wanda Gág's *Millions of Cats* (1928), J. R. R. Tolkien's *The Hobbit*

(1937), Esther Forbes's *Johnny Tremain* (1943), and E. B. White's *Charlotte's Web* (1952). Librarians continue to function as "selectors" of good books, having largely renounced their old role as censors of bad books; *selection* remains a keyword for librarianship (see Asheim 1953).

This American culture of children's book promotion and elevation took place alongside a devaluation of children's literature within the academy. In *Kiddie Lit: The Cultural Construction of Children's Literature in America* (2003), Beverly Lyon Clark points out that whereas in the nineteenth century adults and children enjoyed a shared literary world, by the 1920s a dramatic segregation of children's literature and "adult" literature had occurred, to the decided disadvantage of the former. Even as "bookwomen" and a few bookmen were repackaging old classics and marketing new ones, ushering in something like a modern public sphere of children's books, children's literature was no longer a respectable undertaking for serious men of letters. Serious men of letters in fact demonstrated their seriousness by not writing or otherwise engaging with children's books; such was the attitude of Henry James, Bliss Perry, and others hostile to the genteel tradition of cross-writing. In *Childhood and Art* (1894), Horace Scudder, publisher of *The Riverside* magazine (and the Riverside Literature Series for Young People), envisioned a shared literary heritage in which "[i]t is not the books written expressly for children so much as it is the books written out of minds which have not lost their childhood that are to form the body of literature which shall be classic of the young." By the 1920s,

however, childhood was to be lost at all costs if one wanted to be taken seriously as a scholar.

Children's literature, then, has been defined as a set of classics, but also as the absence or even antithesis of "classic." Given this history, it is no surprise that children's literature critics in English departments have found themselves at once championing and opposing the classic(s). When Francelia Butler founded the first American journal of children's literature criticism in 1972, she called it *The Great Excluded* (it is now *Children's Literature*), implying that children's literature is shut out of the literary canon. Shortly after, Butler and her colleagues founded the Children's Literature Association, in the interest of improving the academic climate and allowing those in the field to network. Jon C. Stott's 1978 presidential address called for the establishment of a canon, which led to a panel discussion in 1980 on "Developing a Canon of Children's Literature" (Lundin 2004). After spirited discussion by members of the association on the merits and problems of canon-construction, the *Touchstones* project emerged, a three-volume collection of essays devoted to sixty-three literary classics, edited by Perry Nodelman (1985–89), with volume one focused on exemplary texts of fiction; volume two, on folk literature, legend, and myth; and volume three, on picture books.

Nodding to Matthew Arnold's use of the term in "The Study of Poetry" (1880), Nodelman and his colleagues chose "touchstone" over "classic" as their keyword. A touchstone helps clarify the quality of a precious stone or substance and is not necessarily itself of great value. The essays were "touchstones," but the more tentative language of excellence here extends to the works themselves—meaning that the *Touchstones* volumes stopped short of declaring those sixty-three titles as canonical. The project was undertaken, as John Cech (1986) explained in his presidential address to the Children's Literature Association, "not to dictate or mandate certain books while ignoring or rejecting others, but rather, to serve as a starting point." Patricia Demers (1985) concurs: "Never ends in themselves, these aids usually serve modest instructional aims: surveying the field for a neophyte and easing the chronological trudge by erecting signposts. Their purpose is initiatory." Even so, the enterprise was not without its critics, some of whom complained that the Association was sending mixed messages about how classics are to be identified and treated. Such are the ambivalences of canon-construction, or better yet, "canontology," to borrow Jed Rasula's (1995) term.

The last few decades, of course, have seen a dampening of enthusiasm for "classic" and "canon," thanks in no small measure to poststructuralist theory and the progressive social movements of the 1960s and 1970s. Adding to the momentum, if further complicating the scene of analysis, are Pierre Bourdieu's (1979) sociological explorations of "distinction" and John Guillory's (1993) analysis of "cultural capital." Literary classics and our relation to them, notes Bourdieu, help keep in place distinctions of social class; Bourdieu points especially to prize-winning literature, treated reverently by those aspiring to elite culture. For Bourdieu, the very

attitude of respect toward "classic" and other rhetorics of distinction prevents them from achieving such.

The hermeneutics of suspicion regarding "classic" have found their way into children's literature studies, to be sure. Jacqueline Rose's *The Case of Peter Pan, or The Impossibility of Children's Fiction* (1984) is, among other things, a dismantling of the idea. Echoing Roderick McGillis (1998), but also applying Bourdieu to the field of children's literature studies, Jack Zipes (2001) argues that the idea of the children's classic—indeed, the larger conceit of children's literature—distracts us from a more expansive understanding of what children actually read as well as write. While Jordan (1976) declared *Alice* the most classic book of all, Deborah Stevenson (1997) asserts that "[e]ventually a children's literature classic masters being loved with actually being read . . . you do not have to read *Alice,* but you will be deemed culturally illiterate should you not acknowledge it as a children's literature classic." O'Sullivan's (2001) study of comparative children's literature is, finally, a deconstruction of "classic" and "canon" alike. She makes a persuasive case that "classic" does not usually survive translation, by which she means translation into another language, but also translation into other cultural contexts and/or narrative forms. "In practice," she writes, "we have a number of disparate texts for which there is not, and cannot be, any single explanation of the (canonical) processes of selection, evaluation, preservation and safe transmission."

A possible conclusion here, one reached by Coetzee (2001), is that while "classic" tends toward reification, the term also encompasses the debate it engenders. "The classic defines itself by surviving," proposes Coetzee, and therefore "the interrogation of the classic, no matter how hostile, is part of the history of the classic, inevitable and even to be welcomed. For as long as the classic needs to be protected from attack, it can never prove itself classic." Coetzee takes the logic further: "[T]he function of criticism is defined by the classic: criticism is that which is duty-bound to interrogate the classic." It remains to be decided whether this function of criticism amounts to a taming of "classic" or yet another refashioning.

I2

Crossover Literature
Sandra L. Beckett

In children's literature scholarship, "crossover" refers to literature that crosses from child to adult or adult to child audiences. While crossover literature is not a new phenomenon, the term itself was not adopted until J. K. Rowling's Harry Potter books gave this literature a high profile. Although the term was in use in the late 1990s, it did not emerge as a common expression until the early years of the new millennium. While the crossover phenomenon actually began earlier in the visual media, with television shows (*Star Trek*, *The Simpsons*), films (*E.T.*, *Toy Story*), comics (*Charlie Brown*), and video games (*Super Mario Bros.)* that had broad appeal with mixed-age audiences, the term is not often used in this sense, except by children's literature theorists and critics.

The website *crossoverguide.com* is one of the few sources to offer a broad definition that embraces several media: "Any book, film or TV programme that appeals to both adults and children is a crossover title." A children's literature encyclopedia entry devoted to "crossover literature" defines it as "books and films that cross from child to adult audiences and vice versa" (Falconer 2004). Some of the most successful crossover films have been adaptations of crossover novels, notably the Harry Potter saga and *The Lord of the Rings*. A much earlier example of a crossover film derived from a children's book is *The Wizard of Oz* (1939). In popular music, the term "crossover" has been used since the 1970s to refer to a piece that finds appeal beyond its niche market with a wider, but not necessarily intergenerational, audience. In children's literature, the term refers specifically to the crossing of age boundaries. One of the earliest articles in the British media to refer to the "crossover phenomenon" in those terms was a 1997 piece titled "Breaking the Age Barrier," devoted to "books that blur the lines between children and adult categories" (Rosen 1997).

Since the 1990s, a number of other terms have been adopted to refer to literature read by both children and adults. Scholars and writers have been responsible for some of these terms, while others have been coined by the book industry. Regardless of the terminology used, theoretical discussions of crossover literature have occurred almost exclusively within the field of children's literature, as theorists of adult fiction rarely "cross over" to children's books and therefore have shown little interest in the subject. The term "cross-writing" (or "crosswriting") was broadly used by critics, even beyond English-speaking borders, before the widespread adoption of the term "crossover" (Beckett 1995; Knoepflmacher and Myers 1997). The two terms are not synonymous, however. Cross-writing includes authors who write for both child and adult audiences in separate works, while crossovers address the two audiences simultaneously. Crossover works are read by young readers and adults, but they are not necessarily written or marketed intentionally for both audiences.

One could perhaps argue that a true crossover title is the somewhat rare book, such as Lian Hearn's *Across the Nightingale Floor* (2002) and its sequels, which is written, published, and marketed for readers of all ages. However, this is not the case for the vast majority of crossovers, which often find an audience of both children and adults with no authorial or editorial intention. Crossovers may initially have been published for a particular audience and subsequently appropriated by another, in a process that has been called "cross-reading." "Cross-writing" and "cross-reading" are both essential facets of crossover literature.

Critics and reviewers have also referred to crossover literature as having "dual address," or as "dual-readership," "dual-audience," or "cross-audience" literature. The contributors to *Transcending Boundaries: Writing for a Dual Audience of Children and Adults* use a variety of these terms to examine diverse aspects of the crossover question (Beckett 1999). The adjectives "intergenerational" or "cross-generational" have also been employed. Other critics prefer to use variations of the term "all-ages audience." Hyperion, the general-interest book publishing division of the Walt Disney Company, was using the term "multipurposed books" to refer to their crossover titles as early as 1997. In the early years of the new millennium, "crossover" became a favorite media buzzword, particularly in Britain. The catchy term was also a handy label for publishers anxious to cash in on the new trend.

A number of countries have adopted expressions to designate this type of literature, some as early as the

1980s. The term *allalderslitteratur* (all-ages-literature) was coined in Norway as early as 1986, and it was adopted slightly later in Swedish. The Spanish-speaking countries refer to *libros para todas las edades* (books for all ages), and the publisher Siruela created the series Las Tres Edades (The three ages) in 1990. Several countries have adopted terms that incorporate the idea of "all-ages books," sometimes using a variation of this anglicism. In Germany, the Anglo-German terms *All-Age-Buch*, *All-Age-Literatur*, and *All-Age-Titel* have been used to refer to crossover works since about 2002, although the term *Brückenliteratur* (bridge literature) has been in use much longer and was probably coined after the 1979 publication of Michael Ende's *The Neverending Story*. The Dutch term *literatuur zonder leeftijd* (literature without age) began to be widely used after it was chosen as the title of a journal, in 1993, in order to reflect the growing importance of literature for all ages. Unlike the catchy English term "crossover," the terms coined in many languages tend to be rather cumbersome. In French, it has been necessary to resort to terms such as *la littérature destinée à un double lectorat* (literature aimed at a dual readership) or *la littérature pour tous les ages* (literature for all ages) (Beckett 1997). The existence of so many terms in other languages serves to remind us that crossover fiction is not a phenomenon limited to the English-speaking world, but rather a widespread, global trend.

"Crossover" has been considered a somewhat "slippery" descriptor, as it is used with a different signification in other fields, such as postcolonial or gender studies (Falconer 2004). The ambiguity or "fuzziness" that Rachel Falconer (2009) attributes to the term, even in the context of children's literature, is reflected in its inconsistent usage. The "crossover writer" has been defined as "the writer who writes for both children and adults" (Cadden 2000b), but the texts produced by such a writer would not necessarily be crossover works read simultaneously by both audiences. Since the success of the first Harry Potter books, the term has generally been adopted for books that cross over in one direction only, that is, from young readers to adults (child-to-adult crossover). Crossover literature is typically defined as "children's books which appeal to adults" (Cheong Suk-Wai 2004). In this sense, it becomes synonymous with the trendy label "kidult fiction." "Crossover" is sometimes reserved exclusively for young adult fiction that is read by adults. Others contend that the term should not refer to novels for older teenagers, but only to children's books that appeal equally to adults. For many, crossover books are genre-specific, being novels only. In Philip Ardagh's (2003) words, "[C]rossover books seem to cross in one direction only, upwards, being novels intended for young readers that adults consider worthy of attention." The crossover novel has been in the limelight, as the title of Falconer's 2009 study suggests. Further, there is a tendency to equate crossover with fantasy. While the super crossovers that have garnered most of the public and critical attention have been fantasy novels, almost every genre can cross between child and adult audiences, including short fiction, poetry, picture books, graphic novels, and comics, not to mention realistic novels and all the novelistic sub-genres, such as mystery, gothic, historical, science fiction, romance, fairy tales, and so forth. Like the term "crossover" in English, those used in other languages have generally been adopted only for a one-way border crossing from children or young adults to adults. A few critics have taken issue with this limited use of the term since its adoption, and a broader application is now generally accepted. Crossover literature also includes adult fiction with appeal for young readers (adult-to-child crossover), which has a much longer historical precedent.

In spite of some misgivings about the word "crossover," it is superior to earlier terms used to describe this literature. Crossover fiction blurs the borderline between two traditionally separate readerships: children and adults. However, it is not sufficient to see these works in terms of dual address or dual audience, especially in light of the burgeoning category of young adult fiction. Crossover texts address a diverse, cross-generational audience that can include readers of all ages: children, adolescents, and adults. Nor is "cross-writing" an adequate term, as it neglects the essential dimension of cross-reading.

Crossover fiction has been seen by many journalists and critics as exclusively a marketing and mass media phenomenon, epitomized by the Harry Potter series. However, in addition to being recognized as a distinct marketing category, it is now being acknowledged as serious literature, deserving of critical as well as popular acclaim. Crossovers such as Philip Pullman's *His Dark Materials* trilogy and Mark Haddon's *The Curious Incident of the Dog in the Night-Time* (2003) have won over the literary establishment. The first two book-length studies to use the term "crossover" in the title appeared in August 2008, although both bear a 2009 publication date (Beckett 2009; Falconer 2009). Recent encyclopedias of children's literature have also included substantial entries on the subject (Falconer 2004; Beckett 2006). In light of the current cultural importance of the phenomenon, "crossover" is likely to become a much more frequently used term in literature, as well as in the various visual media that enjoy mixed-age audiences.

13

Culture

Richard Flynn

"Culture," writes Raymond Williams (1983a), "is one of the two or three most complicated words in the English language." When it is applied to the study of children and their literature, it is certainly one of the most contested as well. The Latin *cultura* is derived from the past participial stem of the root word *colere*: to cultivate, to worship. According to the *Oxford English Dictionary*, later meanings are divided into three branches:

I. The cultivation of land, and derived senses.

II. Worship.

III. Extended uses (from branch I.).

While the second branch meaning is obsolete and rare, many of our extended, metaphorical uses of the term bear some relation to notions of the sacred, particularly when applied to children.

Notions of children's acculturation are often perceived as being either in concert with or opposed to nature, or frequently both. Largely as a result of the influence of a Wordsworthian brand of Romanticism, childhood itself has often been equated with innocence and the primitive, and the socializing and "culturing" aspects of child-rearing and education have often been dismissed. When we think of culturing children in the sense of cultivating them, we extend agricultural meanings metaphorically to the process of educating them. Just as later extensions of the verb

"to culture" applied to microorganisms in biology or to pearls imply that culturing is done under artificial or controlled conditions, the rearing or cultivating of children is often thought of as a similar process involving a delicate balance of the "natural" and the cultural. Even such a radically Romantic text as Jean-Jacques Rousseau's *Émile* (1762) argues that the aim of education is to cultivate the (male) child's natural tendencies in order to avoid the negative effects of "all the social conditions into which we are plunged" because "they would stifle nature in him and put nothing in her place. She would be like a sapling chance sown in the midst of the highway, bent hither and thither and soon crushed by the passers-by." It is clear who has the upper hand here. Even when we grant children some agency in the creation of their own culture, that creation usually takes place under adult supervision.

Until very recently, contemporary notions of culture have tended to exclude children altogether. None of the various keywords volumes upon which the present one is based include children or childhood as a category. Although *New Keywords* (Bennett, Grossberg, and Morris 2005) has an entry for "Youth," it is there defined as "the period between childhood and maturity." The author of that entry, Simon Frith (2005), describes our interest in youth as a problem or a marketing category. If it is a cultural category, it is subcultural at best. Undoubtedly this exclusion stems from a contemporary disdain for notions of childhood that privilege nature over culture. In the past, whether the child was presumed to be originally sinful or originally innocent, he or she was thought to exist in a state of nature, upon which adults and adult institutions imposed culture. Our tendency, then, is to define culture by its presumed opposite.

But what *is* the opposite of "culture"? Like "culture" itself, that which opposes it shifts in meaning according to historical and, well, cultural contexts. I have already suggested nature, but if we understand culture as cultivation, that presumes something natural to cultivate. Of course "nature," according to Williams, "is perhaps the most complex word in the language," even if Romantics in equating childhood with nature emphasize its simplicity. Contemporary scholars tend to reject the idea that childhood is simple; indeed, they tend to define childhood as a cultural invention, as opposed to a "natural" or biological developmental state. Citing the rising interest in childhood in the 1990s by critics in cultural studies, Kenneth Kidd (2002) astutely observes, "[L]ike 'discourse' and 'ideology,' 'culture' is at once a problematic and useful term. On the one hand, the culture idea is so generic or universal that it threatens to mean nothing at all, as some scholars have pointed out. Yet that is exactly why we like it. We rely on its vagueness." One reason for this, Kidd notes, is that in the shift to cultural studies we may also oppose culture to literature, at least insofar as the study of children's material culture seems to provide academics with a more likely route to accumulating cultural capital.

The vagueness of "culture" springs from the contradictory meanings built into the concept, which become even more pronounced when we consider them in terms of children, childhood, or children's literature. The general public assumes that children's literature disseminates cultural norms, and often any suggestion that even classic children's books might be ambivalent about children's literature's socializing function causes great consternation. Alison Lurie's 1990 book *Don't Tell the Grown-Ups: Subversive Children's Literature* was retitled *Don't Tell the Grown-Ups: Why Kids Love the Books They Do* for its first paperback printing; most recent printings bear the title *Don't Tell the Grown-Ups: The Subversive Power of Children's Literature*, allowing that children's books might have subversive power but reassuring the reader that they are not actually subversive. In any event, the perceived conservatism of the children's canon has spurred scholars to explore what might be termed counter-cultures, such as the subversive works represented in Julia Mickenberg and Philip Nel's anthology *Tales for Little Rebels* (2008).

Such works show us that children's culture is historically a site of contest, and that defining children's culture is at least as hard as defining children's literature. "Culture" carries both the elitist connotations of "High Culture" and the populist notions of mass culture (such distinctions were particularly contentious in the 1950s and early 1960s in the United States at the height of the Cold War). While "literature" has always been as much an evaluative term as a descriptive one, "children's literature" has often been relegated to what Williams (1983a) calls the "category of popular literature or the sub-literary." Of course, the study of children's literature, popular literature, women's literature, ethnic literatures, and, indeed, any literature that carries an adjective other than "serious," is itself a result of significant cultural changes that allow us to view "culture" as dynamic rather than a stable collection of monuments.

In his fascinating but cantankerous manifesto, *The Idea of Culture* (2000), Terry Eagleton complains that while "traditionally, culture was a way in which we could sink our petty particularisms in some more capacious, all-inclusive medium," it now means "exactly the opposite . . . the affirmation of a specific identity—national, sexual, ethnic, regional—rather than the transcendence of it." Asserting that culture "has passed over from being part of the solution to being part of the problem," Eagleton lampoons literary critics' interest in cultural studies as having "scrambled out of Tudor drama into teenage magazines, or swapped Pascal for pornography." Eagleton's disdain for a straw figure he names "postmodernism" throughout his book results in nostalgia for capital-C "High Culture" notions of stability and universality:

> Culture is no longer, in Matthew Arnold's exalted sense, a criticism of life, but a critique of a dominant or majority form of life by a peripheral one. Whereas high culture is the ineffectual opposite of politics, culture as identity is the continuation of politics by other means. For Culture, culture is benightedly sectarian, whereas for culture Culture is fraudulently disinterested. . . . We seem

torn between an empty universalism and a blind particularism.

Children's literature, in its ongoing quest for legitimacy, straddles the Culture/culture divide. Especially in its infancy, the study of children's literature sought legitimacy primarily by allying itself with literature for adults, by demanding parity and inclusion in the adult canon of great books. Taking a cursory look at the early issues of *Children's Literature* (then subtitled *The Great Excluded*), one finds in the table of contents, in Francelia Butler's "The Editor's High Chair" column, and in the lists of areas for further research a lot of attention to adult texts, to children's texts by writers who write primarily for adults, and articles with titles like "Milton's *Comus* as Children's Literature." But closer examination reveals that even in the early days of the discipline, the humanities-based study of children's literature was already engaged in what we today recognize as "cultural studies," as Anne Devereaux Jordan's (1974) account of the very first Children's Literature Association conference reveals. The theme of the conference was "Cultural and Critical Values in Children's Literature," and the participants included academics, writers, publishers, reviewers, and even a member of the Newbery-Caldecott committee. At the same time Perry Nodelman and others were constructing the children's literature canon, articles in the *Children's Literature Association Quarterly* often discussed children's culture more broadly conceived, as in a special issue on folklore edited by Priscilla Ord (1981), which contained articles on children's games, toys, folk speech, Disney films, and more.

Early on, critics working in the field of children's literary studies also understood the international scope of children's culture. Volume 3 of *Children's Literature* (1974), for instance, is multicultural in ways "adult" journals of the time were not, with surveys of Chinese, Austrian, Greek, and Norwegian children's literatures. Because children's literature is not confined to a particular historical period, scholars have always paid attention to historical and cultural contexts. In addition, because the genre of children's literature is defined by its audience, and because much scholarship before the establishment of humanities-based criticism was conducted by cultural workers—teachers, librarians, publishers, reviewers—the field of children's literary study was fertile ground for the cultivation of cultural-studies approaches as they gained popularity beginning in the 1980s.

As Kidd (2002) argues, "[C]hildren's culture and children's studies," rather than "venturing into uncharted territory," are more of a "shift in focus from literature to culture [that] attests to the staying power and adaptability of analysis as a vocation, and of 'culture' as an organizing field." The appearance of Jacqueline Rose's *The Case of Peter Pan* in 1984 initiated greater attention to poststructuralist discourses of power, and its sophisticated Freudianism exposed the inadequacies of the tepid psychoanalytic approaches that had long dominated the field. Along with the indictment of Bettelheimian "uses of enchantment" by fairy tale scholars such as Jack Zipes, Maria Tatar, and Ruth Bottigheimer, Rose's case for "the impossibility of children's fiction" was exciting to the new generation of children's literature and culture scholars in that it foregrounded the discourses of power explored in the work of Michel Foucault. While insights derived from Rose's work (and indeed Foucault's) today seem overused to the point that they risk becoming clichés, most would agree that they have had a positive effect in deepening our understanding of children, their literature, and their culture, as well as lending rigor to children's (or childhood) studies.

The turn from literature to culture, as Kidd points out, is a complicated story rooted in the disciplinary history of English departments and in the ethnographic turn in twentieth-century cultural anthropology. Poststructuralist anti-essentialist theory authorized scholars of childhood, beginning with Philippe Ariès's controversial but influential *Centuries of Childhood* (1962), to recognize that childhood is constructed rather than "natural." The acknowledgment that childhood is not a universal, transhistorical, and sacrosanct culture of its own necessitated a turn away from belletristic literary appreciation to a more rigorous consideration of history, ideology, and culture in our discussions of children's texts. Likewise, the shift from the iconic "work" to the concept of "text" in literary studies broadened the range of what was acceptable as an object of study. The recognition that children's narratives occur in a variety of extra-literary media—films, games, the internet, including social networking sites, and even cell-phone text messages—was not so much an abdication to trendiness as a recognition not only that children's culture extends beyond books, but also that children are active participants in that culture. Despite a host of Cassandra-like lamentations over the "disappearance of childhood" (Postman 1982) in the 1980s, critics of children's literature and culture recognized that no stable or fixed idea of childhood exists, and that childhood so defined negates children's agency.

Interestingly, sometime in the 1990s, quite a while after critics working within the field of children's literature began establishing a body of work that recognized and explored the cultural construction of childhood, critics from the burgeoning discipline of cultural studies discovered childhood. Henry Jenkins's anthology *The Children's Culture Reader* (1998) excerpted a number of foundational texts, including those by Ariès, Rose, Viviana Zelizer, James Kincaid, and others, but by the time it appeared it was old news to veterans in children's literature studies. Likewise, while the introduction paid lip service to children's agency, many of the essays therein—with the notable exception of those by media studies scholars Lynn Spigel and Ellen Seiter—relegated children to victim status. For all of its discussion of exploding "the mythology of childhood innocence," Jenkins's book served in many ways to perpetuate that mythology. Finally, the body of children's literature and culture criticism that had been published since the 1970s in *Children's Literature, The Children's Literature Association Quarterly, The Lion and the Unicorn, Children's Literature in Education, Signal,*

and other journals in the field was ignored altogether. Jenkins's assertion that "a surprising number of the essays written about children's media, children's literature, or education manage not to talk about children or childhood at all" shows that he did not really do his homework.

As an object of study, then, children's culture is both shaped and contested by a host of adult institutions, ranging in the academy from scholars in literature and education to those in media studies and social history. Culture is, of course, also created by children—if they are interpellated by adult ideologies, they are nevertheless also capable of resistance and action. Children are also capable of creatively misappropriating the cultural artifacts they inherit from adults and transforming them into their own texts—as anyone who has paid attention to children playing knows. If the study of children's culture often appears to be the province of adult, experience-distant field workers (to borrow the language of ethnography), there are increasing numbers of scholars who respect children's subjectivities and take them seriously. The traditional gatekeepers of Culture have begun to pay more attention to culture, and to acknowledge children's agency in helping to make that culture. Nevertheless, as with the climate, cultural change occurs more rapidly than we expect, requiring scholars to try to become allies rather than gatekeepers, if we hope to keep up.

I4

Domestic

Claudia Nelson

The term "domestic" derives from the Latin *domus* (house), through the Middle French *domestique*. The *Oxford English Dictionary*'s (*OED*) earliest usages are early sixteenth century, by which time the word already had multiple meanings: the achievement of quasi-familial intimacy, as in the 1521 supplication "make hym domestique / Within the heuyns," but also homegrown rather than foreign. While "domestic" always implied closeness, the extent of the sphere of proximity varied. That sphere might be the individual (John Norris's 1707 *Treatise on Humility* defines "domestic ignorance" as "the ignorance of . . . what passes within our own breast," notes the *OED*); the household, for example in the use of "domestics" to describe servants; the nation, as in "domestic policy"; or even humankind at large, since "domestic animal" includes livestock belonging to people in other countries and eras. What the sphere of proximity excludes—the wild animal, the stranger, the foreigner—necessarily partakes of the alien, the other, in a binary that opens possibilities of hierarchy, conflict, and exploitation.

In children's literature, "domestic fiction" describes a genre that emerged in the eighteenth century from writers such as Maria Edgeworth, namely stories of family life in a realist mode. It may be blended with other genres, such as the historical novel or the animal story, but its classic form uses a contemporary setting and a primary focus on a household, perhaps with a sprinkling of neighbors—who, in the sixteenth-century sense of the term, become "domestic" within the principal family. While such tales remain popular, the term is now more commonly applied to the fiction of earlier generations, particularly the nineteenth century. It thus carries a connotation of the old-fashioned, especially of a world in which fiction for middle-class girls was expected to facilitate adjustment to home duties and focused primarily on the interior, both of the home and of the individual, rather than on outdoor adventure or imperial conquest.

The association of the term "domestic fiction" with middle-class Victorian girls occludes not only postmodern tales of alternative domesticity such as Francesca Lia Block's magic-realist Dangerous Angels series (1989–2005) or discussions of nontraditional family life such as Paula Fox's *The Eagle Kite* (1995), which chronicles a boy's response to his father's AIDS, but also the multicultural domestic novels that began to proliferate in the twentieth century (summarized in Nelson 1994). Some of the latter play on the tension between "domestic" and "foreign," such as Rosa Guy's *The Friends* (1973), whose protagonist deals with being an outsider as a West Indian immigrant to Harlem, with her mother's terminal illness and her father's difficult nature, and with her own guilt at failing her best friend; Geraldine Kaye's *Comfort Herself* (1984), in which, after her English mother is killed, Comfort joins her father and grandmother in Ghana and must decide which country to consider home; and even Dori Sanders's *Clover* (1990), which describes how, when Clover's father dies in an accident hours after remarrying, ten-year-old Clover comes to feel kinship with her white stepmother despite community disapproval of the match. Others, such as Joseph Krumgold's *. . . and now Miguel* (1953), situate their protagonists entirely within their community of origin, but use a documentary approach hinting that the anticipated reader will find this group alien. Whatever the culture being described, the issues that domestic fiction raises are often far from cozy. The lighthearted tone of Jeanne Birdsall's *The Penderwicks* (2005) belies its focus on a mother's attempts to dominate her fatherless son, while Kyoko Mori's demanding *Shizuko's Daughter* (1994) describes the difficult adolescence of a Japanese girl whose mother has committed suicide, leaving her upbringing to her distant father and hostile stepmother.

Because "domestic fiction" is often perceived as being for and about girls, many readers from the Victorian period onward have associated it, disdainfully, with the sentimental and lachrymose. Thus Elizabeth Vincent commented in 1924 that Louisa May Alcott appeals to girls with "a natural depraved taste for moralizing" (Keyser 1999); in contrast, Humphrey Carpenter (1985), writing after critics had begun to argue that domestic fiction is subversive, suggests that it would be wrong, but possible, to assume that the Marches are "a rather saccharinely portrayed but otherwise unremarkable family." Providing a useful sample of Victorian male littérateurs' attitudes, an article by Wilkie Collins (1858) in *Household Words* satirically describes the influence of "this fatal domestic novel," Charlotte Yonge's *The Heir of Redclyffe* (1853), on a young female fan: "She reads for five minutes, and goes up-stairs to fetch a dry pocket handkerchief; comes down again, and reads for another five minutes; goes up-stairs again, and fetches another dry pocket handkerchief. . . . [T]he case baffles the doctors. The heart is all right, the stomach is all right, the lungs are all right, the extremities are moderately warm. The skull alone is abnormal."

Since the 1970s, critical interest even in Victorian domestic fiction for the young has been more respectful, owing largely to the influence of feminist critics such as Judith Fetterley, Nina Baym, Nancy Armstrong, and others. Elizabeth Thiel's (2008) argument is characteristic: "The ambiguities that clearly exist within nineteenth-century texts for children—sometimes overt, sometimes implicit, but invariably present—may have been attempts to tell the truth about domestic life in a world that celebrated idealism in all its aspects." Thiel is not the first to see nineteenth-century children's domestic fiction as a covert dialogue among sisters who could not afford to speak plainly about women's pain. This emphasis on femininity is legitimate, since most practitioners and readers of domestic fiction have indeed been female, yet it also tends to obscure the form's connections with masculinity.

Consider Alcott's *An Old-Fashioned Girl* (1870), which uses the adjective "domestic" only once in connection with its title character, who has "unfashionable domestic accomplishments" unacceptable to the citified and female-dominated circle that she visits. The word appears more frequently in connection with male characters. On the one hand, the narrative notes Tom's poor grasp of "domestic affairs," but on the other, it praises Sydney's "domestic traits and virtues[,] which are more engaging to womanly women than any amount of cool intellect or worldly wisdom," and observes that he "was a domestic man, and admired housewifely accomplishments," a trait by no means universal among Alcott's young women.

Moreover, some prominent domestic fictions (among them *The Heir of Redclyffe*) have employed male protagonists, such as Frances Hodgson Burnett's *Little Lord Fauntleroy* (1886) and Dinah Mulock's *John Halifax, Gentleman* (1856), which like Yonge's work found a wide readership among boys and men as well as girls and women. Many classic domestic sagas divide their attention impartially between the genders, as in Eleanor Estes's Moffat series (1941–83), Elizabeth Enright's Melendy quartet (1941–51), Ethel Turner's *Seven Little Australians* and its sequels (1894–1928), and Mary Grant Bruce's Billabong books (1910–42). Contemporary instances of the male domestic-novel protagonist include Judy Blume's Fudge series (1972–2002), in most of which a boy chronicles the doings of his annoying younger siblings, and Sarah Ellis's *Odd Man Out* (2006), in which a boy, given permission to trash his grandmother's home after it has been scheduled for demolition, finds a notebook from his dead father's teenage years and gains a new perspective on himself and his world.

The image of the destroyed house in Ellis's novel reflects our willingness to concede that "domestic," even in a children's book, may not be yoked to "bliss." Kimberley Reynolds (2008) dates to the mid-twentieth century the readiness to perceive "threats to child characters' wellbeing . . . as coming from within the family rather than from sources beyond it," just as "a domestic," per the *OED*, is twentieth-century police slang for a violent altercation between family members. But earlier domestic novels for adolescents also frequently acknowledge that intimacy need not promote peace. *The Heir of Redclyffe* is one of many Yonge novels to make this point, while the "domestic drama" of *Little Women* is heightened by bitter quarrels, particularly between Jo and Amy, and the apparently placid Marmee reveals that she is "angry almost every day of [her] life" (Alcott 1868–69). Jo, especially, chafes at being confined to the home, and while she eventually accepts domesticity, readers remain free to identify with her initial impatience at household demands.

Tracing the concept of "home" in children's literature from the development of the modern family in the eighteenth century to the post-traditional society of the early twenty-first, Reynolds (2008) argues that children's fiction has always identified domesticity as an unstable concept to be contested or redefined at need. This instability is apparent in the shifting emotional connotations that have long surrounded "domestic." Some writers for girls celebrate this word: Mrs. George de Horne Vaizey's *A Houseful of Girls* (1902) contains a mother whose "strong ideas on the subject of domestic education" elicit comments such as "I love rushing about in an apron, using my muscles instead of my brain" (Rowbotham 1989). Others acknowledge that many women despise the concept. In L. M. Montgomery's *Anne of Green Gables* (1907), humor derives from Anne's domestic mishaps—flavoring a cake with liniment, mistaking currant wine for raspberry cordial—which often stem from Anne's letting her mind drift away from her chores. In a later Montgomery work, *Jane of Lantern Hill* (1937), Jane's grandmother sneers that Jane "fancies herself as domestic," inasmuch as "she likes to hang about kitchens and places like that." The narrator adds, "Grandmother's voice implied that [Jane] had low tastes and that kitchens were barely respectable."

The source of the "barely respectable" here is not purely a matter of class, but also an outgrowth of the tension between tradition and progress. In *Marm Lisa* (1896), Kate Douglas Wiggin satirizes activist women's assumption "that no woman could develop or soar properly, and cook, scrub, sweep, dust, wash dishes, mend, or take care of babies at the same time. . . . They were willing to concede all these sordid tasks as an honourable department of woman's work, but each wanted them to be done by some other woman." This comment and domestic fiction both classic and contemporary share a quality from which, arguably, much of the energy of the domestic novel for children derives: the recognition that achieving and maintaining what is domestic, whether defined as intimacy, familiarity, or housewifery, is often neither easy nor pleasant.

15

Education

Elisabeth Rose Gruner

In both *Keywords* (Williams 1983a) and *New Keywords* (Bennett, Grossberg, and Morris 2005), "education" (*Keywords* has "educate") is primarily an institutional practice, which, after the late eighteenth century, is increasingly formalized and universalized in Western countries. Bearing the twin senses of "to lead forth" (from the Latin *educere*) and "to bring up" (from the Latin *educare*), "education" appears chiefly as an action practiced by adults on children. The *Oxford English Dictionary* thus defines the term as "the systematic instruction, schooling, or training given to the young in preparation for the work of life."

Education may be primarily vocational, leading children into their futures as productive adults, or more holistic, nurturing children into, variously, adulthood, gentlemanly status, and/or citizenship. This latter sense of education is often called "liberal education." Either view of education focuses "on the formation of individuals to the benefit of society" (Ferguson 2000)—and, in either case, the concept is intimately connected with children's literature, which is also a product (primarily) created by adults for children. Serving both senses of education, literature for children offers (at the very least) a medium for literacy training—a prerequisite for more and more vocations since the industrial revolution—and provides "morals" or lessons in citizenship and life.

Children's literature as such arises out of an increasingly formalized educational system; Seth Lerer (2008) links the development of a specialized literature for children with education from its very beginnings (for Lerer, in classical antiquity and the education of the elite through adaptations of Homer, Aesop, Virgil, and others). Most histories, however, focus especially on the link between John Newbery and John Locke. In *Some Thoughts concerning Education* (1693), Locke prescribes a regimen of physical fitness, self-denial, and lessons in manners, among other things, to the sons of the gentry as more essential to their education than the classical reading most often emphasized at the time. His emphasis on pleasure in reading, and his rejection of "promiscuous reading" of the Bible, certainly influenced Newbery and other publishers in developing books to both "delight and entertain" child readers. A century later, Mary Wollstonecraft (also the author of an early children's book, *Original Stories, from Real Life* [1788]), in her *Vindication of the Rights of Woman* (1793), made an early claim for education as a "grand national concern." Her prescient argument for coeducational, government-run day schools stresses the importance of universal education for the development of a free citizenry, though it still preserves class distinctions in prescribing vocational training after the age of nine for "girls and boys, intended for domestic employments, or mechanical trades," while "young people

of superior abilities, or fortune" would pursue a more Lockean liberal education.

The tension between vocational and liberal education is omnipresent in the history of the field. While the sons (and later, daughters) of the wealthy have always had access to some kind of education (usually, until the nineteenth century, based on the classics), education for the poor was rudimentary and primarily religious and/or vocational until the eighteenth century. In the British and, later, the Anglo-American tradition, formal education was predominantly religious in nature: between the fifteenth and eighteenth centuries, children first learned their alphabet from hornbooks or primers, and moved very quickly into metrical versions of the Psalms and Bible stories (Avery 1995). Those destined for labor left school (if they attended at all) quite young, and received the remainder of their education in the form of on-the-job training. A gentleman's education, by contrast, served to consolidate class status by providing him with the cultural capital his position demanded. Thus, for Locke and even to some extent for Wollstonecraft, education is primarily a matter of manners and morals; curriculum is secondary.

In eighteenth-century England, charity schools taught reading and writing in order to facilitate religious instruction; similarly, slaves in the United States occasionally learned to read along with their religious instruction, though for most slaves reading was forbidden (see "Literacy," below). Efforts to impose compulsory education in the modern era seem to begin in Scotland in the seventeenth century, though the idea is present in Plato; Massachusetts was the first American state to enact compulsory education legislation (1852), and Mississippi the last to do so (1918). In 1948 the United Nations included compulsory elementary education as a fundamental human right in the Universal Declaration of Human Rights (Article 26.1). Most nations now provide primary and even secondary education freely to their citizens. The content and form of that education continue to be contested, though the Declaration makes liberal education its centerpiece, focusing on "the full development of the human personality" and "the strengthening of respect for human rights and fundamental freedoms," and linking them to the promotion of peace. The Declaration also recognizes a potential conflict between the demands of the state in education and the demands of the family, declaring further that "[p]arents have a prior right to choose the kind of education that shall be given to their children" (Article 26.3).

As the framers of the Declaration may have anticipated, the more the state becomes involved in education, the more certain elements of society are likely to opt out. While in the United States and the United Kingdom, as in other countries, independent schools offer one alternative to state-run schools for the elite and educated classes, their pedagogy and curriculum are markedly similar. However, progressive pedagogies such as Montessori and Waldorf methods, as well as homeschooling and "unschooling" offer alternatives to standard educational models. Put simply, "traditional" institutional education, whether in state-run, religiously affiliated, or independent schools, tends to emphasize control, while Montessori, Waldorf, and especially unschooling methods tend to focus on developing children's agency. (For a discussion of the social functions of institutional education, see Winch and Gingell 1999.) Even the control-oriented institutional education in state-run schools, however, has had the effect of creating opportunities for social mobility, especially in the United States. As Richard Shaull notes in his foreword to Paolo Freire's *Pedagogy of the Oppressed* (2000), education either helps the younger generation conform to the logic of the present system, or it helps them "deal critically and creatively with reality and discover how to participate in the transformation of their world." We might, more radically, suggest that education has always done both things: integration and transformation.

Literature's role in the curriculum mirrors education's dual function. Until the twentieth century, rote learning figured prominently in the school curriculum. In the United Kingdom and the United States, children memorized the "classics," first in Greek and Latin, later in English, as part of the set of "accomplishments" expected of the gentry. As satirized in Lewis Carroll's *Alice's Adventures in Wonderland* (1865), the poetry selected for memorization most often delivered pat morals, behavioral models, or nationalist sentiment. Even so, as both the Alice books and Angela Sorby's *Schoolroom Poets* (2005) make clear, students "read . . . (and then rewrote [the poems they learned]) in ways that served their own local interpretive communities."

While children's literature and other books adapted for children have been the medium of education for centuries, in the nineteenth century education itself became a central theme of children's literature. In addition to the satires of education in the Alice books, Thomas Hughes's *Tom Brown's School Days* (1857) popularized the genre of "school story," in which the school setting provides theme, structure, and plot. Books set in schools continue to be a popular subgenre of children's literature; although they rarely focus on curriculum or specific subjects taught, the school setting and the implicit didacticism of the form make them in many ways a school themselves, an education about education for the children who read them. As Beverly Lyon Clark (1996) notes, "School stories lend themselves to didacticism because they are about schooling. . . . Schooling is, in part, a metaphor for the effect that the book is supposed to have, whether it endorses traditional schooling or tries to school us in subversion." By depicting students within an educational system, books as different as Harry Allard and James Marshall's *Miss Nelson Is Missing* (1977), Andrew Clements's *Frindle* (1996), J. K. Rowling's Harry Potter series (1997–2007), and John Green's *Looking for Alaska* (2005) all advocate certain ideas about the form and content of education. Whether the tone is nostalgic, celebratory, or critical, these and many other stories set in schools generally endorse a liberal educational model with the future-oriented goal of producing a competent citizenry.

In the twenty-first century, debates over both the form and content of education continue. A growing homeschooling movement draws on several strands of education theory as justification: some homeschoolers reject compulsory public education on religious grounds, preferring to isolate their children from modern secularism; others, following American educator John Holt, reject the institutionalization of education, preferring a child-led "unschooling." Holt's (1967) central claim is that "[c]hildren do not need to be made to learn, told what to learn, or shown how. If we give them access to enough of the world . . . they will see clearly enough what things are truly important to us and to others, and they will make for themselves a better path into that world than we could make for them." David Almond's *Skellig* (1997) dramatizes unschooling through the character of Mina, whose curiosity and imagination lead to her to make connections between art, science, literature, and her own life—connections that are denied or at least impeded by her neighbor Michael's schooling. However, Holt's claim that children will learn what they and their society need for them to know undercuts the very basis of institutional education and, especially, the contemporary concern with measurable standards.

In the United States, anxieties about American competitiveness (in science and mathematics education especially) have led to a movement for "standards-based education," enacted into law as "No Child Left Behind" (NCLB) in 2001. NCLB standards require schools to meet certain benchmarks (usually set by the state) in order to maintain their public funding. While controversial, NCLB has focused public attention on debates within the educational community on the value of testing, the desirability of standards, and the place of literature in the curriculum.

The rise of standards-based education reveals a never-long-buried fissure in public debates about education: while many educators believe in and try to practice liberal or holistic education, many taxpayers and legislators are (perhaps understandably) concerned with vocational training. Vocationally oriented education can be more easily tested and measured than can the development of an appreciation for literature, a moral character, or a curious mind. Several recent novels speak to this divide without specifically referencing standardized testing. For example, in Laurie Halse Anderson's *Speak* (1999), "Job Day" bears no relationship to any of the courses the students take, while Mr. Freeman, the art teacher, routinely violates school policies (especially regarding assessment and grading) but introduces his class as "the only class that will teach you how to survive." Like many other young adult and children's novels, *Speak* assumes its readers will be familiar with a standard high school curriculum—thus references to Nathaniel Hawthorne's *The Scarlet Letter* and American suffragists can resonate with the protagonist Melinda's situation without explication. By depicting an internal growth—in John Dewey's (1959) words, a "restructuring of experience"—that remains invisible to (most of) the adults responsible for her instruction and development, *Speak* reminds us that education is often self-directed and takes place alongside, rather than through, the standard curriculum.

Dewey's dictum that "[t]he process and the goal of education are one and the same thing" suggests, perhaps, that the divide between liberal and vocational education need not be impassable. Like the literature that represents it and forms a major part of its content, education forms part of an ongoing process of growth and development, always partial, never complete.

16

Empire

Jo-Ann Wallace and Stephen Slemon

> E is our Empire
> Where sun never sets;
> The larger we make it
> The bigger it gets.
> —Mrs. Ernest Ames, *An ABC, for Baby Patriots* (1899)

A barrage of associated terminology attends the advance of empire, and none of it fires with exactitude. "Imperialism" usually refers to "the practice, the theory, and the attitudes of a dominating metropolitan centre ruling a distant territory" (Said 1993)—that is to say, the politics, the economics, and the enabling ideology behind the promulgation of empires. "Colonialism" is generally understood as the assemblage of ways by which one nation or people imposes direct rule over another nation or people. "Colonization" refers specifically to the establishment of settler colonies in foreign lands. "Neo-colonialism," a term coined by Kwame Nkrumah (the first president of Ghana, itself the first of Britain's African colonies to politically decolonize), refers to that postcolonial condition by which a newly constituted (or now reconstituted and liberated) nation-state is only "in theory independent. . . . In reality its economic system and thus its political policy is directed from the outside" (Hadjor 1992) by its former ruler, or by a new surrogate.

But it is "empire" that shimmered to the schoolboy and, perhaps to a slightly lesser extent, the schoolgirl reader of British children's literature from the 1850s onward. It was empire that flushed pink British pride into a world map shown to be one-quarter "British" in 1897, at the time of the Diamond Jubilee celebration of Victoria, Queen of the United Kingdom of Great Britain and Ireland, and Empress of India. It was empire that breathed fire into an endless stream of memorabilia, collectibles, advertisements, play activities, costumes, and club formations, in Britain and abroad, throughout the late nineteenth and early twentieth century. And it is empire that continues, despite its declared end, to play a foundational role in the subject-formation of the children on both sides of the imperial divide.

From its beginnings, the word "empire" has held a close "etymological connexion" to the ideas of power through, and subjectivity under, militarism (*Oxford English Dictionary* [*OED*]). The word "emperor"—with its attendant sedimentation of Roman centralization, citizenship, and hegemony—entered the English language around 1225, almost a century before the word "empire" (*OED*). "Empire" is rooted in the concept of "supreme and extensive political dominion . . . exercised by an 'emperor,'" and then later, "by a sovereign state over its dependencies" (*OED*). The personal element of the British emperor—"Queen Victoria of the United Kingdom of Great Britain and Ireland, Empress of India [as of 1876], Defender of the Faith"—was sometimes obscured in British children's literature of "the period of high imperialism," and even in children's games and puzzles, where Britannia replaces the body of the emperor/empress (Norcia 2009). That said, an inherent celebration of military supremacy remained a prominent component of imperial pageantry abroad, as evidenced in representations of Victoria's Golden and Diamond Jubilees.

"English" schoolchildren found it relatively easy to identify with the shimmering, overdetermined category of "Britishness" promulgated within the idea of empire, but non-English readers and consumers of empire's ubiquitous address found themselves distanced, and internally split, by the category: "subjects" of empire on the one hand, objects of empire on the other. The idea of a globally inclusive, British subjectivity, promulgated throughout the "British Isles," the "Dominions," and the "Colonies" through publications like *The Boy's Own Paper* (1879–1967) and Nelson's *Royal Readers* (1875–95), rested on an embedded narrative of imperial cultural "progress" wherein non-English traditional practices and languages, celebrated as they were for their exoticism and difference, would necessarily in time give way to a "larger" and emancipatory "Britishness" that empire eventually would bestow. "British," Raymond Williams would write in *Border Country* (1960), his novel of rural south Wales, "was hardly ever used without 'Empire' following, and for that nobody had any use at all" (Gikandi 1996). Nirad Chaudhuri's dedication to his 1951 *The Autobiography of an Unknown Indian* captures this split subjectivity

of empire's ideological force with painful clarity: "To the memory of the British Empire in India," he writes, "which conferred subjecthood on us but withheld citizenship; to which yet every one of us threw out the challenge: '*civis britannicus sum.*'"

In *Keywords* (1976), Williams circumvents empire's splitting impetus, focusing instead on the more stable social concept of "imperialism" as a modern political system developed "especially after 1870," and inevitably associated with a self-proclaimed "civilizing mission." Williams notes a later, early-twentieth-century shift in connotation, where imperialism becomes "understood primarily as an economic system of external investment and the penetration and control of markets and sources of raw materials." Postcolonial literary writers, including writers of children's literature (see Ngũgĩ 1986), have been at pains to retain the ideological force of empire as a divisive and diminishing social message well into the present day. Bennett, Grossberg, and Morris (2005) dropped "Imperialism" from their *New Keywords,* substituting "Colonialism" as "a general term signifying domination and hegemony." In their introduction to that volume, the editors indicate that they have deleted "those of Williams's keywords that we feel have not sustained their importance," emphasizing instead a "shift to a collective and more international mode of production." *Keywords for American Studies*, on the other hand, revives "empire" in a specifically American, post–2003 Iraq War context, tracing "arguments about the possible virtues of U.S.

empire" from the 1803 Louisiana Purchase to the present (Streeby 2007). The sliding fortunes of "empire" in keywords dictionaries suggest a stabilization and diminishment in the term—movements that may be related—and thus it remains useful to interrogate the concept as an organizing principle in American and British children's literature, and as a category of critical analysis. As Williams (1976) notes, keywords not only reflect but also produce "continuity and discontinuity, and also deep conflicts of value and belief."

While "empire" has functioned as a category of critical analysis for literature read *by* children since the late 1970s, with particular focus on adventure novels (see Green 1979), some critics have suggested that it has been insufficiently explored in texts written *for* children. Peter Hunt and Karen Sands (2000) argue that "empire" and "post-empire," that is, colonialism and postcolonialism, are undertheorized in British children's literature: first, because the notion that children's books "were the witting or unwitting agents of the empire-builders" is "so apparently obvious" (a hiding-in-plain-sight argument), and second, because recent postcolonial studies have focused on "the other" and not on "the centre, the imperialist coloniser." Hunt and Sands note the degree to which "empire" lingers as an unvoiced theme in post-1945 children's genres, such as in the animal fantasy (e.g., Michael Bond's Paddington stories, Richard Adams's *Watership Down*) whose characters "learn that the Brits are still on top" (Hunt and Sands 2000).

Like Hunt and Sands, Daphne M. Kutzer (2000) suggests that "little attention has been paid to imperialism and its intersections with literature intended for those 'future rulers of the world.'" As Kutzer's phrasing might suggest, much of what early criticism there was on the topic focused on high imperialist writing for boys (see Richards 1989; Bristow 1991), a trend identified by J. S. Bratton in 1989 but continuing, with some exceptions (see McGillis 1996), until recently. The emphasis on writing for boys—leaving to one side the question of whether the texts were also read by girls, as they almost certainly were—resulted in a critical stress on the genres of the adventure novel and the schoolboy novel, where the interpellation of the boy subject as imperial ruler and/or colonial administrator is often overt. Fueled by scholarship on imperial feminism (Chaudhuri and Strobel 1992; Midgley 1998), on the "New Girl" (as a parallel to the "New Woman"; Mitchell 1995), and, to a lesser degree, by the rise of "girls' studies," especially in the American academy (Kearney 2009), recent years have witnessed new interest in the imbrication of writing for girls and questions of empire. While such writing drew on traditions of masculine adventure (Norcia 2004a; Horne 2004), it also led to the development of new subgenres, like the nursing novel (Smith 2009). Kutzer's claim that "children's literature is highly [she suggests inherently] conservative" (Kutzer 2000) is challenged by the complicated relations between late-nineteenth- and early-twentieth-century feminism and writing for girls.

E

Jo-Ann Wallace and
Stephen Slemon

Further complicating the relationship between writing for children and questions of empire, Jacqueline Rose, Perry Nodelman, and Satadru Sen align the children's writer with the imperialist. *The Case of Peter Pan* (1984), Rose's controversial Lacanian and deconstructive exploration of adult desire for an idea of the child, and of adult "colonization" of childhood, did not of itself launch a rethinking of the relationship between children and their books; it did, however, model rigorous investigation of the uses of children's texts and of relations of power between children and adults. Nodelman (1992) pushed the colonial analogy farther, asserting that "child psychology and children's literature are imperialist activities." More recently, critics like Sen (2004) have begun exploring the nature and affect of writing for colonial child subjects, or "colonized children." An issue that has not yet received significant attention is the question of the relation of class to the project of empire. While this issue has received attention with regard to children's history and childhood studies, with some exceptions (see Boone 2005) it remains largely absent from questions of children's literature.

Regardless of readership and address—child or adult, colonizer or colonized, imperialist or imperial subject—the question underlying writing for children and the matter of empire remains at heart one of interpellation, the calling into being of the child as sovereign or as split subject, hailed into complex social identifications by the seemingly simple but structurally complex, and continuing, literature of empire. As

Mrs. Ernest Ames writes in her *An ABC, for Baby Patriots* (1899),

F is the Flag
Which wherever you see
You know that beneath it
You're happy and free.

17

Fantasy

Deirdre Baker

The history of fantasy in the realm of children's literature has been one of forceful contradictions: on the one hand, fantasy is criticized as being fraudulent, irrational, and overly imaginative; on the other, it is criticized for being formulaic, escapist, and not imaginative enough. The seeds of this debate lie in early uses of the word, which seem to have little to do with literature per se, but nevertheless powerfully influenced the activity of imagination over centuries. Fantasy's potency in relation to children's literature reflects its potency in relation to literature in general: it takes us into the heart of story-making—imagination and reason.

According to the *Oxford English Dictionary* (*OED*), the origin of the word "fantasy" lies in the Greek word *fautasia*, literally "a making visible," "to make visible," or "to show." It begins its career in English as both "fantasy" and "fancy" (derived from its alternate spellings, "fantsy," "phantsy," "fansy," "fancie"). Its earliest and primary meanings belong to scholastic psychology and refer to a faculty of mind: "mental apprehension of an object of perception; the faculty by which this is performed," or "the image impressed on the mind by an object of sense." A primary sense of fantasy in the early modern period is "imagination; the process or the faculty of forming mental representations of things not actually present"—that is, showing oneself,

in the mind, images perceived through sensory experience and retained in the memory. This meaning supplies the silent foundation of its use to describe characteristics of twenty-first-century fantasy literature—a literature distinctive for its abundant visual imagery.

"Imagination" is the Latin translation of the transliterated Greek "phantasia": in the seventeenth and eighteenth centuries, "fantasy," "fancy," and "imagination" were virtually interchangeable and related not just to the faculty of forming mental representations, but to the way the mind examines and orders those images—that is, turns them into story, or into sense (Svendsen 1956; Stevens 1984). "Fantasy, or imagination . . . is an inner sense which doth more fully examine the species perceived by common sense, of things present or absent . . . it is subject and governed by reason, or at least should be," Robert Burton explains in *The Anatomy of Melancholy* (1621). When fantasy is distinguished from imagination, it is understood to be the creative faculty of the mind that combines, as opposed to receives, images provided through sensory experience—a distinction made in Peter de la Primaudaye's *The French Academie* (English translation 1618): "then doth [Fantasie] as it were prepare and digest [received images], either by joyning them together, or by separating them according as their natures require" (quoted in Svendsen 1956). Thus, in the seventeenth century, fantasy, fancy, or imagination—as involuntary as the senses of taste and touch—were considered necessary to reason and to our apprehension of reality. And since fantasy is how we order data we receive from the "real world," the images it produces and the logic with which it orders them presents us with something that is "real"—a potency that fantasy and imagination exercise in their roles in poetry and prophecy (*OED*; Stevens 1984).

But early modern scientists of the mind recognized that in sleep, fantasy can "misjoin shapes" and produce the "wild work" of dreams, as John Milton's Adam tells Eve in *Paradise Lost* (1667). Fantasy's dream-work is "sudden," De la Primaudaye writes, "for it . . . taketh what pleaseth it, and addeth thereunto to diminisheth, changeth and rechangeth, mingleth and unmingleth so that it cutteth asunder and seweth up againe as it listeth. . . . [F]ancie breeds the fact which it imagineth" (quoted in Svendsen 1956). Fantasy is thus fundamental to reason, but is also volatile, operates by caprice and pleasure, and can make one susceptible to its own artful constructions, befuddling reason. It is associated with desire and delusion, or an inability to distinguish the imagined from the "real" (note the *OED*'s definitions for both "fantasy" and "fancy": "illusory appearance; delusive imagination; a whimsical or visionary notion or speculation; caprice; inclination, liking, desire").

The operation of fancy/fantasy is central to debates over children's literature. In the eighteenth century, the valorizing of science and utility, as well as the exercise of prudence, moderation, and reason, tussled with children's enjoyment of reading materials that some educators felt undermined rationality and proper understanding (Summerfield 1984). Early in the century,

English translations of Charles Perrault's fairy tales and Antoine Galland's version of the *Thousand and One Nights* brought new, rich fodder to the chapbook trade, augmenting its fare of romances, fairy tales, and adventure stories such as *Guy of Warwick, Jack the Giant-Killer*, and legends of Arthur. Such tales found an avid audience in children, although rationalist educators such as Thomas Day and Maria Edgeworth (and, earlier, John Locke) sometimes deplored them as dangerous and confusing to mind and soul. "Why should the mind be filled with fantastic visions instead of useful knowledge?" wonders Edgeworth (1796), who criticizes fairy tales for their improbability and for stimulating unhealthy desire. Similarly, Sarah Trimmer (1805) declares that "for the most part, [fairy tales] answer no better part than to amuse the fancy, and not infrequently at the hazard of inflaming the imaginations and passions of youth." They are, she notes, likely to confuse "little children whose minds are susceptible of every impression; and who from the liveliness of their imaginations are apt to convert into realities whatever forcibly strikes their fancy" (Trimmer 1803). The understanding evident in De la Primaudaye's warnings about fantasy's dream-work—that fantasy/fancy can wildly, freely "mingle and unmingle" images it receives from the sensory world and also affect behavior—underlies Edgeworth's and Trimmer's uneasiness with fairy tales, as well as their notions of how the mind processes literature and the images it presents to the mind's eye.

Rationalist arguments against the desirability of fairy tales as young people's reading point to the forcible tide of opinion for its benefits—a tide in which Samuel Johnson, Thomas Carlyle, George Crabbe, James Boswell, and Samuel Coleridge are only a few notable examples (Johnson, quoted in Edgeworth 1796). By 1802, William Godwin (writing under the pseudonym William Scolfield) complained, "The modern improvers have left out of their system that most essential branch of human nature the imagination . . . everything is studied and attended to, except those things which *open the heart*. . . . They would not for the world astonish the child's mind with a giant, a dragon, or a fairy; but their young people are all so good . . . that no genuine interest can be felt for their adventures." Godwin's articulation of the value and function of imagination and fairy tale in children's moral and intellectual development presages William Wordsworth's claims for the regenerative powers of poetry and his romantic characterization of the child as a pure, abundant font of imagination and fancy.

Wordsworth's and Coleridge's division of imagination from fancy underlies subsequent developments in views of children's literature and fantasy. They judged fancy to be a creative activity inferior to that of imagination. In his preface to the 1815 volume of "Poems of the Fancy" and "Poems of the Imagination," Wordsworth claimed that "Fancy is given to quicken and beguile the temporal part of our nature, Imagination to incite and to support the eternal." For Coleridge (1817), "primary imagination" is "the living power and prime agent of all human perception, and as a repetition in the finite mind of the eternal act of creation in the infinite I am." Echoing Burton, De la Primaudaye, and Milton's claims for fantasy, Coleridge says the "secondary imagination . . . dissolves, diffuses, dissipates, in order to re-create . . . it struggles to idealize and unify." Fancy, on the other hand, has no originating power and functions by consciously moving around and recombining materials that are "ready made from the law of association." Coleridge calls fancy the "drapery" of poetic genius, while imagination is its "soul." Fancy is a conscious, voluntary activity and rearranges, but does not create; imagination, reflecting God, creates *ex nihilo*, coexists with conscious will, and has an element of the unconscious, the involuntary, in it. Both George MacDonald and J. R. R. Tolkien consciously adapted Coleridge's ideas on "primary" and "secondary" imagination for their fantasies for children.

In the mid-Victorian period, fancy was valued in association with imagination, sympathy, and understanding; it was considered essential to the development of the child's mind and even to the success of the British nation. Publishing his elegant *Home Treasury* editions of fairy tales and nursery rhymes—partly to counteract the plethora of "improving" rationalist children's literature—Henry Cole (1843), under the pseudonym Felix Summerly, claimed that "the many tales sung or said from time immemorial" appeal to important elements in a child's mind: "its fancy, imagination, sympathies, [and] affections." Charles Dickens defended "the fairy literature of our childhood" because "a nation without fancy, without some romance, never did, never can, never will, hold a great place under the sun" (quoted in Cruikshank 1854). Anxieties about how a child's fancy might be wounded or lead it astray give way in these writers to the critical role fancy and imagination play in the development of morals and understanding.

Trimmer, Cole, Dickens, and others associated fancy and the fantastic with a particular kind of literature—fairy tales and nursery rhymes. Edgeworth (1796) argued that the fairies, giants, and enchanters of fairy tales fill the mind with "fantastic visions"; a reviewer praised Cole's (1843) nursery rhyme book saying, "We rejoice that the beautiful, and the fantastic (the nonsensical, if the reader please) are now to have a turn." In 1818, Benjamin Tabart's *Fairy Tales and the Lilliputian Cabinet* carried the subtitle *Containing Twenty-Four Choice Pieces of Fancy and Fiction*. George MacDonald, while using the word "Fancy" with Coleridgean depreciation as the generator of "mere inventions," prefaced *The Light Princess and Other Fairy Tales* with an essay entitled "The Fantastic Imagination" (reprinted in MacDonald 1882/1893). The fantastic and fancy are thus constantly associated with fairy tales, but "fairy tales" is an expansive category, lumping together folk and traditional fairy tales; adventure stories such as *Jack the Giant-Killer*, *Guy of Warwick*, and *St. George and the Dragon*; nursery rhymes; Arthurian romances; versions of Gulliver's visit to Lilliput; and contemporary literary fairy tales. In his preface to *The Heroes; or Greek Fairy Tales for My Children*, Charles Kingsley (1856) considered "the Eddas, and the Voluspa, and Beowulf, and the noble old Romances" equally to be fairy tales

(quoted in Kamenetsky 1992). Twenty years later, Lewis Carroll referred to *Through the Looking Glass and What Alice Found There* (1871) as "the love-gift of a fairy tale," demonstrating that "fairy" also encompassed new, longer, and untraditional works of fancy.

By the middle of the nineteenth century, "fairy literature" was understood to pertain to children and to the "childhood of man." "All nations [love fairy tales] when they are young: our old forefathers did, and called their stories 'sagas,'" wrote Kingsley (1856), reflecting prevailing attitudes toward civilization and cultural maturity. Studies in anthropology and folklore throughout the nineteenth century (the Grimm brothers, Andrew Lang, Joseph Jacobs) brought fairy tales into publication as never before, acknowledging the rich relationship between fantasy, imagination, childhood, and culture. For George MacDonald (1882/1893), fairy tales' appeal for the young relates to spiritual openness: "[F]or my part, I do not write for children, but for the child-like, whether five, of fifty, or seventy-five," he wrote; "he who will be a man, and will not be a child, must . . . become a little man, that is a dwarf." MacDonald virtually sanctified the fantastic, and his endorsement of fairy tale as the way to "awaken meaning" and inspire spiritual maturity is the underpinning of Tolkien's and Lewis's defense of fantasy.

Tolkien reclaimed the fairy tale for adults, taking both it and the term "Faërie" in the broadly inclusive sense. He also reinvigorated the word "fantasy" in his influential essay "On Fairy-Stories" (1938/1947), restricting "Imagination" to "the mental power of image-making" and spurning the Romantic definition of fancy. Art is "the operative link between Imagination and the final result, Sub-creation," and is responsible for achieving "the inner consistency of reality" in ideal creations. Fantasy embraces "both the Sub-creative Art in itself and a quality of strangeness and wonder in the Expression, derived from the Image." His definition of "fantasy" combines "its older and higher use as an equivalent of Imagination" with "the derived notions of 'unreality' (that is, unlikeness to the Primary World), in short of the fantastic." Like Joseph Addison, who comments on the difficulties of "the fairy way of writing" and its demands on fancy (Summerfield 1984), Tolkien acknowledges that "'the inner consistency of reality' is more difficult to produce, the more unlike are the images and the rearrangements of primary material to the actual arrangements of the Primary World." Here fantasy is again, with images and rearrangements—cutting asunder and sewing up—this time not with the effect of helping to order the experience of the sensory world, but with the hope of sub-creating a "living, realised" Secondary World distinguished by its very unlikeness to ours. It is an exercise of consciously joining together what the human mind allows us to separate, Tolkien says, noun and adjective: "[W]e may cause woods to spring with silver leaves and rams to wear fleeces of gold, and put hot fire into the belly of the cold worm . . . in such 'fantasy' . . . new form is made; Faërie begins; Man becomes a sub-creator. An essential power of Faërie is thus the power of making immediately effective by the will the visions of

'fantasy.'" Fantasy thus retains its sense of "making visible" as well as its quality of "putting together images"; by the end of his essay, Tolkien also uses "fantasy" as a synonym for "secondary world." Thus he opens the way for understanding fantasy as a form of literature itself: a written, secondary world.

The *OED*'s first citation for "fantasy" as "a genre of literary compositions" dates to 1949, in the *Magazine of Fantasy and Science Fiction*. In 1952, C. S. Lewis wrote that "within the species 'children's story' the sub-species which happened to suit me is the fantasy or (in a loose sense of that word) the fairy tale," and went on to refer repeatedly to "fantasy or fairy tale" as if they are synonyms. He includes in his consideration of fantasies, among other works, *Odysseus,* showing the same broad inclusiveness in his definition that Kingsley showed earlier in his umbrella term "fairy tales" for the Greek myths, Norse sagas, *Beowulf,* and so on. Thus, by the middle of the twentieth century, Carroll's *Through the Looking Glass* (1871) had ceased to be "the love-gift of a fairy tale" and had become a fantasy; indeed the primary meaning of fantasy within children's literature, henceforth, was "fantasy literature," rather than fantasy as a faculty of mind or creativity.

The ground prepared by Victorian fantasists (Kingsley, Carroll, MacDonald, Rudyard Kipling, Christina Rossetti, Juliana Horatia Ewing, Mary Louisa Molesworth) and further tilled by the Edwardians (E. Nesbit, J. M. Barrie, Kenneth Grahame) broke forth with new abundance in the burgeoning industry in children's publishing that developed from the 1950s to the present. In the United Kingdom, C. S. Lewis, Eleanor Farjeon, William Mayne, Philippa Pearce, L. M. Boston, Leon Garfield, Susan Cooper, Alan Garner, Joan Aiken, and Diana Wynne Jones; in the United States, Edward Eager, Carolyn Kendall, Norton Juster, Elizabeth Marie Pope, Lloyd Alexander, and Ursula K. Le Guin—among many others—published their works in the decades after World War II. There is a freedom and playfulness in the exercise of fantasy in these writers, a willingness to take the data of sensory perception and cut, rearrange, and conjoin as a way to explore ideas ranging from the personal to the political and philosophical, in manners subversive and sometimes conservative. In the wake of the popularity of *The Lord of the Rings,* Tolkien-derivative "epic" or "heroic" fantasies have proliferated—and fantasy was given another enormous boost with the sensational popularity of J. K. Rowling's Harry Potter series at the turn of the millennium.

In great part, the children's fantasies of the 1950s to the present function as poetry: the images invented through the mingling and unmingling of the imagery of the "real world" are an attempt to convey truths that cannot be encompassed by language. Thus, in David Almond's *Skellig* (1997), a decrepit, winged man found in a derelict garage becomes a lens through which we get a partial glimpse of the grief and fear of loss. In *Howl's Moving Castle,* by Diana Wynne Jones (1986), the magical aging of a young woman becomes a way to approximate an inner condition, just as the physical dream land of Elizabeth Knox's *Dreamhunter* (2005) offers an image of the territory of the adolescent psyche.

Such fantasy acknowledges the inability of language to convey fully the puzzling aspects of being human; at the same time, it acknowledges the supreme fitness of fantasy—of metaphor—as the best means through which to explore and attempt to understand them. Some postwar fantasy playfully brings together the fanciful with the unanswerable, the incomprehensible. On the other hand, the unprecedented response to the Harry Potter series (1997–2007)—a backlash, perhaps, to the "gritty" realistic fiction that dominated children's publishing from the 1970s to the 1990s—shows a desire for the reinstatement of a comfortable old regime: a boy wonder who triumphs; untroubled gender roles; a narrator who has everything under control; and a world in which material and consumer culture, unsatisfying as it may have proven to be in the real world, has an extra, desirable, unattainable quality: magic.

In the face of the many thousands of children's fantasies that have been written, sold, and read in the past fifty years, adults still show some fear that fantasy literature will draw the young into unhealthy escapism and an inability to manage in the "real world." Some protest the "occult" or heterodox content in stories of magic—most recently targeting Philip Pullman's *His Dark Materials* and the Harry Potter stories. But critical debate now centers on how we categorize fantasy literature, as well as what exactly fantasy literature is and does—a conversation which, thanks in part to the legacy of MacDonald, Tolkien, and Lewis, is one of the few in which literature for children and adults are considered together (Attebery 1992; Mendlesohn 2005).

With the tentative entrance of fantasy literature and children's literature into the realm of the academy, efforts to define fantasy have proliferated. For Brian Attebery (1992), following Tolkien's template means that "non-formulaic" fantasies involve some violation of what the author believes to be natural law; they are comic in structure; and they provoke a response of wonder, or estrangement, in the reader. For Sheila Egoff (1988), "[P]erhaps all that can be said with conviction is that fantasy is a story in which the sustaining pleasure is that created by the deliberate abrogation of any natural law, no matter how slight, or by the taking of a step beyond it." In Diana Wynne Jones's work, Farah Mendlesohn (2005) finds many key definitions of the fantastic, including Tzvetan Todorov's "moment of hesitation" between the *marvelous* and the *uncanny*, Attebery's "treats impossibilities without hesitation," and Gary K. Wolfe's idea that fantasy's "collective world view" is "the geography of desire." Natalie Babbitt (1987) claims that fantasy "aims to define the universe"; and in her *Fantasy Literature for Children and Young Adults*, Ruth Lynn Nadelman (2005) cites myriad examples of attempts to define fantasy in relation to literature, from Jane Langton's "fantasy novels are 'waking dreams'" to Susan Cooper's fantasy is a "most magnificent bubble." Trying to wrest fairy tales from fantasy in an ironic reversal of earlier usage, Maria Nikolajeva (2000) writes: "[F]antasy is one of the most ambiguous notions in literary criticism, and it is often,

especially within the context of children's literature, used to denote anything that is not straight realistic prose. It has been treated as a genre, a style or a narrative technique, and it is sometimes regarded as purely formulaic fiction. In many handbooks fairy tales and fantasy are discussed together without precision, and no totally satisfactory and comprehensive definition of fantasy literature has been conceived so far."

The failure to define "fantasy" lies, perhaps, with its current primary meaning as a type of literature instead of as a faculty of mind. Echoing the latter idea, Le Guin (1973/1979) writes that fantasy is "a different approach to reality, an alternative technique for apprehending and coping with existence. Fantasy is nearer to poetry, to mysticism and to insanity than naturalistic fiction." Le Guin claims that the role of the child is central to the creation of fantasy worlds, and likens fantasy to play—"pure pretense with no ulterior motive whatever . . . the game played for the game's sake." Lloyd Alexander (1987) refers to fantasy as "transformative imagination, and also notes that "if a work of fantasy can fail through a lack of realism, a work of realism can fail through lack of fantasy." Both fantasists hark back to fantasy's earlier, powerful meaning as the mind's creative ability to apprehend sensory data, present images to itself, and rearrange those images into a narrative that interprets the world. Trimmer worries about the effects of fairy tales on children's fancy because in children, who are still acquiring data from the sensory world, the faculty of fantasy is particularly active in arranging and rearranging images, finding out the sense in the world. Fairy tales (fantasy literature) thus amplify and augment an activity that is already especially vigorous in children. In the second half of the twentieth century and into the twenty-first, the artists who write children's fantasy literature and the children who read it are exceptionally free to enjoy this imaginative activity.

18

Gender
Erica Hateley

The *Oxford English Dictionary* (*OED*) informs us that "gender" has at its root the Latin *genus*, meaning "race, kind," and emerges as early as the fifth century as a term for differentiating between types—especially those of people and words. In the ensuing 1,500 years, "gender" appears in linguistic and biological contexts to distinguish types of words and bodies from one another, as when words in Indo-European languages were identified as masculine, feminine, or neuter, and humans were identified as male or female. It is telling that gender has historically (whether overtly or covertly) been a tool of negotiation between our understandings of bodies, and meanings derived from and attributed to them.

Within the field of children's literature studies, as in other disciplines, gender in and of itself is rarely the object of critique. Rather, specific constructions of gender structure understandings of subjectivity; allow or disallow certain behaviors or experiences on the basis of biological sex; and dictate a specific vision of social relations and organization. Critical approaches to gender in children's literature have included linguistic analysis (Turner-Bowker 1996; Sunderland 2004); analysis of visual representations (Bradford 1998; Moebius 1999); cultural images of females (Grauerholz and Pescosolido 1989); consideration of gender and genre

(Christian-Smith 1990; Stephens 1996); ideological (Nodelman and Reimer 2003); psychoanalytic (Coats 2004); discourse analysis (Stephens 1996); and masculinity studies (Nodelman 2002), among others. In the adjacent fields of education and literacy studies, gender has been a sustained point of investigation, often deriving from perceived gendering of pedagogical practices (Lehr 2001) or of reading preferences and competencies, and, in recent years, perceptions of boys as "reluctant readers" (Moss 2008). The ideology of patriarchy has come under critical scrutiny primarily because it has been used to locate characters and readers within the specific binary logic of gender relations, which historically subordinated the feminine to the masculine. Just as feminism might be broadly defined as resistance to existing power structures, a gendered reading might be broadly defined as a "resistant reading" in that it most often reveals or contests that which a text assumes to be the norm.

From its eighteenth-century inception, children's literature addressed itself through particular narrative strategies as male *or* female, and, in doing so, enacted an entangling of bodies and words in the sources and objects of gendered understandings. Within the liberal-humanist project of socialization through literature, works for children affirmed values of consciousness and experience as distinctly masculine or feminine. Reading not only created literate citizens, it also located them in a gendered social order.

We can clearly see ideological gendering of children's literary culture taking place within serial magazines such as *The Boy's Own Paper* (1879–1967) and *The Girl's Own Paper* (1880–1956). The intersections of language, bodies, and socialization performed by such periodicals linked femininity with stories of romance and domesticity, and masculinity with stories of adventure and empire. Not coincidentally, such publications appeared roughly contemporaneously with the so-called "Golden Age" of children's literature, which produced children's books that are still canonical. Beatrix Potter's *The Tale of Peter Rabbit* (1902), L. M. Montgomery's *Anne of Green Gables* (1907), Kenneth Grahame's *The Wind in the Willows* (1908), and J. M. Barrie's *Peter and Wendy* (1911) all demonstrated that, even when its characters are represented as animals or fantastic figures, children's literature inculcates a range of gendered norms. While these books both shape and are shaped by their context of production—for example, Grahame's privileging of male homosocial bonds or Barrie's conceptualization of motherhood—their continuing popularity suggests that such models of gendered behavior are still perceived as normal (and thus work as normative).

In keeping with nineteenth-century ideologies of "separate spheres" and "biology as destiny," children's texts "presented boys in fiction as movers, doers, explorers, adventurers, creatures of action, guile, mischief, intellect, and leadership. It presented girls as tag-alongs, subordinate to boys in initiative and daring, relatively docile, passive, emotional, and unimaginative; as restraining influences on male daring and excess; as objects of an ambivalent (if not schizophrenic) male adulation and contempt (mirroring that which was prevalent in adult society); as domestic souls in training to be housewives and mothers" (Sutherland 1985). Such representations work to shape readers' understandings of the "naturalness" of specific behaviors being attributed to sexed bodies, and implicitly link the adherence to such ideas with a cohesive, productive, and forward-moving society.

On the one hand, a relatively stable set of signifiers or codes of gender across several decades of children's literature might suggest a similarly stable understanding of gender in the surrounding social contexts; on the other hand, the extent to which children's literature produced and reproduced these codes may also signal an anxiety about any such stability. Certainly, the fin de siècle cultures of the New Woman/Girl (Mitchell 1995) and dandyism (Moers 1960) suggest that "gender" was far more troubled in the decades preceding the Golden Age of children's literature than that literature might itself seem to suggest. In turn, it would be problematic to suggest that child readers passively or unthinkingly took on the gender roles prescribed to them, even in times of seemingly stable gender codes. As Mitzi Myers (1989) has pointed out in discussions of eighteenth-century children's texts, there are almost always possibilities for resistance encoded within texts as well as in actual readers. Even so, the success of series fiction such as the Stratemeyer syndicate's Hardy Boys (1927–) and Nancy Drew (1930–) books perpetuate and reveal tensions in inherited modes of gendering children's texts and changing social contexts. There seems to be no doubt in the Stratemeyer universe that male bodies should exhibit masculine traits and female bodies feminine traits.

Women's movements in contemporary Western cultures have challenged and disentangled historical conflations of gendered bodies and language in order to re-imagine bodies and the bodies-politic they make up. What is now known as the First Wave of feminism in the late nineteenth century sought bodily equality in order to achieve social equality, and in doing so laid the groundwork not just for a politics of sex but for a challenge to the sex-gender model that dominated Anglophone cultures. Second-Wave feminists in the 1970s and beyond have extended the object of critique to a politics of language that seeks to enact and enable a politics of bodies. The *OED* notes that modern "(esp. feminist) use" of "gender" has been as "a euphemism for the sex of a human being, often intended to emphasize the social and cultural, as opposed to the biological, distinction between the sexes." In understanding gender as distinct from sex, the goal is at least in part to recast the dyad of male/masculine and female/feminine as a non-binary opposition. If the ideology of patriarchy both derives from and scaffolds a binary logic of sex and gender identities and relations, then it makes sense that critiques of gender in and around children's literature have focused on individual and social levels. That is, gender critics have focused both on representations of characters "as" gendered, and on the ways in which cultural texts produce a gendered effect by socializing readers into specific ways of thinking and being in relation to gender.

Bob Dixon's influential 1977 contribution to the debate about gender and children's literature encapsulates anxieties about socializing young readers into rigid gender roles:

> There's no foundation, at present, for any of the fierce sex-role indoctrination we've seen in children's fiction. Nor need it go on in life. There's no reason why girls shouldn't play football, climb trees and get dirty, no more than there's any reason why boys shouldn't play with dolls if they want to and take an active interest in cookery. Why shouldn't boys, or men, for that matter, cry? (35)

Published in the same year as Dixon's critique, Gene Kemp's *The Turbulent Term of Tyke Tiler* offered a fictional illustration of Dixon's assertions that all behaviors should be seen as available to all young people, regardless of their sex. Kemp's novel deploys familiar genre tropes—the school story, individual development, and friendships—to tell, seemingly, the story of a group of schoolboy friends. The novel shows Tyke engaging in a range of stereotypically masculine behaviors, but near the novel's end Tyke is revealed to the reader to be a "naughty, disobedient girl" (120). By inverting the patriarchal binary of male/masculine and female/feminine as active/passive, superior/inferior, such texts engage politically with the question of gender, marking a shift away from gender being

understood as deriving from sexed bodies and toward understanding it as a set of socially constituted practices, as a repertoire of behaviors, actions, and ideas—or, as Stephens puts it, "schemata" (17)—whereby "socially desirable" (19) gendered subjects are both interpellated by and represented in children's fictions.

The late-twentieth-century combination of theoretically literate critical communities of librarians, teachers, and scholars and a creative community conscious of gender politics resulted in children's books that explicitly sought to challenge preconceptions about gendered schemata. Robert Munsch's well-known picture book *The Paper Bag Princess* (1980) exemplifies the strategy of recasting and regendering traditional narratives in its account of Elizabeth, a princess who decides "to chase the dragon and get [her paramour] Ronald back" after he is abducted. The inversions of familiar fairy-tale tropes are obvious and powerful in Munsch's text, but the book still works to naturalize "feminine" traits such as outwitting rather than physically overpowering the dragon. Similar attempts at inverting gender roles appear in Anthony Browne's *Piggybook* (1986), which tells the story of Mr. Piggott and his sons, Simon and Patrick, who must learn to contribute to the housekeeping when Mrs. Piggott abandons them, leaving only a note reading, "You are pigs." In her absence, the house becomes a pigsty, and the males literally become pigs; once Mrs. Piggott returns, the domestic duties are shared equally, leaving Mum free to happily work on mending the car—so inadvertently re-inscribing the belief that it's better to be a dirty boy than a clean girl.

More complex engagements with theories of gender and subjectivity emerge in recent children's fiction that engages self-reflexively with debates about identity and gender. The extent to which such models have become normalized in understandings of gender can be seen in the self-conscious (and playful) deployment of Freudian tropes in Neil Gaiman's *Coraline* (2002). Gaiman's parodic psychoanalytic plot enables an equally parodic plot of gendered subjectivity, when Coraline realizes she can defeat her enemy by a pretense of juvenile femininity: "[S]he served each doll a slice of invisible cake on an invisible plate, chattering happily as she did so. From the corner of her eye she saw something bone white scamper from one tree trunk to another, closer and closer. She forced herself not to look at it. . . . She pretended to clean up spilled cake and then to get Jemima another piece" (166–67). In strategically deploying stereotypes of girlhood, Coraline achieves empowerment and agency within a novel clearly conscious of its critical and social contexts.

Interventions in feminist discourse that have shaped this shift in theory and practice include Judith Butler's enormously influential conceptualization of gender as performative. Her *Gender Trouble* (1990) revolutionized gender studies across a range of disciplines through its use of linguistic and psychoanalytic theory to postulate that gender is constantly called and re-called into being through performative strategies of which individuals are likely to be unconscious. Butler's point that "performativity is not a singular act, but a repetition and a ritual, which achieves its effects through its naturalization in the context of a body, understood, in part, as a culturally sustained temporal duration" (xv) returns us to the bodily and linguistic contexts of gender that have been present since its coinage. Children's literature can itself be seen as a site of such performative action, as it constructs and reconstructs often seemingly neutral or natural representations that are in fact gendered representations (cf. Nodelman and Reimer 2003). The complexity of a performative understanding of subjectivity can be seen in Lauren Myracle's *ttyl* (2004), wherein one young woman seems conscious of the performative aspect of subjectivity when she wonders, "how much of other ppl r just images they made up. like maybe ppl lie about all kinds of things—how would we ever know?" (68). However, this same character participates unthinkingly in performative policing of femininity when she writes, "i could never not shave my pubes. that is just gross. but even if i did have a pubic hair problem, which i do not, u and zoe would still luv me, right?" (3).

Just as feminist theory and practice has been affected by contributions from poststructuralism such as those by Butler, so too has postmodernism (Flax 1987) and postcolonialism (Spivak 1985; Mohanty 1988) challenged models of gendered subjectivity that fail to take into account the ways in which gender is necessarily modified by categories such as race, nationality, class, and sexuality. By extension, the imagination or realization of "equality" narratives that fail to take such intersections into account becomes problematic. When Amal, the adolescent female protagonist of Randa Abdel-Fattah's *Does My Head Look Big in This?* (2005a), decides to wear her hijab full-time in Melbourne, Australia, she and the reader quickly realize that familiar feminist narratives of "all women are equal" may not be as true as one might wish. Amal's access to agency is affected by her visible difference from the imagined "woman" of liberal, white, Second-Wave feminism, and thus reminds readers that there can be no "one size fits all" approach to gender or subjectivity. Intersectional consciousness can also be traced in Markus Zusak's *Fighting Ruben Wolfe* (2000), which illustrates that particular modes of privileged masculinity are determined as much by the protagonist's working-class location as they are by his male body. Such novels respond to increasingly diverse sociocultural sensibilities just as surely as complex theories of gender and subjectivity do. They also suggest that for all of the stereotypical or normative gendering of children's literature, progress has been made since the birth of children's literature: in short, for every *Gossip Girl* there is a *Does My Head Look Big in This?* (even if the former enjoys far greater commercial success than the latter).

Just as "feminist" studies have evolved into "gender studies," a shift mirroring moves from essentialist to constructivist understandings of gendered subjectivity, one highly visible development in the meaning of gender has been the relatively recent development of "masculinity studies" (Connell 2005). This field has engaged specifically with children's literature in works such as John Stephens's edited collection of essays, *Ways of Being Male* (2002), or Kenneth Kidd's *Making American Boys* (2004). Such work, rather than viewing "masculinity" as a stable category against which femininity might be measured and critiqued, seeks to challenge the very meanings of "male" and "masculinity," just as feminism sought to redefine the meanings of "female" and "femininity." Most importantly, masculinity studies has invited consideration of masculinity as a gendered spectrum of behaviors and ideas that may or may not be linked with a male body.

The results of such interrogations can be seen in the young adult novels of authors such as John Green, who makes heroes of young men who may historically have been viewed as "unmasculine" or "effeminate," as in the case of Colin, the intellectual protagonist of Green's *An Abundance of Katherines* (2006). One particularly resonant narrative of masculinity as constructed or acculturated can be seen in Frank Portman's *King Dork* (2006), when the protagonist Tom tells the reader, "I suppose I fit the traditional mold of the brainy, freaky, oddball kid who reads too much" (5). Recognizing his lack of hegemonic masculinity, Tom seeks guidance from his dead father's copy of the canonical novel of adolescence, *The Catcher in the Rye*, and thus Portman's novel foregrounds alternative models of masculinity at the same time that it engages the ways in which young people acquire their understandings of acceptable masculinity. Both Green and Portman complicate masculinity within a white,

American, middle-class, heterosexual milieu, which suggests that our understandings of gender in general and masculinity in particular still have some way to go before children's literature can be seen to truly reflect the fluid complexities of lived gender for most people.

Although the effects of mainstream feminism can be felt in anxieties about stereotypes of sex and gender in children's literature, one need only cast the most cursory eye over lists of recent bestsellers and prize-winners to note a continuing, deep investment in gender as stable, essential, and "safe." For all of the theoretical and cultural debates about the meanings of gender, the field of children's literature continues to reflect and shape young people's understandings of themselves as the occupants of sexed bodies and as the bearers of gendered identities that are seen as "most appropriate" when "least unstable." Tracing competing meanings of gender from essentialist, biological, dyadic sex roles through to constructivist, social, fluid gendered subjectivities (in critical or creative fields) does not, by itself, alter the lived experiences of those young people who continue to be socialized and acculturated by texts written for them. As long as "gender" is understood to be a constituent aspect of identity or subjectivity, what and how gender "means" must continually be queried, challenged, redefined, and recast. Doing so offers hope for shifting from the *OED* definition of gender as a noun, toward its definition of gender as a verb, to "come into being," without reference to being male or female, masculine or feminine, but instead, as human.

Girlhood

Jacqueline Reid-Walsh

According to the *Oxford English Dictionary* (*OED*), "girlhood" has been in use from the mid-eighteenth century until the present day as both a singular and a plural noun. From the first cited use—notably, in Samuel Richardson's *Clarissa* (1747–48), a novel concerning the paragon of virtuous adolescent girlhood—the term "girlhood" has had a history as an ideologically loaded term in Western culture. As the following brief definitions indicate, several meanings overlap: "The state of being a girl; the time of life during which one is a girl. Also: girls collectively." Its different denotations and connotations make for a fuzziness of meaning surrounding an apparently simple term: a state of being, a developmental or chronological phase of existence, as well as girls as a collective group. This variability of meaning and ideological loading continues in contemporary research on girlhood. Some academics emphasize only age and psychological development, others consider girlhood almost exclusively a cultural construction, and still others maintain an approach based on a balance between the two.

The term "girlhood" is, of course, based upon the noun "girl," which begs the question, Who is a girl? The *OED* again reveals complex and contradictory meanings for this apparently simple noun—a lengthy set of definitions and examples (amounting to some twenty pages of printout) traced back to the Middle Ages in English and German. These definitions undermine the idea of "girl" being associated with a set chronological age or even sex or gender; in the 1300s, the term (usually in the plural) referred to a child or young person of either sex. From the late 1300s on, "girl" also began to be associated with the female sex, in ways both matter-of-fact and derogatory, including: a young or relatively young woman, a woman of any age, a female child, a sweetheart, a prostitute, a female servant, a female slave, and an effeminate man.

The *OED* offers two theories about the subsequent history of the word. F. C. Robinson (1967) proposed that the term "girl" derives from the Old English word for dress or apparel, *gyrela*; the other theory suggests that it is a diminutive of the Middle Low German word for small child, *Gör, Göre*. The first theory, linking "girl" and "apparel" or fashion, may be startling to the modern reader, but it underscores the problematic associations between two terms that have been linked in Western culture ever since Jean-Jacques Rousseau's *Émile* (1762) connected girls to fashion-doll play and argued that this play predicated a girl's life-course: "The doll is the special plaything of the sex. Here the girl's liking is plainly directed towards her lifework. For her the art of pleasing finds its physical expression in dress. . . . Look at the little girl, busy with her doll all day long. . . . She is absorbed in the doll and her coquetry is expressed through it. But the time will come when she will be her own doll."

The question of who a girl is continues to be asked today, and the variability of chronological age is a constant feature. Does it matter if a girl is of preschool age, between the ages of ten and fourteen (a young adolescent as defined by the Population Council), eighteen (at the age of consent in many countries and at the far edge of American adolescence)? Another question is begged as well: Who is included and who is excluded from being a girl? In other words, according to which definitions are used, who is not experiencing girlhood? In addition to the varying ages at which girlhood ends, geography, culture and race also determine who is included and who excluded from the term. A young female in Sub-Saharan Africa may spend her childhood looking after her siblings because her parents have died of AIDS. Her girlhood is not the same as other girlhoods at all, especially in the West, so whether she is experiencing what we understand "girlhood" to be becomes a question. At the other extreme, if the United Nations definition of childhood is applied to a girl, the age limit rises to twenty-nine and young and not-so-young women are included, making their experiences valid to an understanding of girlhood. If participating in the popular culture of girls or in commercialized girl culture is considered an aspect of girlhood, then the age rises even further to include middle-aged women (Fuchs 1989, cited in Mitchell and Reid-Walsh 2002). Indeed, these multiple meanings and contradictions provoked Anita Harris to ask this question in an appendix to her book *Future Girl: Young Women in the 21st Century* (2004).

If we move from a discussion of girlhood as lived experience to its representation in fiction, a more ideologically loaded set of meanings appear, codifying and reinscribing a specific vision of girlhood. In British children's literature, the earliest novel addressed to girls and describing their behavior is Sarah Fielding's *The Governess: or, Little Female Academy* (1749). This didactic novel about female education concerns Mrs. Teachum, the headmistress of a boarding school with different ages of girls. Notably, the fourteen-year-old Jenny Peace is the main maternal influence on the girls (Vallone 1995). The culture of the school then becomes a self-regulating, girl-centered moral economy. Considering that the first commercial children's books were not issued until the 1740s, by the British publisher John Newbery, it is very striking how early in the history of children's literature a girl's book was produced. Significantly as well, given the linking between the earliest use of the term "girlhood" and the novels of Richardson, whose heroines are presented as female exemplars for their adolescent girl readers, in 1756 the first abridged version of Richardson's novels for younger girl readers appeared. Called *The Paths of Virtue Delineated*, the subtitle indicates the scope and aim: *or, the History in Miniature of the Celebrated Pamela. Clarissa Harlow, and Sir Charles Grandison, Familiarized and Adapted to the Capacities of Youth.* For its part, the publisher Newbery and Caran issued a popular abridgement of *Pamela* for children in 1769; in terms of intended readership, the relatively low price of one shilling enabled the spread of the moral didacticism of ideal girlhood conduct both to children of the middling classes and to working-class readers (Vallone 1995).

The genre of didactic school and domestic girls' fiction became more evident at the end of the eighteenth century with writers such as Mary Wollstonecraft and Maria Edgeworth, and was continued in England in the nineteenth century by Catherine Sinclair and Charlotte Yonge (Avery 1975; Cadogan and Craig 1976). "Girls books" flourished in the nineteenth and early twentieth century, especially in the United States: *Little Women* (1868–69), *What Katy Did* (1872), *Rebecca of Sunnybrook Farm* (1903), *A Little Princess* (1905), *Pollyanna* (1913), and so on. In Canada the famous *Anne of Green Gables* (1908) and the subsequent Anne series extended and transformed the genre, notably introducing the theme of higher education. These books explore the vitality, playfulness, and unconventional childhood of the heroines (Reynolds 1990). Many are initially tomboys, but eventually they all grow up to accept and extol conventional female norms. In this way the books serve as fictive conduct manuals for girls, teaching normative values in terms of morality, behavior, and religious beliefs for white, middle-class girls (Vallone 1995).

In the United States in the 1920s and 1930s, girls' books began to present more action and adventure for female readers. They offered girls new choices in the public sphere by casting them in careers or as detectives solving mysteries (as in the ongoing Nancy Drew series), or by extolling frontier values, as in the Little House books. After World War II, the junior novel and, later, the problem novel dealt with contemporary social issues. Changing concepts of girlhood now encompassed tomboys as a youthful identity, not simply a phase to be passed through on the way to mature womanhood (Renold 2008). Authors such as Judy Blume and Louise Fitzhugh often addressed issues of sexuality. In the later twentieth century, girls' novels by Nancy Garden and Francesca Lia Block began to explore lesbianism and polymorphous sexuality. During the same period, race and ethnicity became another focus of didacticism in girls' novels, such as those by Belinda Hurmence and Jane Yolen (Nelson 2001).

Looking through a historical lens at girls' material culture such as dolls and toys, these artifacts and their use both parallel and diverge from or even subvert the conservative and didactic path of girls' fiction. In the eighteenth and nineteenth century, doll houses and dolls were intended to teach girls how to be good housekeepers and seamstresses by organizing a kitchen and other rooms of a miniature house, and by making dolls' clothes and house furnishings. Female educational theorists such as Maria Edgeworth and Catherine Beecher extolled these practical applications, while other educators, following the influential Rousseau, stressed the importance of girls' toys to teach the player how to become conventionally feminine in appearance and behavior. In the second decade of the nineteenth century, hybrid texts that crossed the boundary between book and toy began to be published, such as the paper doll book *The History of Little Fanny* (1810), which adapted the conduct-book logic to the reading and play patterns of young, middle-class girls (Reid-Walsh 2008).

At the same time, the didactic intent of the object and the lack of agency of the implied player is much weaker with a toy than with a narrative. Scholars of girls-and-doll play in nineteenth-century America have studied doll production, the doll as object, and consumption or play with dolls. In the process, they have encountered black dolls and rag dolls that were the opposite of the didactic fashion or lady doll, as well as recorded incidents of unladylike and boisterous play by the girls, such as turning tea parties upside down by sliding on the tray or staging doll funerals instead of doll parties (Forman-Brunell 1993).

Debates about girls, dolls, and fashion play continue today in academic and popular circles. Concerns center on body shape, provocative clothing, sexuality, and the ideologies of Western girlhood promoted to younger and younger girls, particularly through Barbie and Bratz dolls (Driscoll 2008; Peers 2008). Moreover, the dolls are not only material artifacts, but are featured in other media forms such as comic books, cartoon shows, videos, live action films, and as virtual dolls on the web or in computer games. These "moral panics" about girls and their fashion dolls indicate that "girlhood" remains a vexed and elusive term harkening back to the two very different root meanings of the word: dress or apparel and small child.

Golden Age

Angela Sorby

The "Golden Age" is a Greco-Roman concept, introduced in Hesiod's *Works and Days,* which pictures a race of men who "lived like gods without sorrow of heart, remote and free from toil and grief: miserable age rested not on them; but with legs and arms never failing they made merry with feasting beyond the reach of all evils" (2007). In children's literature, the term was first proposed by the mid-twentieth century British biographer (and Inkling) Roger Lancelyn Green, whose use of it was ideologically freighted but historically useful. Since Green, however, the term has spread and morphed to become a designation of generic excellence: there is a "Golden Age" of children's book illustration, a "second Golden Age" of children's fantasy, and a "Golden Age" of African American children's books. As Raymond Williams (1976) notes of every keyword he included, "Golden Age" seems "inextricably bound up with the problems it was being used to discuss." In the case of "Golden Age," does the paradigm tint—or even obscure—the picture?

The first Golden Age of children's literature began, more or less, with *Alice in Wonderland* (1865) and ended with *Winnie-the-Pooh* (1926), although some would start earlier, with Catherine Sinclair's *Holiday House* (1839), or end earlier, with *Peter Pan* (1911). In *Tellers of Tales* (1965), Green is less interested in marking boundaries than in describing the underlying cultural shift that allowed excellent children's books to be produced. He sees Kenneth Grahame's *Golden Age* (1895) as a watershed text: "Suddenly children were no longer being written down to any more—they were being written up: you were enjoying spring in its own right and for itself, not looking on it anxiously as a prelude to summer." It makes sense that Grahame and Green, as Oxford-educated Englishmen, would seize on a classical metaphor to describe the pastoral, pagan world of childhood. But it is vital to remember that this metaphor did not describe the whole world, but rather the middle- and upper-middle-class strata of the British Empire. This limitation is also a strength because it implies that the "Golden Age" was not a mythic space but an historical time period.

In his landmark study *The Romantic Ideology* (1977), Jerome McGann complains that "the scholarship and criticism of Romanticism and its works are dominated by a Romantic Ideology, by an uncritical absorption in Romanticism's own self-representations." Grahame's *Golden Age* draws on Romantic assumptions about childhood, but so does Green's "Golden Age." From his Marxist perspective, McGann would describe both Grahame and Green as engaging in Romantic dramas of displacement and idealization, in which the vision of a timeless utopia elides textual conflicts and contradictions. *Tellers of Tales* thus emerges, not as a critical text, but as a wonderful example of the phenomenon it seeks to explain. The question then becomes: Does the term "Golden Age" always, and in every context, re-inscribe Romantic assumptions, or can it be used to unpack the Romantic ideologies that structure classic children's books?

According to Green, "Golden Age" authors such as Lewis Carroll, George MacDonald, and Frances Hodgson Burnett realized for the first time that children were not just undeveloped adults. This allowed them to understand childhood as a life-stage with positive attributes that should be creatively celebrated, not didactically squelched. Childhood thus became "a good thing, a joyous thing—a new world to be explored, a new species to be observed and described, a precious experience to be recaptured out of the past and presented truly and lovingly for its own sake" (Green 1965). Like Charles Darwin's Galapagos turtles and birds, it was thought that children "naturally" inhabited a Neverland—a separate sphere—that was cut off from civilization. Green presents this "new world" as a place that was discovered, not invented, by mid-century Victorians. Children, he suggests, were suddenly seen *as they really are*. Tellingly, Green locates this perceptual shift at the moment children exited the workforce *en masse* and retreated into the segregated spaces of the school and the nursery. To lose "the child" as a productive laborer was to gain "childhood" as a productive metaphor, one that Green so eloquently describes precisely because he shares its cultural assumptions. He did not fully account for the "Golden Age," but by naming it he opened the door to later critical assessments of both the term and the historical period.

At its height, the collective dream of childhood as a "Golden Age" generated British fairy tales, fantasy, and nonsense verse. Realist American novelists such as Louisa May Alcott and Mark Twain fit only awkwardly into the paradigm, and American poets like Henry Wadsworth Longfellow were problematic because they continued to write for a dual readership of children and adults. The core group of "Golden Age" writers is thus comprised of Edward Lear, Lewis Carroll, George MacDonald, Kenneth Grahame, Beatrix Potter, Frances Hodgson Burnett, J. M. Barrie, and A. A. Milne, with grudging nods to Alcott (whose children spend too much time with adults) and E. Nesbit (who was rather too commercial). Unlike Green, Humphrey Carpenter, in *Secret Gardens: The Golden Age of Children's Literature from Alice's Adventures in Wonderland to Winnie the Pooh* (1985), attempts to historicize the "Golden Age," asking, "What was it that possessed the late Victorians and Edwardians to create a whole new genre of fiction"?

For Carpenter, childhood during the "Golden Age" was not a newly discovered country but rather a newly constructed utopia, created by adults who wanted to question mainstream society. He divides authors into two categories: "destroyers," such as Carroll and Lear, whose impulse was to attack social conventions; and "Arcadians," such as Barrie and Potter, who imagined alternative realms. These categories are useful because they allow readers to see both destroyers and Arcadians as engaged in social critiques. Curiously, however, Carpenter's wider historical analysis recapitulates the myth of a "Golden Age" even as he attempts to analyze that myth. In his final chapter, he argues that World War I destroyed the possibility of Arcadia; he thus posits the Victorian/Edwardian era as a walled garden in which smaller walled gardens could be cultivated. In Carpenter, the boundaries between the nineteenth and twentieth centuries become as reified as the boundaries between Victorian children and Victorian adults.

One critical tension in the term "Golden Age," then, stems from the ideal of self-containment. How unique and separate is (or was) the experience of childhood—or, for that matter, the nineteenth century? Fredric Jameson (1981) has argued that most narratives function as "strategies of containment" that mask economic processes. From this perspective, the "gold" in "Golden Age" might be traced to a mine in South Africa. Exploring these questions in *Empire's Children*, M. Daphne Kutzer (2000) notes that "the rise of imperialism is roughly contemporaneous with the golden age of children's literature (approximately 1860–1930), and the two grew up together." While Kutzer does not explicitly unpack the term "Golden Age," she does modify its sense of self-containment. Imperialism, Kutzer argues, not only organizes the British Victorian imagination, but it continues to influence children's literature today: "The longing for empire, or at least for national importance, is reflected in children's books both of the golden age and of our age." Moreover, the bordered gardens and Neverlands of Arcadia were products of a British middle class that was in turn supported by an almost borderless imperial economy, so that even when "Golden Age" utopian authors were unconscious

of their privilege they still drew on that privilege. The "Golden Age," Kutzer implies, drew on global resources even as it championed British isolationism, and the ideologies it embraced resonate beyond the world wars and beyond the borders of the British Empire.

Although Kutzer and Green map the spaces and territories of the "Golden Age," it is crucial to note that the term imagines not just children's spaces but also children's bodies. Romantic poets and philosophers discarded the notion of infant depravity, moving to the opposite extreme: children were now spotless innocents trailing clouds of glory. Seen from a Romantic perspective, characters such as Mary Lennox, Peter Rabbit, Winnie-the-Pooh, and even Peter Pan can be mischievous or wrongheaded, but they cannot be evil and they cannot be sexual because they are living their own golden ages. "Golden Age" literature features protagonists of a certain "Golden Age"—not just prepubescent but also prelapsarian, and thus presumably walled off from base urges and adult agendas. Moreover, unlike first-generation Romantic texts, which were aimed at adults, "Golden Age" texts speak to readers who themselves represent, albeit temporarily, an innocent "golden age."

The status of the Victorian/Edwardian child's body points to another question raised by the "Golden Age": Precisely who, if anyone, counts or once counted as innocent? In *Child-Loving: The Erotic Child and Victorian Culture* (1992), James Kincaid argues that conventional "Golden Age" images—of a walled garden, say, or a band of lost boys—are essentially erotic because they fetishize the border between childhood and adulthood. Unlike Carpenter, Kincaid does not see "Golden Age" authors as dissenters; instead, they emerge as mainstream Victorians who were popular because they tapped into the libidinal energies of their child and adult readers. If the term "Golden Age" works to displace imperial forces, Kincaid suggests that it also displaces (but does not dissolve) the Victorian impulse to repeatedly erect and then violate the boundaries between children and adults.

Similar issues are raised by the debates surrounding Charles Dodgson's portraits of children, which are literally bathed in the golden light of mid-century photographic technology. Dodgson's nude photograph of nine-year-old Ellen Hatch might invite us to see her (and ourselves) as innocent, protected by the developmental "golden age" that she embodies; or, that "Golden Age" boundary might contain the ideological complications that make Dodgson's photography—and his fiction, and indeed his era—so compelling.

If the "Golden Age" conjures images of Arcadian spaces and prelapsarian bodies, it also draws a line between the walled garden and the free market. An explosion of middle-class book-buying power may have spurred the production of "Golden Age" fictions, but within the stories themselves the Victorian mercantile economy is barely in evidence. A major exception is the work of E. Nesbit, whose Bastable children are unabashed "treasure-seekers," but Nesbit's status as a "Golden Age" writer is wobbly. In classical mythology, the "Golden Age" ended when Pandora opened her jar full of chaos and discord. For the "Golden Age" of children's literature, one perceived source of chaos and discord (along with sex) was explicit commercialism—which was not, incidentally, associated with women writers. Even in latecomer A. A. Milne's work, commercially produced toy animals might walk and talk but they do not discuss their origins in a department store. Nesbit's celebration of commerce (and commercial success) inspired criticism that she was a purveyor of "prosaic magic" (Green 1965) or a "hack" whose effects on children's literature are "questionable" (Carpenter 1985). Green and Carpenter assume that authentic Romantic children should not be depicted or treated as consumers, or Arcadia will be at risk.

In sum, then, the term "Golden Age" contains or displaces late-Victorian cultural anxieties about the empire, the body, and the rise of consumerism. However, by identifying a historically specific canon, the term has also enabled later critics such as Kutzer and Kincaid to move beyond Romantic recapitulation. The key, perhaps, is historicization: if the notion of a "Golden Age" stages an escape from history, then the task of the critic involves acknowledging that no one escapes.

21

Graphic Novel

Charles Hatfield

Nowhere has the fissure between adult-sanctioned and self-selected children's reading been more boldly marked than in regard to comics, an internationally popular form that has often been seen as the province of amoral profiteers rather than a domain of children's literature. If comics have at last "arrived" as a children's genre, then this new acceptance has been spurred by enthusiasm for the graphic novel, the bulwark of comics' recent claims to literariness.

The term "graphic novel" has fuzzy borders and origins. The *Oxford English Dictionary* (*OED*) defines "graphic" as "of or pertaining to drawing or painting," and "novel" as "a long fictional prose narrative," but the phrase "graphic novel" means more than the sum of its parts. Although the equation, minus the requirement of prose, is not far off the mark, the term's popular usage more closely reflects a desire to ditch the troublesome word "comics" than it does any semantic nicety. Perhaps because "graphic novel" is the kind of phrase that might be independently coined in different times and places, it has three main origin stories. The better-known story centers on Will Eisner's *A Contract with God and Other Tenement Stories* (1978), among the first books to bill itself as a "graphic novel," and certainly the first self-styled graphic novel by a veteran comics artist with a strong reputation (who, though

credited with legitimizing the term, knew he had not created the genre). Yet *Contract* is not a novel per se but a short story cycle centered on a common locale. While it is the most celebrated of the candidates for "first" graphic novel, its novelistic character is doubtful, and that fundamental uncertainty has stayed with the genre since. From the start, then, the phrase represented less a precise analogy to the literary novel than a bid for status.

Another, lesser-known origin story centers on fan historian Richard Kyle, who, around 1964–65, began using the phrases "graphic story" and "graphic novel," a practice encouraged by a fanzine to which Kyle contributed, Bill Spicer's *Graphic Story Magazine* (from 1967). It may also center on George Metzger, whose underground-style comic *Beyond Time and Again* (1976) billed itself as a graphic novel two years before Eisner's *Contract*. (Regarding the disputed origins of the term, see Harvey 2001.) In the years after Eisner, myriad other publications that had not originally been billed as graphic novels came to be remembered, and sometimes republished, under that tag. At the start, none of this publishing activity had children or children's books in mind.

The term "graphic novel" describes neither a discrete literary genre nor a specific publishing format. Rather, it denotes a sensibility: an attitude taken toward comics. As cartoonist-historian Eddie Campbell (2001) has said, the acceptance of the term "embod[ied] the arrival of an idea." This "idea" aligns comics with a literary aesthetic, a seriousness as expressed by readers who come from multiple, sometimes competing, perspectives, including those who see in comics a form deserving literary recognition; aesthetes interested in comics as a species of visual art; confirmed participants in comics subculture, for whom the term offers a way of talking about their interests without needing to go on the defensive; publishers and booksellers, for whom the graphic novel is promising new turf for commercial exploitation; and proponents of children's reading, who may see in comics either an emergent genre, perhaps even the linchpin of a new visual literacy, or the welcome return of an old genre. The "graphic novel" label is not so much a single mindset as a coalition of interests that happen to agree on one thing—that comics deserve more respect.

Respect for the genre may derive from standards that presuppose artistic autonomy from the marketplace: literariness, aesthetic delectation, or avant-garde experimentalism; or, respect might be conferred by the market, wherein artistic creation is assumed to be subject to and legitimized by the test of popularity. In some instances, advocates of the graphic novel are contrarily driven by both standards—that is, by both a Romantic assertion of the individual artist, in spite of any commercial considerations, and by a desire that comics should participate, in the noisiest way possible, in the larger free-for-all of mass culture. These competing interests have found common cause only because comics, morphed into graphic novels, have become recognized as a "serious" form. This consensus has come just in time to align with other trends in our culture, including abiding concerns about children's putative illiteracy, the hyping of "new" visual literacies, and growing anxiety among publishers about the decline in book-reading. Together these factors have legitimized comics as a new focus of publishing in general, and children's publishing in particular.

Given the long-standing exclusion of comics from children's literature, the recent touting of the graphic novel as a children's book genre is paradoxical and ironic. The world's most popular and influential comics have always been rooted in ideas about childhood, and they have had millions of child readers. For comics to arise now as a newly recognized children's genre—against a neglected backdrop of comics for and about children that spans Wilhelm Busch, R. F. Outcault, Winsor McCay, Grace Drayton, James Swinnerton, Harold Gray, Hergé, André Franquin, Crockett Johnson, Osamu Tezuka, Carl Barks, Leo Baxendale, John Stanley, Charles Schulz, Hank Ketcham, Tove Jansson, Quino, Warren Kremer, Bill Watterson, and countless others—requires an act of historical amnesia. If interest in the graphic novel has resolved the long-standing border dispute between comics and children's book publishing, it has done so, arguably, at the cost of eliding the very history of children's comics.

In the United States, the comic book was father to the graphic novel. For more than half a century, comic books, as developed in the early to mid-1930s, were America's definitive medium for long-form comics narrative. Unfortunately, this medium, which at the outset was frankly mercenary in character, attracted moral panic and public opprobrium, coming to a head in the early 1950s. The comic book industry reacted by collapsing into severe self-censorship. The Comics Code, adopted by most comics publishers from late 1954, was a desperate, rearguard move by the publishers to shield themselves from the consequences of their own carelessness—for the comic book business was a benighted one, unable or unwilling to follow the curve of its development by making honest distinctions between children's and adult comics. In the early 1950s, *Walt Disney's Comics and Stories* had sat on newsstands alongside Grand Guignol horror and titillating romance comics, all of them accessible ten-centers tossed together higgledy-piggledy in a generative, arguably subversive, stew. In response, a massive and censorious moral campaign—in which children's publishing professionals, teachers, and librarians played no small part—served to corner the comic book medium, damp down its troublesome vitality, and confine it to the margins of the culture, where it languished (Beaty 2005; Hadju 2008; Nyberg 1998).

Other factors were involved too: the mushrooming influence of television; the destabilization and shrinking of magazine distribution; and falling profit margins brought on by prices stubbornly fixed at what, it was assumed, a young child could afford. This perfect storm of factors wounded the medium practically beyond mending, and memories of the million-selling comic books of the glory days (the 1940s to early 1950s) quickly dimmed. This postwar furor was not confined to the United States, but was mirrored by moral panics elsewhere, for example, in Canada, Britain, and Western Europe (Lent 1999). In America, recovery from this tempestuous period would be long, strained, and never quite complete.

When recovery came, it did so, ironically, due to developments in areas from which young children were pointedly excluded: the hippyesque hedonism and radical ideological fury of underground comix, which vented a long pent-up reaction against comics' self-censorship; the growth of a connoisseur culture via a network of comic book shops for older hobbyists, which depended on a specialized distribution system known as the *direct market*; and the resultant rise of alternative comics for adults. Together these factors nurtured an ethos of individualistic, at times radically Romantic, self-assertion among comics artists, as well as an intense sense of belonging among members of the subculture—that is, fans (Hatfield 2005). With its roots in these decidedly adult venues, the graphic novel's recent emergence as a work for children is paradoxical.

The example of Jeff Smith's series *Bone* (the inaugural offering in Scholastic's Graphix line) underscores this paradox. *Bone* was published by Graphix between 2005 and 2009 in nine volumes. Yet the series, comprising one epic fantasy story, had previously been published by Smith's own imprint, Cartoon Books, over some thirteen years (1991–2004). A small, self-publishing outfit, Cartoon Books depended on the direct market's unusual trade terms—essentially, a subscription system. Cartoon Books released *Bone* first as a series of traditional comic books (fifty-five issues,

1991–2004), then as a series of trade-paperback compilations (nine volumes, 1993–2004), and finally as a single 1,300-page volume (2004). In essence, Smith and company were able to gain traction by taking advantage of the direct market's specialized distribution apparatus, which served to bring to market independent, small-press comics as de facto heirs to the underground. *Bone* was thus a "children's" comic birthed in an underground tradition, and, as such, enjoyed the loyal support of comic book hobbyists with an ideological commitment to individual self-expression and "creators' rights." The series has since sold millions worldwide, in sixteen languages, and its Graphix editions have been very successful. *Bone* thus clearly demonstrates the process of moving from esoteric comic book fandom to mainstream book-trade success. Its republication by Scholastic marked a signal moment in the emergence of graphic novels for younger readers.

Besides shifts in readership and reading habits that may be affected by making novel-length comics available to children, the fact that we now pay serious attention to comics at all is important. Genres, after all, are socially as well as aesthetically founded; therefore, changes in reception are changes in genre. Inasmuch as graphic novels are now being recognized inside the borders of American children's literature, a new genre is being willed into existence. This is not to say that children's comics have never existed until now, but rather that graphic novels *as a genre of American children's book publishing* are just now coming into their own. Consider the launching of publishing programs like Scholastic's Graphix imprint, Papercutz (2005), First Second Books (2006), and TOON Books (2008); librarians' initiatives such as the Young Adult Library Services Association's "Great Graphic Novels for Teens" program (2007); the plethora of recent books designed to facilitate collection development (e.g., Lyga 2004; Pawuk 2007; Weiner 2005) or classroom teaching with comics (e.g., Cary 2004; Gorman 2003; Thompson 2008); and literacy learning initiatives such as The Comic Book Project (2001) and the Maryland Comic Book Initiative (2004). Such attention is a new phenomenon for comics in the United States.

Granted, the graphic novel ideal may hide as much about comics as it discovers; for example, it gives us no way to understand or value vintage comic strips and panel cartoons. This may explain why so many comics enthusiasts, among them cartoonists, editors, publishers, and curators, dislike the "graphic novel" label. No matter: the phrase helps get things done. Witness this introductory pitch from a 2007 pamphlet for Scholastic's Graphix line:

> Graphic novels are hot! No longer an underground movement appealing to a small following of enthusiasts, graphic novels have emerged as a growing segment of book publishing, and have become accepted by librarians and educators as mainstream literature for children and young adults—literature that powerfully motivates kids to read. (Crawford and Weiner 2007, 13)

Clearly, the graphic novel represents for children's publishing a way of eliding the controversies that once clung so stubbornly to the idea of children reading comics. What has changed is not so much the comics themselves (though projects like *Bone* are something new) as their positioning in children's culture. After all, comics-reading has never been strictly an "underground movement" appealing only to "enthusiasts." Even novel-length comics are not new: witness the European album tradition, or collected Japanese manga. But what has emerged from the underground movement—from the discourse of enthusiasts—is the graphic novel ideal as a way of conferring legitimacy on comics. The genre's new invocation of literariness has served to bring comics into the fold of children's publishing. Although it is the product of an underground and disreputable subculture, the graphic novel has, ironically, negotiated for comics a new visibility as a children's genre.

If the graphic novel ideal in some ways effaces the history of comics, it also, potentially, opens new possibilities for appreciating comics and comics history from around the world. Graphic novel culture, besides representing myriad interests, also represents a dovetailing of traditions drawn from myriad centers of comics worldwide. Yes, the label "graphic novel" is American in origin, but not nearly everything now touted as a graphic novel hails from America. The American graphic novel market is part of a global circulation of comics that has served to educate readers in many countries. Readers of English-language comics are increasingly aware of European comics, even those produced by small presses and avant-gardists—an awareness fostered by North American publishers of graphic novels such as Drawn and Quarterly, Fantagraphics, and NBM. Even more obviously, consider the assertive exportation of Japanese manga in many markets, including East Asia, Latin America, and Western Europe, where manga is said to have as much influence as it has had in the United States—which is considerable. Indeed, manga constitute a new "mainstream" in the marketing of comics; they are largely responsible for the recent mushroom growth of graphic novel sections in large U.S. bookstore chains.

These myriad traditions come from cultures where the label "graphic novel" has had little or no impact—where indeed the idea of the graphic novel has not been necessary. After all, francophone *bande dessinée* albums and collected Japanese manga preceded the Anglophone graphic novel culture. Yet such comics have been and will continue to be claimed as part of the creative inspiration for graphic novels in English. They are commonly included in the artistic family, if not the immediate historical lineage, of the graphic novel genre. Eisner, "father" of the genre, claimed as inspiration the so-called woodcut novels of the Depression era, such as Lynd Ward's *Gods' Man* (1929), which were part of an international genre of graphic narrative launched in Western Europe with the seminal works of the Belgian Frans Masereel (see Beronä 2008). More recently, other American artists such as Art Spiegelman and Chris Ware have taken an interest in the pioneering graphic albums of the Swiss Rodolphe Töpffer (1820s–1840s), claimed by many scholars, particularly in Europe but also increasingly in the United States, as the architect of modern comics and even of graphic novels (Juno 1997; Kunzle 2007). Today, some would cite the pioneering manga of Osamu Tezuka and his successors as another source of inspiration for graphic novels (one can see this debt in, for instance, Scott McCloud).

If, as Jorge Luis Borges observed, artists create their own precursors, then it is safe to say that the past of the graphic novel is continually being re-created and extended, not in a way that obeys a strict historiography, but in an unpredictable accumulation: a continual layering of precursors and inspirations that takes in a huge range of cartooning and comics originally far distant from today's graphic novel ideal. The graphic novel has been independently invented or anticipated in multiple nations and cultures; work conceived without graphic novels in mind has since been claimed as part of the genre's inheritance. The eclecticism of the graphic novel, then, extends not only to what is being made available, often across national boundaries, today; it also extends to the very history of the genre, which is no history and all comics histories at once. Positing something as a forerunner or early example of graphic novels is a radical act of reframing that has become common: a move that historically decontextualizes but also makes possible the discovery of new lineages, new lines of influence, and, ultimately, new histories.

The graphic novel ideal may yet provide us with ways of taking varied historical traces and international influences seriously, of exhuming and reviving interest in old comics, of awakening awareness of comics across cultural borders, and of discovering the rudiments of an international visual language. Hopefully, we will see in the years ahead much more historical and critical work on the traditions and lines of influence that have fed into the contemporary graphic novel for children. The acceptance of the graphic novel promises not only the continuing creation of splendid long-form comics, but also the historiographical recovery and critical appreciation of a vast, complex, too-little-studied international narrative tradition for younger and older readers alike.

22

Home
Mavis Reimer

The word "home" comes into English through the Teutonic languages of northern Europe, carrying with it the multiple meanings of world, village, homestead, dwelling, and safe dwelling, as well as indicating a direction, as it continues to do in a phrase such as "go home." The primary meaning in contemporary usages of the word is "the seat of domestic life and interests." In this sense, the word is close to the Latin *domus*, from which the adjective "domestic" is derived. As well as referring to a building or place, however, "home" also refers to the quality of feelings associated with that place, so that home is, as the *Oxford English Dictionary* (*OED*) notes, "the place of one's dwelling or nurturing," which can include members of a family or household, "with the conditions, circumstances, and feelings which naturally and properly attach to it."

A nurturing and safe family home is a primary setting of many texts of children's literature, with kitchens and bedrooms within that dwelling often used metonymically to convey the core emotional qualities ideally associated with home. Maurice Sendak's picture book *Where the Wild Things Are* (1963), for example, neatly compresses the qualities of nurturance and safety into the space of the bedroom to which Max returns from his imaginary voyage to find his hot supper waiting for him. The implication that it is his mother who has prepared his supper points to the connection common in children's texts between the maternal and the home. In L. M. Montgomery's *Anne of Green Gables* (1908), for example, Anne can claim the house of Green Gables as home only after she has roused the latent maternal instincts of the spinster Marilla Cuthbert. In the more displaced version of this story in Frances Hodgson Burnett's *The Secret Garden* (1911), Misselthwaite Manor becomes a place of belonging to Mary Lennox when she has learned to see and then to coax into blossom the potential beauty of her dead aunt's enclosed garden. As Burnett's narrative demonstrates, houses are often used as both literal and figurative sites for young people to mother or nurture themselves in children's books, as they do in two quite different ways in Astrid Lindgren's *Pippi Longstocking* (1945) and Philippa Pearce's *Tom's Midnight Garden* (1958). The metaphorical equivalence between the house and the mother can also be exploited for more unsettling effects in children's texts. In Neil Gaiman's *Coraline* (2002), Coraline's passage through the brick wall behind the locked door in the front parlor—which her mother has shown her as the absolute limit to her desire for exploration—takes her into the world of her other mother, which is horrifying in both its resemblances to and differences from her originary home. Such a text instantiates Sigmund Freud's (1919) observation that the experience of the uncanny (*Unheimlich*) resides precisely in that which is most familiar (*heimisch*), the primal example of which he assumes to be the body of the mother.

The linkage of the house to the psychology of the self and the family has a long history in Western cultures, according to Witold Rybczynski (1986), who observes that the evolution of domestic comfort is co-incident with "the appearance of the internal world of the individual, of the self, and of the family." The common use of the family home as a primary setting in children's literature, then, can be understood as one indication that the project of this body of texts is to facilitate the development of the sense of self in young readers. In this reading, the feelings of being "at home" that typically attend the resolution of narratives for young people are privileged over the ultimate arrival at a dwelling place.

Whether as place or feeling, "home" continues to mark the narrative closure of many, arguably most, texts for children. As a place of origin or departure, it also marks the beginning of many of these texts. Indeed, the circular "home-away-home" story has been understood as the central organizing principle of the genre of children's literature (Nodelman and Reimer 2003). This use of "home" as holding a structure in place is consonant with its use as both destination and direction in the language of games and computers.

Psychological interpretations of children's literature typically privilege the emotional over the material and, in doing so, screen the socioeconomic implications of linking house and home. The idea that a house is, or should be, the center of family life is at the foundation of the contemporary systems of consumer capitalism that are taken to be normative in many of the societies of the developed world. Seen in this light, the intense interest in home in children's literature situates this literature within the dominant ideologies of its societies. Rosemary Marangoly George (1996) has argued that imagining home in fiction within the English tradition should be understood as "a display of hegemonic power" and characters who can claim or return home analyzed in terms of "the power wielded by [their] class, community and race." Such interpretations of the homes represented in children's literature often require critical readers to read against the grain of the texts, looking for the unspoken assumptions on which the narrative is premised. A few children's narratives themselves perform such readings. Jan Needle's *Wild Wood* (1981) rewrites Kenneth Grahame's *The Wind in the Willows* (1908) to reveal the arrogant assumptions about his entitlements that underwrite Mr. Toad's claim to his eponymous home, Toad Hall. In *M.C. Higgins, the Great* (1974), Virginia Hamilton, by restricting the narrative view to what the young mountain boy sees, feels, and understands, builds a picture of a home that is not safe but nevertheless is nurturing. While readers become aware of some of the judgments of the "normal" world of town and city through M.C.'s conversations with the strangers he meets, the cabin on Sarah's Mountain clearly occupies the place of home at both beginning and end of the narrative. A novel such as David Almond's *Skellig* (1997), however, is more typical. Much of Almond's story focuses on Michael's complicated relationship with the indeterminate being—part human, part animal, part angel—whom he finds in the garage behind his house, but the story ends with the reconstitution of his family and his silence as the adults around him conclude that a vagrant has been squatting in the dilapidated outbuilding and that this is reason to demolish it.

Almond's novel is one of a large number of recent narratives throughout the Anglosphere that demonstrate the structural linkage between ideas of home and ideas of homelessness. The first use of "homelessness" recorded in the *OED* is by Charles Dickens in *Dombey and Son* (1848); now, as then, homelessness designates the lack of the condition of being at home, and, in this opposition, secures the idea of home as one of plenitude. Contemporary texts for young readers—from *Breaking the Wishbone* (1999) by Irish writer Siobhán Parkinson, to *Tom Finder* (2003) by Canadian writer Martine Leavitt, to *Sleep Rough Tonight* (2004), by Australian writer Ian Bone, to *Paranoid Park* (2006) by American writer Blake Nelson—are exploring, and in some cases challenging, the borderlines between the inclusions and exclusions used to build the idea of home in discourses in English. The interest of these novels in itinerant "street kids" and in the institutional homes that claim to serve them suggests that one of the boundaries being tested for its permeability is that between staying and going, between dwelling and journeying. Itinerants and vagrants are, of course, only two of many categories of subjects on the move in the globalizing world: others include migrants, immigrants, refugees, travelers, and tourists. In the context of these times, David Morley (2000) suggests, home

is being re-theorized as "a mobile, symbolic habitat, a performative way of life and of doing things in which one makes one's home while in movement." But the controversy generated by the publication of Sendak's *We Are All in the Dumps with Jack and Guy* (1993), a picture book about homeless men and children, suggests that confounding the borders between home and homelessness in books for children continues to be understood by many adults as a challenge to fundamental cultural values.

The current interest in mobile subjects and in the relation of mobility to home is not unprecedented. Postcolonial theorists have demonstrated the ways in which European explorers, adventurers, and travelers prepared the ground for colonization, settlement, and other imperial practices. In fact, the sense in which "home" is used to designate "one's own country, one's native land" or "the mother-country" is identified in the *OED* as formulated by British subjects abroad and residents of former British colonies, with instances of such usage clustered in the nineteenth century, the time during which the generic patterns of children's literature in English were set. Both the boys' adventure stories and the girls' domestic stories that proliferated during this period participate in linking the political project of home to the psychology of home. That the British Empire might be understood as a large-scale homemaking project is an argument that has been made in relation to Daniel Defoe's *Robinson Crusoe* (1719)—notoriously the only novel Jean-Jacques Rousseau thought to be suitable for children (O'Malley

2008). For the colonized inhabitants of the places being claimed as home by the colonizers, the consequence of such imperial homemaking was displacement—a loss of home whose consequences are being explored in the work of contemporary Aboriginal writers for young people in Australia and Canada. But home also functioned as a site of resistance to public imperial culture in colonial India: its status as a private sphere permitted it to nurture the birth of Indian nationalism, according to Tony Bennett (Bennett, Grossberg, and Morris 2005).

Bennett's comments are a reminder that a culture's keywords not only assert a meaning, they also circulate various meanings simultaneously and accrue new ones in their passages. The ways in which the auratic connotations of "home" can be pressed to serve the production of nationalism can be seen in quite a different way in the recent deployment and institutionalization of "homeland security" in the United States in the aftermath of the events of September 11, 2001. The children's texts about 9/11 now being published cite tensions and contradictions already evident in the overlapping structural, historical, psychological, gendered, economic, and political meanings of home. It is likely that these texts will also shift the meanings of home available in contemporary culture.

23

Identity
Karen Coats

In the various branches of the natural, mathematical, and human sciences, "identity" has a range of uses related to the property of sameness or consistency of an element regardless of the influence of other variables. "Personal identity," the subset most relevant to studies of children's literature, is defined in the *Oxford English Dictionary* (*OED*) as "the sameness of a person or thing at all times and in all circumstances; the condition or fact that a person or thing is itself and not something else." This definition has a rigidity that most contemporary scholars of children's literature will find objectionable. Rather than being an invariant condition or a fact, identity is more likely to be conceptualized as a goal or an achievement. It is usually thought of as developmental, and is entirely dependent on the influence of variables such as race, culture, religion, family, ideology, and embodiment.

Moreover, the concept of identity is a product of its time, or at least of the dominant epistemological stance in which it is being considered. The *OED* definition is marked by its modernist heritage, and it rests on assumptions of the outward display of an autonomous, unified, authentic self that remains consistent over time. Postmodern critique has taken these assumptions to task, arguing that identity is instead provisional and fluid; that it is more dependent on external forces than inner potentialities; that it is fundamentally discursive and performative, and thus any appearance of sameness over time is merely the result of the repetition of certain kinds of performances. Rather than a condition of sameness emanating from an inner core, identity has become more of an outward show seeking recognition and uptake; hence a more felicitous definition for contemporary thinkers might be that offered by Mark Bracher (2002): "the sense of oneself as a more or less coherent and continuous force that matters in the world."

John Locke (1690) provides the first extended exploration of the concept of personal identity, and his ideas about the development of personhood have become inescapably important for scholars of children's literature. Locke's idea of the self as a *tabula rasa*, a blank slate, makes understanding the images and ideologies of children's culture crucial to understanding the contours of modern identity. Locke's view culminates a way of thinking initiated by Augustine (397–98 C.E.), who established the notion that the self possessed inner depths that one must navigate in one's search for self-knowledge and, ultimately, for God. Developing further this methodology of looking within, René Descartes (1641) sought to strip away the contingencies of sensual experience in order to locate the eternal truths of our existence, and he took subjectivity itself as an object of disengaged investigation. While both Augustine and Descartes believed that humans possess innate tendencies toward truth, Locke believed that our reason is clouded with superstitions, customs,

and traditions learned largely through childhood experience. He concluded that the developmental and educational process of children must be carefully controlled and scrutinized, because lessons absorbed in childhood remain forever imprinted on the self unless scrupulously interrogated. He was particularly concerned to limit children's exposure to stories of ghosts and other supernatural horrors so that such fantasies would not interfere with their growth into rational adults. Developmental psychologists and children's literature theorists would argue against such a rigid prohibition, and thinkers since Sigmund Freud would disagree with the notion that children's minds are blank slates or that rationality is the reigning disposition in the development of the person. However, Locke's premise that identity parameters are deeply influenced by childhood experience remains unchallenged. Further, his commitment to the rigorous interrogation of identity has remained a persistent area of inquiry across multiple disciplines.

By posing the questions "Who am I?" and "How do I know what I know?" philosophers, theologians, psychologists, and sociologists have established a split in the self, between the self who is the object of study and the self who is asking the questions, testing the hypotheses, and reflecting on the process. The answers to the first question lead to the establishment of a sense of identity as a series of identifications and dis-identifications, many of which are based in fantasy and willed assertion—I am strong like my father, I am not a crybaby like my sister, I am smart like my teacher, I am beautiful like a princess, I am not at all like the stinky kid in my class—most of which involve some sort of performance, complete with costume, and almost all of which are mediated through feedback from others. Whereas modernist culture saw the outcome of these identifications as ideally leading to an integrated, composite whole, postmodern culture emphasizes the provisionality of these identifications and performances; the goal is not to discover or even craft some core truth of who we are, but to fashion an identity that gives us the kind of recognition we crave. Frank Portman's *King Dork* (2006) is exemplary of this sort of identity construction through continual self-examination and revision; his protagonist talks of kids going to school in music-themed Halloween costumes and continually changes the name of his band, reflecting the lack of a stable, continuous identity.

Sociologist Charles H. Cooley (1902) developed the notion of what he called "the looking glass self," whereby our sense of identity emerges through how we imagine others see and react to us. Recognition of this reflected self is situated in children's literature as a key element on the road to a desirable identity. Mary Lennox, in *The Secret Garden* (1911), has no idea of how she appears to others when she first arrives at Misselthwaite Manor, nor does she care. Learning to care, and to adjust her behavior accordingly, is part of her becoming a likable young woman. Jamilah, a Lebanese Muslim living in Australia in Randa Abdel-Fattah's *Ten Things I Hate about Me* (2006), dyes her hair blonde and wears blue contact lenses in an attempt to hide her ethnicity from her peers. Each of these books acknowledges the importance of society in the construction of identity, and while many children's books offer an explicit message that their protagonists should embrace their individuality rather than conform to the group, there is almost always an implicit undercurrent of identity management according to group ideals. Abdel-Fattah seems to lead her protagonist through a process of liberation from the tyranny of the looking glass self, but ultimately simply repositions the looking glass so that it reflects a different community for Jamie to respond to—the community of Lebanese Muslims of whom she should be proud, rather than the bigoted high school classmates whom she should reject.

Because children do use their literature for sites of identification, both authors and critics often focus on identity with a qualifying adjective—gender identity, national identity, racial identity, ethnic identity, class identity. Adults have long believed that it is crucial for children "to see themselves in the book" so that their particular identity structures are validated and affirmed. Black girls need stories about black girls, gay boys need to read about gay boys, and so on, so that they do not have to adopt alienating and oppressive subject positions or feel invisible as they read. Identity in a global, highly and multiply literate culture, however, cannot be essentialized quite so completely. People draw their identifications, and hence craft their identities, from a range of models, often taking the values of the dominant culture as an important component of their identity structure, even when that culture could be viewed as historically or culturally oppressive. For instance, a person from a nonwhite culture with strong communitarian values may internalize individual achievement, a prominent feature of mainstream white culture, as a core identity component. Such is the identity crisis explored by Sherman Alexie in *The Absolutely True Diary of a Part-Time Indian* (2007). In his desire to get a good education and escape the soul-deadening atmosphere of the reservation, Junior leaves his best friend, Rowdy, behind. Rowdy condemns him as a traitor, not only to their friendship, but to his people, whom he has abandoned in favor of white culture through white education. Junior questions his desires, but he also questions the values of those around him. Eventually, Rowdy validates Junior's choices by connecting him with the nomadic side of his Native heritage: according to Rowdy, Junior can still own his identity as an Indian because there is a stronger tradition of Indians as nomads than there is of Indians staying in one place, as they do now on the rez.

The answer to the second question of the philosophers—"How do I know what I know?"—is of crucial importance to scholars of children's literature, as our subject is one of the key sites of ideological interpellation through which children are called to identify with models and ideals, but also through which they learn what counts as an identity and the processes whereby one achieves one. In other words, literature is one avenue through which we learn what we know. It is certainly one of the most important ways that we learn about identity. In postmodern culture, identity is no longer conceived as something one achieves through looking inward for the eternal, unchanging truth of oneself, but instead emerges at the nexus of a set of discourses—of race, gender, ethnicity, class, and so on—that one uses with degrees of submissiveness or subversion to fashion a provisional performance of the self. The discourses—their rules, their costumes, their vocabulary, their gestures—often come from literature, and we know how they're supposed to work because of the ways the stories end. Feedback is also critical: if our performance gains us recognition, we are likely to repeat it, at least until we find a new model worth trying. The models are variable, and that in itself lets us know that there is no guaranteed path to success, and that it is okay not only to follow different trajectories, but also to end up in different places. The primary goal of identity construction in contemporary culture is recognition from others; ultimately, what we desire is to matter to the people who matter to us.

24

Ideology

Elizabeth Parsons

Based on the classical Greek words *ideo*, meaning idea, and *ology*, referring to a branch of knowledge, a systemic set of ideas, or a form of discourse, the concatenated word "ideology" derives from the French *ideologie*. The concept arose as part of a French philosophical movement in the late eighteenth and early nineteenth century period of Enlightenment, and its original meaning was to denote a science of ideas. In the nineteenth century, the term was taken up by Karl Marx to label the unconscious system of beliefs in a social group, and specifically socioeconomic class structures (Bennett, Grossberg, and Morris 2005). Louis Althusser (1971) then revised the concept by using Jacques Lacan's theories of psychoanalysis, principally his concept of the imaginary, to explain the role of language and representation in producing ideological positions. Althusser's work was taken up by later Marxist scholars, notably by Fredric Jameson in relation to capitalism and modernity.

While the Marxist usage of the term has been employed in the analysis of children's texts—for example by Jack Zipes (1980), Ian Wojcik-Andrews (1993), and Elizabeth Parsons (2005)—the more general definition of "ideology" employed in children's literature analysis is "the system of ideas that define a culture." This system includes the larger scale of political, cultural, and economic ideas like democracy, Christianity, capitalism and individualism that dominate in the Western world, but also the more intimate identity politics within a culture, in particular those that surround gender, sexuality, race, and class and that effect the distribution of power among individuals in a society. All cultures have ideologies. Sometimes these are recognizably very different from those of the West, particularly in societies that adhere to different religious traditions or in cultures that see the society or the family as more important than the individual. All things produced in a culture are expressions of that culture's ideology—from architecture, to fashion, to laws, to scientific endeavors, to children's literature.

Peter Hollindale's (1998) early essay on ideology in children's literature was instrumental in generating debate in the field. He works outward from the *Oxford English Dictionary* when he describes ideology as "[a] systematic scheme of ideas, usu. relating to politics or society, or to the conduct of a class or group, and regarded as justifying actions, esp. one that is held implicitly or adopted as a whole and maintained regardless of the course of events." As he indicates, ideologies also work to justify the system they underpin; they are usually normalized and seem to be naturally "the way things are." That is, they appear unquestionable to the people who belong to that culture. As Perry Nodelman (1992) explains, "Ideology works best by disappearing, so that people simply take their ideological assumptions for granted as the only whole, and unquestionable truth." For example, in the past white people felt that having black slaves was simply part of the natural order of the world, and based on an assumed "natural" superiority, slavery therefore went unquestioned. Depictions of nonwhite people in children's literature from such periods reiterate that belief, as in the case of *Elsie Dinsmore* (1867) (see Sekeres 2005). Even when government policies change, attitudes can remain in place in the culture. Although British imperialism had halted by the time Maurice Sendak wrote *Where the Wild Things Are* (1963), the story shows a white boy who travels to foreign lands where he easily suppresses the natives and becomes their king in an unproblematic rehearsing of the colonial project (Ball 1997; see also the entry on "Postcolonial").

Children's literature tends to be a largely ideologically conservative genre in that it often upholds the values of the culture in which is it produced and consumed as part of an inherently didactic agenda. This is typically the case because, as John Stephens (1992) argues, "[c]hildhood is seen as the crucial formative period in the life of a human being, the time for basic education about the nature of the world, how to live in it, how to relate to other people, what to believe, what and how to think—in general, the intention is to render the world intelligible." The tensions this produces in children's literature scholarship, then, can emerge at the fundamental level of a contest over what we, as a society, wish to teach children to believe and value. This teaching can come through language, image, and plot-structures: a story usually rewards or celebrates a character because he or she is acting (or learns to act) in line with the kind of values espoused by the empowered adult culture. Some narratives, however, work to reject the social norms (or the dominant ideological positions) of a culture, such as M. T. Anderson's *Feed* (2002), set in a dystopic future where the protagonist gradually learns to question the ways in which capitalism is destroying the world.

The core conflict for the "ideology" in children's literature analysis is politicized around this question of values. The work becomes implicated in the so-called culture wars—that is, the battle between the religious and secular conservative right versus leftists who seek greater equality for women, nonwhites, queers, and lower-class peoples (with the inbuilt left assumption that the white, male, middle-class powerbase has employed capitalism to maintain its position of power). Feminist, queer, and postcolonial theorists, as well as theorists who focus on classism, employ ideological modes of interpreting stories. The social/political right denounces them, branding this kind of reading as overtheorizing what the general public often assumes to be the innocent fun of children's texts. These criticisms of ideological analysis can also be linked to a social belief in the idea that children are, or should be, apolitical beings, and that the stories adults give them, and the analysis of such texts, should be somehow outside politics. Although ideology itself is the neutral description of the system of beliefs that underpin a culture, conservatives wish to claim that children's literature is not ideological (a position that conveniently works to mask ideology), while those on the left argue that revealing the ideological nature of children's texts will help readers perceive structural imbalances of power. As T. Purvis and A. Hunt (1993) explain, ideology "always works to favour some and to disadvantage others."

Ideological scholarship is also criticized because it rejects a focus only on the book/text and instead looks at the real world in which stories are being consumed in order to ask "what children's literature does to its readers by, for instance, encoding ideological assumptions or disseminating strategies for resisting them" (Reynolds 2007). To interrogate a text's ideological stance is to use a theoretical framework that pays less attention to the aesthetic qualities of the story because the critique is more interested in the embedded ideological messages of the narrative than in the literary merit of the work. Research therefore does not demarcate high- versus popular-culture texts—unsurprisingly, since those interested in a text's impact on children are more likely to focus on the most popular or highly trafficked works, regardless of their perceived quality. Ideological analysis might be less concerned with the literary ideas J. K. Rowling "borrowed" in *Harry Potter and the Philosopher's Stone* (1997) than on the ways in which the narrative privileges the dominance of a white, middle-class boy as the hero whose quest is supported by the lower-class Ron Weasley and "Mudblood" female character Hermione. Similarly, ideological analysis would consider the way the fantasy dimension of the novel (the "wizarding world") uncritically reproduces a male-run society with the same educational, governmental,

economic, and consumer-driven environment of real-world contemporary Britain. The story thus confirms and naturalizes the current state of the world as both typical and impossible to imagine in different terms—even with all the potential a fantasy location offers for reimagining social orders and structures.

Ideological interpretations of children's literature also tend to be less interested in the views or biographical details of the author and instead focus on the ways in which a story positions the reader to accept a set of values. In addition, the ideological landscape of a fictional story may unconsciously reproduce the author's values and assumptions without the author's direct awareness of her or his own biases (Hollindale 1998). Given this, the author's view of what the story is about or what it teaches children may not give access to ideological positions in the text, many of which exist as covert curricula beneath the overt story. The difference between the surface message and the deeply embedded ideologies in children's stories can also be at opposite poles. On the surface, the film *Shrek* (Adamson and Jenson 2001) appears to reject fairy tale norms with a feminist-inspired, empowered princess. On closer examination, Fiona is only able to fight emasculated men like the camped-up Monsieur Hood and his merry men (in tights) and still requires her prince, Shrek, to rescue her and enable their happily-ever-after ending, in a reversion to old-fashioned (or conservative) gender norms.

Given that ideology is often hidden beneath the narrative surface, academics engaging in ideological analysis of children's literature are criticized for intellectualizing about stories in ways that would not be part of the reading experience of the child. This causes tensions between practitioners of ideological analysis and scholars working with a reader-response paradigm for children's literature research, and these same tensions also circulate in the popular consciousness, which pits "ideology'" against "common sense" (Sarland 1999). Proponents of ideological analysis, however, agree that no text is innocent of values. They also agree that ideology is always connected to politics, social relations, language and representation, and the distribution of power. In this sense, ideological analysis scrutinizes the cultural work a children's story does: who it rewards or punishes (and why), how it depicts stereotypes and power-relations, and how it is oriented (as celebrating or critiquing) the existing social, political, and economic structures of the society in and for which it has been written or produced.

25

Image
Nathalie op de Beeck

Depending on the speaker (children's author, literary critic, art historian, advertising designer, painter) and the venue (bookstore, literature conference, gallery, marketing meeting), the term "image" implies an array of connotations, purposes, and audiences (Mitchell 1986). In the hybrid contexts of the twenty-first century—where visual culture, visual studies, and visual literacy are related but contested terms—"image" crosses disciplinary boundaries and characterizes multimodal activities in classrooms and communication. For children's literature, an interdisciplinary field drawing upon many scholarly discourses, pedagogical approaches, and modes of creative expression, "image" is a complex and provisional term, always at play and in flux.

Appropriately, the *Oxford English Dictionary* (*OED*) variously defines "image" in terms of the likeness and the statue, the "mental representation due to any of the senses," and the phantom and the apparition, indicating an irreconcilable tension between concrete and abstract. While the earliest meaning of the word, according to Raymond Williams (1976), was "a physical figure or likeness," a secondary meaning developed around sets of ideas or "mental conceptions, including . . . seeing what does not exist as well as what is not plainly visible." These concepts were given physical form in art, writing, and other media, abstractions meant to instill or reinforce images. Williams further relates "image" to fiction, idealism, and realism. Building on these bases, the term connects to ideas of truth, trust, and faith; shifting artistic and literary conventions; consciousness, perception, and dreams; "objects of religious veneration" (*OED*); and the mythic. Williams notes *image*'s "unfavourable connotations overlapping with *idol*," which resonates with W. J. T. Mitchell's example of the biblical golden calf. This graven image was worshiped as a false god before its original was destroyed, yet the icon lived on in cautionary tales and representational artifacts; the "image" of the golden calf persists in collective memory. "Image," writes Mitchell (2008), is "a highly abstract and rather minimal entity that can be evoked with a single word. It is enough to name an image to bring it to mind."

Thus, to use the term "childhood" or produce a likeness of "the child" is to activate and test a mutable image. Any figure of the child or childhood will contradict or coincide with a national imaginary or a commonly held conceit among the members of an organization or system of belief. For example, considering "image" in terms of veneration and idolatry, the image of childhood is held sacred by some and deemed secular by others. Lauren Berlant, in *The Queen of America Goes to Washington City* (1997), indicts the American fascination with the material and symbolic fetus—a symbol of vulnerability, innocence, and pregnant women's options—as a potent political image. James Kincaid, in his controversial *Child-Loving* (1992), notes

a pedophilic component in the fascination with actual children and eroticized images of childhood, inviting accusations of obscenity and even blasphemy for activating such a troubling image. William Blake's *Songs of Innocence* (1789) and *Songs of Experience* (1794) and William Wordsworth's "Prelude" (1805) establish a foundation for the nineteenth-century Romantic child, while Vladimir Nabokov's *Lolita* (1955) presents one of our most indelible images of exploited twentieth-century childhood. All these artists and critics call upon audience recognition of cherished, or disturbing, notions of childhood that feed the construction of an ideal or troubling image.

An image, then, is not strictly a picture, although terms such as "picture," "illustration," and "image" tend to be used interchangeably. As James Elkins (1999) explains, terms like "word-image" are inaccurate due to "*mixtures* of reading and seeing. . . . [T]here is 'reading' in every image and 'looking' in every text." In order to theorize the image, critics must perform "not only a semiotic, formal analysis, but also a historical and ideological contextualizing" (Mitchell 2008). The ability to grasp the image in a given text is both a formal and a cultural exercise, "a matter of an almost anthropological knowledge" (Barthes 1977); a picture is not "worth a thousand words," but instead serves as a complement to words in an intimate chain of signification (Miller 1992). A lone picture cannot narrate without context (Sontag 1977). Instead, a word-and-picture combination, a captioned illustration, or a graphic sequence—presented to the reader via some physical medium, whether a book, a canvas, or a living body—helps the active reader generate the image. "[T]he transformation of a medium into an image continues to call for our own participation" (Belting 2005).

Istvan Banyai's picture book *Zoom* (1995) serves as an example of how images arise from textual form and content. The book's title implies the workings of a zoom lens, and its pages offer a series of illustrations-within-illustrations that mime snapshots. There is no written narrative, just an ever-expanding frame that pulls back or zooms from the tiny scale of a toy to the scale of outer space. *Zoom* is not simply a related series of pictures. Readers attempting to narrate this wordless book find themselves considering the camera apparatus, the human eye, and their place in an infinite universe—in other words, exploring the connotative image beyond the denotative word and picture. Gilles Deleuze (1983/1986, 1985/1989), who theorized the movement image and time image in cinema, conceived of a multifaceted crystal image, alternately transparent and reflective on its surfaces. *Zoom* operates on such multiple levels.

More so than an isolated illustration, an image functions as a changing collective conceit, determined by culture and situated in time and place. For example, Helen Bannerman's *The Story of Little Black Sambo* (1899) once was deemed an appropriate, humorous story for young audiences, and its words and pictures laid the foundation for an insulting image of colonial Indian subjects and people of African heritage alike. In an effort to interrogate the book's clownish image of blackness, recent scholars have debated the ethno-racial basis of the story, and children's author-illustrators have revised it. Julius Lester and Jerry Pinkney's *Sam and the Tigers* (1996) interprets the tale as African American folklore and nonsensically names all its characters "Sam," while illustrator Fred Marcellino's *The Story of Little Babaji* (1996) gives Bannerman authorial credit while renaming *Sambo*'s trickster hero and providing affirmative depictions of India. Such countertexts, which tactically alter the words and pictures of a problematic original, have the potential to establish new ideological images.

Many critics of literature, art, and cinema examine "image" through Ferdinand de Saussure's sign/signifier/signified triad and Charles's Peirce's formalist semiotics (which revisit Saussure's tripartite structure of signification). For his part, Jacques Derrida (1967) sharply distinguishes between sign and image in his account of the codification of written language. For Derrida, reading and vocalizing alphabetical writing depends upon a prior understanding of the images conveyed by the writing, since written communication necessarily has become concise and abstract over generations and across the distances between agricultural and industrial communities. Although his examples come from pictographs, hieroglyphics, and alphabet systems, Derrida might well have considered the commonplace abstractions in ABCs for young readers. The "A" in Crockett Johnson's *Harold's ABC* (1963) stands for "Attic" and takes the shape of the attic itself; the "C," a typographical character originally colored tan, "turns green" with seasickness as ocean waves get rough in Michael Chesworth's *Alphaboat* (2002). Examples like these exploit the slippage between writing, pictures, and the images conjured by literate readers.

Further, it is precisely this slippage that authors and illustrators seek to exploit as they create a text for young readers. Roland Barthes (1977) locates "a linguistic message, a coded iconic message, and a non-coded iconic message" in a commonplace advertisement or comic book, and off-handedly remarks that children learn to negotiate this complex verbal-visual information at an early age. He acknowledges the urge to stabilize interpretation "in such a way as to counter the terror of uncertain signs." The word-picture text's creator attempts to manage the formal arrangement and cultural reception of the constructed image, and the spectator is eager to make sense of it too. Therefore, picture books with puzzling imagery (e.g., Maurice Sendak's goblin-infested *Outside over There*, 1981) or lack of closure (e.g., Dr. Seuss's ambiguous *The Butter Battle Book*, 1984) defy the stability some readers expect from the literature of childhood and the ideal image of the child.

Like Barthes, picture-book critics such as Perry Nodelman (1988), William Moebius (1986), and Joseph Schwarcz (1982) note the sophistication of young readers and the interpellative codes that operate in the most elementary picture books. A board book labels cartoon animals, and a typical counting book provides a 1-2-3 order and a set of quantifiable items. Yet the process of signification in these texts, in a picture book's sequential narrative, or in the paratext (cover, frontispiece, etc.) of a chapter book, is as complex as any commercial sequence or brand logo. The transmission of an image depends upon a level of clarity for the implied young audience. This is not to say that children's textual imagery is unmediated or automatically perceived. As children learn to read multimedia sequences of words and pictures, they develop and begin to reproduce the images particular to their cultures. We might say that the iconic peaked-roof house, front lawn, sunshine, and stick-figure family associated with children's crayon drawings acknowledge a collective Western image of home (and, further, challenge what idealistic thinkers have called the "innocent eye" by suggesting how our subjectivities are interpellated at a young age). Mental images, thought but not necessarily articulated in words or an artistic medium, shape and are shaped by material artifacts, including literary and visual images.

Central images of childhood persist despite changes in sensibility and technology, and despite significant changes in the construction of childhood itself. Nostalgia is a potent force in determining cultural ideals, especially when it comes to infancy and childhood, and anachronistic images can "resurface in new media. . . . Images resemble nomads in that they take residence in one medium after another" (Belting 2005). As a result, critics of children's literature may operate as iconoclasts or as supporters of favorite collective notions. Jacqueline Rose, in *The Case of Peter Pan* (1984), argues that the image of childhood is a slippery notion and children's literature "impossible" as a mode, due to the instability of childhood itself as a collectively held ideal. Anne Higonnet, in *Pictures of Innocence* (1998), attends to the consumption and construction of childhood through sentimental images from Thomas Gainsborough's *Blue Boy*, to John Everett Millais's *A Child's World* (which became a Pears soap advertisement, *Bubbles*), to Ann Geddes's photographs of plump babies as flowers. Scholars and mainstream pundits alike lament the marketing of toys, stories, and other commodities for and about children, which helps stabilize a capitalist, corrupted image of childhood on a global level.

Children's literature itself deploys competing and provocative images of childhood. The visceral image of adventurous childhood posited by Sendak in iconic picture books like *In the Night Kitchen* (1970, with its famously naked Mickey) and *We Are All in the Dumps with Jack and Guy* (1993, with its allusions to homelessness and genocide) differs substantially from the image of privileged but solitary Manhattan childhood purveyed by Kay Thompson and Hilary Knight's "Eloise" books (1955–59, 1999–2001) or the inventive, indulged child of Ian Falconer's "Olivia" series (2000–present). The Romantic, Anglo-American image of childhood represented in appealing work by Randolph Caldecott, Kate Greenaway, and A. A. Milne is at odds with the pragmatic, equally lively image of racially and ethnically diverse childhood. Texts such as Langston Hughes's astute *The Dream Keeper* (1932b) exemplify authors' attempts to interrogate and provide a corrective to a dominant, oppressive child image. Hughes's legacy in challenging what Nancy Larrick (1965) called "the all-white world of children's books"—and its attendant ideal image of a flaxen-haired, blue-eyed, English-speaking child—resonates in the more recent picture books of Allen Say, Faith Ringgold, Christopher Myers, Julius Lester, Ana Juan, and Chris Raschka, as well as in bilingual and international texts.

Of course, the image need not be conjured by a commodity or a political movement. A powerful image of childhood is perpetuated by the professional elementary school teacher, working with young people on a daily basis and concerned with the quality of their education. This image competes with that held by the stay-at-home parent, primarily focused on raising his or her own children. The teacher and parent, in turn, will have differences with the scholar of children's literature and culture, whose focus is on the critical concept of childhood as well as the sociopolitical status of children at some particular historical period and geographical location. All of the aforementioned share a deep concern for actual children and for the quality of childhood, yet their distinct images of childhood influence their behavior and motivate the opinions they express in their everyday endeavors. Their ideologies around factors like race, ethnicity, class, gender, nationality, and age—influenced by their lifelong encounters with loaded images of childhood and real children alike—are brought to bear upon their praxis, which in turn contributes to popular images of the child, childhood, and children's literature.

26

Innocence

Marah Gubar

Pondering the immense popularity of young starlets such as Deanna Durbin and Shirley Temple, Grahame Greene (1993) declared in 1939, "Innocence is a tricky subject: its appeal is not always so clean as a whistle." While Temple's charm ostensibly lay in her perfect purity, he argued, in fact she functioned as a highly eroticized figure. Indeed, Temple's first films were a series of shorts known as "Baby Burlesks" that placed tiny children in compromising positions. "Boy, she's hot stuff!" remarks one of Temple's male admirers in one of these shorts (*War Babies* [Lamont 1932]), and her later films likewise situate her as an object of intense desire. Building on and extending Greene's argument, James R. Kincaid contends in *Erotic Innocence* (1998) that "our culture has enthusiastically sexualized the child while denying just as enthusiastically that it was doing any such thing." He piles up compelling proof that the physical makeup of the child—big eyes, a narrow chin, waiflike slightness—now coincides with our vision of what is sexually alluring. Providing further support for this claim, Hugh Hefner has noted that the *Playboy* "Playmate of the Month" (a distinctly juvenile appellation!) was inspired by the "Good Girl Art" of George Petty (1894–1975), whose pin-ups in *Esquire* "had the wholesomeness of the girl next door, but acknowledged her sexuality as well" (Edgren 2005).

Petty's image of a voluptuous girl swathed in a pink rabbit outfit may well have inspired the creation of the Playboy Bunny, that iconic marriage of cute and sexy, the innocent and the erotic.

Is this habit of sexualizing purity a mere quirk of our own culture, or is there something about innocence as a concept that makes it especially open to association with its opposite? Certainly, it is extremely difficult to define this quality without invoking its antonyms. Thus, the *Oxford English Dictionary* describes "innocence" as "freedom from sin, guilt, or moral wrong . . . freedom from cunning or artifice." Innocence is all about what you lack (guilt, guile, knowledge, experience) or what you cannot do; etymologically, *innocens* means "not harming" (being unable to injure anyone). Kincaid posits that it is this emptiness that makes innocence such a problematic category. When we insist that young people are unsullied, he says, "this hollowing out of children by way of purifying them of any stains (or any substance) also makes them radically different, other. In this empty state, they present themselves as candidates for being filled with, among other things, desire. The asexual child is not . . . any the less erotic but rather more" (1992). In other words, characterizing children as alien, exotic beings who are completely different from adults renders them mysterious and "heartbreakingly attractive" (Kincaid 2000). Like Kincaid, many scholars who study the history of childhood and children's literature adopt a critical stance toward the association of children with innocence: working against the powerful and frequently articulated conventional wisdom that childhood purity is both natural and wholly admirable, they prod us to recognize that this way of conceiving of children is historically contingent, culturally constructed, and potentially damaging to the wellbeing of actual young people (Bruhm and Hurley 2004; Egan and Hawkes 2010).

Childhood and innocence have not always been inextricably linked. On the contrary, prior to and during the nineteenth century many people subscribed to the doctrine of original sin, which held that human beings are born already tainted by depravity inherited from Adam (Bunge 2001; Clark 1994; Jacobs 2008). Anxious for children to attain the ability to seek salvation, adults who believed in original sin did not celebrate the child's difference from adults, but instead strove to speed young people's passage into maturity and enlightened piety. Precocity was thus highly prized. Prior to the eighteenth century, painters often represented children as miniature adults, eliminating or downplaying any babyish characteristics of child subjects because such qualities were viewed not as adorable, but as undignified shortcomings: the primitive "inadequacies of infancy" (Calvert 1992; see also Ariès 1962; Schorsch 1979). Many seventeenth-century parents considered crawling animalistic and tried to prevent it by placing infants in leading strings and standing stools, which forced babies to adopt an upright position (Calvert 1992). Early intellectual development was also encouraged. The child speaker in Isaac Watts's children's poem "Praise to God for Learning to Read"

(1715) calls himself "A wretched Slave to Sin," but finds comfort in the fact "that I was taught, / And learnt so young / To read [God's] holy Word." Other early children's writers, influenced by the philosopher John Locke (1632–1704), moved away from the notion of the child's innate depravity and instead embraced the idea that the child's mind resembled an "empty cabinet" or "white paper, void of all characters" (Locke 1690). Yet they too assumed that the child was admirable insofar as he or she obeyed and emulated adults, absorbing their teachings and modes of thinking and being.

Many historians of childhood point to the eighteenth century as the time when Western culture started to shift decisively away from conceiving of children as imperfect adults-in-the-making and toward the notion that they were exemplary beings to be cherished for their primal innocence and authenticity (Cunningham 1995). Philosopher Jean-Jacques Rousseau (1712–1778) and Romantic poets such as William Blake (1757–1827) and William Wordsworth (1770–1850) played key roles in inspiring this revolution in sentiment (Garlitz 1966; Richardson 1994; Myers 1999). "Trailing clouds of glory do we come / From God, who is our home: / Heaven lies about us in our infancy!" wrote Wordsworth in his influential "Ode: Intimations of Immortality from Recollections of Early Childhood" (1807). Rejecting the notion that aging and education constitute a positive process whereby adults help children to attain an ideal state of rationality and virtue, both Wordsworth and Rousseau suggested that the child arrives into the world in a natural state of liberty, free from the constraining, corrupt norms of civilized life. "Everything is good as it leaves the hands of [God]," Rousseau (1762) declared, but "degenerates in the hands of man, [who] wants nothing as nature made it, not even man; for him, man must be trained like a school horse." In *The Prelude* (1805), Wordsworth likewise disparages the learned, socialized child, contrasting the monstrous "dwarf man . . . engendered by these too industrious times" to the far more appealing Boy of Winander, a solitary figure who roams the natural world, blissfully uninfluenced by adult ideas, practices, and discourse. If children must read, Wordsworth suggests, let them peruse fairy tales and fables; such stories, he felt, arose organically from ancient, folk sources and were thus as natural and primitive as children themselves.

Despite the Romantics' own distrust of literary and cultural artifacts, the increasingly popular view that childhood was a separate stage of life that should be enjoyed rather than rushed through inspired an unprecedented explosion of products aimed at children, including toys and books (Plumb 1975). Catherine Sinclair attested to the growing influence of Romantic ideas on children's literature by including a fairy tale in her children's novel *Holiday House: A Book for the Young* (1839). Echoing the Romantic critique of rationalist education in her preface, she bemoans adult attempts "to stuff the [child's] memory, like a cricketball, with well-known facts and ready-made opinions" and characterizes her own fiction as a form of "innocent" amusement that sets before child readers the model of happy-go-lucky child characters who are "like wild horses on the prairies, rather than like well-broken hacks on the road." Many nineteenth-century children's authors promoted the Romantic notion that all children, regardless of their class status, deserved to experience childhood as a holiday from the demands of adult life, a period of "delight and liberty" (Wordsworth 1807). Like Blake, Charles Kingsley protested against the plight of young children forced to labor as chimney sweeps in *The Water-Babies* (1863). This children's novel provides an example of how "emotional appeals to the idea of corrupted innocence" did sometimes improve the condition of actual children (Mitchell 2000); Kingsley's book helped to ensure the passage of The Chimney-Sweeper's Act of 1864, one of many pieces of legislation passed during this era that aimed to protect children from adult exploitation.

This way of conceptualizing children seems both familiar and laudable to us today, yet there are also drawbacks to adopting the ideology of childhood innocence. To begin with, assuming that all children everywhere (and in all time periods) share this trait is dubiously essentialist: it presumes that childhood purity is an innate, eternally present quality, rather than recognizing the central role that adult thinkers, writers, and visual artists played in creating and promoting the ideal of the innocent child (Higonnet 1998; Pointon 1993; Steward 1995). More specifically, as Judith Plotz (2001) notes, the Romantic "Child of Nature" was largely a creation of male artists, who detached child characters from the domestic realm, portraying them as solitary, autonomous beings, existing apart from family, school, and society. Such fantasies erect a barrier between child and adult, reifying the child as a race apart. Indeed, George Boas (1966) sees the increasing tendency to idolize childhood purity in the nineteenth century as a form of anti-intellectual primitivism, whereby the child replaces the Noble Savage as the human ideal, a stance that entails valuing nature and instinct over art, intelligence, and acquired knowledge. Adults who viewed education, acculturation, and even growth itself in negative terms were naturally drawn to the idea of arresting the child in place. For this reason, many nineteenth-century child characters die young, so that their perfect purity remains forever unbesmirched.

It is easy to see how the notion that life goes steadily downhill after childhood—expressed so clearly in Wordsworth's Immortality Ode—could be disabling for both children and adults. Idealized and sanctified by such discourse, actual children might encounter pressure and even anger from adults if they fail to live up to this static, angelic ideal, while adults who accept the idea that maturity is a dead end might experience depression and envy, resenting children for their ability to inhabit such an (ostensibly) idyllic state. Turn-of-the-century writers were attuned to these negative possibilities. The narrator of J. M. Barrie's novella version of *Peter Pan* (1911) expresses both nostalgia for childhood and rage at the "rubbishy . . . brats" lucky enough to inhabit that "careless" state, while the murderous behavior of the governess in Henry James's *The Turn of the Screw* (1898) illustrates the dangers of being so committed to the ideal of innocence that one cannot allow children the luxury of a complicated inner life. Like his contemporary Sigmund Freud (1856–1939), James characterizes purity as a quality that adults project onto children, and he further suggests that the ideology of childhood innocence does not enable the child but rather stifles agency and individuality. He thus anticipates Kincaid's point that adult efforts to "protect" the child's purity can constitute a kind of assault in which innocence is forcibly imposed onto young people, even as he illustrates how easily this quality can become eroticized: the governess breathlessly describes her appreciation of "the real rose-flush" of her pupils' innocence as a form of "infatuation," a dazzling "romance."

My account here of the historical development of the concept of innocence is seductively linear, and much good evidence exists to support it. Yet it is important to acknowledge that some thinkers and writers before the Romantic period championed the child's innocence, including Pelagius (d. circa 418), Julian of Eclanum (d. circa 455), Henry Vaughan (1621–1695), and Thomas Traherne (1637–1674). Moreover, it is a mistake to view the nineteenth century as the era when everyone finally agreed that childhood should be a protected time of dependence and delight. Borrowing Mary Poovey's influential description of how gender norms developed during this era, Karen Sánchez-Eppler (2005) observes that it is more accurate to think of the implementation of the ideology of childhood innocence as a "gradual and uneven" development, since

"Calvinist conceptions of 'infant depravity' . . . , Lockean conceptions of childhood as a 'blank slate' upon which parental authority must write, [and] Romantic visions of the child as natural and innocent as nature vied and mingled with each other." Golden Age children's literature reflected this confused state of affairs. Texts such as *Holiday House* and *The Water-Babies* bear distinct traces of older ways of conceiving of the child, and the child-related prose and practices of authors such as Barrie and Lewis Carroll have inspired controversy precisely because their attitude toward youth seems so contradictory; they simultaneously endorsed and subverted Romantic notions of childhood innocence (Gubar 2009).

Indeed, it is tempting to accuse Carroll—and the Victorians in general—of being hypocritical in their stance toward young people. How, we wonder, could a society both celebrate the celestial purity of children and drag its heels when it came to outlawing exploitative child labor practices and mitigating the miserable living conditions of the juvenile poor (Pinchbeck and Hewitt 1973; Horn 1997; Lavalette 1999)? How could Carroll (1979) at once enthuse about his reverence for the "simple-minded child of Nature" and take erotically charged photographs of scantily clad and even naked young girls? Yet we could level the same accusatory questions at ourselves, even though today the ideology of innocence is much more widely accepted than in Carroll's time. Why are tiny girls tarted up to perform in beauty contests and invited to don minuscule bikinis and midriff-baring tops in everyday life, while advertisers, filmmakers, and fashion designers bank on the appeal of the nymphet as the icon of American beauty (Mohr 1996/2004; Walkerdine 1997; Kincaid 1998; Giroux 2000)? How do we reconcile our actual treatment of young people with our stated commitment to shielding all children from the cares and rigors of adult life? Throughout the twentieth century, Judith Sealander (2003) observes, "[m]uch American support for children and those who spent the most time with them took the form of earnest words of praise, not adequately funded budgets." Whereas federally sponsored programs to benefit America's elderly—a valued voting block—greatly reduced the percentage of aged poor over the course of the twentieth century, the child poverty rate soared: by 2008, 1 in 6 American children were poor (Sealander 2003; Children's Defense Fund 2008). Worldwide in 2007, approximately 9.2 million children under the age of five died from largely preventable causes. According to UNICEF (2009), "The world knows what it takes to improve child health and survival but millions still die because they lack access to these basic services."

Even as more and more children drop below the poverty line and find themselves subjected to "savage inequalities" in terms of the kind of schooling they receive (Kozol 1991), Romantic notions about childhood innocence continue to permeate children's literature. The child hero of Jane Yolen's picture book *Owl Moon* (1987), who journeys out into nature to commune with owls, is an updated version of Wordsworth's Boy of Winander, who hoots "to the silent owls / That they might answer him. / And they would" (Wordsworth 1807). Yolen seems intent on offering a feminist revision of this paradigmatic Romantic figure, since she pointedly refuses to detach the child narrator from a specific social and familial context: fusing the natural and wild with the domestic and industrial, she has the child go owling with a parent, compare the untouched snow in the woods to "milk in a cereal bowl," and listen as the farm dogs "s[i]ng out" in response to train whistles. Yet her nameless, genderless child seems even more blank and drained of agency than Wordsworth's boy. In Yolen's version, it is the father who orchestrates and participates in the close encounter with the owls; the silent child merely trails along behind, watching him and mimicking his actions. "I was a shadow," s/he admits, thereby revealing that even in this revised form innocence constitutes emptiness.

Meanwhile, in keeping with Rousseau's warnings about the dire effects of puberty, books and films for and about adolescents often suggest that the advent of mature sexuality makes you a monster. In Brian de Palma's 1976 film of Stephen King's *Carrie* (1974), the teen heroine's first period coincides with her sudden ability to use her mind as a weapon to murder and destroy. Likewise, in the phenomenally popular Twilight books (2005–8), Stephenie Meyer portrays her heroine's sexual coming-of-age as concurrent with her transformation into a terrifyingly powerful vampire. The moment Bella begins to have sex, she gets pregnant and dies a spectacularly gory death, consumed from within by her monstrous unborn child (though her lover quickly manages to reincarnate her as a vampire). The Twilight series thus offers its own variation on the "sex equals death" theme that film critics detect in so many late-twentieth-century horror movies, whereby teen characters survive only if they remain sexually pure.

Despite the repressive message sent by such texts, commentators such as Neil Postman (1982) blame popular culture for what they see as the wholesale destruction of innocence in the electronic age, citing new media (television, video games, the internet) for eroding the dividing line between childhood and adulthood. Postman acknowledges that childhood is a culturally constructed category. Indeed, he claims that the existence (or nonexistence) of childhood entirely depends on the kinds of cultural artifacts a society produces, asserting that the printing press "created childhood" by requiring the young to serve a segregated apprenticeship in schools, slowly learning to read and interpret complex texts, whereas the rise of "total disclosure" media such as television destroys childhood because it prematurely exposures children to sex and violence in a form so simplistic "that it requires no instruction" to grasp its meaning. And yet, in making his argument, Postman heavily relies on the Romantic notion that children are essentially innocent, as when he declares, "In having access to the previously hidden fruit of adult information, [children today] are expelled from the garden of childhood."

As Henry A. Giroux (2000) notes, blaming the loss of childhood innocence on new media "conveniently absolves Postman . . . of the need to examine how the political dynamics of a changing economic climate—rather than popular culture—result in cutting the funding for public services for young people while simultaneously cutting short their freedoms and future." Postman's work thus proves Giroux's point that embracing the ideology of innocence can positively harm children, since such a stance demands that we view young people as existing at a remove from political and economic forces. If we deny that such circumstances shape the lives of children, how can we accept the responsibility of changing them? In other words, deploying the ideology of innocence does not protect children; instead, it mystifies the actual conditions in which they live, making it more difficult to offer the right kind of aid and assistance.

In *Harmful to Minors: The Perils of Protecting Children from Sex* (2002), Judith Levine provides further proof that the story Americans have chosen to tell about children has deleterious effects. After detailing how adults invested in the idea of childhood purity have succeeded in blocking young people's access to information about sexuality, Levine points out that compared to European countries that offer more comprehensive sex education, the United States has a much higher rate of unwanted teen pregnancies, abortions, and sexually transmitted diseases. Levine also observes that children caught engaging in eroticized play are being pathologized and stigmatized, despite the fact that research indicates that such behavior is normative; one recent study found that 77 percent of children engaged in masturbation or some form of sex play with peers before the age of six (Okami, Olmstead, and Abramson 1997; see also Constantine and Martinson 1981; Martinson 1994). As Richard Halpern (2006) notes, the blanket ascription of purity to children constitutes a denial or disavowal of uncomfortable things that we know to be true: for instance, that carefree innocence is still a luxury many children cannot afford, or that children are not devoid of sexuality. Reminding us that childhood innocence is an adult construction, these scholars suggest that perhaps we should start telling a different story about children, although it is still less than clear what that other story should be. But surely it will involve a move away from the binary thinking that sets children up as blank, alien others, and toward a more flexible paradigm which acknowledges that they are akin to adults in their diversity, complexity, and embeddedness in particular sociocultural milieux.

27

Intention

Philip Pullman

"What was your intention when writing this book?"
"What did you mean by the passage on page 108?"
"What did you want the reader to feel at the end?"
"What message did you intend the book to deliver?"

Authors of novels, especially novels for children, know that questions such as these are not uncommon. This might be surprising, in view of the fact that more than sixty years have gone by since William K. Wimsatt and Monroe C. Beardsley published their famous essay "The Intentional Fallacy" (1946), except that somehow it isn't surprising at all to find that lengthy and passionate discussion among literary critics has not the slightest influence on the way most readers read most books. Clearly, for many readers, the author's intention still does matter, and getting it right, or at least not reading against this supposed intention, is an important part of the satisfaction, or perhaps the relief from anxiety, they hope to feel. Recently I answered online a number of questions from readers of *His Dark Materials,* including this one: "Is a reader 'allowed' to have a Christian/religious reading of a text that is supposed to be atheistic?"

What seems to be going on here is the feeling that reading is a sort of test, which the reader passes or fails according to how closely the interpretation matches the one the author intended. It would be easy to criticize or mock this feeling, but it is genuine. It comes from the same source as the indignation readers feel when a text they believed was a truthful memoir turns out to be fiction, and it's almost certainly related to the anger felt by a child who learns what the rest of the family has known for years, namely that he is adopted. It's the desire not to be made a fool of: the wish not to be shown up as ignorant of a truth that everyone else knows. In fact, it's a natural human feeling. People think there really is an answer. I should probably qualify that by saying that it's young readers, or unsophisticated readers, who seem to be most anxious to know the author's intention. English literature graduates will have at their fingertips all the arguments about the intentional fallacy, and a dozen other fallacies besides. But do we expect all readers to have that sort of knowledge? It would be absurd. There are plenty of other things for people to be interested in. The question is how we deal with this one.

What I want to examine here is what part intention really plays in the writing of a book, and whether it really helps readers to know what that intention is. Unfortunately, writers are not always trustworthy when they tell us about their intentions. Firstly, they might not remember; secondly, they might not want to reveal their true intentions anyway; thirdly, the context of the question sometimes determines the sort of answer it gets. Questions like this tend to be asked at events such as literary festivals, where the task in hand is that of entertaining an audience rather than revealing deep and complex truths, and faced with that task, the storyteller's instinct in front of an audience takes over and shapes a few scraps of half-remembered fact and a sprinkle of invention into a coherent and interesting narrative: a story about their intentions.

But they—they? I mean we. I mean I. I, we, and they do that with most questions, especially the old favorite, "Where do you get your ideas from?" We do it because it's necessary. One of the occupational hazards the modern writer has to negotiate is the book tour, and it's in the course of such a tour that we have most need of such instant stories about telling a story, because the same questions come up in every interview, at every bookstore, with every audience, twenty, fifty, a hundred times; and in sheer self-defense we develop a performance, with a set of neat anecdotes, one-liners, and pat answers. And one of the consequences of this anti-madness strategy is that our audiences, which consist for the most part of people who like reading but don't necessarily follow the convolutions of literary theory, come to believe—or are confirmed in an existing belief—that there really is a simple answer to such questions as "What did you intend when you wrote this book?" and that that answer matters to their reading of it.

But here, I hope, I can abandon the pat answers and tell a little more, or as much as I know, anyway, of the truth about my intentions when I wrote one of my books, *The Scarecrow and His Servant* (2004). The book tells the story of a scarecrow who miraculously comes to life, engages a young boy called Jack as his servant, and wanders about a land that seems to be a sort of fairy-tale Italy. After several adventures, during which they are followed without their knowledge by a lawyer representing the obviously villainous Buffaloni Corporation, they discover that the Scarecrow, thanks to the will that his maker had hidden in his stuffing, is the real owner of a farm in a place called Spring Valley. The Buffaloni Corporation, which had illegally taken possession of the land, is foiled and evicted, and the Scarecrow and his servant live happily ever after.

The story forms a book 230 pages in length, and is illustrated by delicate pen-and-ink drawings by Peter Bailey. I mention that because it was part of my intention to write a story with pictures, and because Peter Bailey had done such delightful illustrations for some of my previous books. So I had his talent in mind from the start, and I intended to write a story that would suit his light and fantastical style.

But as I write those words I know that "intended" should really have been "hoped." And this is perhaps the first thing to say about writing and intention: intending to write a particular kind of story is not the same sort of thing as intending to rake up the leaves on the lawn, or telephone one's cousin, or buy a present for one's grandchild. We know we can do those things. We don't know we can write a story that will be funny, or moving, or exciting, though we hope we can. All we can honestly intend to do is try.

Then there is the matter of the subject, the characters, and the setting. This is also difficult to explain in terms of intention. I can recall the moment the notion of this story first came to me: it was during a performance of Leonard Bernstein's *Candide* (1956) at the

National Theatre in London in 1999. I found the relationship between Candide and his servant Cacambo intriguing, and wondered about other such simple master/clever-servant pairs, such as Bertie Wooster and Jeeves. I liked the inbuilt dynamics of the relationship. Did that mean that I *intended* to write a story about such a pair? Not yet, but the possibility was there. However, the observation struck me with a particular resonance, which I've learned means that I probably *am* going to write about it.

There were two other sources of which I was conscious. One was a book of reproductions of the younger Tiepolo's lively and brilliant drawings in pen and brown wash of Punchinello. Punchinello, or Pulcinella, was one of the characters in the *commedia dell'arte*, and whereas the Scarecrow is not Pulcinella, he has this in common with him as well as with the other *commedia* characters: he is flat and not round. I had found that an absence of psychology in my protagonists was a positive advantage in writing fairy tales of the sort this was going to be, and the sort of intense vivid character embodied in the *commedia* mask, its reactions instant and predictable and its attempts at subtlety absurdly obvious, was exactly the sort of personality I could already sense developing when I thought of the Scarecrow. Again, it's impossible to separate what is *intention* here from what is something else—hope, as I've suggested, or simple fascination: here's a new character to play with. And, of course, the *commedia* background suggested Italy, and that soon became inseparable from the rest of the idea.

The second source I was aware of was a book of vivid watercolor sketches sent me by a friend, a poet and painter living in Japan, who had become intrigued by the scarecrows Japanese farmers made for their fields. Anything will do: a pink plastic Wellington boot, a toy plane on a string, a doll trailing scores of colored ribbons. They are a riot of improvisation. My friend had sketched dozens of these, and the infinite transmutability of the Japanese scarecrows certainly played a part in one important development of the plot, when the lawyer for the Buffalonis is trying to prove that the Scarecrow in the witness box is not the Scarecrow mentioned in the will, since every single part of him has now been replaced by something else.

But at what point did I intend to make that idea a part of the plot? From the beginning? I don't think so. I seem to remember I found it with a start of pleasure as I was writing the court scene, but all that might indicate is that my mind had been preparing the way without my being aware of it: that my intention had been unconscious. However, once I had become aware, I could go back and prepare the way by making sure that in the course of each adventure the Scarecrow lost a leg, or an arm, or his clothes, and his servant Jack found a replacement. I definitely remember intending to do that.

In fact it may be that the major decisions are out of our control, and the intentions we're conscious of are concerned with matters of detail. That certainly goes for what we're going to write in the first place. I learned a long time ago that it was a mistake to intend, in a calm and rational way, having looked at a range of options and considered their relative merits and drawbacks, to write a certain book rather than another. The part of me that intended to write that particular book wasn't capable of it, and the part of me that was capable of writing books didn't want to write that one.

Among those major decisions, the ones that are made for me, is the one about voice and point of view. I couldn't truthfully say that I "intend" to write in the third person, though I almost invariably do write like that. Nor did I "intend" to make the voice that tells *His Dark Materials* different in tone from the voice that tells the Sally Lockhart novels, or both of them different from the voice that tells *The Scarecrow and His Servant* and my other fairy tales, though they are. The voice I found, in each case, seemed to be what the story wanted. And although I think those voices are different, I dare say that if anyone were to perform a stylistic analysis by computer of all my various stories, it would show that I have certain habits and mannerisms that would always give me away, no matter which "voice" I was using; but as I don't know what they are, I can't say that I intend anything very much in connection with them.

The aspect of the author's intention that readers are perhaps most concerned about is the one about "message." After the first and second volumes of *His Dark Materials* had been published, but before the third, I was asked many times which of the characters were supposed to be good, and which bad; whom should the readers cheer for, and whom should they boo? They were clearly frustrated by the lack of a clear signal from the author, or the book itself, or the publisher via the blurb, and they felt unmoored, so to speak. The answer I gave was, in effect, "I'm not going to tell you, but the story isn't over yet. Wait till you've read it all, and then decide for yourself. But what are you going to think when someone you've taken for a bad character does something good? Or when a good character does something bad? It's probably better to think about good or bad actions rather than good or bad characters. People are complicated."

Audiences seemed satisfied with that, and the question faded away; it was seldom asked in that form after the final book was published. But anxiety about religion and morality is particularly sharp in the present age, so variants of that question turn up still, such as the one I quoted earlier: Is it all right to think X, when the book is apparently intended to say Y? What's the correct view? What's the right answer? People clearly feel that intention matters a great deal, and that they can trust the author to tell them about it.

The final aspect of "intention" I shall look at here has to do with audience. "What age of reader is this book written for?" is a question that different authors feel differently about. Some are quite happy to say "It's for sixth and seventh graders," or "It's for thirteen and upwards." Others are decidedly not. In 2008 most publishers of children's books in the United Kingdom announced that in an attempt to increase sales they were going to put an age-figure on the cover of every book, of the form 5+, 7+, 9+, and so on, to help adult purchasers in nonspecialist bookstores decide whether a particular book would make a suitable present for a particular child. They met a determined resistance from many authors, who felt that their efforts to write books that would welcome readers of a wide age-range were being undermined by their own publishers, and that the age-figure would actively discourage many children from reading books they might otherwise enjoy. The argument continues, but again it shows the problematic nature of "intention." Does age-guidance of any sort imply that the book is intended for a particular kind of reader? My own view is that the only appropriate verb to use is, again, hope rather than intend. We have no right to expect any audience at all; the idea of sorting our readers out before they've even seen the first sentence seems to me presumptuous in the extreme.

To conclude: a writer's intention with regard to a book is a complicated and elusive matter, and explaining each case truthfully and in full is not always possible. Would a reader want to know that complicated and elusive truth in any case? Would it be any use to them? Possibly, if they were genuinely interested in the process of composition, and prepared for ambiguities and contradictions and uncertainties; probably not, if their desire was for a simple answer that would end their anxiety about whether they'd really understood what the book was saying.

But it would be frivolous to maintain that a writer's intention doesn't matter at all. In other spheres of activity it matters a great deal. If we accidentally dislodge a heavy flowerpot from a sixth-floor balcony onto somebody's head, it's unfortunate; if we intend to do so, it's murder. The courts certainly recognize the difference. There is also the related question of responsibility. If a writer produces a story that has the effect of inflaming (for example) racial hatred, can the writer disclaim responsibility by saying that whatever intention he or she had, it wasn't that, and that in any case the writer's intention is irrelevant? To disclaim intention and responsibility altogether seems to me to regard the author as little more than an elaborate piece of voice-recognition software, taking down dictation from an unseen source. Of course our intentions matter to some extent: it's just rather difficult to say what they are.

In practice, the way we answer questions depends on what we judge to be the needs, the age, the maturity, and the intellectual ability of the questioner, as well as the situation in which the question is posed. If we're lucky enough to have a long line of young customers waiting for us to sign their newly purchased books, we can't spend much time on any of our answers; with a small group of well-prepared university students in a seminar room, the case is different.

But I think that I would try—that I do try—to explain that what I *intended* to do was make up as good a story as I could invent, and write it as well as I could manage. And I try to explain something about the democratic nature of reading. I say that whatever my intention might have been when I wrote the book, the meaning doesn't consist only of my intention.

The meaning is what emerges from the interaction between the words I put on the page and the readers' own minds as they read them. If they're puzzled, the best thing to do is talk about the book with someone else who's read it, and let meanings emerge from the conversation, democratically. I'm willing to take part in such conversations, because I too have read the book, and if I'm asked about my intentions, then any answer I give will be part of the conversation too; but it's hard to persuade readers that my reading has no more final authority than theirs.

In that way, I may not clarify much for people who want to know about my intentions, but I do introduce the idea of reader-response theory, which is probably more helpful.

28

Latino/a
Phillip Serrato

As a proper noun, "Latino" designates a resident of the United States who is of Latin American descent. As an adjective, it renders the noun that it modifies somehow pertinent to or associated with such individuals. While the *Oxford English Dictionary* traces the first use of the label back to the 1940s, it did not gain widespread currency until the 1980s. As Suzanne Oboler (1995) observes, "Latino" emerged as a counter to "Hispanic," an umbrella term resented by many who fell into its fold as "an artifact created and imposed by state administrative agencies." Among other things, "Hispanic" implicitly cleaned up the genealogy of the individuals it subsumed by privileging Spanish descent and disarticulating Latin American origins. The insistence on "Latino" over "Hispanic" that proliferated in the 1980s thus emanated from a desire for self-signification as well as a desire to recuperate a connection to Latin America. Moreover, as Felix Padilla (1985) explains in one of the first (and best) discussions of the emergence, function, and efficacy of "Latino" as a politicized identity category, the moniker has enabled the mobilization of diverse ethnic, cultural, and national groups into an imagined community predicated not just on linguistic and hemispheric affiliations, but also on shared experiences in the United States with racism, poverty, and other social challenges.

As "Latino" came into use in the 1980s, it quickly became supplanted by "Latino/a" and "Latina/o," both of which offered to correct the gendered implications of "Latino." In Spanish, an –o ending, which serves as the default form for adjectives and adjectival nouns, renders a term masculine, while an –a ending renders it feminine. Since default references to "Latino literature" or "Latinos in Hollywood" discursively overlook and exclude women while alleging to accommodate them, the utilization of "Latino/a" or "Latina/o," which are more explicitly inclusive, has become more commonplace. In an effort to circumvent the politics (and messiness) of "Latino" versus "Latino/a" versus "Latina/o," "Latin@" has recently come into use in some sectors, though this concoction can certainly be parsed and problematized, too.

While the terminology has been a hotly contested matter with an array of cultural, political, and personal stakes (Gimenez 1993; Hayes-Bautista and Chapa 1987; Oboler 1995; Chabram-Dernersesian 2003), it is not surprising that it has been handled in different—if not inconsistent—ways in children's literature. As might be expected, one encounters in criticism and reviews published in the 1970s and 1980s recurring references to "Hispanics" and "Hispanic Americans" as well as some mention of "Spanish Americans" (Madsen and Wickersham 1980; Adams 1981). Although this earlier research's use of "Hispanic" evokes the aforementioned issues, and references to "Spanish Americans" perpetuate the inaccurate and fundamentally racist reduction of ethnic identity to language, it is nonetheless sensitive to the portrayals of Latinos/as in children's books as well as to their relative invisibility in the literature available at the time. Notably, one also finds in this earlier period—most prominently in the groundbreaking *Interracial Books for Children Bulletin*—an emergent swerve away from generic labels through specific attention to representations of Chicanos and Puerto Ricans (Council on Interracial Books for Children 1972; Council on Interracial Books for Children 1975; Freundlich 1980).

In more recent years, terminology has remained an unresolved issue: the titles of conference papers, research articles, reference books, and dissertations continue to waver in their negotiation of "Hispanic," "Latino," and "Latino/a." For many researchers and critics, "Hispanic" continues to serve as a conveniently generic and familiar descriptor (Gillespie et al. 1994; Nilsson 2005). Arlene Barry (1998) explains, "[B]ecause U.S. government institutions, such as the Bureau of the Census, use *Hispanic*, I thought it might be more widely recognized and would help to avoid confusion." Yet another contentious dimension of "Hispanic" becomes apparent when Barry adds that she prefers the label because "it places more of an emphasis on integration." Generally, however, researchers today prefer "Latino/a" and "Latina/o" due to greater awareness of the assorted problems with "Hispanic" and the gendered implications of "Latino" (Day 1997; Medina and Enciso 2002; Chappell and Faltis 2007). Not to be overlooked, of course, is the fact that it is becoming increasingly more common for researchers to abandon generic labels altogether and, in the vein of the aforementioned *Interracial Books for Children Bulletin*, to particularize their discussions according to the specific ethnic and cultural ties of the authors under discussion and/or the experiences being depicted.

As occurs with the descriptor "African American," the application of "Latino/a" to children's literature raises a series of questions. In the simplest sense, "Latino/a children's literature" refers to literature for children by Latino/a authors that often portrays and speaks to Latino experiences. Works such as *How Tía Lola Came to Visit Stay* (2001) by Dominican American writer Julia Alvarez and *Friends from the Other Side* (1993) by Chicana legend Gloria Anzaldúa thus easily fit into the category. The parameters of the category must become more flexible, however, when one considers works by authors of mixed backgrounds, including Pam Muñoz Ryan and Matt de la Peña. There is also the matter of books such as *We Are Chicano* (1973) by Rose Blue and *A Day's Work* (1994) by Eve Bunting, which depict Latino/a characters and experiences but are written by non-Latino/a authors. To be sure, cases can be made both for and against the inclusion of these texts in the category. Among others, Alma Flor Ada (2003) acknowledges the trickiness of this issue. Ultimately, Ada makes an overture toward literary merit, but she quickly qualifies it when she cautions, "The merit of a book is determined not by the heritage of the author or illustrator, but by their intention, knowledge, sensitivity, responsibility, and artistry. . . . Yet there is an inner look to a culture that is not easily acquired and requires long contact with people of the culture and its environment. The deep experiences of a people can seldom be told authentically from the outside." At the very least, the hesitancy in Ada's comment—which should not be taken as the definitive statement on the matter—throws into relief some of the challenges and stakes involved in conceiving of Latino/a children's literature.

Publishers and booksellers have certainly added to the lack of consensus about which terms are preferred, accurate, and politically correct by organizing their own categories of literature for children variously around "Hispanic," "Hispanic American," "Latino," "Latino/a," and even "Latin American." In different venues, one finds *Talking with Mother Earth / Hablando con Madre Tierra* (2006) by Jorge Argueta (a Pipil Nahua Indian from El Salvador who now lives in San Francisco) classified as "Latino," "Latino & Hispanic," or, by virtue of its bilingual content, simply (and very unhelpfully) "bilingual." Although in some cases more specific descriptors such as "Mexican American," "Chicano/a," and "Dominican American" have been utilized, largely the institution and promulgation of the more general categories has been a result of publishers and booksellers commodifying multiculturalism and making shopping for multicultural fare as convenient (i.e., as uncomplicated and obvious) as possible.

Unfortunately, inasmuch as categories such as "Hispanic children's literature" and "Latino/a children's literature" readily signify diversity for consumers seeking to broaden children's reading experiences, these categories actually "hide more than they reveal" (Gimenez 1993). On one hand, they obfuscate the specific cultural content and context of a text (assuming it has specific cultural content and context in the first place); on the other, they perpetuate indifference toward the diverse ethnic identities and cultural formations that terms such as "Hispanic" and "Latino/a" actually encompass. Within the children's literature subcategory of "Latino & Hispanic," Amazon.com lists among the top results Spanish-language translations of Margaret Wise Brown's *Goodnight, Moon* (1947, trans. 1995) and Esphyr Slobodkina's *Caps for Sale* (1940, trans. 1995). But to consider Spanish-language editions of classic books "Latino & Hispanic" alongside books that specifically reflect, represent, and speak to Latino/a experiences is a fraught proposition that radically dilutes the category. Elsewhere, the website of Lee and Low Books, a publisher distinguished for its multicultural offerings, describes as "Latino/Hispanic/Mexican Interest" works such as Lulu Delacre's *Arrorró, mi niño: Latino Lullabies and Gentle Games* (2004), Pat Mora's *Confetti: Poems for Children* (1996), and Alexis O'Neil's *Estela's Swap* (2002). Such a grouping again renders the category of "Latino/Hispanic/Mexican Interest" a broad and slippery one. Besides the fact that the three authors hail from different ethnic backgrounds, their texts fit their shared billing in overly general ways. Delacre's book promises to be a collection of "Latino lullabies," but the deployment of "Latino" in this instance completely undoes what the label has come to mean: as a modifier, it suggests that, as in the case of "Latino literature" or "Latino film," the lullabies are products of individuals or cultural formations based in the United States that have ties to Latin America. In actuality, the lullabies have been culled from throughout Latin America. Given the origins of the songs and games featured in the book, a more proper subtitle would be *Lullabies and Gentle Games from Latin America*.

Once Delacre's book is triangulated with Mora's and O'Neill's, additional questions arise about the parameters of and criteria for the "Hispanic/Latino/Mexican Interest" designation. That Delacre is a native of Puerto Rico, Mora is Mexican American, and O'Neill is not of Latin American descent invites the usual question as to whether an author's ethnic background should determine whether her book merits the "Hispanic/Latino" tag (which, to be sure, carries a certain capital within the current marketplace of children's literature). More worthy of attention and concern are the textual and narrative elements that render the three texts "Hispanic/Latino," including the incorporation of Spanish (to different degrees), the integration of a few culturally specific references, the deployment of many more culturally indeterminate references, and illustrations that feature distinctively brown bodies. As these kinds of elements come to serve as a shorthand for "Latino/Hispanic/Mexican Interest," they reflect and reify a broader slippage in the popular American imagination and media in which "Latinos are perceived primarily in terms of assumed patterns of cultural behavior, of stereotypes reinforced by vaguely defined and ahistorical interpretations of the meaning of 'Hispanic ethnicity'" (Oboler 1995).

Although many books for children play into the homogenizing, essentializing effects of popular labels by reenacting Latino/a ethnocultural indeterminacy (Soto 1995; Rodríguez 1999; De Anda 2004; Herrera 2004; Pinkney 2007), many others defy such complicity by featuring specific ethnocultural contexts. In *The Rainbow Tulip* (1999), Pat Mora smoothly establishes that the family in the story is of Mexican origin, while René Colato Laínez makes it clear in *I Am René, the Boy / Soy René, el Niño* (2005) that the narrator has come to the United States from El Salvador. One refreshing example is the *Sports* volume of the Latino Life nonfiction series published in the mid-1990s by Rourke Publications. In spite of the series' name and broad chapter titles such as "Latinos in Baseball," the author of the *Sports* (1995) installment, Jeffrey Jensen, is careful to identify the ethnic background of each individual that he profiles. As in the books of Mora and Laínez, Jensen's gestures toward specificity offer to interrupt popular tendencies (including that of his own publisher) to lump Latinos/as into a homogenous ethnocultural bloc.

Since the very convenience of terms such as "Hispanic," "Latino," and even "Latino/a" is the root of the problem with them, it behooves scholars, teachers, librarians, and consumers to understand these terms as superficial descriptors and not as signifiers of a homogenous ethnocultural formation. Rubrics such as "Hispanic children's literature" and "Latino/a children's literature" encompass too easily a spectrum of unique texts that embody diverse and distinctive mixtures of cultural, historical, political, and artistic specificity, influence, and significance. Attending to the distinguishing characteristics of texts that otherwise tend to get grouped together—either because of convenience or because the texts lend themselves to it—can yield more nuanced understandings that reveal the limits of the terms upon which popular categories turn.

29

Liminality

Michael Joseph

Although the phenomenon of liminality appears in the earliest children's texts, it doesn't appear in children's literature scholarship until the beginning of the twenty-first century, chiefly in the adjective form, "liminal," a polyseme whose other meanings relate to psychology and mysticism. "Liminality" is a coinage from the Scottish anthropologist Victor Turner (1969), who drew on "liminaire," a term used by Arnold Van Gennep (1909) in his ethnographical writings on preindustrial societies to designate the middle, transitional stage of a three-stage paradigmatic rite of passage ("rites which accompany every change of place, state, social position and age"). Joseph Campbell adapted this construct as a basis for *The Hero with a Thousand Faces* (1949), an instance of Van Gennep's influence on literary studies, although Turner's influence has proved deeper and more pervasive.

Liminality describes the quality of being socially segregated, set apart and divested of status, and relates to associated characteristics and qualities: indeterminacy, ambiguity, selflessness, and becomingness. Although Turner gives the Latin *limen* as its root, the origins of "liminality" have been traced back to the early Bronze Age, to the Egyptian word for port, harbor, haven, and port city—*mni*—which appears during the second millennium B.C.E. in the Middle Kingdom

and later becomes transposed into the Greek *limen*, also meaning harbor. It is the root of the modern word "limnology," defined as the study of inland waters.

As Campbell adapted the rite of passage to a Jungian interpretation of myth and fantasy, Turner adapted liminality to the study of religious patterns in contemporary culture, elaborating on Émile Durkheim's theory of religious functionalism. Like Campbell, Turner's work was informed by literary interests, which included children's literature. Edith Turner notes that her husband Victor saw liminality in works by C. S. Lewis, Mark Twain, and Robert Louis Stevenson, as well as in the innumerable children's stories with passage to adulthood as their theme (Turner 1990).

During the 1990s, "liminal" appeared frequently in research touching on adolescence, generally qualifying an adolescent subject with regard to the ambiguousness of his or her social position and/or sexual identity. Reuven Kahane (1997) employed the phrase "postmodern liminality" in arguing that postmodernity had institutionalized liminality, providing adolescents a buffer zone in which to move playfully and spontaneously between normative and antinormative behaviors, and thereby offsetting the tensions of a complex society. Thus postmodern liminality becomes a metonym of adolescent agency, which continues to resonate in the criticism of young adult literature.

What may be the earliest yoking of liminality and preadolescent children appeared in 1995, in Dennis Todd's discussion of objects acquired by gentleman collectors—specifically "[m]onstrous children, in their deceased form." Todd calls these gruesome collectibles "liminal creatures," because they straddle boundaries between categories and thus neutralize conventional definitions. The identity of children and monsters is an ironic commonplace in contemporary culture, and, indeed, in children's literature. Like monsters, literary children dismayingly breach boundaries, and in their passage into adulthood (Turner's phrase), they symbolize both chaos and order, antistructure and structure. One glimpses the face of invisible affiliation in the historical shifting of the similarly transitional gothic romance (such as Mary Shelley's *Frankenstein* [1818]) into children's literature and the congeries of monsters in fairy tales: Madame LePrince De Beaumont's "Beauty and the Beast," perhaps the earliest fairy tale composed for children, asks the question, What is a monster?—a question containing the question, What is a child?

After 2000, scholars began to discuss liminality in representations of childhood, children, and child culture. The adjective "liminal" appeared with greater innovation and richness of use, generally indicating "in between," "bounded," or "hybrid." "Liminal space" emerged as a flexible concept in which "space" can refer (extensively) to literary time/space or to something more abstract: For example, Hogwarts and Crusoe's island are both liminal spaces because they are projected outside of society and symbolize a borderland through which the protagonist or the community of liminal beings, "the *communitas*," passes to reenter structure (Turner 1969). On the other hand, liminal space can also be used (intensively) to signify an interior state—a projection of creative power, a metaphor of the imagination. One can begin to appreciate the broadly pervasive importance of liminal space to children's literature by noting its iteration in the titles of canonical texts: *Alice's Adventures in Wonderland* (1865), *The Wonderful Wizard of Oz* (1900), *The Chronicles of Narnia* (1950–56).

Recent scholarship has blended a separate application of liminal with liminality. "Liminal consciousness" appears (Knoepflmacher 2005) partly to describe Randall Jarrell, who, "obsessively revisiting his grim recollections of a childhood trauma," envisions an escapist fantasy scene of a boy lying abed, between sleeping and waking, in whose "liminal consciousness" the terrifying details of a Grimm's fairy tale his mother is telling him become woven into a dream. Liminal consciousness, like liminal space, is intended to represent a condition of interiority. This usage of liminal evokes the late-nineteenth-century psychological notion of the *limen* as a "threshold of consciousness," though it challenges the customary dyadic psychological structure that recognizes only "subliminal" and "supraliminal" states. In so doing, a compound or fused liminality forms, one that modifies the self with a condition of contingency that is both private, or phenomenological, and public—relating to socially constructed identity.

Liminal has two common usages when coupled with being. The primary one, implying a person or character experiencing liminality, has a robust and growing presence in discussions of multicultural children's literature, often pendant to the phrase "liminal existence." The second usage, a variant of "liminal character," appears in the domains of folklore and speculative fiction and defines a fantasy character who combines antithetical states. These doubled beings are granted wisdom by force of their unique perspective, but they are also unpredictable and dangerous. Gandalf, the wizard who leads Bilbo and then Frodo away from the Shire in *Lord of the Rings* (1954–555), is considered a liminal being because he is both dead and alive (Clute and Grant 1997). Cyborgs such as Ted Hughes's Iron Giant (1968) are also liminal beings. Posthumanist theorists map this derivative meaning of liminal being onto the original, so that cyborgs symbolize women and, potentially, other social categories disempowered or liminalized by normative humanistic values.

Children's literary critics such as Roni Natov (2001) and Christopher Parkes (2006) have described Harry Potter, Robinson Crusoe, and Alice as liminal characters (symbols of liminality), thereby echoing Turner, who thought Tom Sawyer and Huck Finn liminal characters. Turner also considered Lewis Carroll, "with his dream world," a "liminal person," an appellation by which liminality steps beyond the boundary of ritual and representation.

Someone whose personhood is liminal lives beyond the pale of society, or structure. For such persons, liminality is neither ritual nor transitional, but an open-ended way of life qualified by sets of cultural demands, ethical systems, and processes that are irreconcilable. In contrast with ritual liminality, which anticipates the reincorporation of the liminal being

into social structure (Alice steps back; Wendy and Dorothy fly back; Willow Rosenberg turns back—from witch to girl), outsiderhood and marginality defy reincorporation. Much adolescent literature of the last twenty years has explored these latter two types of liminality by imagining lives that are permanently or semi-permanently de-structured. The "outsider" (a term readers will identify with S. E. Hinton's *The Outsiders* [1967], said to be the first work of young adult fiction) retains an element of choice. Lewis Carroll typifies outsider liminality because, according to Turner, he set himself apart—he governs his dreamworld. Holden Caulfield, in J. D. Salinger's *Catcher in the Rye* (1951), is more problematic: Does he reject society for its phoniness and hypocrisy, or is he unable to resolve social ambiguities and hence inassimilable into structure—a "marginal"?

Multicultural children's literature interrogates the "marginal" category of liminality in narratives of the adolescent children of immigrants or indigenous people, often paired with the phrase "liminal existence." "Existence" connotes continuity rather than status or any comparably finite term, and thus reinforces the idea that a marginal's daily life is determined by a crucial disjunction, even opposition, between the values and expectations of the vanishing homeland and those of the looming new world. For marginals, liminality is all-consuming and a priori: liminality precedes existence. The term also catches at the ontological contractedness of such a state. In contrast to the (one might say) landscaped liminal spaces of native-born adolescents, the circumscribed existence of first- and second-generation adolescent immigrants or of indigenous peoples is brutally imposed by a social order whose absorptive rites of passage allow, possibly even demand, a hostage population of permanent exiles.

Sherman Alexie's *The Absolutely True Diary of a Part-Time Indian* (2007), winner of the National Book Award for 2007, depicts the youth of the Spokane Tribe living lives characterized by the absence of hope. Arnold Spirit, the book's protagonist (whose alternative name, Junior, suggests secondary status), enrolls in a high-school away from the reservation, exchanging hopelessness for hope—or marginality for outsider status. Arnold's eventual passage into the social structure from which Indians are generally excluded is symbolically predicted by his acceptance into the *communitas* of the high-school basketball team. Although multiculturalism has centered marginality in contemporary children's literature, troping children as marginals is nothing new. In his popular *Cries of New York* (1808), the Quaker Samuel Wood exhorts child readers to see themselves in the honest, hard-working indigent street vendors. The dying children in James Janeway's *Token for Children* (published in 1671–72 and reprinted often thereafter) exemplified marginality for a seventeenth-century Dissenter readership inasmuch as their passage into adulthood is conspicuously barred by their premature deaths. In both cases, marginality is valorized by a religious worldview that perceives in it, and in the idealized rite of passage, potential transcendence.

30
Literacy
Lissa Paul

In *Keywords*, the term "literacy" does not have an entry of its own. Instead, Raymond Williams (1976) traces its evolution from its fourteenth-century root, "literature." For the first three hundred years of its life, "literature" was an all-purpose word referring sometimes to "being well-read," and at other times to "the books in which a man is well-read" (Williams 1976). Gradually, this common-ancestor word divided into several distinct species: the root-word, "literature," strengthened its links to nationhood (as in English literature or French literature); "literate" came to describe being well-read; "literary" became associated with the "profession of authorship"; and "literacy" arose in the late nineteenth century as a social concept "to express the achievement and possession of what are increasingly seen as general and necessary skills" (Williams 1976). In the definition of "literacy," the operative word is "skills," suggesting a low-order, mechanical, even superficial ability related to the simple decoding of black letters on a white page. But by situating "literacy" as an outgrowth of "literature," Williams reminds us to respect its tough root as well as all its more intellectual branches, including "literary," "literate," "reading," and "writing."

The term "literature," as Williams carefully explains, has as its Latin root *littera*, the letter "L" of the alphabet. Learning to be literate begins with the alphabet. From the "Christ-cross row" of letters on a sixteenth-century hornbook to the animated letters and alphabet songs from the twentieth-century children's television program *Sesame Street*, ABCs initiate children into reading. Teaching children their letters has always been the bedrock on which literacy is founded. In the early nineteenth century, poor children in Joseph Lancaster's monitorial schools (the prototypes for compulsory, universal education) were taught to trace their letters with their fingers in sand-tables (flat trays filled with wet-sand, set into child-sized tables). First they learned letters with straight lines (H, L, T), then letters with angles (A, V, W), then those with curves (O, U, B) (Lancaster 1805).

Children's book history itself arguably begins with a picture book alphabet: *Orbis Sensualium Pictus* (1658) by Johann Amos Comenius. Ever since, alphabet books have functioned almost as barometers, reflecting and constructing images of children, society, and culture. From "In Adam's Fall, We sinned All" (signaling the link between the letter *A* and the fall of humanity) in the *New England Primer* (1777), to the secular graphic puzzles of Mitsumasa Anno's *Anno's Alphabet: An Adventure in Imagination* (1974), to the attention to African children in Muriel and Tom Feelings's *Jambo Means Hello: Swahili Alphabet Book* (1974), alphabet books contribute to the beginnings of identity formation. Being literate means being "lettered." A "lettered" person comes to mean a person "of wide-reading." Until the fourteenth century, a literate person was a well-read person, one who had acquired "polite learning through reading" (Williams 1976).

The word "literacy" did not merit a definition of its own until 1883 (the date the *Oxford English Dictionary* [*OED*] gives as its earliest use), when it was explained only as "the antithesis of *illiteracy*." The *OED* gives 1660 as the first use of "illiteracy," and defines it as "ignorance of letters, absence of education, esp. the inability to read and write." Here, in the attention to writing as well as reading, the *OED* alludes to the way in which being able to read is no longer enough to qualify as being literate.

Through the Reformation, reading was important particularly as it pertained to the Bible—and so to salvation. People sentenced to hang for theft could literally save their lives by demonstrating what was called "benefit of the clergy," that is, the ability to read the "neck verse" (Psalm 51:1). In late-eighteenth-century England, the rise of the Sunday School movement focused attention on teaching children to read the Bible so they would learn industry, piety, and obedience. The Religious Tract Society, founded in 1799 as an evangelical publishing house, successfully supplied the Sunday school market with suitably religious stories, including those by Hannah More. The late eighteenth century, marked by the seismic cultural shifts of the American and French revolutions, saw the religious reasons for reading give way to political reasons: literacy became the key to being enfranchised. As only a literate population could determine its own destiny, voters had to be able to both read and write. In colonial America, however, in order to maintain the fiction that slaves were somehow between animals and people, several states enacted contortionist legislation that made it illegal for slaves to learn to read. Those who attempted it risked punishment—or even death.

Until the mid–fifteenth century, when the increasing adoption of the printing press began the slow process of universalizing letter forms, the shaping of letters was the sole province of scribes and copyists. Writing was a skill, a craft taught separately and serving a different ideological agenda. Whereas reading was something that could be used to keep people tractable, writing proved to be a potent political weapon—and so gave rise to the pen as mightier than the sword. In colonial America, indigenous (Native) Americans were taught to read in order to make them obedient Christians, but those who learned to write used their skill to orchestrate their resistance to colonial power (Monaghan 2005).

By the nineteenth century, "literacy" conventionally came to mean both reading and writing, but was no longer primarily used for religious or political purposes. Instead, it was becoming a powerful cultural tool, used to inculcate ideas of national identity. Elementary schoolchildren in the United States were taught to memorize and recite writing by nationalist, quintessentially American poets such as Henry Wadsworth Longfellow and John Greenleaf Whittier (Sorby 2005).

Over about a five-hundred-year period, being literate played a vitally important role in a person's social and cultural matrix. It could save your life; it could save your soul; it could enable you to be politically enfranchised; and it could confirm your cultural identity. Only in the mid–twentieth century did being literate undergo a significant change of meaning.

In the Cold War America of 1955, Rudolf Flesch set off a firestorm of controversy over the definition of "literacy" with his influential book *Why Johnny Can't Read—And What You Can Do about It.* He shifted the definition of literacy away from being well-read toward something about the process of learning to read. Flesch was horrified at the way the "look-say" or "controlled-vocabulary" reading instruction had gradually come to dominate the induction of schoolchildren into literacy. In the United States, *The Eclectic Readers* by William Holmes McGuffey (first published in 1836) marked the change toward the mass-produced-textbook model of reading instruction. By the mid–twentieth century, limited vocabulary, or "basal" readers as they were called, came into vogue. In 1940, *Fun with Dick and Jane*, by William S. Gray and May Hill Arbuthnot, heralded the ascendance of the characters, Dick and Jane, who became virtually synonymous with reading instruction in America. British children learned to read with "Janet and John." The concentration on learning to read a restricted number of words effectively shifted attention away from learning to read the words of God, of the revolution, or of visionary writers, and toward sentences never uttered by a native English speaker. Educational publishers recognized that mass-market readers were, metaphorically speaking, golden-egg-laying geese: the literacy education of virtually every school-child in America and England would be founded on their books. Although Flesch was an influential advocate for the break-up of their monopoly, a revolt had clearly been brewing. The American journalist John Hersey, in a famous *Life* magazine article titled "Why Do Children Bog Down on the First R?" (1954), had also argued against the banality of basal readers.

Through the late 1950s and early 1960s, several publishers embarked on a compromise venture. They attempted to marry the conformist reading-specialist model of literacy instruction with the free-thinking individuality of authors of genuine works of imaginative literature. Dr. Seuss (Theodor Seuss Geisel) came onto the reading primer market as a one-person army of liberation. Although his first book for children, *And to Think That I Saw It on Mulberry Street*, had been published in 1937, it was the two-hundred-and-thirty-six-word *The Cat in the Hat* (1957) that made him famous and launched the Random House series of controlled-vocabulary, imaginatively vibrant Beginner Books. That same year, Harper and Brothers also successfully launched their I Can Read Books with Else Homelund Minarik and Maurice Sendak's *Little Bear* (1957). Other attempts to marry reading specialists with authors were unsuccessful. The Crowell-Collier house in New York (Collier-Macmillan in London) launched the Modern Masters Books for Children series in 1962 to much fanfare. The series fizzled out within a couple of years, despite the fact that that the famous American poet and anthologist Louis Untermeyer had managed to attract manuscripts from some of the literary giants of the day, including Arthur Miller, Robert Graves, Theodore Roethke, Richard Wilbur, and William Saroyan. The reading specialists employed for the project had no qualms about sending controlled vocabulary lists to famous authors. Those who obeyed wrote terrible books. Those who resisted often wrote terrific books—which, sadly, sank with the series. One of the successful contributors, the poet Richard Wilbur, explains the genesis of his book, *Loudmouse* (1963), and his resistance to what he described as the "hog-tying" of authors: "[T]he word-list which I was sent by the publisher (and which I ignored) was full of cow and barn and grandpa, and clearly meant to coerce me into writing about a visit to grandpa's farm, whereas the story I had in mind was about a hollering mouse and a robber" (2008).

In the early twenty-first century, literacy increasingly became the focus of government policies designed to improve test scores on large-scale assessment exercises. The British National Literacy Trust (established in 1997) stresses its "commitment to evidence-based policy" (National Literary Trust 2009). The American Reading First program (established in 2002; U.S. Department of Education 2009) promotes and funds only "scientifically based reading research" geared to improving achievement scores. The United Nations Educational, Scientific and Cultural Organization (UNESCO) defines "literacy" as akin to saving the world, saying it "is at the heart of basic education for all, and essential for eradicating poverty, reducing child mortality, curbing population growth, achieving gender equality and ensuring sustainable peace and democracy." However, it too turns to test scores, acquired from PISA (Programme for International Student Assessment), to demonstrate success.

For the first time in history, "literacy" is defined not by reading and/or writing, but by grading. Because the economies of scale necessitate tightly defined grading rubrics, "literacy" is more narrowly monitored and controlled than it has ever been. That's what literacy looks like at one end of the spectrum. At the other, literacy has blossomed into literacies, including adult literacy, adolescent literacy, balanced literacy, computer literacy, critical literacy, cultural literacy, early childhood literacy, emotional literacy, family literacy, information literacy, mathematical literacy, media literacy, technical literacy, and visual literacy, among others. Some of the above are subsumed under the umbrella term "new literacies." And, in a curious twist on back-to-basics movements, "literature circles" (essentially book groups for schoolchildren) are being recommended to improve literacy scores.

As the description and measurement of ever tinier particles of literacy skills continue to constrict educational discourse, redescriptions—to use Margaret Meek's (1991) preferred term—of literacy grow increasingly labyrinthine. Nearly two decades ago, Meek recognized that literacy had become "a maze of studies to match a multitude of practices, full of contradictions and paradoxes." She also recognized that understanding "literacy" increasingly means acknowledging contributions from a range of disciplines, including "history, anthropology, sociology, philosophy, linguistics, [and] psychology"—all clamoring for attention but ultimately eluding any "final description."

31

Marketing

June Cummins

At its most basic level, the word "marketing" refers to the "action of buying or selling" (*Oxford English Dictionary* [*OED*]) and always implies some sort of exchange, usually involving goods, services, or ideas—and money. A common usage of "marketing" that directly affects children's literature is "the action, business, or process of promoting and selling a product" (*OED*). Since the advent of the printing press, literature has been intimately related to marketing. It is self-evident that developing technologies made widespread literacy possible; what may take some explaining is that marketing is as essential to the development and dissemination of children's literature as technology was.

"Marketing" is a term that arouses both suspicion and admiration. John Clarke in *New Keywords* (2005) explains that "a certain ambivalence persists towards markets. Perceived as necessary, they are not to be trusted. . . . This creates a sense of refusal—the view that not everything can or should be commodified." At the same time, others focus on the benefits of marketing, either implicitly or explicitly linked to capitalism as a system, and see it as essential to the progress and development of civilization. Indeed, to library historians Brian Alderson and Felix de Marez Oyens (2006), the modern concept of childhood came about not because philosophers such as John Locke and Jean-Jacques Rousseau argued for changes in the understanding of childhood—they only came up with the ideas—but because of the "economic base and the continuing momentum of a specialist publishing industry" that put those ideas into culture through marketing. In addition to childhood, even "'children's literature' was a genre mostly created by publishers."

Publishers also helped create a reading public. As historian Kathleen Rassuli (1988) argues, "[E]arly printers were engaged in practices similar to those of present-day marketers." Using the first printing press in England, William Caxton became a publisher, printing books in vernacular English, not Latin: he wanted to serve "popular tastes" and announced the intended audience on the first pages of many of his publications, a strategy Rassuli links to the contemporary marketing practice of segmentation. He printed such instructions as "not for a rude or uplandish man," "for every man," for "alle Englisshmen," and for "yonge children" (quoted in Rassuli 1988). Included in Caxton's publications for children were the first hornbooks, early primers intended to teach children to read, which were responsible for making widespread literacy possible.

Perhaps the most famous name to be associated with the marketing of children's literature is John Newbery, the eighteenth-century publisher credited as the first person to recognize that children's literature was a *market*, in the sense of being a product ideally poised to be abundantly sold and purchased. His bibliographer Sydney Roscoe explains, "John Newbery's achievement was not to invent . . . juvenile books, not even to start a fashion for them, but to so produce them as to make a permanent and profitable market for them, to make them a class of book to be taken seriously as a recognized and important branch of the book trade" (quoted in Rose 1995). Such laudatory descriptions of Newbery's importance contrast with the more restrained comments of Betsy Hearne (1986–87), who argues that "John Newbery's early publishing efforts were seen as an extension and booster of toy sales, not a new literary vision." While Hearne's seeming dismissal of Newbery reveals that he is not universally revered, it also corroborates that the perception of Newbery as a marketer is a commonplace.

A consummate marketer and one of the first publishers for children, Newbery employed selling strategies that persist, and which are sometimes seen as coercive today, such as advertising his other books within the pages of the bound children's book. Newbery may have been the first to use the "tie-in"—that is, he would include playthings along with the books he sold. A child's copy of *A Little Pretty Pocket-Book* came with a ball or pincushion, depending on the sex of the child for whom the book was purchased. In other books, Newbery would have a character mention additional items he sold. The famous character Goody Two-Shoes is orphaned because her father was "seized with a violent fever in a place where Dr. James's Fever Powder was not to be had"—Dr. James's Fever Powder being Newbery's own patent medicine (quoted in Rose 1995). Today, this sort of cross-marketing is called "product placement" and is often treated with suspicion. Whether or not

Newbery's reading public shared that suspicion, *The History of Little Goody Two-Shoes* was Newbery's most popular book, running through twenty-nine editions between 1765 and 1800 (Rose 1995).

The award that bears his name furthers Newbery's legacy as a marketer. Conferred annually by the American Library Association since 1922, the Newbery Award goes to the best children's book published in the United States. Newbery's prominence in the library world demonstrates the extent to which libraries and librarians themselves are wrapped up in the marketing of children's literature: receipt of the award guarantees sales because libraries buy Newbery winners.

American librarians' influence on children's book marketing dates to the late nineteenth century. Jacalyn Eddy's *Bookwomen: Creating an Empire in Children's Book Publishing, 1919–1939* (2006) begins with discussion, not of a publisher, but of a famous librarian, Anne Carroll Moore of the New York Public Library (NYPL). Moore, whose librarian career began in the late 1890s and extended through much of the twentieth century, saw herself and other librarians as public servants of democracy who were responsible for "providing a crucial foundation for citizenship." Moore believed that only certain kinds of books produced model citizens, and she accordingly privileged those that were "traditional," "classics," "soothing," "idyllic," and "reinforcing positive qualities ([such as] courage, loyalty)" (Eddy 2006). With money to spend for the NYPL children's collection, Moore wanted to purchase only books that met her standards. Believing that publishers were "careless" and were producing "mediocre" books, Moore set out to influence them. In 1918, she became the children's book reviewer for the magazine *Bookman* and argued for "good" children's books. Eddy demonstrates how publishers responded to Moore's column, bringing out more books of the sort Moore advocated.

Although some librarians continued to view publishers with suspicion and disdained "commercialization," Louise Seaman—who in 1919 at Macmillan became head of publishing's first children's division—and other editors knew that librarians' expertise was not only "good for business" but "indispensable . . . to the process of making books for children" (Eddy 2006). During the 1920s, children's book editors often consulted librarians. For her part, while Moore "remained associated with the noncommercial library enterprise, [she was] astutely, if ambivalently, aware that an expanded market was crucial to enhanced quality for children's books" (Eddy 2006). Book editors had to market their books directly to librarians, and librarians needed publishers.

At this time, publishing was a growing industry that encompassed the full range of reading options for children. While "gentleman publishers" and the young women editors they began to appoint in the 1920s saw themselves as public servants who, like librarians, were responsible for democracy and good taste, other publishing companies happily produced comic books, "cheap" paperbacks, dime novels, and Stratemeyer series books. Most of the time, these books could not be found in libraries. Despite trade publishers' and librarians' best efforts, an American Library Association survey undertaken in 1926 found, after asking 36,000 students in thirty-four states what their favorite book was, that fully 98 percent named a book issued by the Stratemeyer Syndicate, publisher of series such as Nancy Drew and the Hardy Boys (Marcus 2008).

The books that would ultimately undo the power of the librarians to influence the book-buying public, however, were not Stratemeyer's but the Little Golden Books, first published in 1942 by Simon and Schuster in conjunction with the Western Printing and Lithography Company. Sold in five-and-dime, grocery, and department stores, Little Golden Books cost a mere twenty-five cents, much less than other hardcover books. Parents were attracted to the bright colors, seeming durability, and low cost of the books, and many appreciated not having to go to high-end bookstores or libraries to find them (a situation that aptly illustrates that marketing to children often, if not always, includes marketing to adults, as they are the ones with the purchasing power). The books were as available as apples. Despite first going on sale in the midst of World War II paper shortages, the Golden Books were a smashing success. Heretofore, if a book failed to be reviewed in the *Horn Book* magazine, or if it wasn't mentioned in the New York Public Library's annual holiday list, librarians could not know of it, and the book had almost no chance of selling (Marcus 2008). But Little Golden Books "bypassed the old review system altogether" by appearing on grocery store shelves, and a publishing phenomenon was born (Marcus 2008).

The conflict between reviewers and marketers flourished, courtesy of another cultural behemoth, The Walt Disney Company. For example, in the early 1930s, Disney gave Western Printing exclusive rights to publish books featuring its cartoon characters. Leonard Marcus (2008) explains that Disney's huge marketing successes were "the realization of [Anne Carroll Moore's and other librarians'] worst nightmares." Despite librarians' nightmares, "old school" publishing did not die out. Throughout the twentieth century, major publishing houses continued to produce high-quality children's books, in steadily increasing numbers. To be competitive, these publishing houses had to develop marketing strategies. By the mid-1960s, all large publishing companies had a promotions department, separate from the editorial department (Marcus 2008).

Marketing books, especially children's books, can be a tricky business. It's rare to see a commercial for a children's book on television, and most children don't read the kinds of print publications, like book review sections in newspapers, that carry book advertisements. Marketers of children's books have to use marketing techniques other than the traditional mainstays popular since the mid-twentieth century. Today, trade publishers borrow heavily from Stratemeyer, Golden Books, and Disney.

One common strategy, "branding," involves "the application of a trade mark or brand to a product; the promotion of consumer awareness of a particular brand of goods or services" (*OED*). Dr. Seuss was an early branding expert, using his artistic creation, the Cat in the Hat, "as a logo not only for his own early reader titles but also for those he commissioned from others as publisher of the Beginner Books imprint" (Marcus 2008).

Series books serve publishers well because when successful they encourage repeat customers. Marketers are particularly interested in "relationship-driven marketing, which emphasizes serving the customer over the long term" (*Encyclopaedia Brittanica* 2009, s.v. "Marketing"), and series books obviously lend themselves beautifully to long-term relationships. Spectacular series successes, such as the Babysitters' Club books of the 1980s or the Stratemeyer books of earlier in the century, turned huge profits for their publishing companies.

As major publishing houses consolidated into a few media powerhouses in the late twentieth century, new marketing strategies either unleashed children's imaginations or exploited them, depending on one's perspective. In what Kimberly Reynolds and Nicholas Tucker (1998) call "asset stripping," book characters are valued only in terms of how they can be merchandised. Popular fictional characters such as Harry Potter leap easily from one medium to another, including not just other forms of art, such as films and video games, but also myriad material objects, ranging from lunch boxes to toothpaste. Seeing such marketing "synergy" as "troubling," Daniel Hade (2002) notes "that the book and each spin-off piece of merchandise and each retelling across another medium becomes a promotion for every other product based upon that story." While Hade and many others chafe at the seemingly endless extension of the book's boundaries, others applaud the permeability of the fictional construct, seeing such extension as a kind of liberation of the child's imagination. Marketers themselves believe that branding is actually good for children, allowing them to feel "joy," "warmth," "friendly," and "empowered" (Del Vecchio 1998). Successful brands, argues Gene del Vecchio, are "defined by aspirations obtained, fantasies fulfilled, or senses gratified. Such brands make a child *feel* something on the inside." Regardless of the intellectual or emotional reactions to the highly elastic book character, one thing is certain: the more a character is seen, heard, or used, the more money the companies producing the character make.

Voicing the concern that that these character proliferations and cross-pollinations might destroy books themselves, Reynolds and Tucker observe, "Many of today's editors watch in dismay as characters from books are moved into independent profit centres and turned into products whose sales are often so much in excess of the fiction that they threaten the very existence of the format for which they were originally conceived." Others are more sanguine, pointing to the huge Harry Potter tomes that children willingly haul about and read. Children are reading despite the massive marketing of the fictional character; some might argue they are reading *because* of it.

In 2009, a "watchdog group," the Campaign for a Commercial-Free Childhood, determined that fully one-third of the items sold through Scholastic's book-buying club service, in which the huge publishing company distributes catalogues to children through their classrooms, were not books but toys, posters, makeup, jewelry, and other nonliterary products. Parents complained that their children were offered these products under "the guise of a literary book club that is promoted in classrooms" (Rich 2009). In fact, Scholastic reports that more than 75 percent of elementary school teachers participate in the book-buying clubs by distributing the catalogues to their students. Although knowledge of the long association between marketing and children's books might not soothe these parents' anxieties, Scholastic's history of marketing nonbook items with their books continues a practice begun hundreds of years ago with John Newbery.

Historian Ronald Fullerton (1988) reminds us that "Modern Western Marketing is a historical phenomenon, not a universal one. . . . That this variant of marketing did not always exist in the past implies very strongly that it may not always exist in the future." The same might be said for children's books. As difficult as it might be for Americans and Western Europeans to imagine a wholly new economic system that would supplant capitalism, it would be equally difficult to imagine a world without children's books. Yet both conditions are ultimately imaginable. What does seem impossible to envision, however, is how children's books could be produced and distributed in our contemporary democratic society without money and marketing. It seems worthwhile, finally, to imagine a world where marketing's major success was to bring literature to as many children as possible.

32

Modernism

Kimberley Reynolds

Arguably no word maps the kind of cultural shifts in language that Raymond Williams (1976) was documenting better than "modernism." At its simplest this is because of its roots in the word "modern." Inevitably, what is modern at one time eventually becomes dated and of its time, and so from the first recorded use of that root word in 1500, through the appearance of the word "modernism" itself in 1737, to the fin de siècle, it was a shifting signifier, referring to the present of any given period, rather than a specific historical moment or movement (*Shorter Oxford English Dictionary*). There have been, then, many modernisms, all at some level suggesting "a sense of forward-looking contemporaneity" (Wilk 2006). Toward the end of the nineteenth century, however, a new set of understandings started to come into play, and eventually the meaning of modernism became more fixed. It is now widely used to refer to a movement from the late nineteenth century to the middle of the twentieth century across all the arts, in which many practitioners, critics, and philosophers turned away from classical and traditional forms, styles, and modes of expression and creativity. Their aims were far from cohesive, and the word embraces both those groups who were pessimistic about a technologized future and those who saw science and technology as capable of realizing utopia for

all. Nevertheless, together they comprise a "movement towards sophistication and mannerism, towards introversion, technical display, internal self-skepticism, [which] has often been taken as a common base for a definition of Modernism" (Bradbury and MacFarlane 1976).

If modernism itself pulls in several directions, the relationship between children's literature and modernism is convoluted and contradictory. This condition came to the attention of those who teach and research in the area of children's literature studies when Jacqueline Rose (1984) argued that writers for children have consciously rejected literary modernism as part of a strategy to resist cultural change. The result, she suggests, is that by the middle of the twentieth century, children's literature provided a bolt-hole for writers in retreat from modernism. As evidence, Rose cites Isaac Bashevis Singer's declaration, "I came to the child because I see in him the last refuge from a literature gone berserk and ready for suicide" (1970). Since Singer makes clear through references to Franz Kafka and to James Joyce's *Finnegans Wake* that it is specifically the impact of modernism from which he is retreating, his views support her case. She might also have pointed to the fact that some modernist writers deliberately excluded children from their audience. Henry James (1899; cited in Hughes 1978), for instance, dismissed both juvenile and female readers as "irreflective and uncritical" and so incapable of appreciating the intellectually driven, self-conscious, work of modernist writers like himself.

But Rose and Singer fail to recognize not only many examples of modernism in publishing for children throughout the last century, but also the fact that modernism itself is highly indebted to the idea of the child as transcendent and inspirational. For instance, modernist artists and practitioners around the globe turned to ideas, activities, and attributes associated with children and childhood in an effort to break away from traditional ways of seeing, thinking about, and representing the world. Foremost among the characteristics of childhood that spoke to modernist sensibilities and aspirations was play, which came to be seen as the basis for imagination, fantasy, creativity—all vital for the modernist project of re-visioning the world. Charles Baudelaire was one of those who pointed to the way: "Children see everything afresh. . . . There is nothing that more closely resembles what is called inspiration than the joy with which children absorb shape and color. Genius is merely childhood rediscovered at will" (quoted in Lloyd 1998).

Like Baudelaire, modernists in all media became interested in ideas of play, the untrained eye, and the intuitive, intense perceptions of childhood. The first half of the last century saw the publication of numerous fully modernist children's books in many countries that make use of objects familiar to children through building sets and educational toys to create stories that do not flinch from the ideological or aesthetic extremes of modernism. A good example of a modernist picture book is the Russian-born artist El Lissitzky's *About Two Red Squares* (1922), a suprematist tale about two squares in six constructions. Lissitzky's short tale, dedicated "[t]o children, to all CHILDREN" (the repeated and capitalized use of "children" elevating the term and including all who retain the capacity to be childlike), uses geometric shapes and flat planes to celebrate revolution and resulting social reforms as symbolized by the appealing red squares, which triumph over the grayness of disorder. Better known in Anglophone countries is Leo Lionni's *Little Blue and Little Yellow* (1959), which uses irregular circles of primary color to create a parable about friendship and tolerance. Both stories have underlying utopian themes, a powerful strand in modernist thought equally evident in Lewis W. Hine's *Men at Work* (1936). This collection of photographs showing muscular men working with machines to create the architectural future also speaks to modernist preoccupations with the healthy body and the heroic nature of workers.

Modernist writing's concern with the nature of writing—the problem of rendering subjective experience on the page—and its engagement with science and technology as forces that are reshaping and destabilizing the world are evident in children's literature from the 1920s onward. Richard Hughes's *The Spider's Palace and Other Stories* (1931), Gertrude Stein's *The World Is Round* (1939), Norton Juster's *The Phantom Toll Booth* (1961), Russell Hoban's *The Mouse and His Child* (1967), and the picture books created from stories extracted from Eugene Ionesco's memoirs (1967, 1970, 1971) are predicated on wordplay that calls into question the tenets of realism—particularly its dependence on chronological linearity. All testify to the vital and enduring relationship between children's literature and modernism. This affinity is rooted in several characteristics of children's literature, especially its tendency to play with language and meaning; its combination of visual and textual elements in illustrated and picture books; and the willingness of children's writers and illustrators to bypass or subvert conventions, not least those associated with the book as an object, paper as a material, and words as a medium.

The visual aspects of children's literature have been a particularly important area of modernist experimentation as they allow precisely the kind of fusion and cross-fertilization of the arts that so interested the early modernists. Colors, graphics, cut-outs, and images work with text to produce what appear to be simple works that nevertheless succeed in conveying complex ideas. For instance, Tove Jansson's *The Book about Moomin, Mymble and Little My* (1952) uses cutouts to bring past, present, and future times (pages) together on a double-page spread, demonstrating the potential for picture books, pop-ups, and movables to explore ways of representing aspects of time and motion on the page. The book's antinaturalistic palette conveys atmosphere and emotions without recourse to language. Illustrations can also organize space, experiment with design, and provide glimpses into internal worlds beyond what is offered by the text. In so doing—especially in combination with elements such as flaps, overlays, and similar devices that break up images—they can disrupt linearity, juxtapose incongruous elements

to inhibit straightforward readings, and offer multiple viewpoints. These devices may function in ways similar to dream sequences, internal monologues, framing narratives, focalization, and other techniques used to render interiority and the fragmented nature of experience in modernist fiction for adults. The combination of words, images, textures, and even scents ("scratch and sniff") and sounds (with accompanying cassettes, CDs, or sounds stored on chips) mean picture books in particular can be highly innovative and synaesthetic, qualities central to modernism.

There is, then, a well-developed if largely unrecognized tradition of modernist children's literature; indeed, arguably modernism itself is a product of children's literature (Dusinberre 1987). As Juliet Dusinberre explains, those in the forefront of literary modernism were also the generation that grew up reading *Alice's Adventures in Wonderland* (1865) and its successors; modernists' concerns with "mastery over language, structure, vision, morals, characters and readers" are based upon their childhood reading. Since the 1990s, critical work on the relationship between children's literature and modernism has tended to follow Dusinberre's lead, demonstrating that far from turning its back on modernism, children's literature has been a fertile area for modernist thinking and experimentation (Boethius 1998; Natov 2003; Reynolds 2007; Westman 2007a). Natov's discussion of Stein's *The World Is Round* concludes, for instance, that it embodies "the aesthetic principles of the modernist hybrid form in an extended children's nursery rhyme and picture book."

In reading such accounts, however, it is important to distinguish between works that are about or draw on childhood and those at least purportedly for children.

Despite recent evidence of the interplay between modernism and writing for children, modernism has not been a highly visible, widely accepted part of publishing for children or the infrastructure around it. As Karin E. Westman (2007a) observes, for the most part "children's literature has not found its way into most conversations about modernism as a literary movement or modernism as a literary period." This silence has much more to do with a failure to recognize the relationship between the two than a lack of interaction or shared history. Often it was assumed that the ideas behind modernism were too demanding for children, though over time this attitude has become outmoded. Appropriately, given that a strong area of conviction in modernist ideology focused on the extent to which mechanical reproduction could bring art to the masses, popular media such as film, television, and graphic novels have helped to accustom even quite young readers to narrative strategies derived from modernism. Writing that employs devices such as mise-en-abyme, chronological fluidity, sophisticated wordplay, metafictive self-consciousness, unreliable or limited focalizers, and stream of consciousness, which would once have been regarded as beyond the comprehension of young readers, is now widely available and readily understood. From the picture books of Jon Scieszka and Lane Smith through the novels of Aidan Chambers, writers and illustrators now make use of modernist elements for readers of every age. At times these cross from pure modernism to postmodernism; for now, it suffices to say that the length and breadth of the relationship between children's literature and modernism is currently being explored more vigorously than ever before. As scholars work to identify who, what, how, and where it has been iterated in publishing for children, there will be yet another change in the cultural meanings attached to this term. This process can be understood as one of rehabilitation; while for early users the term "modernism" was often pejorative, relating to the peculiar, elitist, or meaningless, it is now used to refer to a much more comfortable and familiar body of work and ideas. As the role played by children's writers and illustrators in shaping a modernist aesthetic is documented and developed, the once-challenging associations surrounding modernism will no doubt continue to atrophy.

33

Multicultural

Debra Dudek

The term "multicultural" and its associated "-ism" have been the focus of many debates in literary, educational, political, and sociological circles since the terms were coined. "Multicultural" first appeared in the *New York Herald Tribune* in 1941: "A fervent sermon against nationalism, national prejudice and behavior in favor of a 'multicultural' way of life" (*Oxford English Dictionary* [*OED*]). The second usage, in 1959 by the *New York Times*, both narrows and broadens the definition by connecting a culturally diverse city to cosmopolitanism. In 1965, the adjective "multicultural" expanded into the noun "multiculturalism" in the *Preliminary Report of the Royal Commission on Bilingualism and Biculturalism*: "The answer they often gave was 'multiculturalism' or, more elaborately, 'the Canadian mosaic'" (*OED*). The first three usages of the term "multiculturalism" offered in the *OED* relate to North American society, but the fourth, from a 1973 edition of Scotland's *Stornoway Gazette*, demonstrates the term's potential to migrate into any society in which diversity is of primary importance to its cultural narrative: "A Gaelic Society that has outgrown its original meeting place in just a few short years and enabled the Gaels to meet the new and promising challenge of Multiculturalism." The final two usages represent some of the controversies associated with the term: A 1988 *Courier-Mail* (Brisbane) story cites "Professor Blainey's claim that multi-culturalism is another name for ethnic discrimination," and a 1990 *Marxism Today* article notes that the "policy of multiculturalism . . . has been widely adopted as a more tolerant way forward than full integration into a 'British way of life'."

These quotations allude to and name keywords that intersect with the term "multicultural," predicting and representing tensions that emerge within and around it. "Multicultural" aligns with "nation," "nationalism," "language," "culture," "ethnicity," and "race." While in the first quotation, multicultural exists in opposition to the national, offering heterogeneity as a solution to a homogeneous nation-state, subsequent criticisms connect multicultural ideologies directly to nations and indeed to "national prejudice." These tensions are apparent in multicultural children's literature, which succeeds in varying degrees to represent cultural differences to young readers. In the best cases, such as Shaun Tan's wordless picture book / graphic novel *The Arrival* (2006), readers negotiate a complex, culturally diverse community and may emerge with a stronger understanding of and respect for cultural differences and the effect they have on individual and group identities. At the other end of the spectrum are books that gesture toward an acceptance of cultural difference but reinscribe an ideological position in which one culture has superiority or power over another, as in Michael and Rhonda Gray's *The Stew That Grew* (1990).

However, as David Theo Goldberg (1994) states, "Broadly conceived, multiculturalism is critical of and resistant to the necessarily reductive imperatives of monocultural assimilation." This frequently rehearsed opposition between assimilation and multiculturalism is posited as a linear progression. That is, nations—such as Canada, the United States, and Australia—progress from a racist ideology of assimilation to an ideology of tolerance embodied in a multicultural society. Yet, as Randa Abdel-Fattah (2005b) says, "tolerance" is a dubious objective of a multicultural society: "there is something worse than being demonised, stigmatised, theorised. It's being tolerated."

A rhetoric of tolerance often does not go far enough toward describing and enacting an ethical citizenry based on a deep respect for cultural difference. As Stuart Hall (1996) notes, "Far from being the opposite ends of a pole so that one can trade the rise of one against the decline of the other, . . . both multiculturalism and racism are increasing at one and the same time." Criticizing this dynamic within multicultural societies, Ghassan Hage (1998) cites the picture book *The Stew That Grew* (Gray and Gray 1990) as an example of how "Evil White Nationalists" seek control over national space and over the "ethnic/racial" other.

This existence—and representation—of an ideal multicultural society as one in which people accept cultural differences in each other is one of the most crucial yet fraught tenets of multiculturalism. In his influential "Boutique Multiculturalism, or Why Liberals Are Incapable of Thinking about Hate Speech," Stanley Fish (1997) distinguishes between boutique and strong multiculturalisms and argues that a boutique multiculturalist accepts cultural difference at a surface level of food and festivals and sees such aspects of identity as secondary to a universal humanity, whereas a strong multiculturalist understands cultural differences as central to human identity. Fish goes on to argue that multiculturalism cannot exist because an acceptance of cultural difference at a deep level cannot hold when it is tested at its most extreme, and therefore most important, sites, which include hate speech and female genital mutilation.

While Fish claims that "no one could possibly *be* a multiculturalist in any interesting and coherent sense," his idea of boutique multiculturalism can be fruitfully put to work to analyze whether a text represents only surface versions of an acceptance of cultural difference (McInally 2007, 2008). Food is often an initial way in which child readers see cultural difference represented, with varying degrees of complexity. Rosemary Wells's picture book *Yoko* (1998) tells of a young cat, Yoko, who is teased at school because she eats sushi, which the other children (young animals) find disgusting. To encourage the students to try Yoko's food, the teacher arranges an International Food Day, and asks everyone to "bring in a dish from a foreign country." While Yoko's name and her mother's kimono indicate her Japanese heritage, there is no attempt to represent the richness of her cultural background. Furthermore, the fact that each student makes a dish from a "foreign country" to which they have no cultural belonging suggests that cultural difference can simply be whipped up in the kitchen overnight. In this narrative, food is represented too simplistically as the primary signifier of cultural difference, and the narrative resolves the tensions within multiculturalism too cheerfully.

In contrast, the complexity of Gary Soto and Susan Guevara's *Chato's Kitchen* (1995) draws the reader into a deep engagement with Chato's culture at the levels of language, clothing, art, music, style, and individual and communal taste. Also, although the main culture being represented is Chato the cat's, the reader is privy to the lifestyle of the mice, who have just moved into Chato's neighborhood and whose good friend is a dog. The picture book ends with cats, mice, and dog together eating the food they all prepared, overcoming—yet not erasing—their differences to enjoy a good feast, and encapsulating what Stuart Hall (1996) believes to be one of the most difficult, urgent, and important tasks: "to live with difference without eating the other." The sequel *Chato and the Party Animals* (2000) demonstrates that they have maintained their friendship at a deep level.

Using food and dance strategically, Australian author and illustrator Narelle Oliver's picture book *Dancing the Boom-Cha-Cha Boogie* (2005) could be read either as tokenism or as committed multiculturalism in its metaphoric representation of how three refugees enrich a host culture. The obviously intended reading is to celebrate how a new culture might enhance a host culture, but this enhancement arguably occurs primarily at the level of food, dance, and play—a boutique multiculturalism. Further, the illustration accentuates

the sameness of the two groups, suggesting that multicultural harmony occurs at the expense of the host society's culture. This reading, however, is at odds with the spirit and the politics of the book, which opposes a much-rehearsed rhetoric about the dangers of new cultures negatively changing the "face" of a host culture, and criticizes the Australian federal government's policy of mandatory detention for asylum seekers who arrive without proper documentation.

Oliver's picture book is one of more than a dozen books published in Australia between 2003 and 2006 that advocate against mandatory detention (Dudek 2006b). This engagement with and, often, criticism of government policy may be seen as recurring feature of multicultural children's books, evidenced by a range of books written in response to anti-Muslim sentiment that emerged in the wake of 9/11, such as Rosemary Hayes's *Mixing It* (2007) and Deborah Ellis and Eric Walters's *Bifocal* (2007). The relationship between government policy and the publication of children's books is two-fold. On the one hand, these books may be read as oppositional texts. On the other, government policies of multiculturalism create a ready market for multicultural children's books. School curricula must include books that represent cultural diversity in order to foster an environment that is hospitable to multiculturalism. A number of resources exist to assist educators and parents with selecting suitable books, ranging from individual articles such as Jack Hasegawa's "What Is Fair? Books That Help Children Understand Diversity" (2002); to the comprehensive *PaperTigers* website, selected by the American Library Association as one of its "Great Web Sites"; to monographs designed as references for educators and parents, such as *All for the Children: Multicultural Essentials of Literature* (Finazzo 1997). While some of these resources provide useful and insightful perspectives, many of them promote criteria that offer uncritical, simplistic representations and include texts that "tend to romanticize Aboriginal peoples and their traditional ways of life" (Wolf and DePasquale 2008) and are "emptied of all specific social, cultural, and historical content" (Paul 2000).

Multicultural education grew out of ethnic studies in the late 1960s and early 1970s in America (Schwartz 1995). However, as early as 1938, African American librarian Augusta Baker began listing books that were appropriate for African American children. Following Baker's lead, in 1953, the Jane Addams Book Award recognized books that "most effectively promote peace, social justice, world community, and the equality of the sexes and all races" (Rudman 2006). This effort to call attention to the dearth of children's books that represented African-American characters in positions of power came to the foreground with the publication of Nancy Larrick's oft-quoted and reprinted article, "The All-White World of Children's Books" (1965). Larrick calculated that books with African-American characters accounted for only 6.7 percent of the children's publications issued between 1962 and 1964, and that almost 60 percent of these characters were represented as living outside the continental United States. Since 1970, the Coretta Scott King Awards have been given annually to children's books by American authors and illustrators of African descent.

Similar to Larrick's criticism of books published in America, Karen Sands-O'Connor (2003) finds a tendency to represent racialized characters as originating from outside England in books published in Britain in the 1950s, 1960s, and 1970s. She argues that "fiction for older children and young adults remained steadfastly uniform in their depiction of white characters only," and notes that in Susan Cooper's *Silver on the Tree* (1977) and John Christopher's *Tripods* trilogy (1967–68), "nonwhite people all originate *outside* the borders of England. Citizens of England—and saviours of the planet—are white." Sands-O'Connor posits that since only the mid-1990s has literature for children addressed the idea of Britain as an inclusive multicultural society, even though British cities have been culturally diverse since at least the end of World War II. Ingrid Johnston, Joyce Bainbridge, and Farha Shariff (2007) see a similar yet earlier trend in Canadian children's books, which in the 1970s privileged a Eurocentric perspective, but in the late 1980s and early 1990s began to represent cultural diversity beyond a white mainstream with the publication of Freda Ahenakew's *How the Mouse Got Brown Teeth: A Cree Story for Children* (1988), Paul Yee's *Tales from Gold Mountain* (1989), and Michael Kusugak's *Baseball Bats for Christmas* (1990).

If the mid-1990s saw a rise in the publication of positively inflected multicultural children's books in Britain and Canada, they also may be posited as the beginning of academic criticism of multicultural children's books in North America. It was not until the late 1980s and 1990s that sustained criticisms, analyses, and mappings of multicultural literature and education emerged. Multicultural policy created a market for educational resources, children's literature, and academic publications to aid curriculum development (Schwartz 1995; Carpenter 1996). In North America, these discussions were concerned primarily with multicultural education, and with how children's literature was being used to represent the cultural and racial diversity of Americans and Canadians and to teach children about cultures that were different from their own (Schwartz 1995; Hill 1998).

In the then relatively new field of children's literature research, John Stephens's influential "Advocating Multiculturalism: Migrants in Australian Children's Literature after 1972" (1990) argued that Australian children's literature kept with the Australian educational and political ethos of the 1970s in promoting an acceptance of difference, but did not examine multiculturalism itself. This article opened a conversation about Australian multicultural children's literature, demonstrating how it includes books that represent cultural diversity from Anglo-Celtic Australian perspectives, normalize multiculturalism as an aspect of everyday life, criticize multiculturalism as fractured and characterized by social alienation and dysfunction, represent multiculturalism as "incidental rather than pivotal," and offer a model of reading that reveals how race underpins multiculturalism (McCallum 1997;

Stephens 2000; Pearce 2003; Dudek 2006a; Bradford 2006; Dudek and Ommundsen 2007).

These debates are also concerned with the question Ruth Starke asks in her 1995 article of the same name: "What Is a Multicultural Book?" In her answer, she addresses authorship, authenticity, appropriation, indigeneity, tokenism, and social realism, as well as foregrounding the role that schools and school librarians play in creating demand for books that might serve curriculums and/or award criteria. In other words, some books represent multicultural themes at only a cursory level without engaging with more meaningful ideological tensions. Another criticism aimed at such multicultural children's books is that, in their attempts to reflect cultural diversity in natural, authentic, or truthful ways, they sacrifice art and literariness to social realism (MacCann 2001).

This type of criticism paints too broad of a stroke across multicultural children's books; a number of publishers, authors, and illustrators directly address these concerns, and critics and readers who refuse this binary distinction between literariness and realism include Louise Saldanha (2008) and Perry Nodelman (2008a). Publishers such as Groundwood in Toronto and Lee and Low in New York aim to produce high-quality books that address diversity, and, as the Groundwood website states, to "tell the stories of people whose voices are not always heard." Joseph Kertes and Peter Perko's *The Gift* (1995) examines tensions between Christian and Jews, which are subtly represented as inherent in the experiences of cultural displacement.

Perhaps an even more controversial issue relates to how indigeneity circulates or does not circulate around multiculturalism. Given both the etymology of multiculturalism—which includes the fact that Indigenous peoples in Canada were excluded from the *Preliminary Report of the Royal Commission on Bilingualism and Biculturalism* in a footnote—and the way it has been used in political practice to deal with post–World War II immigration, it is no surprise that, for the most part, Indigenous concerns and multiculturalism exist as separate portfolios. As Starke summarizes, however, the Australian Multicultural Children's Literature Award (AMCL) elides this division: the first award went to Jennifer Inkamala's book *The Rainbow Serpent* (1988), and between 1991 and 1995, Indigenous characters appear in twice as many books as the next most frequently represented group, which Starke defines as "non-specific Asian." Similarly, in the United States and Canada, multicultural book lists include texts by Indigenous writers and about Indigenous issues. In their article "Home and Native Land: A Study of Canadian Aboriginal Picture Books by Aboriginal Authors" (2008), Doris Wolf and Paul DePasquale normalize the inclusion of Aboriginal texts within a multicultural framework when they include the phrase "other multicultural books" alongside their analysis of Aboriginal picture books. Regardless of whether or not texts by Indigenous authors and illustrators—or about relationships between Indigenous and non-Indigenous characters—belong under the umbrella of multicultural children's books, the best of these narratives bring to the foreground issues that are core to discussions about the representation of cultural differences in books for children, while the more problematic texts occur when tourists "fake" their way into someone else's culture (Hade 1997).

Indeed, one of the most serious criticisms of multicultural children's literature is that, until recently, representations of cultural diversity were written and illustrated by white artists. Melina Marchetta's *Looking for Alibrandi* (1992) is considered the first book for young adults in Australia whose author and protagonist are from the same non-Australian culture—in this case Italian. Other Australian examples include Hoa Pham's *Forty-Nine Ghosts* (1998a), *No One Like Me* (1998b), and *Quicksilver* (1998c) and Randa Abdel-Fattah's *Does My Head Look Big in This?* (2005a). In the United States, authors such as Yoshiko Uchida, Walter Dean Myers, Laurence Yep, and Gary Soto are central to an American literary history of multicultural books for children (Bader 2002, 2003a, 2003b), and the Pinkney family are a continued presence in American publishing as creators of African American children's books. In a Canadian context, *Home Words* (Reimer 2008) brings together essays that analyze how notions of belonging and inclusiveness—two words that are key to a vision of ideal multiculturalism—are represented in varying degrees in Canadian children's literature and can be extended to multicultural children's literature more generally.

34

Nature

Peter Hollindale

For the environmentalist and literary critic alike, "nature" has multiple meanings. The zoologist Colin Tudge (2005) observes that "*all* definitions of nature are simply for convenience, helping us to focus on the particular aspect that we happen to be thinking about at the time." Of the General Prologue to Chaucer's *Canterbury Tales* (1387), the literary critic John F. Danby (1961) notes that for Chaucer, the word has three dimensions: Nature is a kind of goddess, the collective force of animate life; it is the material world of organic growth and change; and it is the responsive disposition in the hearts of individual creatures, including humankind—external nature stimulates human nature. In Shakespeare's *King Lear* (1608/1623), however, Nature is (for Lear) the embodiment of Reason as ordained by God, and human nature's task is to act in accordance with a metaphysical absolute: children will love their parents, subjects obey their king. For Edmund, a disobedient and disloyal subject, Nature is instead the urges of ungoverned, self-assertive, individualist human nature, ruled by appetite and will-to-power, and recognizing no constraints.

These early usages feed into subsequent literature, and eventually children's literature. Conceived as a deity, nature may be a kindly dame, an arbitrary, cruel tyrant, or simply not exist. Conceived as the material world, nature can be either a garden or a wilderness, hospitable or inimical to humankind. Conceived as "human nature," it may be rational or bestial, "naturally" inclined to good or evil, or to neither.

The eighteenth century picked its way among these various meanings. It is a crucial period for later writings, since this was the century when ongoing debate about childhood and education first caught fire, and when children's literature emerged fully as a genre. Among the time's many enquiries, two stand out as vital to the treatment of children and the emergence of children's books. One concerned human nature: Was the nature of the human being at birth to be seen as raw material, in need of nurture, education, and socialization, or as an "innate disposition" that would grow most healthily when left to itself? The other concerned external nature: A growth of scientific interest in the natural world immediately stimulated activity in the new genre of children's books, in the form of factual works and stories about animals, the relations between animals and human beings, and the way "dumb creatures" should be treated (Summerfield 1984). Three writers are conspicuously important in this debate: Daniel Defoe, Jean-Jacques Rousseau, and William Wordsworth.

Defoe's *Robinson Crusoe* (1719) was quickly adopted as a children's book, and its huge influence continues to the present day. The boy in Gary Paulsen's *Hatchet* trilogy (1987, 1991, 1996), who survives alone in the Arctic after an aircrash, using whatever he can salvage from the wrecked plane, is a direct descendant of Defoe's shipwrecked sailor and celebrates the same human qualities. But these are not the qualities of un-educated, inborn "nature." Defoe wrote an essay titled "Mere Nature Delineated" (1726) in which he considered the famous case of Peter the Wild Boy of Germany, a celebrated "feral child," and argued, as Michael Seidel (1991) notes, that "nature is not a state that necessarily produces its own progress." Crusoe survives by his ingenuity, his prior knowledge and values, and the products of civilization he retrieves from the wreck. "Mere nature" is not enough.

Although Rousseau in *Émile* (1762) applauded *Robinson Crusoe* as the first book a growing boy should study, his stance is far more radical and his view of original human nature far more optimistic. He argues that children should grow up in accordance with "nature, who does everything for the best," learning from (frequently painful) experience, without interference from the premature harmful influences of civilization. Carried to its logical extreme, this means that every child should be a feral child, although Rousseau knew, of course, that this was impossible. His radical program was lastingly influential. As Hugh Cunningham (1995) notes, "The child-nature link was being forged, with enormous implications for the future of childhood." Its effect was "to mark off childhood as a separate and special world," the most striking evidence being "the development of a special genre of literature for children."

Wordsworth in *The Prelude* (1805, 1850), especially in Books I, II and V, celebrated a childhood of free encounters with nature, which he saw as a teacher and a moral force, in natural and equal harmony with books and reading. Benign and educative, nature for him is that "regulative physical power" which is the "cause of all phenomena" (*Oxford English Dictionary* [*OED*]), or, in his own words, "Nature's self . . . is the breath of God."

Among the *OED*'s extensive definitions of "nature," several stand out as covering this range of meanings, and as early as the end of the eighteenth century children's literature—in the person of the influential Sarah Trimmer—illustrates the scope for irreconcilable quarrels between them. The *OED* gives as one definition, "The material world, or its collective objects and phenomena, especially those with which man is most directly in contact; frequently the features and products of the earth itself, as contrasted with those of human civilization." Trimmer's *Fabulous Histories. Designed for the Instruction of Children, Respecting Their Treatment of Animals* (1786, later known as *The Robins*), is largely compatible with this definition. It firmly places human life above the animals, distinguishes domesticated and familiar creatures from the wild, and is designed, she says, to "excite compassion and tenderness for those interesting and delightful creatures, on which such wanton cruelties are frequently inflicted." Her book is an ancestor of the "nature study" familiar to more recent generations of children.

However, a second *OED* definition of nature as "[t]he creative and regulative physical power which is conceived of as operating in the material world and as the immediate cause of all its phenomena" is a different matter. In modern times this power may be variously titled God, Mother Nature, Gaia, or Evolution, according to belief. But in her periodical *The Guardian of Education*, Trimmer, a conservative evangelical, had already detected the perils of such liberal definition, and attacked books for the young that "lead the minds of children into the idea that all things come by chance, and that there is no *God* but *Nature*" (Trimmer 1802).

Two further definitions given by the *OED* are also significant for children's books. Nature is "the inherent and inseparable combinations of properties essentially pertaining to anything and giving it its fundamental character," and it is the "inherent and innate disposition or character of a person (or animal)" or (with less implicit fixity) "a thing, or person of a particular quality or character." Janni Howker's story *The Nature of the Beast* (1985) effectively plays on these definitions, its title referring interchangeably to the capitalist industrial economy, an escaped leopard, and the character of a disaffected adolescent boy.

These varied definitions feed directly into children's literature, including works in which the word itself is virtually omitted. The children's classics *Bevis* by Richard Jefferies (1882) and *The Secret Garden* by Frances Hodgson Burnett (1911) include Wordsworthian experiences of mystical bonding between child and nature, and both works recruit "Magic" as the term for nature's power. They also celebrate independent, secret, and unsupervised play in natural settings, seen as fostering health and self-reliance. Kenneth Grahame's *The Wind in the Willows* (1908) similarly includes a mystical invocation of Nature as goddess, but also contrasts a dangerous world of "Nature in the rough" with a gentler riverside pastoral: nature is both wilderness and garden.

The coming together of nature as science and as children's literature and art moves forward again with Beatrix Potter. Linda Lear's admirable biography of Potter is aptly subtitled *A Life in Nature* (2007) and quotes Potter as remarking, Wordsworth-like, "I have always found my own pleasure in nature and books." Potter was a distinguished mycologist, and in her "little books" for children she combined witty anthropomorphism with meticulous observation of wild creatures. No one has worked with equal finesse on the ill-defined border between human and nonhuman nature.

Nature as "innate disposition" or "particular character" (not synonymous phrases) has a similar active development in children's literature. Charles Dickens in *Great Expectations* (1861) presents a definitive exchange between Pip and Estella. When Estella declares her inability to feel or understand love, Pip remonstrates, "Surely it is not in Nature." Estella replies, "'It is in *my* nature' . . . And then she added, with a stress upon the words, 'It is in the nature formed within me.'" In two sentences are invoked Nature as a general and essential human quality, as a particular innate disposition, and as the product of experience. A comparable trio of meanings appears in Louisa May Alcott's *Little Women* (1868–69). The dying Beth is represented as unchangeable ("nothing could change the sweet, unselfish nature"), Jo as volatile and mobile ("she just acted out her nature . . . as the mood suggested"), while the March family sustains a benign, encompassing view of general human nature such as that appealed to by Pip. In both texts, and in many others, several usages compete and interplay.

This repertoire of established definitions is now under stress because human overpopulation and technology, together with resultant climate change, have transformed the relationship between humankind and the natural world. The environmentalist Bill McKibben (1990) has argued that "nature" in the traditional sense (a biodiverse world independent of human beings) no longer exists, because no life-forms or natural phenomena are now uninfluenced by people. Everything that happens is "the awesome power of Mother Nature as it has been altered by the awesome power of man." This radical perception is reflected strongly in numerous dystopian novels for children (many of which take the form of bleak, futuristic Robinsonades). Perhaps the most powerful of these is Peter Dickinson's *Eva* (1988), which depicts a world in which nearly all nonhuman life is either captive or extinct and human overpopulation is rampant. At the end, the human race itself develops a self-corrective suicidal urge, which a scientist ascribes to "old Dame Nature who we keep forgetting we're children of cutting the population back to a sane kind of size." *Eva* is set many years in the future, but the growing urgency of recent debate about climate change is now generating dystopias set in the very near future. In Saci Lloyd's *The Carbon Diaries 2015* (2008),

the weather, physical environment, and human nature are overwhelmed by sudden consequences of man-made global warming, taking place far earlier than predicted.

Whatever the future, there is little doubt that "nature," both human and environmental, is now forcibly acquiring new meanings, calling for critical address as they permeate literature for children.

35

Nonsense

Michael Heyman and Kevin Shortsleeve

In his introduction to *The Chatto Book of Nonsense*, Hugh Haughton (1988) comments that "nonsense is a bit of a problem." Haughton is alluding to a set of semantic and literary "difficulties" that have surrounded "nonsense" since the term came into common usage in the seventeenth century. At first the word was used mostly in its literal sense, meaning that which makes no sense, or that which is useless, but a new meaning emerged over the next two hundred years, referring to a particular literary phenomenon. The interactions between these senses of the word are at the heart of some of the difficulties we face with the term "nonsense."

What today we classify as literary nonsense has an ancestral connection to medieval carnivalesque traditions—material that Mikhail Bakhtin (1968) examines in *Rabelais and His World.* Bakhtin describes a genre of "absurd compositions" that revel in "linguistic freedom," illogical sequences, and the "inside out." Bakhtin would categorize this material as the "grotesque." According to the *Oxford English Dictionary* (*OED*), the earliest usage of the word "grotesque," dating from the sixteenth century, refers to a painting that is "rugged" or "unpolished." In the seventeenth century the term was used as an adjective meaning that which is distorted, irregular, fantastically extravagant, or bizarre. In this same period the word "grotesque" was used to describe literary works that were considered "quaint" or "immaterial." By the eighteenth century the term also meant that which is ludicrous or "fantastically absurd," and by 1822 the term was used to describe a person who was "very amusing."

Thus, when literary nonsense was popularized in Victorian England, it was frequently associated with the term "grotesque." In 1868, when Lewis Carroll was casting about for illustrators for *Through the Looking Glass*, W. S. Gilbert came to mind, because, as Carroll wrote, "his power in grotesque is extraordinary" (quoted in Stedman 1996). In 1926 Emile Cammaerts, in *The Poetry of Nonsense*, uses the term "grotesque" almost interchangeably with the word "nonsense" to describe that which is rough, childlike, sketchy, or exaggerated.

Bakhtin's study in the grotesque suggests that in the eighteenth and nineteenth centuries a splintering occurred in the meaning of the term "grotesque," with one version, an ascendant gothic vision, referring to that which is horrifying or disgusting, and the other, to that which is merely joyful and gay. Critical and lay visions of what we now label "nonsense" can be split along similar lines. By its association with the word "grotesque," the term "nonsense" is understood to mean something unnatural, distorted, bizarre, ludicrous, or fantastically absurd; at the same time, it is understood as amusing, quaint, immaterial—a place for simple, joyful fun.

In the early- to mid-seventeenth century, as Noel Malcolm (1998) illustrates in *The Origins of English Nonsense*, there was a fashion to produce what today we can retrospectively identify as "literary nonsense"— poems such as John Taylor's "Sir Gregory Nonsense His Newes from No Place" (1622), or "Mercurius Nonsensicus" (1648). Yet the poets of the time were just as likely to use other terms to classify their works, such as John Hoskyns's "Cabalistical Verses" (1611), or Taylor's "Poem in the Utopian Tongue" (1630). Seventeenth-century anthologies of light verse would include some nonsense pieces, yet the volumes were often labeled "drolleries" and made no distinction between nonsense and other humorous pieces.

In this period the word "nonsense" was predominantly used in the literal sense of the first *OED* definition: "that which is not sense; spoken or written words which make no sense or convey absurd ideas." While the concept of absurdity complicates the issue, this definition emphasizes the "non" in "nonsense"— meaning that nonsense must be that which has no sense at all, or which is contrary to sense. This was and is the common meaning of the word, but it sometimes acquired the additional meaning of "unsubstantial or worthless stuff or things" (*OED*).

Because the word "nonsense" sometimes meant "worthless," the term was used dismissively in literary circles as the ultimate critical put-down (Haughton 1988). A critic would use the word "nonsense" to describe a piece of writing as useless or entirely without redeeming qualities. This unfortunate semantic connotation, combined with the fact that nonsense poems usually make a great deal of sense, suggests that, as a genre, "literary nonsense" is poorly named. (Nonsense literature, then, might better be described with an original portmanteau phrase, a phrase freed from the semantic shackles of its overly negative cousin-meanings. We would suggest "literwordsy absurdifusion." Really.)

The transformation of the term "nonsense" from these simple negatives to a descriptor of a specific kind of artistic creation for adults and children occurred slowly over a two-hundred-year period. While nursery rhyme publishers of the mid- and late eighteenth century such as John Newbery used the word "nonsense" to advertise their publications, the first two *OED* quotation entries for the phrase "nonsense verses" occur in 1799 and 1819. The first comes from the text *Public Characters*: "Although few *men* in England could equal him in writing *sense* prose, yet many *boys* might surpass him in writing *nonsense* verses." John Keats, in an 1819 letter, used the phrase similarly. Even though in both cases "nonsense" had made the leap to being attached to "verse," it still denoted an inconsequential, lesser art form. Both the 1799 and 1819 examples also seem to have shifted the word from representing what was once the sophisticated, adult parodic nonsense of the seventeenth century, to a child's creation, a move that parallels the development of new conceptions of childhood that had been emerging throughout the eighteenth and early nineteenth centuries. In this association with children, nonsense aligns itself with another troubled term, "innocence."

It can be claimed that the vision of the "innocent" child was created in part in relation to nonsense literature. John Morgenstern (2001) throws doubt on the popular notion that the emerging vision of the "innocent" child gave birth to the children's book industry in the eighteenth century. Instead, Morgenstern argues, the children's book industry gave rise to the idea of the innocent child. With the spread of literacy in the late seventeenth and early eighteenth centuries, Morgenstern posits, there grew a larger population of adults seeking more sophisticated texts; thus, the novel arose. Children's literature, he says, is defined by the "gap" in complexity between adult and children's texts. In this development, children were not simply cast as "other" but specifically as "pre-literate." This new "species," if you will, required "special" texts for pre-literate people. But consider what it might mean to be cast as pre-literate in the dawning days of the British Empire. Morgenstern asserts that there is an "intimate connection" between children's literature popular in the eighteenth century "and some lost, 'original' oral culture." As Jean-Jacques Rousseau (1762) claimed, to be "pre-literate" was to be like the noble savage, to be pure and Edenic—and thus, one may assume, children were associated with texts from pre-literate societies. Newbery's success, then, came from responding to and creating the vision of the pre-literate child with texts from oral traditions, including folklore, fairy tales, country rhymes—and nonsense. Thus a semantic connection between innocence and nonsense was established (Shortsleeve 2007). This connection has led to trouble in how nonsense literature is perceived and discussed. Just as we

routinely underestimate the resilience, independence, rebelliousness, and sexuality of a supposedly "innocent" child, it is argued that critics correspondingly underestimate the complex nature of nonsense literature (Shortsleeve 2007). Edward Lear biographer Vivien Noakes (2001) denies any provocative qualities to Lear's nonsense and describes his works instead as a haven of "safety and imagination." Nonsense, imagination, and innocence thus come tumbling together in a semantic muddle.

The most influential step in the evolution of the term "nonsense" came when Edward Lear featured it prominently in the titles of his books: *A Book of Nonsense* (1846); *Nonsense Songs, Stories, Botany and Alphabets* (1871), *More Nonsense, Pictures, Rhymes, Botany, etc.* (1872), and *Laughable Lyrics: A Fourth Book of Nonsense Poems, Songs, Botany, Music, etc.* (1877). However, while his work further redefined "nonsense" in terms of audience and genre, the transition was paradoxical, as his use of the term worked in opposing ways: while he maintained its literal, pejorative definition and its association with children, he simultaneously refocused its meaning to designate the products of his own style of approach to literary and artistic creation. Most significantly, in the introduction to his third volume, *More Nonsense, Pictures, Rhymes, Botany, etc.* (1872) he published a defense:

> [I]n no portion of these Nonsense drawings have I ever allowed any caricature of private or public persons to appear, and throughout, more care than might be supposed has been given to make

the subjects incapable of misinterpretation: "Nonsense," pure and absolute, having been my aim throughout.

Lear's claim, along with similar statements by the other master of nonsense, Lewis Carroll, swayed many to accept the idea that nonsense had no meaning, no politics, no context, and therefore no *consequence*—an art of pristine nonsensical purity. The condition of nonsense being "pure and absolute" became for many critics and authors an integral part of the genre's definition and a further seed of its later diminution.

From Lear's first volume in 1846, *The Book of Nonsense*, to his final publication in 1877 the descriptor had shifted from "nonsense" to "nonsense rhymes" to "nonsense poems," an indication of its elevation from the lowest level of literary output—nonsense in its literal meaning—to the highest, poetry. In 1888 Edward Strachey noted this trend, proclaiming, "The late Mr. Edward Lear was the creator of a new and important kind of that Nonsense for the honors of which the pen and the pencil contend; and at the same time he fixed the name of Nonsense to the Art." In 1925 Cammaerts suggests that, despite Lear's apparent "humble disparagement" of his own works, his progressive use of the word implies "a very different meaning . . . something else, something which is rather difficult to explain."

While the late-nineteenth-century critics and reviewers were clearing the way for more intense work on literary nonsense, the public, hungry for nonsense but unable to articulate what exactly it was, reveled in certain misunderstandings on its nature. Starting in the 1860s, Lear's books sparked limerick contests (Baring-Gould and Hart-Davis 1969), but the texts submitted were almost always of the modern limerick form rather than of the kind made famous by Lear. These modern limericks were really stylized jokes, complete with a witty punch line, while it has since been established that the defining features of nonsense limericks are an absurd circularity and linguistic, graphic, and logical tension, rather than wit and ingenuity of rhyme. To the uninitiated, or those who might take the *OED* to heart, there is a tendency to assume that fantasy, riddles, and light verse are nonsense. Yet even by the widest possible definition, merely as forms, they are not. Even today, editors, authors, and critics continue to misrepresent nonsense in so-called "nonsense anthologies." Collections such as William Jay Smith's *Laughing Time: Collected Nonsense* (1990), which includes the poem "Round or Square / Or tall or flat / People love / To wear a hat," and Carolyn Wells's *Nonsense Anthology* (1902), which includes Alfred Lord Tennyson's "Minnie and Winnie," offer examples of nonsense being confused with other forms.

In the post-Lear period critics have not been able to agree on how to classify nonsense as a literary and cultural creation. They have called it a genre, a mode, a device, a cluster-concept, and a quality. The genre approach is the most commonly used, though the term "genre" was not applied in regard to nonsense until the 1950s (Tigges 1988). Critical discussions that broach the topic suggest subcategories such as "literary" nonsense and "folk" nonsense (Heyman, Satpathy, and

Ravishankar 2007). Some attempt to describe a canon supposedly composed of "pure" nonsense; in Tigges's forty-eight-page chapter "What Nonsense Is Not," nursery rhymes find themselves excluded from the nonsense canon, while Elizabeth Sewell (1952) drops from the canon certain poems by Lear and Carroll that she finds too emotional. Inevitably, the aggregate of nonsense definitions proves too exclusive to include the vast variety of nonsense and nonsensical texts. This is the situation today. As Strachey remarked in 1894, echoing Saint Augustine when asked about the definition of time, "What is Nonsense? I know when you do not ask me" (Lear 1894).

36
Picture Book
William Moebius

No keyword in children's literature could be quite as fluid in its application as the one word "picturebook" or the two-word "picture book." The cultural medium to which this locution refers is itself quite malleable and can be stretched to include: nonprint pictorial media for children or adults on the internet; picture-book "format" or, following the German cognate, *Bilderbuch*, "a type of visual encyclopedia"; humorous simulacra for adults such as the recent *Goodnight Bush* (Origen and Golan 2008); or the once risqué *Home Sweet Zoo* (Barnes 1950). Or it can simply be a book with pictures in it; Henry James in 1900 called his illustrated travel book *A Little Tour in France* a "picture-book," a hyphenated form recognized by the *Oxford English Dictionary* (*OED*), and defined as "a book consisting wholly or partly of pictures, esp. for children."

Linking the words "picture" and "book," after *Bilderbuch*, some academic specialists (e.g., Bader 1976; Nikolajeva and Scott 2000; Moebius 1986) have attempted to zero in on a particular configuration or historical modality of books for children in which pictures and words together are treated as semi-autonomous and mutually attractive chains of meaning, rather than as fixed images serving as a supplement to meanings fixed in words. This particular configuration emerges with the advent of cinema and the comic book, and may have ties with theater, opera, vaudeville, and dance. While this working hypothesis has gained adherents, those who retain the separation of "picture" and "book" in a collocation (hyphenated or not)—still recognized by the *OED* and print media such as the *New York Times* and the *New Yorker*, as well as critics like David Lewis (2001) and a host of librarians—may well have the history of the book itself in mind. One reason to keep the two words separate is to retain traces of that history of the "book" as one that, at least in Europe, while favoring the written word, seems to foster images in the margins, at the incipits of verses, and intermingled with text. This practice diversifies the reader's experience, as a stimulus and call to reading, and enhances the reader's memory, as has been noted by philosopher Paul Ricoeur (2004), and by medievalists such as Carruthers and Ziolkowski (2002).

What, as part of print media, is to be called a "picture book" or "picturebook" depends very much on a particular reader's memories, expectations and affinities; an artist/writer's intentions and historical moment; the marketing strategies of book editors and publishers; and the trade or academic connections of book critics, librarians, or children's literature specialists. As a keyword, "picture book" is a loaded gun, especially once it has gone from being an artifact of childhood (evoked by the French locution *album de jeunesse,* as something of a memory book long out of print) to a staple of print culture, mass marketing, and official scrutiny, a sustainable commodity ratified by national media and local teachers and librarians as well as parents. In this respect, the picture book becomes malleable in a different way. If it is *Little Black Sambo* (Bannerman 1899)*, Curious George* (Rey 1941), or *Heather Has Two Mommies* (Newman 1989), if its stereotypes and caricatures are perceived to cast a shadow on a particular population or demographic, it may cease to own its place in the world of the picture book and become an instant cultural artifact available only to historians and specialists in children's culture. Despite the vulnerability of such texts, the picture book has proven to be more resilient and fungible than the comic book, itself a kind of "picture book." Although comics have influenced picture books (notably Maurice Sendak's *In the Night Kitchen* [1970] or Raymond Briggs's *Snowman* [1978]), the comic book until recently has been deemed to be in a register unworthy of the American Library Association or the professional organizations of educators and critics, and, as McCloud (1993) once pictured it, confined to the lower regions, while the picture book hovered on the wings of cherubs.

Such medieval theodicy aside, the picture book may be seen as a descendant of the European propaganda wars that paradoxically attached the Counter-Reformation spirit of the Baroque, as French critic Jean Perrot (1991) has documented so well, and its pictorial turn to the ardent advocacies of literacy that followed the spirit of the Reformation, notably in the compendious proto–children's picture book of Jan Amos Comenius, *Orbis Sensualium Pictus* (1658). The hieroglyphic turn of the pre-seventeenth-century alchemy book or grimoire (cognate with grammar) may also anticipate the rebus and alphabet books for children of later centuries. Whether in the service of nation, culture, or religion, the picture book has tended, no matter where it has emerged as a medium for children, to be identified with public decency and right-thinking, even if the message, as in a Dr. Seuss book, seemed to be subversive. But in France and Belgium what in the United States would be called a kind of comics has enjoyed no such stigma; whether as *Bécassine*, *Astérix*, *Suske en Wuske*, *Tintin* or *Lucky Luc,* the *bande dessinée* has shared respectability in the public sphere since the 1900s with what in Anglophone countries is called the picture book.

In the United States this defining of the picture book as a public asset, requiring a certain regulation by educational authorities, heralds also the public influence of female voices rather than those of men. Led by librarian Anne Carroll Moore, this establishment would frown on comics, to which, nonetheless, young male readers such as John Updike and W. T. J. Mitchell would gravitate, whether as Disney comics or *Mad Magazine*. In coming to terms with the picture book in its historical evolution in the United States, it is important not to overlook the gendered face of the educational institutions that once granted the picture book most favorable status. Barbara Bader's definition of the picture book in 1976 is still the most comprehensive, making room for the child reader's experience while acknowledging the book's physicality ("an item of manufacture"), exchange ("a commercial product"), and historic value ("a social, cultural, historical

document"). Her definition is also still worthy of qualification and extension, particularly when one addresses the picture book as an "experience for a child" with its "interdependence of pictures and words," and "the simultaneous display of two facing pages."

There are two prevailing views in the critical literature of what this experience means to be. On the one hand, it is seen as one of "the drama of the turning of the page," and thus conducive to notions of theatricality, dynamism, performance, presentational process, staging, miniaturism, ritual, choreography, carnival, and the allure of advertising, in which the play of the body in motion is key. Such a view may be found in Bader's own treatment, but also in Moebius (forthcoming), Reinbert Tabbert (1999), Maria Nikolajeva and Carole Scott (2000), Catherine Renaud (2007), and Sophie van der Linden (2000). On the other hand, some readers and producers of picture books, led by Jane Doonan, Molly Bang, and, paradoxically, Quentin Blake, see the picture book as a site for "absorption." For this school, the turning of the page is not as urgent as the lingering on the single image on each page, plumbing its depths, understanding its multiple dimensions and messages, interrogating the feelings of its characters. While one school seems to favor the exciting possibilities of montage, the jump cut, the close-up, the panorama, the other favors a respect for color, shape, texture, and artistic medium as sufficient rewards for the picture "beholder," a word Doonan (1993) chooses over "reader." Certain picture books—those of Allen Say, Mitsumasa Anno, Jane Birkert, or Molly

Bang herself, for example—would appear to meet the absorption/contemplation test. Recent picture books by Quentin Blake (1995, 2001) highlight the significance of the traditional tableau or easel art as something worth pondering. Other picture books, such as those of Dr. Seuss, William Steig, Posey Simmonds, or Tomi de Paola, lend themselves to a comedic response for which turning the page is an indispensable part of the book's success. It is not necessary to choose sides in this case (the paradigm for which may be found in art historian Michael Fried's *Absorption and Theatricality: Painting and Beholder in the Age of Diderot* [1980]), but to take the picture book's aesthetic as a guide to its own best reading and to acknowledge the tension described by Lawrence R. Sipe (1998): "There is thus a tension between our impulse to gaze at the pictures—to forget about time in creating an 'atemporal structure'—and to not interrupt the temporal narrative flow. The verbal text drives us to read on in a linear way, where the illustrations seduce us into stopping to look." As a subtext in this contest, the rivalry of the museum school and the commercial art academy plays itself out.

Picture books do not arise *ex nihilo* out of a picture-book generator; they draw on thousands of years of human visual representation, filtered through the creative facilities of the adult imagination of a picture-book maker—or makers. In picture book discourse, authorship is often a collaboration between word-maker and image-maker. In such a collaboration, how does one assign credit? In questions of authorship of Broadway showtunes, it is usually the composer (George, not

Ira, Gershwin; Hoagy Carmichael, not Sydney Arodin) who earns the credit. Until recently, the author of the verbal text was deemed to hold chief responsibility for the picture book, while the image-maker was viewed as secondary.

Another complex issue related to picture book discourse is derived from the presumption of adult authorship and the recognition that the picture book experience is "constructed," the result of multiple acts of representation that cannot be credited to the mind of a child. The suggestion of what has been called "cross-writing" is an inevitable consequence, especially since adults usually judge which books get published, reviewed, or bought. However "constructed," a picture book in circulation for more than one generation may also come to be revered as a site of memory, despite invidious stereotypes, power relations, or questionable representations of violence (e.g., Wilhelm Busch's *Max und Moritz* [1865]).

An abiding faith in linearity in the guise of sequential narrative may lead some critics to assume that a picture book, in order to mobilize the reader, must adhere to a narrative logic, and that the picture book is therefore subject to linear models of narrativity. However, a given picture book may not be beholden to any narrative logic but rather to processes associated with poetry, rhetoric, and choreography, such as repetition, alternation, augmentation, and diminution. It is not uncommon in the picture book world to bump up against the non sequitur, the "good night nothing" of Clement Hurd and Margaret Wise Brown's *Goodnight*

Moon (1947), or the provocative juxtapositions of Chris Van Allsburg's *The Mysteries of Harris Burdick* (1984). The critical question here is whether such representational gambits mimic child behavior and thought for adult amusement (the child as ignorant savage) or engage in and address the cognitive uncertainties of the child as a thoughtful future survivor of childhood.

Critical vocabularies for the picture-book experience are now fairly well established, but some debate remains in respect to the application of critical analogies to other practices, whether hermeneutics, music, or translation. While some critics (Nikolajeva and Scott 2000; Moebius [forthcoming]) find these critical analogies useful and edifying, others, like Lewis, find them anathema. Is a picture in a picture book an "interpretation," or an illustration, or a silencing of a few words? Is the interplay of pictures and words a kind of "counterpoint" (Nikolajeva and Scott 2000), or is it best described as a kind of "ecology" (Lewis 2001)? What is the role of culturally specific images and verbal formulations in the translation of the picture book? The epistemology of the picture book is still being written, but it is clear that the verbal text alone will not suffice, and the term "iconotext" may eventually take its place in common parlance.

In this regard, the picture book may be best viewed as an experiment for the child and even for an adult student of literature. Picture books such as those of Arnold Lobel or Peter Catalanotto may serve as testing grounds for thought about the world. Philosopher Gareth Mathews has shed light on the potential of the picture book in this regard, and his work has been seconded through applications in public schools. The uses of the picture book—be they psychotherapeutic, sedative, role modeling (gender), mathematical skill-building, or as memory books for geography, cultural heritage, or history—are, to echo Barbara Bader, limitless.

37

Popular

Julie A. S. Cassidy

While the definition of the term "popular" has remained relatively unchanged for over four hundred years, its connotation certainly takes on new meaning when applied to children's literature. In *Keywords*, Raymond Williams (1983a) reports that the term "popular" was "originally a legal and political term" that first came into the English language in the late fifteenth century. Within the domain of the legal system, an "action popular" was any suit that was open to or brought forth by anyone who was part of the general public. According to the *Oxford English Dictionary* (*OED*), in the early sixteenth century the term "popular" defined the "common people" or people of "lowly birth" as opposed to people of the aristocracy. By the late sixteenth century (the *OED* cites 1599), the intention behind the word shifted slightly to invite negative similes such as low, vulgar, and plebeian. Nine short years later, in 1608, "popular" appeared for the first time as a positive attribute indicating that a subject was a favorite, acceptable, and pleasing to numerous people. The change from a pejorative to a complementary connotation reflected the beginning of the "common" people's effect on culture. Well into the twentieth century, the term "popular" continued to contain these diametrically opposed negative and positive connotations, particularly when describing texts created for and read by children.

As early as the 1920s in the United States, the term "popular" was held in direct opposition to the term "literature" in the children's book world because the former indicated "not only those creations of expressive culture that actually had a large audience" but also "those that had questionable artistic merit" (Levine 1988). At the same time, "literature" signified a masterpiece that inherently contained a high degree of worth and value. In this regard, the term "literature" maintained an attachment to its definition as "polite or humane learning," which the *OED* deemed "rare and obsolete" by the late 1800s. In *Literary Theory* (2000), Jonathan Culler further emphasizes that "literature is "an institutional label that gives us [the readers] reason to expect that the results of our reading efforts will be 'worth it.'" According to these standards, a mass-produced, popular text must have "questionable artistic merit" by the very definition of its consumer-driven nature, and therefore cannot simultaneously contain literary merit or be labeled as "literature." Beginning in the 1920s and persisting for decades, the rift between these two ideologies fueled a debate among public school teachers and librarians over what types of texts children in the United States should be reading.

In 1916, Lucy Sprague Mitchell indirectly challenged the standards librarians placed on children's literature by establishing the Bank Street College of Education in New York City (originally named the Bureau of Educational Experiments before its move to Bank Street). Mitchell promoted experimenting with and adopting new educational techniques. She also encouraged authors to test the popularity of new books on the students who attended Bank Street's School for Children before they were published (Bank Street School for Children 2006). Rather than base their teaching materials solely on the educational value of the "classics" of children's literature, teachers emerging from the Bank Street College understood that a popular children's text could also trigger the imagination and intelligence of a child. In challenging the standards by which librarians judged texts for children, public school teachers also brought into question the librarians' larger ownership of children's literature.

In contrast, librarians championed the merits of "literature" over "popular" children's texts. Due to a secondary, audience-based divide between books for adults and books for children, librarians in the early twentieth century had only recently become the cultural gatekeepers of children's literature. Unfortunately, this division of reading audiences further diminished the importance of texts for children by categorizing all books read by children as "kiddie lit." (Often books enjoyed by women were also forced into this same category in order to indicate their perceived lack of literary merit.) Prior to this division, a book's movement between child and adult audiences was rarely questioned. According to Beverly Lyon Clark in *Kiddie Lit: The Cultural Construction of Children's Literature in America* (2003), "[C]hildren and childhood were less segregated from adults and adulthood in the nineteenth century, before the split between high culture

and low, before literary authority shifted from genteel editors to the professoriate [*sic*]." By the early twentieth century, as "gatekeeping shifted from literary journals to the academy," this split forced children's literature out of the hands of "genteel editors" and into the hands of librarians, since "academics ignored it" (Clark 2003). This shift placed librarians in a position to dictate which children's texts contained the proper amount of moral fiber and artistry to be deemed literature worth reading. Thus, while librarians fought for the importance of literature over popular texts, they also struggled against the pejorative connotation of the term "kiddie lit" (a controversy people in the field of children's literature still face).

During this time, the United States witnessed a proliferation of popular series books such as Dick and Jane, the Bobbsey Twins, Betty Gordon, the Blythe Girls, Nancy Drew, Tom Swift, Perry Pierce, the Hardy Boys, and the Riddle Club. The Stratemeyer Syndicate produced many of these series books; if not, other publishers followed the Syndicate's example by hiring ghostwriters who could churn out multiple texts under a pseudonym. According to Leonard Marcus's *Golden Legacy* (2007), the 1920s clash between traditional librarians and progressive educators deepened into the 1940s as librarians regarded "all juvenile fiction published in series form" with "deep suspicion." Most (but not all) librarians in the early twentieth century disapproved of these popular texts because the dominant discourse among librarians dictated that an inexpensive, highly popular children's text could not possibly contain high-quality literature or artistry. Librarians feared that the consumption of popular children's texts would diminish a child's moral fiber and social consciousness. Thus, on a certain level "popular" became synonymous with "lowbrow."

At the turn of the twentieth century, a basic social assumption that cultivation and class could be achieved through literature complicated the debate surrounding the merit of popular children's texts. The growth of a middlebrow culture blurred the simplistically defined, either/or parameters of highbrow and lowbrow culture as the people in a growing middle and working class strove for self-improvement regardless of their class status and educational background. In response to the desire for self-improvement, book distribution was largely based on the conclusion that culture "could be acquired" through the process of "reading certain books and avoiding others" (Rubin 1992). For example, John Steinbeck's *Of Mice and Men* was first circulated in 1937 through the Book of the Month Club. Since then, the literary status of Steinbeck's novel has transformed from that of a new book through which adults could acquire culture to a "classic" piece of literature for children, thereby avoiding the negative connotations of the term "popular." Quite commonly, texts that move from an adult to a child reading audience are labeled as "classic" while texts that crossover in the opposite direction are designated as "popular."

Currently within American children's literature and culture, "popular" connotes a widespread appreciation for and love of the object itself when appended to a text, object, or person. Yet, the same question still resonates: Can a popular children's text also contain literary merit? Children's and young adult authors are deemed "popular" when the general public shows great admiration for them and their work. This question has faced numerous greatly admired, commercially successful authors, including Dr. Seuss, Judy Blume, J. K. Rowling, and Shel Silverstein. Popular texts, movies, toys, and the like can prove their popularity through sales figures. In 2000 Janette Sebring Lowrey's Little Golden Book *The Poky Little Puppy* (1942) was ranked the number one selling hardback book on the *Publishers Weekly* "All-Time Best-Selling Children's Books" list ("All-Time" 2006). The top ten slots on this list included three additional Little Golden Books: at #3 is *Tootle* (1945) by Gertrude Crampton, at #7 is *Saggy Baggy Elephant* (1947) by Kathryn and Byron Jackson, and at #8 is *Scuffy the Tugboat* (1946) also by Crampton. Furthermore, *Harry Potter and the Goblet of Fire* (2000) ranked at #5 and *Harry Potter and the Chamber of Secrets* (1998) claimed #10 on this same list. In June 2008, the final book in Rowling's wildly celebrated Harry Potter series, *Harry Potter and the Deathly Hallows* (2007), had reportedly sold over 15 million copies within its first twenty-four hours on the market in the United States (Forbes.com 2008). As a result of their sudden and continued popularity, the literary merit of books like Harry Potter or the Little Golden Books remain in question.

If online dictionaries offer any gauge of contemporary use, then the term "popular" has largely been freed of its negative connotations with definitions like "regarded with favor, approval, or affection by people in general" or "widely liked or appreciated." At face value, the term indicates that a person's work is worth reading or that a text is worth buying because it is loved and embraced by the general public. Yet, describing an author or a text as simply "popular" still brings into question the literary merit of the work. Here, the term becomes a conflicted selling point. Do authors sacrifice some of their own literary reputation if their books are marketed as popular? Can a book ranked highly on a best seller's list also be a "good" book of literary merit? What makes a children's book an instant classic as opposed to a marketing success? The establishment of both cultural studies and children's literature as legitimate fields of inquiry has created a space for academic dialogue about topics that are "popular" in American culture but have "questionable artistic merit" in the eyes of the critics (Levine 1988). Moreover, the exploration of consumer culture has opened the door for projects that recognize mass-marketed children's books as a significant part of American culture and children's "literature," not in spite of, but certainly because of, the books' widely popular appeal.

38

Postcolonial

Clare Bradford

The word "postcolonial" refers (1) to a period or state following (that is, "post") colonialism, and (2) to the effects of colonization upon cultures, peoples, places, and textuality. The terms most often associated with "postcolonial" are "imperialism," which denotes the formation of an empire, and "colonialism," which refers to the establishment of colonies by an imperial power that maintains control over them. The first usage of "postcolonial" (or "post-colonial") identified in the *Oxford English Dictionary* (*OED*) occurs in 1883 in the *Century Illustrated Monthly Magazine* (White 1883), where it denotes "occurring or existing after the end of colonial rule." This association of the word with practices whereby history is divided into distinct periods (periodization) is sustained well into the twentieth century; for instance, the *OED* cites the following quotation from Gavin Black's *The Golden Cockatrice* in 1975: "If there's one thing worse than . . . rampant colonialism . . . it's post-colonial dictatorship." By the late 1970s "postcolonial" was used by literary critics to refer to the effects of colonization, and to reading strategies capable of interrogating the (often naturalized) manifestations of colonial discourse that appear in texts of all kinds and times. Although Edward Said did not use the term "postcolonial" in *Orientalism* (1978), his characterization of Orientalism as the discourse that constructed the Orient for Europeans afforded a model for the analysis of relations between colonizers and their colonized others (Dirks 2005). "Discourse" in this sense follows Michel Foucault's (1980) treatment of the term as a body of social and cultural knowledge transmitted through language and establishing what is regarded as true in particular cultures.

In their seminal text *The Empire Writes Back* (1989), Bill Ashcroft, Gareth Griffiths, and Helen Tiffin use the term "post-colonial" to "cover all the culture affected by the imperial process from the moment of colonization to the present day," and this usage is, by and large, accepted within postcolonial theory and postcolonial literary studies. Nevertheless, in contemporary nations where indigenous peoples experienced the traumatic events of colonization, their descendants generally resist the idea that they live in a postcolonial state, since they experience the lasting consequences of colonization through poverty, loss of territory, injustice, and other effects that are not yet resolved, or "post" their lived experience (Logan 1999; Lucashenko 1999; MacCann 2001). Texts for children are caught up in these tensions, since they construct ideas about colonization, about individual and national identities, and about postcolonial cultures (Bradford 2001, 2007). While it is never safe to generalize across all postcolonial societies, these societies commonly manifest a sense of unease about their nations' origins. Graham Huggan (2007) suggests that an acceptable response to the question "Is Australia postcolonial?" is that "while Australia is postcolonial with respect to its former British colonizers, it remains very much colonial or, perhaps more accurately, *neo*-colonial in its treatment of its own indigenous peoples." Critics are divided on whether the United States is a postcolonial society. Elleke Boehmer (1995) argues that the United States is not postcolonial because it gained independence long before other former British colonies and its literature developed along a different national trajectory. However, Peter Hulme (1995) and other scholars maintain that the doctrine of American exceptionalism merely covers over the imperial and colonial history that shaped the national identity of the United States and (arguably) provided the preconditions for its neo-colonial enterprises in modern times (Janiewski 1995; Hage 2003).

In Europe and the New World, publishing for children developed rapidly during the nineteenth and early twentieth centuries, when European imperialism was at its peak. It is thus inevitable that children's texts of this time engaged with some of the key concepts and ideologies that informed colonialism. Chief among these were a belief in the superiority of European culture, a high regard for "progress" (especially in industrial and economic terms), and a conviction that indigenous peoples did not deserve territory because they failed to use it to generate wealth (Seed 2001). Authors such as G. A. Henty, Frederick Marryat and W. H. G. Kingston produced stories of empire featuring boy heroes; school stories beginning with Thomas Hughes's *Tom Brown's Schooldays* (1857) were directed toward boys who would grow into imperial men; Daniel

Defoe's *Robinson Crusoe* (1719) spawned scores of robinsonades, narratives in which young adventurers both engaged in colonial enterprises and also domesticated the New World by reproducing British, middle-class homes in the midst of unhomely territories (O'Malley 2008). If "postcolonial" refers to all culture from the moment of first contact between colonizers and indigenous peoples, these are postcolonial texts; but they are informed by a colonial discourse that advocates the values of imperialism. Nor are contemporary texts necessarily exempt from colonial ideologies, which retain their potency long after nations have achieved political independence.

As Bill Ashcroft says (2001), "postcolonial" refers to "a *form of talk* rather than a *form of experience*"—a form of talk that moves beyond historicist approaches in which texts are analyzed in relation to whether they depict life as it "really" was (Fisher 1986). Postcolonial discourse theory, drawing on the work of Foucault and Said, adopts poststructuralist methodologies by refusing to locate "truth" or "reality" in societies, institutions, or textuality. Rather, postcolonial readings of texts (whether historical or contemporary) seek to dismantle the signifying systems of colonialism by identifying the tropes and rhetorics whereby texts construct "truth"—for instance, the "truth" of colonial hierarchies that rely on binaries such as civilized/savage or modern/premodern. In addition to the historicist approaches commonly used in children's literature criticism, discussions of colonialist texts (that is, texts that directly concern themselves with colonial expansion) often treat the authors of these texts as merely "men [*sic*] of their time"; thus, Dennis Butts (2003), discussing Henty's *With Clive in India* (1884), notes that Henty's historical novels "reflected the ideology of a late-Victorian British imperialist." Rather, postcolonial discourse analysis considers the strategies of concealment and denial that manifest in even the most self-confident colonialist texts. Colonial authors were not necessarily conscious of the fissures and inconsistencies that marked their writing, since the power of colonial discourse is such that it "constructs the colonizing subject as much as the colonized" (Ashcroft, Griffiths, and Tiffin 2000).

Textual production for children by indigenous authors and illustrators (sometimes originating from indigenous publishers) now comprises a sizable body of postcolonial children's literature. Some of these texts, like Louise Erdrich's *The Birchbark House* (1999), Thomas King and William Kent Monkman's *A Coyote Columbus Story* (1992), and Gavin Bishop's *The House That Jack Built* (1999) reclaim indigenous histories, telling the past from the perspectives of peoples formerly objectified by colonial discourse. Erdrich's depiction of Anishinabe life when Europeans were beginning to occupy ancestral lands focuses on how the Anishinabe held on to their practices and beliefs in the face of colonial violence and the ravages of introduced diseases. In *A Coyote Columbus Story,* King and Monkman engage in what Stephen Slemon (1987) refers to as postcolonial counterdiscourse through its mockery of Christopher Columbus and his colonial enterprise; and Bishop's treatment of the wars that raged between Maori and European invaders in *The House That Jack Built* dismantles triumphalistic accounts of settler achievements in New Zealand.

The continuing influence of colonialism upon the lives of indigenous people in contemporary postcolonial societies is increasingly addressed in novels by indigenous authors. Alexie Sherman's *The Absolutely True Diary of a Part-Time Indian* (2007), Lee Maracle's *Will's Garden* (2002), and Meme McDonald and Boori Monty Pryor's *Njunjul the Sun* (2002) locate their Aboriginal protagonists in cross-cultural settings. The concept of hybridity is a complex one in postcolonial theory (Bhabha 1994), and these novels refuse to accede to simplistic notions of an untroubled "mixing and matching" of values and practices from European and indigenous cultures. Rather, their protagonists are shown to construct new ways of being Aboriginal as they engage in multiple negotiations, positive and negative, with the dominant culture.

Researchers in children's literature have been slow to adopt postcolonial theory: aside from a scattering of journal articles (Paul 1990, Slemon and Wallace 1991), postcolonial approaches have been used in a few collections of essays (Khorana 1998; McGillis 1999) and monographs (Logan 1999; Bradford 2001, 2007; Jenkins 2006). Although Perry Nodelman's 1992 essay "The Other: Orientalism, Colonialism, and Children's Literature" has been influential, its central premise—that relations between Orientalists and Orientals offer a parallel to relations between adults and children—has been accepted far too uncritically, leading to assertions such as that "children are colonized by the books they read" (Kutzer 2000). It is, of course, the case that colonial discourse constructs colonized peoples as children, lacking the intelligence or autonomy of their (colonizing) superiors. However, the reverse paradigm—that children are similar to colonized peoples—is highly problematic. The comparison between children and colonized people tends to produce a homogenized version of childhood and "the child," denying the possibility of childhood agency. (Ironically, this effect is similar to Said's account of how Orientalism operates.) Moreover, the analogy occludes any reference to race and racism, whereas the concept of "race" as a system of classification based on genetics and physical appearance was a founding principle of imperialism from the early modern period. The worst effect of the analogy is its capacity to trivialize the violence and oppression of colonization and its lasting effects on indigenous peoples; the white, middle-class child readers who comprise the principal audience of children's literature do not occupy a comparable position either politically or symbolically.

Like many other critics, Donnarae MacCann (2001) notes that postcolonial studies can be regarded as an abstract body of theory far removed from the lived experience of colonized peoples and their descendants, and carried out by European scholars who conduct a form of neo-colonialism whereby they exert power over colonized peoples (Parry 1987). In her famous essay "Can the Subaltern Speak? Speculations on Widow

Sacrifice" (1985), Gayatri Spivak argues that the voices of subaltern people are lost in the noise of Western theorists as they talk *about* the colonized; and Dipesh Chakrabarty (1992) contends that postcolonial theory is inevitably incorporated in a Eurocentric historical master narrative. Nevertheless, contemporary work in postcolonial literary studies is strikingly syncretic, drawing upon indigenous knowledges and epistemologies in conjunction with European theories. In addition, postcolonial theory now aligns itself with critical race theory and whiteness studies, thus enabling comparative and historicized approaches that consider both national literatures and the global conditions in which they are produced.

39

Postmodernism

Philip Nel

"Postmodernism" denotes an historical period, a style, or a cultural logic. If an historical period, then the word means *after modernism*—although when, precisely, modernism ended is debatable: 1939, 1945, and 1950 are common dates, but the term "postmodernism" crops up well before then. The *Oxford English Dictionary* (*OED*) finds J. M. Thompson in 1914 using "Post-Modernism" to describe a shift in Christian thinking that would "escape from the double-mindedness of Modernism." A still earlier example eluded the *OED*: circa 1870, the English painter John Watkins Chapman spoke of "postmodern painting," which he alleged was more avant-garde than French impressionism (Storey 2005). To denote a new period in literature or architecture, however, the term gained wide use in the 1960s, with the earliest such uses occurring in the 1940s.

In the 1980s and 1990s, children's literature witnessed the rise of a postmodernism characterized by three different but related strands of stylistic play. Popularizing the *narrative fragmentation* strand displayed earlier by Remy Charlip and Jerry Joyner's *Thirteen* (1975), David Macaulay's *Black and White* (1990) launches simultaneous narratives that both compete with and complement one another. Evenly dividing its two-page spreads into quadrants, *Black and White* refracts a story into four perspectives, each unfolding in its own half-page. Though it also presents multiple overlapping stories, Jon Scieszka and Lane Smith's *The Stinky Cheese Man and Other Fairly Stupid Tales* (1992), which self-consciously plays with and comments on the book's form, best embodies a second strand—the *metafictional*. As the protagonists of David Wiesner's *The Three Pigs* (2001) would later do, *The Stinky Cheese Man*'s characters walk out of their narratives, slice up stories, and even alter the physical form of the book. A third but less prominent strand emerges in the *metapictures* of Ann Jonas's *Round Trip* (1983), in which each two-page spread can be read right-side up or upside-down. The book deploys the simplest metapictures—illustrations of the Duck/Rabbit type, in which figure and ground perpetually oscillate, positioning (as W. J. T. Mitchell [1994] says) the audience as the subject of the experiment. All three of these stylistic approaches challenge readers' expectations of what a book is or should be.

However, a focus on formal traits collides with the periodizing definition. Although their "meta" excursions may be of a slightly lesser degree, children's books that experiment with form date to at least the early part of the last century. E. Nesbit's "The Town in the Library, in the Town in the Library" (1901) presents two children who, in their family's library, build a town out of books; they enter the book-town, and find a duplicate of their house, with a book-town in *its* library. Prefiguring Jorge Luis Borges's "Library of Babel" (1941), *that* town contains another duplicate, and so on, "like Chinese box puzzles, multiplied by millions and millions for ever and ever" (Nesbit 1901; Rosenberg 2008). Each page of Peter Newell's *Topsys & Turvys* (1902) offers a metapicture, framed by a couplet—the first line appears below the image and right-side up, the second line above and upside-down. Turn the book 180 degrees to complete the rhyme, and perspective completely alters the picture's meaning. Newell's *The Hole Book* (1908) and *The Rocket Book* (1912) exhibit metafictional tendencies. Courtesy of the printer's hole punch, a bullet has blown a neat circle through each page of *The Hole Book*, and a rocket has blasted an oval through each page of *The Rocket Book*. These explosions alter the pages on which they are printed, much as the cheese's rank smell causes one illustration to melt in *The Stinky Cheese Man*, or as the caterpillar's appetite knocks holes in the pages of Eric Carle's *Very Hungry Caterpillar* (1969). In fiction for grown-ups, the metafictional impulse emerges well before Newell and Nesbit—at least as early as the second half of Miguel de Cervantes' *Don Quixote* (1615), where we meet characters who have read the first half of the novel.

A second stylistic trait suggested by the term "postmodern" fits more succinctly with its temporal location (postmodernity), but readers disagree on whether this trait is critically productive or critically bankrupt. Smith's pastiche of styles in the *Stinky Cheese Man* might be "visually arresting" and parodic, its metafictive traits serving a "critical consciousness-raising function" (Cox 1994; Stevenson 1994; Peters 1996). In contrast, *The Grim Grotto* (2004), Lemony Snicket's "pastiche of *Moby Dick*" may be "like the white whale,

. . . present[ing] a blankness on which readers can project their longings" (Langbauer 2007). This latter quotation invokes Fredric Jameson's definition of postmodern pastiche as "blank parody, a statue with blind eyeballs," and therefore lacking parody's "satiric impulse" (Jameson 1991). Critics are divided on whether postmodernism's playfulness engages or fails to engage with the culture in which it was produced—that is, "postmodernity," a period of global capitalism beginning in the 1960s and dominated by service industries that provide consumerism as a (false) compensation for economic and political impotence. So, for example, some have read the Harry Potter phenomenon as a symptom of postmodernity, offering a pastiche of influences and celebrating consumption (Zipes 2001; Gupta 2003); others see Potter as consciously playing with its source material and delivering a viable political critique (Westman 2002; Nel 2005). Both analyses figure Rowling's work as "postmodern," but each posits it as advancing diametrically opposed aims.

One means through which postmodernism may engage political realities is historiographic metafiction, a self-conscious critique of the material relationships under which hierarchies of power are sustained and perpetuated (Hutcheon 1989). Walter Dean Myers's *Monster* (1999)—told primarily through screenplay, courtroom transcript, and personal journal (but also via marginalia, mug shots, and video stills)—juxtaposes genres to raise questions about racism, responsibility, and the U.S. criminal justice system. By its end, the book does not answer whether its sixteen-year-old

black protagonist was guilty of being an accessory to a robbery that ended in murder. Readers must discover their own complex, contingent truths. Underscoring the trickiness of truth-seeking, Geraldine McCaughrean's *A Pack of Lies: Twelve Stories in One* (1988) blurs the line between fact and fiction. Near the novel's end, a mysterious storyteller—whose tales were both persuasive and probably false—leaves. Shifting perspective, the characters discover his stories to be true, and themselves to be his creations (he is their author). In a final twist, the raconteur enters the story he has written. Like René Magritte's *The Human Condition* (1933), Crockett Johnson's *Harold and the Purple Crayon* (1955), and Anthony Browne's *Bear Hunt* (1979), *A Pack of Lies* destabilizes the boundary between real and imaginary, leaving readers to ponder where fictions' truths lie.

Yet, deploying varied genres and narrative perspectives to challenge objectivity is as much an aesthetic feature of modernism as it is of postmodernism. There are so many formal continuities that postmodernism might be seen more as an extension of modernism than as a break from it. Both use collage, densely layer a work with interwoven motifs and allusions, and strive to represent disordered contemporary experience. Though described as postmodernist (McMillan 2003), Browne's *Voices in the Park* (1998)—a rewriting of his *A Walk in the Park* (1977)—could also be called modernist. It is richly allusive, weaving in art by Magritte and Edvard Munch, as well as images of the *Mona Lisa*, Mary Poppins, and King Kong. Amid its visual play, it offers, in succession, four different accounts of a trip to the park: Mrs. Smythe, Mr. Smith, Charlie Smythe (son of Mrs.), and Smudge Smith (daughter of Mr.). The book destabilizes any central narrative, as its competing stories develop a contrast between adults and children, females and males, upper class and lower class (the Smythes are wealthy, the Smiths poor).

However, to read *Voices in the Park* as modernist is to efface three important distinctions between modern and postmodern: the historical moment (modernity or postmodernity) to which the work responds, the *degree* of formal play, and its resistance to metanarratives. In the context of postmodernity, one might read *Voices* as making visible the class inequalities that Tony Blair's New Labor sought to ignore *or* as offering up a proliferation of cultural allusions to distract us from these very concerns. In other words, depending on whether Browne's particular postmodernism offers incisive analysis or playful escapism, the book might offer a materialist critique of postmodernity or it might aestheticize politics. Certainly, the degree of its visual allusiveness—and many allusions have at best a tangential connection to the work's social themes—mark its aesthetic as more postmodern than modern. Yet, in valuing some narratives above others, its structure is more modern than postmodern. As Cheryl McMillan (2003) notes, the tale's four voices "move from the position of lowest truth status to fullest truth status": having the parents speak first grants "both children a right of reply, which may act as corrected versions."

If, in contrast, we seek works that resist metanarratives, then Macaulay's *Black and White* and Chris Van Allsburg's *The Mysteries of Harris Burdick* (1984) are better candidates for the postmodern picture book, because they do not privilege any one particular story. Having all four stories develop simultaneously, *Black and White* gives them each the same pictorial and narrative weight and never explicitly underscores the connections between them (Lewis 2001). Further flattening the sense of which information may be most important, each motif resonates in many directions. The title serves as an ironic reminder that the book is anything but "black and white" (it's not straightforward); winks at the punch-line to the old joke "What's black and white and read all over?" (newspapers, which figure prominently in the stories); and provides a unifying visual motif, uniting the bandit, the Holstein cows, and the dog. His "Chris" nametag suggests an allusion to Macaulay's friend Chris Van Allsburg, who always hides a bull terrier somewhere in each of his books (Trites 1994). Van Allsburg's *The Mysteries of Harris Burdick* creates a similar leveling of hierarchies. Offering a single illustration from and caption to each of fourteen stories, all allegedly abandoned by Burdick, the book invites readers to solve two sets of mysteries—the missing narratives, and the missing author. Both Van Allsburg and Macaulay compel the reader's active participation.

In this sense, *Harris Burdick*, *Black and White*, and *The Stinky Cheese Man* highlight the branch of postmodernism that draws its energy from the historical avant-garde, which works to "re-integrate art into the life process" in order to engender in the audience "a critical cognition of reality" (Bürger 1984; Huyssen 1986). *Harris Burdick*'s Magritte-inspired juxtapositions and *The Stinky Cheese Man*'s Dadaist montages derive the style of their provocations directly from that modernist avant-garde. In *The Stinky Cheese Man*'s "Giant Story," the Giant creates an exquisite corpse–style surrealist collage of fairy tale clichés, accompanied by Smith's collage of images from different children's stories—Madeline's hat, Pinocchio's nose, Aladdin's lamp, a just-bitten apple. In *Burdick*'s "The Third-Floor Bedroom," Van Allsburg animates the wallpaper's pattern of birds: the first bird has gone, presumably through the window at left; the second is prying itself free from the pattern. The text says only: "It all began when someone left the window open." What began? Why? Like the enigmatic titles of Magritte's paintings, Van Allsburg's text does not explain the image; similarly, Smith does not tell us what to make of his juxtaposed images. Readers must intervene, creating meanings themselves.

For some, this is the central critical problem of postmodern representational strategies: they presume that the reader, having perceived the irony or made sense of the ambiguity, will then arrive at an enlightened conclusion. For others, there is instead strength in subtlety: pushing readers toward a specific social critique may meet resistance; encouraging independent thinking is a more persuasive approach. Though there is no guarantee that nurturing an inquisitive outlook will lead to supporting a particular political program, the vast majority of children's literature scholars and

reviewers remain unconcerned. Most embrace the possibility that postmodern literature for children will foster active, thoughtful readers who are ready to raise questions about the world and their role in shaping it.

40

Queer

Kerry Mallan

The word "queer" is a slippery one; its etymology is uncertain, and academic and popular usage attributes conflicting meanings to the word. By the mid-nineteenth century, "queer" was used as a pejorative term for a (male) homosexual. This negative connotation continues when it becomes a term for homophobic abuse. In recent years, "queer" has taken on additional uses: as an all-encompassing term for culturally marginalized sexualities—gay, lesbian, bi, trans, and intersex (GLBTI)—and as a theoretical strategy for deconstructing the binary oppositions that govern identity formation. Tracing its history, the *Oxford English Dictionary* notes that the earliest references to "queer" may have appeared in the sixteenth century. These early examples carried negative connotations such as "vulgar," "bad," "worthless," "strange," or "odd," and such associations continued until the mid-twentieth century. In the early nineteenth century, and perhaps earlier, "queer" was employed as a verb, meaning to "to put out of order," "to spoil," "to interfere with." The adjectival form also began to emerge during this time to refer to a person's condition as being "not normal" or "out of sorts." To cause a person "to feel queer" meant "to disconcert, perturb, unsettle." According to Eve Sedgwick (1993), "the word 'queer' itself means *across*—it comes from the Indo-European root—*twerkw*, which also yields the German *quer* (traverse), Latin *torquere* (to twist), English *athwart* . . . it is relational and strange." Despite the gaps in the lineage and changes in usage, meaning, and grammatical form, "queer" as a political and theoretical strategy has benefited from its diverse origins. It refuses to settle comfortably into a single classification, preferring instead to traverse several categories that would otherwise attempt to stabilize notions of chromosomal sex, gender, and sexuality.

From the late 1980s, "queer" began to take on a more political function. AIDS activist groups in the United States such as "Queer Nation" demanded recognition of the severity of the AIDS crisis, and challenged homophobic social attitudes and government policies. Children's and young adult (YA) literature responded to these social-political contexts by incorporating "queer" themes and issues into their narratives. The reappropriation of "queer," changing it from an insult to a "linguistic sign of affirmation and resistance" (Butler 1993), was an important precursor to the radical theorization that was to follow, namely, "queer theory." Teresa de Lauretis coined the phrase "queer theory" in 1991, as "a working hypothesis for lesbian and gay studies" (De Lauretis 1994). However, "queer" and the theories that support it are in constant formation, being redeployed, taking twists and turns from previous usages, while always expanding their political purposes (Butler 1993).

Queer theory continues to be a contentious and contested field of academic study. All scholarly attempts have only revealed the impossibility of finding a static, mutually agreed-upon meaning. Resistance or inability to settle on a clear-cut definition is itself part of the inherent radical potential of queer theory. Michael Warner (1993) refers to this lack of specificity as the preference for "queer" as representing "an aggressive impulse of generalization." An inevitable effect of this impulse is that "queer" permeates discourses that go beyond GLBTI lives, reaching more broadly into Western urban cultures and the marketing of consumer products, including entertainment and fashion accessories. This kind of "market fetishisation" of the word "queer" threatens to dissipate its political valency, which, in turn, results in the ironic situation of making it "a site of privilege *par excellence* . . . that only the most privileged can afford or achieve" (Winnubst 2006). The so-called "culture of childhood" has also become an area whereby researchers have examined "queerness" in the lives of children, with respect to children's sexuality and sexual desires, gay and lesbian parenting, pedophilia, cross-dressing, and transgenderism (Owens 1998; Bruhm and Hurley 2004; Kidd 2004; Flanagan 2007; Mallan 2009).

While the uncritical adoption of "queer" in popular culture has certainly domesticated the term to some extent, it retains its conceptually radical challenge to normative structures and discourses. Drawing on feminist, poststructuralist, Foucauldian, and psychoanalytic theories, queer theory began to investigate and deconstruct categories of gender, sex, and sexuality, arguing the indeterminacy and instability of all sexed and gendered identities. In troubling gender categories and their support of gender hierarchy and compulsory heterosexuality, Judith Butler developed the notion of "performativity" in her influential books: *Gender Trouble: Feminism and the Subversion of Identity* (1990) and *Bodies That Matter: On the Discursive Limits of Sex* (1993). Butler's proposition of the performative considers that gender is not what one is but what one does. It is in doing one's gender that subjects repeat and reiterate prior norms that constitute them as a boy or a girl. Gender can be performed differently when one refuses to conform to these norms by blurring the gender boundaries, as does the eponymous character in Gene Kemp's *The Turbulent Term of Tyke Tiler* (1977). The concept of the performative has provided ways for thinking about the processes by which discourse and language construct identity, the functioning of social norms, and how disruptive performances of gender and sexual identity (e.g., drag and parody) can subvert identity categories, as well as reinforce existing heterosexual structures.

While queer theory draws attention to questions of sexuality and the power that "heteronormativity" exerts on individuals in naturalizing and privileging heterosexuality, a story about a gay character does not makes it *ipso facto* a queer story, though such stories may indeed be queer. In the nineteenth century, books emerged with child or adolescent characters who harbor, even covertly, same-sex desires. In these texts, the doomed, sacrificed, or dismissed figure of the "erotic child" (Kincaid 1998; Moon 2004) provided narratives of "childhood sexuality." According to Steven Bruhm and Natasha Hurley (2004), these narratives ultimately resolved in affirmation of "secular gender normativity." Examples from this period include Constance Fenimore Woolson's short story "Felipa" (1876), which considered the fate of lesbian desire for its eponymous young character, and the homoerotic romances of the "ragged boys" created by Horatio Alger in the popular *Ragged Dick* (1868).

The publication of books for young people that deal with same-sex desires or active or implied gay or lesbian sexuality has expanded significantly. Since the first YA novel with gay content—John Donovan's *I'll Get There. It Better Be Worth the Trip* (1969)—there have been numerous titles published that can be broadly classified as "gay or lesbian children's or YA fiction." Realistic fiction with gay or lesbian characters attempts to reflect the diversity of sexuality within society as well as the divergent attitudes toward nonconformity. Consequently, some of these fictions perpetuate or debunk stereotypes about gay people (*Uncle What-Is-It Is Coming to Visit!!* by Michael Willhoite [1993]), provide affirming "coming out" stories (*Annie on My Mind* by Nancy Garden [1982]), and offer a neo-liberal agenda of gay assimilation (*Heather Has Two Mommies* by Lesléa Newman [1989]).

From the 1990s, attempts to classify these texts as either "queer fiction" or "GLBTI fiction" have become blurred, when "gay" and "queer" are treated synonymously. While many may see "queer" as "a newer or hipper synonym for gay" (Carlson 1998), others such as Donald Hall (2003) contend that "queer fiction" exhibits particular "queer qualities." These include a refusal of a naturalized binary of hetero- and homosexuality; a politicizing of the interplay of sexuality and identity (or at least allowing the reader/critic to politicize this interplay); and a resistance to facile closure on questions of sexual identity. Despite the proliferation of GLBTI fiction, not all of it offers a "queer aesthetic or sensibility" (Morris 1998). Integral to this aesthetic or sensibility are the narrative processes that draw readers' attention to the incoherencies in a binary system of sexual identity, and to "the oppressive regulation of sexual desire and practice in a social order" that is dominated by metanarratives of heteronormativity (Pennell and Stephens 2002). In Ellen Wittlinger's *Parrotfish* (2007), Grady, the female-to-male transgender protagonist, questions why such a binary must exist. Like *Parrotfish*, Julie Anne Peters's *Luna* (2005) demonstrates the impossibility of any "natural" sexuality and invites readers to join the characters in their questioning of seemingly unproblematic categories such as "man" and "woman." Queer YA fiction often deals with the subject of desire as a counter-approach to mainstream identifications and pleasures that dominant culture denies or prohibits to GLBTI subjects. In some instances, the narratives use humor as a strategy of subversion, as in Will Davis's *My Side of the Story* (2007). Picture books and novels for younger readers deploy masquerade and cross-dressing, but often the effects of these strategies do not necessarily subvert dominant discourses about gender and sexual dualisms. The picturebook *Odd Bird Out* (2008) by Helga Bansch offers a queer aesthetic or sensibility through the character of Robert, a cross-dressing raven. Through his flamboyant clothes and lifestyle, Robert flaunts social convention: he not only triumphs against the social constraints, but is the motivator for change within his community. By contrast, other humorous cross-dressing novels, such as *Bill's New Frock* (1989) by Anne Fine, offer a closure that returns to the social order of naturalized binaries of sexual identity, depoliticizing the interplay between gender, sexuality, and identity.

Queer fiction for children and young adults remains, like queer theory, a contentious and confused area for many. It also offers pleasures for readers, who may gain insights into the lived realities of diverse individual characters, whatever their sexual identity may be. Queer fiction turns identity politics on its head, shifting from "queer" as a noun to a verb "to queer." From a queer perspective, the most successful fiction for children makes visible the processes that seek to enforce heteronormative categories and binaries, and that foreground subjectivity as multifaceted and shifting. The most successful queer stories "queer" their readers by provoking them to query the assumptions that underpin notions of normal and abnormal identity, especially sexual identity.

41

Race

Katharine Capshaw Smith

A term with a variety of charged meanings and purposes, "race" arose in English in the sixteenth century from the French "race" and the Italian "razza" and has been employed as a means of grouping individuals by ethnic, social, or national background. While the term has been applied generally to a range of collective identities—including the "human race" (Williams 1976) or the "German race" (Murji 2005)—at present the term invokes categorization attached to imagined physical similarities or to a group's own sense of collective ideals and history. "Race" as a term points both backward toward injurious histories of eugenics and physiognomic pseudoscience (Gombrich 1970; Rivers 1994), and forward in its reclamation and revision within liberationist social movements, like the U.S. civil rights movement of the 1960s and 1970s and postcolonial movements in the Caribbean and Africa.

Within children's literature and culture, representations of "race" often reflect history's problematic racialist thinking. Hugh Lofting's *The Story of Dr. Dolittle* (1920) and the series that followed are probably the most familiar examples of canonical children's books containing race-based stereotypes. One might consider the ways in which racial stereotypes of the "other" emerge in children's literature during periods of white anxiety about social domination, as in the cases of

George A. Henty's books, which articulate a British imperialist imperative, and Thomas Nelson Page's texts, which attempt to ameliorate Southern American post-Reconstruction uneasiness. Focusing on representations of African Americans, Donnarae MacCann (1998) addresses "race" in American children's literature, explaining that the rewards of emancipation were "neutralized in public consciousness by racist tale-telling. And the other institutions that impinged on children's lives—schools, churches, libraries, the press—joined in promoting the notion of race hierarchies." It is difficult to underestimate the pervasiveness of racist representations of nonwhite characters in children's literature before the mid-twentieth century. Aside from the conspicuous examples of racist thinking in children's literature, some of the most respected texts in the canon of children's literature contain representations that offer prejudicial constructions of race, including Frances Hodgson Burnett's *The Secret Garden* (1911), Laura Ingalls Wilder's Little House series, and J. M. Barrie's *Peter Pan* (1911).

Some contemporary texts representing race perpetuate conceptualizations that homogenize and belittle people of color, as in the case of Lynne Reid Banks's *The Indian in the Cupboard* (1980). Some celebrated modern texts call up racist stereotypes from literary tradition, as does William H. Armstrong's 1970 Newbery Award winner, *Sounder*. One might consider the purposes of invoking stereotypical representations of race. For *Sounder*, published during the Black Arts movement, images of racialized passivity may have deflected white anxiety about black activism (Schwartz 1970). Modern representations that invoke stereotypical representations of race sometimes attempt to justify or erase historical white oppression, as Magda Lewis (1988) explains about racist representations of Native Americans in children's books: "[T]hat the invader's treatment of the Native people, both through physical and cultural abuse and extermination, may be justified, in their minds and historically in the minds of their children, these books serve as a vehicle for Dehumanization of the Native in the eyes of non-Native children and for Mystification of the Native in the eyes of Native children." On the topic of dehumanization, racialized characters have sometimes been used as a vehicle for the transgressive in white-authored children's texts. "Dark" characters invoke fears of violence, for example, allowing white child characters to displace and distance themselves from their own violent impulses, a pattern that surfaces in some depictions of Native Americans, as in Alice Dalgliesh's *The Courage of Sarah Noble* (1954) and others. Characters of color have been associated with libidinal energies and immoderate physical urges, as in the case of pickinniny figures, and are often set in contrast with white characters who seem ethereal in contrast. Racialized characters also enable white children to imagine themselves as liberated from restrictive social structures—by "going native," for example—or become the occasion for white children to test social boundaries. Perhaps the most familiar example of experimentation with social boundaries comes at the end of *The Adventures of Huckleberry*

Finn (1884)—a "boy's book" according to Mark Twain— through Tom Sawyer's sadistic treatment of Jim. In service to white child fantasies of power and agency, the racialized character becomes the site through which white children play out their suppressed desire to dominate, confine, and exploit the "other," all under the cover of setting the African American man free.

Voices from within ethnic communities have been decrying the representation of race in children's texts since early in the twentieth century. Writing in the 1932 *Children's Library Yearbook*, Langston Hughes, premier poet of the Harlem Renaissance and an active children's writer, protests the dearth of respectful literature for black children: authored by whites, most books, he explains, "have been of the pickaninny variety, poking fun (however innocently) at the little youngsters whose skins are not white, and holding up to laughter the symbol of the watermelon and the chicken." The African American librarian Charlemae Rollins speaks at length against *Little Black Sambo* in her National Council Teachers of English publication, *We Build Together* (1941): "The illustrations in many of the cheap reprints and animated editions of this story have also done a great deal towards making it offensive. In some cities, it is reported, Negro children mutilate and destroy this book, showing in their own way their rejection and disapproval." Antiracist efforts in the field of children's literature came to fruition in the 1960s and 1970s, and included the organization of the Council on Interracial Books for Children (CIBC) and the publication of Nancy Larrick's landmark article "The All-White World of Children's Literature" (1965) in the *Saturday Review*. Of late there has been resistance to antiracist efforts to reform the canon of children's literature and intervene in educational, social, and political structures that affect the young. Critics claim that antiracist efforts create rancor and divisiveness, privilege political correctness, and sideline aesthetics in service to social justice (MacCann 2001). Oyate, a Native American group, presently issues children's book evaluations in order to redress reductionist and derogatory race-based representations. Individual writers have interacted creatively with representations of race and childhood by white writers, whether that be staking a claim to children's traditions that have largely excluded race (as do the representations of black fairies and brownies in W. E. B. Du Bois's *The Brownies' Book* [1920–21] magazine) or recasting and recouping familiar texts (as do Julius Lester and Jerry Pinkney in *Sam and the Tigers* [1996]).

While the term "race" in the context of children's literature conjures up a variety of injurious uses, the other main valence of the term emerges through efforts at communal self-articulation. As Roderick A. Ferguson's "Race" entry in *Keywords for American Cultural Studies* (2007) reminds us, twentieth-century civil rights movements "intersected with sociological arguments that displaced notions of race as a strict biological inheritance and forced scholars to confront it as a category with broad political and economic implications. . . . Race emerged out of these movements as an expression of cultural and political agency by marginalized groups." As critics and writers have recognized that "race" as a concept is a social construct, and have worked to displace the idea of race from biology, the concept has been claimed by communities as a way to articulate shared history, culture, and political goals. Children's texts often emerge during periods of cultural nationalism, such as the Harlem Renaissance and the Chicano, Black Arts, and American Indian movements, as a means to articulate and inculcate qualities that define "the race." Within these contexts, debates about inclusion and exclusion sometimes blur the line between understanding race as cultural legacy and adhering to the sense that race involves biology, particularly when using blood as a signifier of racial inclusion. The question of whether one is "black enough" or "Indian enough" based on blood or on cultural context surfaces in texts like Virginia Hamilton's *Arilla Sun Down* (1976).

The distinctiveness of children's literature within larger racial-political movements becomes apparent when considering the masculine cast of many civil rights efforts. Ferguson explains, "Anti-racist social movements within Africa, Asia, the Caribbean, and North America not infrequently became sites where women, especially, were subject to gender and sexual oppression and regulation." Children's literature on race enabled women writers to participate in movements, as did Effie Lee Newsome during the Harlem Renaissance; by framing authorship as an extension of child-rearing, women appeared to adhere to conventional expectations for female domesticity. While there are a range of approaches to race literature for children,

women writers often used children's texts as a means to resist the patriarchal restrictions of race movements, and to reshape the race by resisting sexism as well as racism. Sonia Sanchez wrote the children's column for the Nation of Islam's newspaper, *Muhammad Speaks*, in the early 1970s, issuing texts like "Rashada Receives a Gift" (1975) in which women fight valiantly: "[T]he women had slain thirty . . . and someone said loud, 'Lo what women are these that do battle like men?'" As Sanchez's example makes clear, resistance to sexism sometimes comes through claiming male qualities. If, as Cynthia Enloe notes, "Anger at being 'emasculated'—or turned into a 'nation of busboys'—has been presumed to be the natural fuel for igniting a nationalist movement" (quoted in Ferguson 2007), race-nationalist children's literature frequently presents a construction of childhood that invokes typically adult concerns, sometimes by invoking militarism and masculinity, as does Nikki Giovanni's "Poem for Black Boys" (1973): "a company called Revolution has just issued / a special kit for little boys / called Burn Baby / I'm told it has full instructions on how to siphon gas / and fill a bottle." Even if militarism in service to social revolution is not the goal, many children's texts emerging from race movements figure the child as aware of exploitation and injustice, as does Tomás Rivera's " . . . *y no se lo tragó la tierra / And the Earth Did Not Devour Him* (1971). Such constructions reject the idea of childhood as innocent and sheltered, preferring instead to spotlight the child's investment in adult concerns, sometimes with the goal of demonstrating child capability and leadership, and sometimes with the intention of rendering child exploitation in order to inspire social change.

Currently, several small presses are issuing texts that work to represent the lived experience of children who identify through race, including Lee and Low (New York), Cinco Puntos (Texas), Children's Book Press (California), Groundwood (Toronto), Northland (Arizona), and Fulcrum (Colorado) (Gangi 2005). Study of race in children's literature can turn in productive directions, toward recovery of lost writers as well as reinvention and reassessment of the canon. Attention to race can problematize discussions of childhood that tilt toward the universal or that assume a white, middle-class subject. As a site of inquiry, however, race presents numerous challenges, since critics and writers struggle to define "insiders" and "outsiders" in ways that do not reflect biological determinism and that respect the multiplicity of expressions of identity within communities. There is not one monolithic "black" identity, for example, and literature for children reflects a variety of African American cultural expressions. As sensitivity to individuals of mixed backgrounds increases, any simplistic use of "race" as a critical category dissolves.

42

Reading

Margaret Meek Spencer

As recent classical scholarship makes plain, reading is a human, deictic invention. Evidence comes from the evolution of ancient alphabetic writing systems: Sumerian (cuneiform), Akkadian (*Gilgamesh*), Ugaritic (a fine, delicate script), and Egyptian hieroglyphs. Texts on stone and papyrus proved to be more lasting ways of recalling past events than human memory. Long, long before twentieth-century educators would debate whether reading should be taught by phonics or meaning-based methods, the Sumerians showed their young writers how to make word lists on clay tablets by incorporating elements of both of these pedagogies in their instruction. The later, successful Greek alphabet was made by matching speech sounds with symbols, paying explicit attention to oral language. That is what we still encourage children to do when they learn to read. However, my mental picture of biddable Greek children interpreting meaningful texts was dispelled by this recent note: "Much as we may lament the fact, written language, where it appeared more than 5,000 years ago, is not the creation of poets, but of accountants. It comes into being for economic reasons, to keep stock of facts, of possessions, commercial dealings of purpose and sale" (Manguel 2008).

In his account of how he collected terms for *Keywords* (1976), Raymond Williams (1983b) explains the limitations of "the great Oxford Dictionary." For his Keyword vocabulary, he wanted clusters of words. The *Oxford English Dictionary* (*OED*), with its twenty-four-column entry for "read" and "reading," was my starting place. The core sense of "read," as a verb, is "to look at and comprehend the meaning of written matter by mentally interpreting the characters or symbols of which it is composed." The noun form is expressed in sentences such as "I like a good read.'" The origin of the word is *raedan*, an Old Saxon or Old High German word related to a Dutch form, *raden*, to "advise." The *Concise Oxford Dictionary of English Etymology* (Hoad 1986) adds Germanic original meanings of "to inspect or plan," "taking or giving counsel," or "explaining something." *Reden* is Chaucer's word for "read," with the past tense *redde* or *radde*.

Reading has other extensions of meaning: to discover information (*I like reading newspapers*), to discern (*She was reading the fear in his eyes*), to peruse (*He is apt to read all the accounts*), to study for exams (*What are you reading at Oxford?*). The mental-state verbs associate silent reading with thinking. Other glosses include "to interpret, study and give an account of." As formal acts of reading, the *OED* offers the recital of a Bill before the UK Parliament, the reading of a will, a lecture, and a social entertainment where the audience listens to a reader. Reading of a non-deliberate kind is part of ordinary social habits associated with the gas meter, cooking recipes, advertisements, magazines, timetables, medicine packaging, and posted letters. Children's early encounters with these provoke the

repeated question: "What does it say?" This is their acknowledgment of meaning. In school, reading becomes a "subject." Those who look up "reading" in a dictionary already know what it is. The current query "Do you read me?" means "Do you understand?" Only in the *OED* have I discovered "reading" as the interpretation of musical scores, a matter taken up by Peter Kivy in the essay *The Performance of Reading* (2006). He reminds us that the origins of read literature are in performed literature: "There are two kinds of reading," he says, "the one when you do it, the other when someone else does it." Reading—the word, the text, the act, and our explanations of what we do when we do it—are all at the heart of literature for children. It not only extends their linguistic competences, their cognitive growth, and their cultural belonging, but also changes their views of the world and of other people.

The general agreement is that all children must learn to read. The nature of this obligation is bound up with literacy and the "active social history" examined by Williams. There is no entry for "reading" in *Keywords* (1976), but in his collection of essays, *Writing in Society*, we can see him reading Charles Dickens's *Hard Times* (1854)*:* "What is being generally described," Williams writes, "is the uniformity and monotony of the new kind of nineteenth century industrial town and of the new kind of systematic labour process which it embodied" (Williams 1983b). Williams reads Dickens so that the focus is on characters changed by the industrial town and by the events of the narrative. Readers of Williams's insights are, in turn, given accomplished reading lessons on reading Dickens.

There is no dictionary acknowledgment of children in the exemplified contexts of reading. Perhaps, as Jonathan Culler (1980) wrote, experience excludes young people: "Reading is not an innocent activity, nor a moment of analysable communion between a self and a text. It involves a complex series of operations which ought to be described." One of these operations is thinking about thinking. What counts, but is rarely counted, is the life experience that each reader brings to making texts mean—an idea that the great eighteenth-century man of letters Samuel Johnson took to heart. He believed that the contents of books should be brought "to the test of real life" (Boswell 1791).

As reading was a way of life for Johnson, he distinguished "professional" from "unprofessional" readers. The latter are those "whose sheer market power would nevertheless be the first most effective form of criticism," the continuing awareness of all publishers. Johnson read all the languages that were considered either "learned" or "polite" in his time, and upheld "extended critical writing" for which "the foundation must be laid by reading." However, when he used "reading" to mean literacy, he did not include women or the poor, whose skills he deemed inadequate. He is reported as saying that the Chinese had reading difficulties because their language had no alphabet.

On the matter of reading, Johnson's view was that a young person (always a boy) should not be discouraged from reading "anything he took a liking to from a notion that it is beyond his reach." In effect, he had no great sense of children as readers before they had learned the alphabet for writing and spelling. Later he confirmed: "I am always for getting a boy forward. I would let him at first read any English book which happens to engage his attention. I would put a child into a library . . . and let him read at his choice." He was adamant that adults should hide from the young all the current ABCs and the manuals of French and Latin used in school. Instead, they should entertain the young with "whole words," which they would "retain with far more ease." John Newbery, famous as the first successful publisher of books for mothers to read with their children, was Johnson's friend and occasional employer. Newbery introduced Mrs. Trimmer (six sons and six daughters; Queen Charlotte called her to Windsor for a consultation about Sunday Schools) to Dr. Johnson: "To confirm a disputed quotation from *Paradise Lost* for his benefit, she produced a Milton from her pocket; which so pleased the lexicographer that he gave her a copy of *The Rambler*" (Darton 1932/1982).

Reading flourished during the Enlightenment partly because the publishing industry flourished. Newspaper broadsheets circulated accounts of local events. Flyers, gazettes, and almanacs all increased reading as a middle-class habit. *Robinson Crusoe* (1719) and *Gulliver's Travels* (1726) were the novels that, in their chapbook form, reached thousands of readers. Intense demographic growth, as well as intellectual changes in women's writing, social roles, and music, brought about the Enlightenment. The essayist Richard Steele summed up his view of the scene: "Reading is to the mind what exercise is to the body" (quoted in Fischer 2003). His fellow editor at *The Spectator*, Joseph Addison, insisted on the importance of reading history, because it "informs understanding by the memory" (quoted in ibid.).

Male commentators on female reading (such as John Bennett, who wrote two volumes of *Letters to a Young Lady* in 1795) defined women's reading in ways that kept the female reader in the realms of "taste, fancy and imagination" and excluded them from the realm of acknowledged wisdom and understanding (Bennett 1795). Middle-class wives and mothers, released from certain household duties, were expected to complete the first stage of their children's learning to read. The boys, at about age seven or eight, went to boarding schools, while girls continued to be taught at home by reading their brothers' books, sometimes with a governess to promote good manners.

Wherever reading is regarded as a key to educational achievement, it is accompanied by a concern to ensure children's success in early school learning. In England, class distinction still separates those who are most likely to succeed. Home teaching has increased. Government-backed search for "the best methodology" to be used by all teachers in primary schools continues, with emphasis on synthetic phonics. Children's reading of their preferred texts, which might include comics and Japanese manga, is rarely considered relevant evidence of their progress. An international study reports that, despite "good reading results in England, many children no longer enjoy reading" (Twist, Schagen, and Hodgson 2006). At all stages, the multifaceted nature of reading confounds the notion that there could be a single, efficient method for teaching all children. There is also a curious reluctance to admit publicly that good readers read a lot and enjoy it. "Book weeks" and other events urging people to read are supported by the media. The Children's Laureate has but three years of promotion time in which to make a difference. Very few research inquiries seem to take seriously the influence of what children are expected to read and what they may have already read, but a great deal of fuss is made if test results and standards do not improve.

A highly detailed consideration of these and other language matters is being carried out at the Centre for Literacy in Primary Education (CLPE) in London. Founded in 1970 to promote a new approach to in-service for teachers, it has always regarded classroom experience and teachers' observations as important evidence of the personal meanings of learners. Current CLPE work in schools, a program called "The Power of Reading," focuses on the period of time between a young person's awareness of being helped to read in school and the different feeling of "becoming literate." The recorded results show clearly the part played by the texts of important children's books in this transition.

The great reading perplexity is this: reading is best discussed in relation to texts, especially when the implied readers are inexperienced. Never before have books for the young been so imaginative, artful, subtle, subject-extensive, and seriously reviewed for growing readers, and yet, the graded books (called "readers") for beginners are still used in the belief that they offer the safest instruction for the compulsory tests.

My interactions with children's books, their authors, and other teachers who read them to good effect are countered by prophetic writing about reading in the imminent electronic age. In his *Gutenberg Elegies* (1994) Sven Birkerts considered whether the prospects for reading were "dire or merely different." He decided that the outcome would depend on the readers' "own values and priorities." We are already fifteen years into Birkerts's scene-setting with more books than ever and more attention to reading in general. Think of all those who now read comfortably as the result of their accurate eyeglasses. Children rehearse the shape of things to come in their preferred reading matter. Not many of them know that their keyboards are dependant on the same old Latin letters.

More inspiring than interactive technologies is the progress in effectively understanding how the human brain learns to read, and when it can't. With the appearance of Maryanne Wolfe's *Proust and the Squid: The Story and Science of the Reading Brain* (2008), the problems posed by dyslexia have come under different kinds of scrutiny, particularly in the parts of the brain related to reading. Those who are close to children, parents, and teachers in primary schools now know that they cannot simply assume that the persistent difficulties afflicting young learners will disappear in time. Instead, we are to intervene as soon as possible in ways described and demonstrated. At the end of her scientific exploration of the reading brain comes a fascinating reassurance: Dr. Wolf and her colleagues at the Center for Reading and Language Research in Boston discovered that they were "reinventing a program" with some of the same principles used in the first-known reading pedagogy—that of the Sumerians. As she notes, "Unlike the Sumerians, we also use multiple strategies for fluency and comprehension. Like the Sumerians we want every struggling reader to know as much about a word as possible." This work seems more optimistic than some other prognostications about the future. For my part, I still have great faith in the practice of reading stories aloud to those who need to know what "reading" is all about.

43

Realism

Cathryn M. Mercier

Unlike the term "fantasy," "realism" (or "realistic fiction") doesn't always appear as a distinct category in reference books about children's literature. The *Norton Anthology of Children's Literature* (Zipes et al. 2005) includes sections on legends, myth, fairy tales, fantasy, and science fiction, but no single entry on realistic fiction. The *Norton Anthology* does devote sections to adventures, school stories, and domestic fiction, and excerpts from seminal titles that have realistic qualities, such as *From the Mixed-Up Files of Mrs. Basil E. Frankweiler* (Konigsburg 1967). Similarly, Perry Nodelman and Mavis Reimer's *The Pleasures of Children's Literature* (2003) includes sections on poetry, picturebooks, fairy tales, and myth, but not on realism. No separate entry on realism is found in *Children's Books and Their Creators* by Anita Silvey (1995), nor in *The Cambridge Guide to Children's Books in English* (Watson 2001). Instead, realism tends to be discussed as an attribute of other kinds of fiction. Part of the difficulty about how and where to place realism (or realistic fiction)—as a distinct genre or as attribute to other categories of children's literature—rests on this lack of definition.

This lack of definition is ironic, given realism's function in separating children's literature from literature for adults. As Felicity Hughes (1978) notes, Henry James was anxious that the future of the novel was jeopardized by the rise in its popularity, especially among women and children. In 1899 James fretted that this audience interfered with the novelist's pursuit of seriousness and the ability "to select his material from the whole of life." Hughes identifies this moment as "the segregation of children's literature . . . in general aesthetic theory, in literary theory, and in the theory and criticism of children's literature and in the literature itself." As apologists for the novel based their argument on realism, they also cast children's literature away from adult literary concerns and positioned it as separate entity. Such a position has fueled not only the production of literature for children, but also the interrogation of that literature, in theory and practice. Grappling with the definition of children's literature parallels similar difficulties in defining realism.

Raymond Williams writes that "realism is a difficult word, not only because of the intricacy of the disputes in art and philosophy to which its predominant uses refer, but also because the two words on which it seems to depends, real and reality, have a very complicated linguistic history" prior to the nineteenth century. In the nineteenth century, "realism" was a new word but already had four identifiable meanings, only one of which "describe[d] a method or attitude in art and literature—at first an exceptional accuracy of representation, later a commitment to describing real events and showing things as they actually exist" (Williams 1983a). In literature for children and young adults, each of the three parts of this description touches other contested territory in the field. Debates in and around identity, especially those involving race, class, gender, religion, and sexuality, consistently refer to the responsibilities of creators for accurate representation. The debates run along a spectrum that, on one end, views identity as essentialized, and, on the other, sees it as a social construction. The debate polarizes those who believe that only someone from a particular nondominant group can present a character, language, or setting familiar that group at all, never mind accurately, and those who believe that it is the expectation of a creative work to imagine lives other than those lived by its creator.

Hazel Rochman (1993) argues that there is a responsibility to assure that the imaginative representation is accurate on all counts and, as Graciela Italiano (2010) exemplifies, that issues around accuracy of representation have centered on the writer's/illustrator's "authority" to represent; similarly, Donnarae MacCann (1998) and Rudine Sims (1982) point to the reviewer's and critic's authority in assessing such presentations. In the first of three *Horn Book* essays about multiculturalism in children's literature, Barbara Bader (2002) traces the controversies of representation adhering to Ezra Jack Keats's *The Snowy Day* (1962) as part of the "revolutionary breakthrough" of an African-American children's literature by voices of authority, accuracy, and authenticity, including Virginia Hamilton, Mildred Taylor, Eloise Greenfield, and Walter Dean Myers.

Historiography presented a way to interrogate fictional representations as well as readers' interpretations of those fictions, suggesting that "real events"

do not have knowable, exclusive, and essential qualities. In the *Social Construction of Reality* (1966), Peter L. Berger and Thomas Luckmann argue that reality is a social construction, as the complex "relationship between human thought and the social context in which it arises." Although students and readers of children's literature often talk about the people and events in books as if they were 'real," readers and writers alike know the fictional or imagined nature of what they're reading. Unlike writers or readers of history, writers and readers of literature perceive the book's limitation in presenting an objective view. It constructs a reality in which to believe—or not; it constructs a reality that becomes part of an intertwining of many "dialectic[s] between social and individual existence" (Berger and Luckmann 1966). In *The American Novel and Its Tradition*, Richard Chase (1957) cites one primary attribute of the American novel's engagement with realism, namely its ability to

render reality closely and in comprehensive detail. It takes a group of people and sets them going about the business of life. We come to see these people in their real complexity of temperament and motive. They are in explicable relation to nature, to each other, to their social class, to their own past. Character is more important than action and plot, and probably the tragic or comic actions of the narrative will have the primary purpose of enhancing our knowledge of and feeling for an important character, a group of characters, or a way of life. The events that occur will usually be plausible, given the circumstances, and if the novelist includes a violent or sensational occurrence in his plot, he will introduce it only into such scenes as have been, in the words of Percy Lubbock, "already prepared to vouch for it."

S. E. Hinton's *The Outsiders* (1967) and Robert Cormier's *The Chocolate War* (1974) are cited as social realism and psychological realism, respectively, not only because they portray young adult characters who struggle to define identities within and from families, personal tragedy, and socially disadvantaged social status, but also because they include violence as a central aspect. Violence works in these realistic novels precisely because such actions can be understood in terms of the dialectic between the individual and the social. Chase notes that realistic fiction privileges character over plot and creates those complex characters from the web of their social relationships and the ethical decisions they face. One of the first reviews of *The Chocolate War*, a black-bordered box in *Booklist,* challenged the book's ethical position and what it told young adults about identity, charging that the book presented identity in essentialized terms. Later, more substantial critical work coming out of postmodern interpretations, most convincingly in Roberta Trites's *Disturbing the Universe: Power and Repression in Adolescent Literature* (2000), sees the novel's multivoiced narrative as offering readers multiple subject positions from which to assemble their own ethics. Such ethical negotiation stands as one of the central qualities of today's realistic fiction. Narratology's interest in polyphonic novels (see Nikolajeva 2002b) and in multiple narrative stances (see Schwenke-Wylie 2003) gives frameworks for grappling with the realisms of texts such as Walter Dean Myers's *Monster* (1999), in which Stevie exposes his own uncertainty about his guilt or innocence as he writes a script of his trial; or Sonya Hartnett's *Surrender* (2005), in which a possibly schizophrenic character speaks in many voices from a present and recent past.

In *The Oxford Encyclopedia of Children's Literature* (2006), Vanessa Joosen's entry on "Realism" discusses varying "degrees of realism" and outlines its subtypes, including the "everyday-life story" for younger children; the problem novel or "social critical literature" that address issues, such as divorce, eating disorders, racism, or war (citing authors such as Anne Fine, Jacqueline Wilson, and Beverly Naidoo); and texts "with documentary value, describing historical events of social problems with numerous accurate details." Nonetheless, realism presenting ethical dilemmas appears in books for younger readers, too, from picture books such as Allen Say's *Grandfather's Journey* (1993); to chapter books such as Eleanor Estes's *The Hundred Dresses* (1944); to middle- and upper-middle-grade novels such as Katherine Paterson's *Bridge to Terabithia* (1977), Nina Bawden's *Carrie's War* (1973), Paula Fox's *One-Eyed Cat* (1984), Brock Cole's *The Goats* (1987), Polly Horvath's *Everything on a Waffle* (2001). Such books often show their characters struggling to forge identity, learning things that change their knowledge of their world or themselves, but still allow some measure of innocence or hope for the reader.

Young adult literature is less invested in protecting the reader's innocence and packaging hope as a take-away for the reader, which has created fluid delineations of realism. In addition to social realism and psychological realism, the terms "'hyperrealism,' 'ultrarealism,' and 'hard' or 'harsh' realism denote novels that depict the darkest sides of (social) reality often refraining from happy endings" (Joosen 2006). These descriptors generally include books that break social taboos. Though such taboos are often mixed in one novel, they typically involve drugs (Melvin Burgess's *Smack* [1997]), sex (Sonya Hartnett's *Sleeping Dogs* [1995] for incest; Barry Lyga's *Boy Toy* [2007] for sexual abuse), and violence (rape in Chris Crutcher's *Chinese Handcuffs* [1989] and Chris Lynch's *Shadow Boxer* [1993] and *Inexcusable* [2005]; beatings, rape, murder, and kidnapping in Tom Feelings's *The Middle Passage*).

In "Interrogating the 'Real' in Young Adult Realism," Joanne Brown (1999) acknowledges the relativistic circularity of measuring a text's realism by its mimesis; she cites Jonathan Culler (1975), who "speaks in terms of 'verisimilitude' rather than 'realism,' by which he means a text's artificial resemblance to the external world." But even then, talking about the qualities of realism quickly leads to assumptions about the purpose/s of children's and young adult literature held by the field's gatekeepers: Why show things as they actually exist, some adults will ask; the adult role is not at all to show children what actually exists, but to protect children and their presumed innocence from that reality for as long as possible. At the 2009 Edinburgh National Book Festival, former British children's laureate Anne Fine created a stir when she said that perhaps "realism has gone too far in literature for children" and fretted about the hopefulness and aspirations in bleak, realistic stories published for children. While fantasy suffers book challenges because of its departures from the world of the known and its disconnectedness from teaching practical knowledge to its readers, realism comes under attack when its artificial vision of things as they actually are counters a gatekeeper's ethical sensibilities. Mike Cadden (2000a) argues that one strength of the polyphonic realistic narrative, such as *The Chocolate War*, is its ability to present multiple ethical viewpoints, enabling the reader to come to his/her own determination. Such an expectation of young adult readers troubles some gatekeepers—and delights others—as readers of realistic fiction move out of adult mediation, away from protection, away from innocence.

44

Science Fiction

A. Waller Hastings

The term "science fiction" denotes a genre of imaginative literature distinguished from realism by its speculation about things that cannot happen in the world as we know it, and from fantasy by abjuring the use of magic or supernatural. In science fiction, all phenomena and events described are theoretically possible under the laws of physics, even though they may not at present be achievable. Stated in this way, it would appear that works belonging to the genre would be easily identifiable. However, critics of science fiction have struggled to find an adequate definition almost since the term was coined and applied to a certain kind of fiction, supplanting an earlier, even less satisfactory term, "scientific romance," which had been applied to some nineteenth-century British works as well as to the novels of Jules Verne. As Paul Kincaid (2005) has said, "The critical test for any definition is that it includes everything we believe should be included within the term, and it excludes everything we believe should be omitted." Identifying thirty-three earlier attempts to pin down the genre, he notes that, "[s]trictly applied, every single one of those definitions would admit to the genre works that we would prefer to exclude, or would omit works we feel belong."

Although the *Oxford English Dictionary* cites one isolated reference to "Science-Fiction" from 1851, the coining of the term is generally credited to the American editor Hugo Gernsback, who first used "scientifiction" to refer to stories built on extrapolations from credible scientific thought when he established the first magazine dedicated to such writing, *Amazing Stories*, in 1926. The precise origin of the genre remains in dispute, with various scholars connecting works of fantastic literature such as Mary Shelley's *Frankenstein* (1818) and Sir Thomas More's *Utopia* (1516) to the developing genre. However, most agree that the development of science fiction, both for adults and for children, is primarily a phenomenon of the twentieth century, while acknowledging the significance of Jules Verne in France and H. G. Wells in England as proto-science fiction writers.

Although it has not usually been identified as such, early science fiction, at least in the United States, was significantly a juvenile genre. Stories of amazing developments in science and technology appeared in magazines that appealed to adolescent boys in particular. Fred Erisman (2000) notes that the first magazine given over entirely to science fiction was the August 1923 issue of Gernsback's *Science and Invention*, a popular journal otherwise concerned with factual science. The Tom Swift adventure stories by "Victor Appleton," one of many juvenile series published by the Stratemeyer Syndicate, began in 1910 and are generally identified with science fiction, although Erisman and others have noted that the Tom Swift books initially did not extend their extrapolation very far, confining the inventions to such existing technology as motorcycles and motorboats; their focus was more on the adventure than on the scientific prophecy. A large portion of the audience for *Amazing Stories* and its successors was adolescents, and important science fiction writers such as Isaac Asimov and Ray Bradbury published their first stories while still in their teens.

Various definitions of science fiction have been advanced, ranging from extremely prescriptive arguments that many of the best-known pop-culture examples of the genre (e.g., *Star Wars*) are not, in fact, science fiction at all, to Damon Knight's somewhat flippant and not very helpful, "Science fiction is whatever we point to when we say 'this is science fiction'" (Malzberg 2005) or Brian Aldiss's flat statement: "There is no such entity as science fiction. We have only the work of many men and women which, for convenience, we can group together under the label 'science fiction'" (Aldiss and Hargrove 2005). A number of critics of the field have suggested that identification of a work as science fiction depends more on the reader than on any intrinsic quality of the writing. James Gunn (2005) claims, "The kinds of questions we ask determine how we read" an imaginative narrative; only if answering the question "How did we get there from here?" is a significant element of the work's appeal can it be truly science fiction.

Many academic critics turn to Darko Suvin's formulation "cognitive estrangement" to distinguish science fiction from other fictional genres. Suvin (1972) argues that science fiction takes a fictional hypothesis and develops it to its logical end; because such a fiction employs a different concept of "normal" than one finds in the everyday world, the story causes the reader to feel alienated or estranged. Some degree of estrangement is not unique to science fiction, however; both myth and fantasy also present their audiences with worlds that do not conform to ordinary normality. In science fiction, there is also an expectation that the alternative world will conform to the reader's cognitive understanding of reality—things that are impossible in the real world, given our understanding of the universe (e.g., magical persons or objects) are just as impossible in the science-fictional world. Paul Kincaid (2005) recognizes that the concept of cognitive estrangement is central to most academic criticism, but observes that it "is a prescriptive definition that works fine as long as we are comfortable with what it prescribes, but can lead to extraordinary convolutions as we try to show that certain favored texts really do conform to the idea of cognitive estrangement, and even more extraordinary convolutions to reveal that familiar non-SF texts don't."

Several of the common tropes seen in both juvenile and adult science fiction would seem to violate one or the other halves of the "cognitive estrangement" definition. Faster-than-light (FTL) travel is generally understood to violate the physical laws governing mass and energy, and Albert Einstein showed that velocities approaching light speed would cause time dilation—yet FTL travel between stars with no time dilation has been a mainstay of science fiction almost from the beginning, especially in the genre of "space opera," into which adventure stories like *Star Wars* fall. Many science fiction purists would argue that space opera is in fact not science fiction at all, but a variation on traditional adventure story tropes. But even works that are unequivocally recognized as science fiction, such as Robert A. Heinlein's juvenile novel *Citizen of the Galaxy* (1957), employ FTL space travel without explanation. More recently, science fiction writers have often presented interstellar travel in ways that conform to known physical laws, as in Orson Scott Card's *Ender's Game* (1985), where the fleet of starships seeking out the enemy planet takes many years to span the distance between stars, or have employed unproven hypothetical formulations such as "wormholes" that take advantage of the Einsteinian curvature of space-time to create shortcuts between solar systems. Such methods of space travel were exploited in juvenile science fiction as early as 1955 in Heinlein's *Tunnel in the Sky*.

On the other hand, some science fiction presents a world so close to our own as to cause little estrangement. William Sleator's young adult (YA) novel *Test* (2008) presents a society in which the emphasis on testing in schools has become more rigid than is currently the case in the United States, though not unlike that of some other countries, and in which overpopulation and a reliance on the automobile has resulted in perpetual traffic jams—again, not terribly unlike the case at rush hour in many cities.

In an important and provocatively titled essay, Farah Mendlesohn (2004) uses the concept of cognitive estrangement to ask, "Is There Any Such Thing as Children's Science Fiction?" Although her answer is a heavily qualified "yes," she concludes that few works of juvenile science fiction meet the rigorous academic standard she is applying, primarily because the circularity of much children's fiction is fundamentally incompatible with the narrative arc required of science fiction. As she argues, children's fiction focuses on the individual child, who moves out from home (or a position of stability) only to return at the end of the novel. Calling science fiction a fiction of ideological rules, she says that it cannot be circular; it "does not accept that change can be undone, or the universe returned to its starting place," although human beings do have the capacity to influence the nature of that change (291). If it is true that children's fiction requires a return to the status quo, while science fiction requires a permanent change in the world as presented in the novel, it does indeed appear that the two are incompatible. Science fiction is mainly concerned with "the political, scientific, or social" ramifications of the work's events (292–93), with individual characters existing to demonstrate those ramifications, not to achieve some kind of personal growth or understanding, as is typical in fiction for young people.

Mendlesohn acknowledges within her essay the objection of an early reader (Michael Levy) that she was imposing a definition that a priori excluded coming-of-age stories from "full science fiction," but says that this is exactly her point: the two genres have mutually exclusive agendas. However, it might be argued that the path of children's fiction is a spiral rather than a true circle; the child returns to a stable situation, but one that has been altered (either in external reality or in the child's understanding), so that a permanent change has occurred. If this is the case, there is no necessary barrier between juvenile fiction and "true" science fiction. The internal dialogue in her essay echoes the conflict between Suvin's strict concept of cognitive estrangement and Kincaid's argument that such a prescriptive definition requires "extraordinary convolutions" to fit accepted science fiction texts within it. Levy suggests that the use of YA or children's literature conventions is a reasonable expectation in juvenile science fiction, and asks for a clearer acknowledgment that the juvenile SF writer is not trying to write the same kind of book as Mendlesohn wants him to. One might go further and suggest that science fiction, like other genres, must undergo a necessary transformation in its manifestation as children's literature, such that "children's science fiction" and "adult science fiction' may, in fact, constitute two related but distinct genres of equal validity.

Ellen Ostry (2004), exploring specific YA science fiction texts that extrapolate developments in biotechnology and computer science, approaches the issue of estrangement in a different way from Mendlesohn, integrating the concept into the norms of YA fiction generally:

> The young adults in these books feel estranged
> not just from their parents and from the society
> that would likely shun them, but from themselves.

The question all adolescents ask—"Who am I?"—becomes quite complicated when one finds out that one is a clone, or otherwise genetically engineered.

Self-definition, the quintessential task of adolescence, often becomes in YA science fiction the problem of defining what it is to be human in an alienating world. Thus, in Peter Dickinson's *Eva* (1988), the title character finds her brain transplanted into the body of a chimpanzee and must decide whether to align herself with humans or apes; in Mary Pearson's *The Adoration of Jenna Fox* (2008), Jenna's mind is first stored in a computer and subsequently implanted into a largely bionic body; in Nancy Farmer's *The House of the Scorpion* (2002), Matt is cloned from the DNA of a drug lord; and in Monica Hughes's *The Keeper of the Isis Light* (1980), Olwen's body has been medically transformed to fit her to life in a hostile environment. In all of these novels, the "if . . . then" extrapolation that Mendlesohn argues should follow the initial "What if?" question of the science fiction novel has been melded with the "Who am I?" question of YA fiction.

This melding results from the differentiation of adult and juvenile science fiction during the post–World War II era. There was little need for such differentiation in the genre's early days—indeed, as Mendlesohn comments, many early "invention stories" are not unlike the less satisfactory juvenile science fiction of today. Other than the Tom Swift books, little or no science fiction was being written specifically for younger readers. By the late 1940s, however, as adult science fiction began to take on its modern shape under the influence of the editor John W. Campbell and his stable of writers at *Astounding Stories*, a separation based on reader age began to appear necessary. Heinlein's *Rocket Ship Galileo* (1947), about three teenage boys who travel to the moon, was the first in a series of highly successful juvenile books, published in hardcover, that provided an alternative to the pulp magazines as an entry point for young science fiction readers. Other writers, including Isaac Asimov and Andre Norton, joined Heinlein in writing for the youth market through the 1950s.

Today, the science fiction world of children and teens has separated significantly from that of adults, with few writers crossing between audiences as Heinlein and Asimov did fifty years ago. One author who does write for both audiences, Orson Scott Card, arrived at the position almost by accident, when *Ender's Game* (1985), originally published as an adult book, found a wide audience among adolescent readers. *Ender's Game* recounts the story of a boy taken from his family at an early age and trained to lead a human space fleet against an alien civilization. Despite the novel's success with teenagers, its sequels did not fare as well with that audience, most likely because they dealt with the adult lives of Ender and other characters. The fate of *Ender's Game*, however, suggests a basic pattern for young adult science fiction not unlike that seen in Heinlein's earlier juvenile novels: a young person, generally with above-average intelligence, is placed into a situation in which he or she must adapt to an alien environment and solve scientific or technological problems in order to survive.

While Heinlein and Card seem to confirm the possibility that Mendlesohn's question can be answered affirmatively, the fact remains that young adult science fiction—whether defined as rigorously as Mendlesohn would have it or more liberally—is comparatively rare in the early twenty-first century. Susan Fichtelberg (2007) observes that only about 12 percent of all YA speculative fiction (a term she uses to include true fantasy, horror, and science fantasy as well as science fiction) currently being published falls under the rubric of science fiction, and she includes a relatively large proportion of adult titles in her YA bibliography. She speculates that most avid readers of the genre discover it around the age of twelve and quickly begin reading science fiction intended for adults.

Whether one follows the strict definition of cognitive estrangement that Suvin outlines, or adopts a more fluid conception, "science fiction" for even younger readers continues to be problematic. *The Wonderful Flight to the Mushroom Planet* (1954), by the children's author Eleanor Cameron, was an early example of the difficulty. The boys create a spaceship from scrap materials and use a mysterious fuel given them by the enigmatic Mr. Bass to fly to a hitherto unknown planet orbiting the earth just one-fifth of the distance to the moon; they complete the entire round trip within a few hours. There is little attempt to provide scientific explanations for details that are implausible at face value; instead, the trappings of the science fiction novel are used to frame a rather conventional story of adventure and active imagination. Similarly, there is nothing intrinsically speculative in the robot of Dav Pilkey's *Ricky Ricotta's Mighty Robot* (2000); it is simply a large, avenging friend who helps the eponymous mouse deal with bullies (along with a stereotypical mad scientist), filling a role that could as easily be given to the golem of Jewish folklore, a *djinn*, or a benign giant. Likewise, the alien of Jon Scieszka and Lane Smith's *Baloney (Henry P.)* (2001) goes to school in a spaceship, but is otherwise indistinguishable from any human child creating an excuse for being late to school. The difficulty in creating believable science fiction for the very young lies in the readers' inadequate knowledge of the world, which arguably does not permit them to distinguish adequately between fantasy and more plausible scientifically informed extrapolations. For the youngest readers, then, "science fiction" appears to be used primarily as a trope to give a veneer of the unusual to everyday activities. As Mendlesohn suggests, we might label such works "analogic books" (295). But are they science fiction?

45
Story
Hugh Crago

Historically, "story" is probably one of the most frequently employed words in relation to children's literature. Yet despite its constant use by reviewers and critics over much of the history of fiction written specifically for young people, it has rarely been defined or analyzed. In its apparent simplicity, taken-for-grantedness, and resistance to deconstruction, the term establishes itself as something unquestioned, like the nature of "childhood" or "the child" itself. "Story" is missing from the index of numerous works where one might reasonably expect to find it—such as Katherine Nelson's *Narratives from the Crib* (1989), a psycholinguistic study of the spontaneous (and sometimes story-like) compositions of a preschool child, or Peter Hollindale's *Signs of Childness in Children's Books* (1997). If, as Jacqueline Rose (1984) has argued, "children's literature" is itself a problematic category, terms like "story" may be an integral part of it. Perhaps significantly, "story" does not appear in Rose's index either.

"A Story for Children" runs the subtitle of C. S. Lewis's *The Lion, the Witch and the Wardrobe* (1950), its wording comfortably placing the book in a line of descent from a century, at least, of other "stories for children." (Nobody to my knowledge has ever subtitled an adult novel "A Story for Adults," although some have come close: Lewis himself did come up with "A

Modern Fairy Tale for Grown Ups" for *That Hideous Strength* [1945], and since the mid-1980s Shel Silverstein's mock-primer *Uncle Shelby's ABZ Book* [1961/1985] has borne the subtitle "A Primer for Adults Only.") In this usage, then, "story" draws a line of demarcation between child reader and adult reader, with the implication that once one attains adulthood, stories have been outgrown (or conversely, that outgrowing a love of stories is one way of becoming an adult).

When John Rowe Townsend titled his 1971 collection of critical essays *A Sense of Story*, it was his contention that adult fiction had forgotten or sidestepped the appeal of story, and that it had been left to children's writers to maintain a tradition of storytelling that went back as far as Homer. At the time, his opinion was widely quoted and admired, and Perry Nodelman (1992) has repeated it more recently. It rests on the assumption that the appeal of "story" has more to do with an exciting or involving *sequence of actions* than with anything else. This seems so self-evident as to require no critical investigation at all. As Lewis put it in his classic essay "On Stories" (1947), "[T]he Story itself, the series of imagined events, is nearly always passed over in silence, or else treated exclusively as affording opportunities for the delineation of character."

In fact, Townsend was comparing children's stories in general with "highbrow" adult fiction, not with what most adults actually read. Adult bestsellers, from *Gone with the Wind* (Mitchell 1936) to *The Da Vinci Code* (Brown 2003), are "stories" in exactly the sense that Townsend and Lewis meant. Likewise, thrillers, crime

novels, spy fiction, and action movies are all "stories." In a more innocent age, they would have been called "adventures"—another word that hardly anyone would now use of any fiction intended for adults (although it survives in the phrase "true-life adventure").

If these adult fictions could all be considered the work of "what-happened-next action-mongers" (Chambers 1978b), there are plenty of examples of what Chambers calls "storytelling by artists-in-narrative" (he instances, among others, Graham Greene, Kurt Vonnegut, John Fowles, and E. L. Doctorow) to give the lie to the assertion that "story" has become largely the province of children's publishing.

So far, then, we have established two related positions on the meaning of the term "story": The first is that story commands attention largely as simple narrative; the second is that this preference for simple narrative is more typical of children than of adults. The second assumption we have already seen to be highly questionable; the first also requires modification, though (as I will later argue) it is not as misleading as the first.

Turning to the word's genealogy, "story" came to us with the Norman Conquest of England as the Anglo-French word *estorie* (the initial vowel eventually was dropped). Thus the anonymous individual who first committed the Anglo-Saxon epic *Beowulf* to writing could not have referred to it as a "story," but the anonymous composer of *Sir Gawain and the Green Knight*, several centuries later, did use the word. "Estorie" derived from the Latin *historia*, which in turn came from the Greek *histor*—a man of knowledge, a "keeper of wisdom," and the one who, traditionally, stood in the marketplace of village or town and declaimed "news" of important events to those gathered there to hear it. Hence, what the *histor* narrated was a "history"—something significant, told aloud. (While it is indisputable that most history has been written by men and chronicles the deeds of men, it is misleading to syllabify "history" into "*his* story," since it is not English components that are in question. The Greek root *his-* actually signified "truth," "wisdom" or "knowledge.")

The Latin-derived "history" and the French-derived "story" ran parallel for centuries, in that both words could refer equally to a record of "true" events (a "history" in our modern sense) and to a record of blatantly fictitious ones. Daniel Defoe's *Life and Strange Surprising Adventures of Robinson Crusoe of York, Mariner* (1719) is a work of fiction, but one based on the true story of Alexander Selkirk. Henry Fielding's great 1749 comic novel was titled in full *The History of Tom Jones, a Foundling*. Fielding was well aware that he had written a work of fiction, but gave it a title that proclaimed its "reality," as did many eighteenth- and nineteenth-century novelists. Playful attitudes to the whole idea of truth did not commence with postmodernism!

The *Oxford English Dictionary* (*OED*) records "story" in the sense of "a theme for mirth, a dupe" from 1603—in other words, a "story" is something not to be taken seriously; and this strand in the word's meaning continues, with "story" being used as the equivalent to "lie" (from 1679), or "a mere tale, a baseless report"

from 1796. Today's adults say to children, "You're telling stories," meaning, "untruths." Hence, "story" has for centuries embodied an edge of fabrication, lying, unreliability, while "history" has gradually asserted its association with "fact." (As Leopold von Ranke famously proclaimed in the nineteenth century, the aim of history was to establish what actually happened.)

Yet the ambiguity persists. To journalists, from 1892, a "story" has meant a purportedly *factual* narrative account in a newspaper (carefully arranged so that the most newsworthy piece of information comes first, thus "hooking" the reader into reading further). The "news" we watch on TV can contain misinformation and myth more reminiscent of "story" than of "fact." To further complicate things, "novel" (now synonymous with "fiction") originally meant "something new" or "news"!

Katherine Paterson, author of *Jacob Have I Loved* (1980), neatly turned the idea of fiction based on truth on its head in her moving autobiographical essay, "My Life Is Based on a True Story" (1989). In fact, the lives of real people often exhibit more powerful patterning than we would allow as "realistic" if they were presented in fiction. So our rules for what makes a "story" credible are more rigorous than those we apply to "real life stories." I believe that our profound hesitation toward the reality status of "stories" reflects something fundamental to the concept's psychological origins (see the final section of this entry).

For all its persistent association with deliberate untruth, "story" in its mainstream sense does not imply a self-serving "fabrication," like those of sociopaths or dementia patients. Rather, a story is something *constructed to give pleasure to others*, whether its raw material be factual or not (*OED* records this sense since 1500). As in the somewhat analogous case of "tale," there is an implication that what is being presented has a shape that compels attention, that *seems* "true" (Erikson 1951).

Like "tale," though less unambiguously, "story" reaches back to the world of oral narration, where a speaker directly addressed a listener (or a group of listeners). Many well-known children's books (among them *The Hobbit* [Tolkien 1937], *The Wind in the Willows* [Grahame 1908], *James and the Giant Peach* [Dahl 1961], and *Watership Down* [Adams 1972]) began life as stories told aloud to children, and even when they were not, written narratives for both children and adults can embody many of the assumptions and techniques of oral composition (Rudd 2000). "Tale" seems at one time to have been used of more substantial narratives, and "story" confined to mere anecdotes or narrated incidents—a usage that survived as late as Beatrix Potter, whose *The Story of a Fierce Bad Rabbit* (1906) and *The Story of Miss Moppet* (1906) were so titled to distinguish them from the longer, more complex *Tale of Benjamin Bunny* (1904) and its like. Today, the relative positions of the two terms have been almost reversed, with "tale" usually implying a shorter, less serious narrative than "story." But, in a similar way to "story," "tale" has rarely been discussed or defined, and is now (insofar as it is used at all) firmly associated with childhood.

"Story" is so ubiquitous in popular usage, and so unquestioned, that academic authors, searching for precision and clarity, have avoided it. In the days of New Criticism, the preferred word was "plot" (which implies conscious design of the sequence of events that *constitute* a "story"). The preferred word today is "narrative," which can embrace both fact and fiction, both products of conscious literary craftsmanship and "spontaneous" or fragmentary compositions. "Narrative," too, directs attention to structure rather than content. Attention to narrative structure began with Vladimir Propp's study *Morphology of the Folktale* (1928), a pioneering work that led to an entire scholarly field, "narratology." How much has actually been gained by this is hard to say. As Peter Hunt (1991) notes, "At worst, narrative theory only rehearses the obvious, and leads to spectacularly pretentious non-statements." Simply replacing "story" with "narrative" does not necessarily take us any closer to understanding what makes *some* "narratives" (but not others) so compelling.

It has taken a scholar from right outside the academic tradition to boldly address that question. Christopher Booker's *The Seven Basic Plots: Why We Tell Stories* (2004) reduces an astonishing range of texts to "seven basic plots" (e.g., "rags to riches") in a way reminiscent of Propp's much earlier analysis of folktales. Booker's organizing paradigm—broadly, Jungian—is not new, but he applies it with authority, and without unnecessary jargon, to stories from all historical periods and cultures, rightly making no distinction between "popular" and critically acclaimed fiction, or between novels and movies. His approach offers a "grand theory" of why we are "held" by stories at a level that operates below conscious awareness—by re-creating archetypal figures and plots that correspond with our own personal psychic structures, stories offer us the opportunity to re-create our internal myths.

"Narrative" is rapidly becoming a debased currency, as the term is used more and more broadly. Academics such as M. M. Gergen and K. J. Gergen (1984) and Jerome Bruner (1986) have popularized the view that narrative is a fundamental device through which human beings cognitively organize their world. That is, we turn our experience into story form as a way of understanding it, or in some degree controlling it. Tiny speech fragments like "I looked in the refrigerator and found two tomatoes" are considered to be "mini-narratives" (Stern 2004). Telling someone else the alarming thing that happened to us on the bus is a way of making sense of it, a way of constructing it as meaningful. As novels such as Laurie Halse Anderson's *Speak* (1999) and Meg Rosoff's *How I Live Now* (2004) demonstrate, trauma victims tell their stories over and over again, as if attempting to master the horrors they have endured. "Narrative therapy" (White 2007) relies on the therapist asking clients a series of questions designed to "thicken" previously weak or undeveloped "plot lines" in their life narratives. The "stories" discerned by contemporary therapeutic approaches are brought into being in the act of conversation between client and therapist. Here we can clearly see the continuity between such a concept of narrative and the origins of "story" and "tale" in oral transmission.

The postmodern emphasis on "the present moment" in which narrative is created or re-created in readers' minds has led to the publication of numerous experimental texts that foreground such processes—among them a number of children's books. Shaun Tan's wordless picture book *The Arrival* (2006) is described in its blurb as a "graphic novel," thus blurring the child/adult boundary. *The Arrival* aims to re-create the experience of migration to a strange country, where nothing makes sense and everything must be learned from scratch (as by a very young child). However, in so doing, Tan forces his readers to confront the way in which they must actively select details for significance, in order to "make a story" out of an ongoing series of pictured actions, set in an almost totally alien landscape. As reader-response criticism asserted (Holland 1975; Rosenblatt 1978), each reader may thus make a different "story" from the ambiguous materials and "telling gaps" (Iser 1974) Tan provides.

In doing so, they will have imposed on Tan's sequence of pictures preexisting "story templates," including *a logically linked series of events*, a structure that includes *a beginning, a middle and an end, characters who remain the center of attention throughout*, and to whom the story happens, and *a resolution that offers some form of resolution or release*. Despite many changes of critical emphasis and terminology, these templates, described originally by Aristotle in his *Poetics*, have never been superseded since he created his theory in fourth century B.C.E. Athens. And interestingly, several of the key components of his story schema appear to evolve in a predictable order as we observe the maturation and development of children.

The typical "proto-narratives" of two year olds (Pitcher and Prelinger 1963; Sutton-Smith et al. 1981) consist only of a seemingly random series of events or assertions, without logical linkage, and often without a consistent protagonist. By the fifth year of life, children are capable of producing a narrative that features a single central figure to whom the events occur. The "plot" itself alternates fortunate and unfortunate events, but its ending tends still to be inconclusive or unconvincingly linked with what precedes it. Children in middle childhood have mastered the need to begin and end the sequence of events that makes up their story, though they lack the empathy that would enable them to anticipate what information readers or listeners might need to relate meaningfully to their characters. Empathic insight, as embodied in description of scenes, characters, and characters' inner lives, develops in adolescence, and continues to develop throughout adulthood (Applebee 1978; Appleyard 1990; Crago forthcoming).

The earliest forms of storymaking reflect the survival-oriented instincts of the Old Brain—the brain stem (the so-called "reptile brain") and the limbic system or "mammal brain" (MacLean 1990; LeDoux 1998). Hence children as young as two years of age recognize and respond strongly to the alternation of "threat" and "no threat," even though they are incapable of fully understanding what the words of a story say, the logical sequence of events that makes up its plot, or the ability of a happy ending to cancel out earlier distressing occurrences (White 1954; Graetz 1976; Crago and Crago 1983; Lowe 2007).

Although constituted in language, story is concrete, image- and action-based, and oriented to survival—although the "threats to survival" in stories are symbolic and vicarious rather than "real" and personal. Story is typically couched in language that is straightforward enough not to detract from the listener's or reader's immersion in the events being narrated. It depends heavily on "pictures and conversations" (as in Lewis Carroll's *Alice's Adventures in Wonderland* [1865]). Story "flows," that is, it unfolds with a sense of inevitability. These components induce a trancelike state in which we do not *think* about what we are reading or seeing, but simply "live" within the world of the story, as long as that story continues. Hence we do not consider its truth status: fiction and real life are not distinguished—to the Old Brain, all experience is "real."

But there also exists a different kind of writing, or telling, made possible by the gradual maturation of the "logical" left hemisphere of the cortex. In this mode, readers and listeners are invited to be consciously aware of their own experience, to question and consider and compare, to reflect and analyze. Typically, in this second kind of composition, readers are invited to pay attention to the *language* in which events are narrated, or things described, rather than simply being swept along by the unfolding events. They are invited to think evaluatively about the characters, instead of unconsciously identifying with them.

This type of fiction, which I have called "New Brain writing" (reflecting brain functions unique to humans), is a taste that readers must acquire (Crago forthcoming). Probably it is only a minority who do so. In children's literature, Aidan Chambers, William Mayne, and Alan Garner's later work exemplify this type of fiction. It is not a byproduct of modernism. Richard Jefferies's *Bevis*, published in 1882, is a classic example. Its subtitle is *The Story of a Boy*, but in fact it invites its readers to *look at* Bevis from the outside, not to *participate with him* in the adventures he tries so hard to create for himself.

Both children and adults instinctively recognize the difference between these two modes—although children, and many adults too, may be at a loss to articulate it. Critics and scholars, in whom the rational, language-based left hemisphere dominates the right, tend to regard "story" as inferior, as offering "mere" excitement, "simple" action, or "primitive" immersion in wonders and surprises. Underlying such judgments is a suspicion of the instinctive, emotive pull of the right hemisphere, through which speak the atavistic, survival-oriented drives of the Old Brain. We *appreciate* thought-provoking, quality fiction, which confronts us with life's ambiguities and resistance to "happy endings"; but we *long for* story.

46
Theory
David Rudd

The word "theory" appears in Raymond Williams's original *Keywords* (1976). He traces its origins back to the Greek *theoros*, meaning "spectator," with its root in *thea*, for "sight," which also gave us "theater." As more recent commentators put it, "[T]he literal sense of looking has then been metaphorized to that of contemplating or speculating" (Wolfreys et al. 2006). The term became increasingly opposed to "practice," not only as something removed from the everyday, but also as something involved in attempts to explain and model the everyday. Although the title of Williams's work—*Keywords*—implicitly underwrites the importance of language, his own humanistic approach became more and more at odds with the "linguistic turn" in literary and cultural studies.

Regardless of the recent shift toward making it more explicit, theory has always been present both in discussions of literary texts and in the texts themselves, even if an awareness of this has been lacking. Readers who declare that they are atheoretical, limiting themselves to the words on the page, are deceiving themselves. Readers always "frame" texts; merely to see a work as "literary" involves certain theoretical assumptions, as does presupposing a text is for "children"—let alone that it is "Romantic," "realistic," "allegorical," "unsuitable," or whatever.

In a similar way, primary texts are themselves interwoven with theoretical notions. Sometimes these are relatively overt—as, for instance, in the many allusions to Charles Darwin's theory of evolution in Victorian works. In Lewis Carroll's *Alice's Adventures in Wonderland* (1865), for instance, we find the various creatures (including a Dodo and an ape in the illustration) swimming around in the pool of tears where the talk is of predation; and, like the first species to leave the sea, once on dry land they engage in a seemingly meaningless, competitive race. At other times, theoretical notions are less obvious, especially with the sort of theory that is linked to commonsense knowledge. For example, philosophers from Aristotle on (males, mostly) have theorized the inferiority of females to males, aligning the former with nature rather than culture; empirically, of course, such an argument could even be supported by pointing to women's comparative absence from the cultural landscape. And such notions are further underwritten in countless social scripts, including many children's stories—think, for example, of the realistic, human characters in E. B. White's *Charlotte's Web* (1952).

Women, standing slightly apart from the cultural center, are more likely to view things differently. And it is this notion of seeing from a particular vantage point that informs much theory; indeed, we are taken back to the word's roots in spectatorship and its links to "theater." Theorizing, therefore, involves the framing, or staging, of a bit of reality, in order to pay it more attention—precisely what we do when we place a word or phrase in quotation marks. Moreover, we could argue that this is precisely what fantasy does: it takes us to another realm, giving us some sort of critical distance on our world. Again, Carroll's work, this time *Through the Looking Glass* (1871), comes most readily to mind, but there is a far older tradition of "topsy-turvydom," of stories where the world is turned upside down, from Ann and Jane Taylor's *Signor Topsy-Turvy's Wonderful Magic Lantern* (1810) right through to modern stories where animals replace humans in society (as in the books of Richard Scarry). Returning to the example of *Charlotte's Web*, then, we might profitably note that the fantasy realm is where gender stereotyping is queried, Charlotte being situated squarely within the realm of culture (as author, manipulator of words, web-designer even), and Wilbur exhibiting a more maternal, nurturing side.

Although Marxist critics had long pointed out that our notions of reality are shaped by our sociocultural situation, it was only in the late 1960s that the theory-laden nature of all discourse was made explicit. Words that had once seemed innocent were increasingly placed in quotation marks ("scare quotes") in order to scrutinize their provenance and implication. Of course, the field of nonsense writing is premised on just such attention, playing up the physicality of words: their shape, the way they can be broken into independent syllables (often containing other words), or have their letters transposed in spoonerism, or simply have their sound prioritized over sense. James Thurber's *The Wonderful O* (1957), Norton Juster's *The*

Phantom Tollbooth (1961), and Dr. Seuss's *Fox in Socks* (1965) are eminent examples of works that celebrate the materiality of words, acknowledging precursors like Carroll and Lear, who pushed language toward the limits of signification.

While such verbal games and inversions of reality are undoubtedly fun, they also have a subversive dimension, which Mikhail Bakhtin (1968) most explicitly theorized in his notion of the "carnivalesque." In other words, simply creating a space in which the normal coordinates of reality are altered opens up the possibility that things could be otherwise—that, for instance, females (like Charlotte) might indeed build, write, or hunt. The Russian formalists, with whom Bakhtin was connected, had the related notion of "defamiliarization" which, in making the familiar strange, captures for many the essence of literary text. Nonsense and fantasy make this process most explicit (and, notably, are particularly associated with children), but realist texts do the same, albeit in a subtler manner. That is, they bracket off a portion of the world, making us view it afresh as a result of the framing. The book itself is a frame, of course, but it contains other lens-like devices, such as narrators, who also help mediate our view; and then there is the framing of the "chronotope," which organizes the story within a particular envelope of time and space.

These mediators perhaps make it clearer why theory is forever present; for, even if not explicitly articulated, each text sets out a certain way of ordering the world according to particular ethical considerations. So if it is claimed that a text is realist, we need always to ask "Whose reality?" Karl Marx, of course, claimed that the ideas of the ruling class always prevailed, that our reality was always ideologically charged. It is certainly the case that most children's books are written from a middle-class perspective, and some critics, building on F. J. Harvey Darton's (1932/1982) seminal work (e.g., Leeson 1985; O'Malley 2003) have even suggested that their very origin as a separate commodity lay with the rising bourgeoisie, who sought to define and promulgate new codes of behavior, as exemplified, for instance, in Thomas Day's *History of Sandford and Merton* (1783–89).

What we now think of as theory, sometimes termed "critical theory," emerged in the late 1960s on the back of the Civil Rights movement in the United States and, both there and elsewhere, the general challenging of elitist higher education—most vociferously in Paris in May 1968, where an alliance of students and workers sought to overthrow the government. Different social groups then began to theorize their situation. Aside from class, race was a key area. Why were there so few black characters in books for children, for example, and even when present, why were they represented in such stereotypical ways (see Broderick 1973; more recently, Martin 2004; Smith 2004)? Concerned readers scrutinized classics previously seen as respectable, such as Mark Twain's *Huckleberry Finn* (1885) or Helen Bannerman's *Little Black Sambo* (1899), sometimes resulting in revised versions. This focused attention led to wider questions about the treatment of different races and nations, with works such as Daniel Defoe's

Robinson Crusoe (1719) being seen as archetypal in establishing the initial colonizer/colonized relationship—though the books in question were by no means historical only. Roald Dahl's original Oompa-Loompas in *Charlie and the Chocolate Factory* (1964), for instance, were revised to avoid the criticism that they were effectively black slaves.

Women equally protested their second-class status and, like the other groups mentioned, found that Marxism provided a useful terminology with which to articulate (that is, to show linkages, to spell-out) their situation. They reworked (and often removed from their original economic context) notions of ideology, false consciousness, hegemony, consciousness-raising, and fetishization. Clearly, this process of a group protesting its marginalization will continue as long as people experience injustice: they frame their situation, to use that term again, separating themselves out from the background. So, out of disability arose disability studies (see Lois Keith's *Take Up Thy Bed and Walk* [2001]), from the gay community came queer theory (see Bruhm and Hurley 2004), and so forth.

While these theoretical concerns arose from particular interest groups (that is, they all had humanist roots), at the end of the 1960s there was a shift towards an antihumanist way of thinking. This shift could itself be rooted in Marx, with many separating out an earlier, more humanist Marx (the one preferred by Williams) from a later, structuralist thinker, the latter being most prominently theorized by Louis Althusser (1971); in the latter's hands, ideology becomes all-pervasive, with individual agency downgraded.

Structuralism modeled itself on linguistics, attempting to read everything in society as though it had an underlying grammar. The movement was influenced by the work of Russian formalists like Vladimir Propp (1928), who explored the structure of Russian folktales, noting that they all made standard moves, and that they featured a select few, functional character types (a hero, a helper, a villain, and so on). Jean Piaget, another well-known structuralist, sought to show how humans at different stages of their development understood the world. His work was particularly popular with children's literature critics (Tucker 1981), as it seemed to answer the vexed question of what books might be suitable for children of a particular age. If, say, a child thinks in "preoperational" terms (as Piaget argued was common before age seven), then it should appreciate characters in books who do the same. Winnie-the-Pooh regularly exhibits preoperational thinking, imagining that "living under the name of Sanders" must entail Pooh being situated precisely under just such a named sign (Singer 1972). Unfortunately, Piaget's model could not explain why many children did not enjoy these texts, or why many adults did. Moreover, because Piaget's theory was extensively used in education, influencing the age-grading of classes and even the structure of the curriculum, studies conducted in his name almost by default found supporting evidence (Walkerdine 1984).

However, although these early structuralists tried to understand the human mind—Claude Lévi-Strauss, for example, pointing out how we ordered the world in terms of binary opposites—later writers picked up on the theory's latent antihumanism. Namely, if the categories of language precede individuals, then people are actually just "subjects" fulfilling society's functions, much like the folktale characters Propp analyzed. Notions of individuality and agency are undermined; rather than instigating action, we are, as Althusser puts it, "interpellated" or "hailed" by society, with ideology simply making us believe that things are otherwise.

In retrospect, structuralism's lasting contribution seems to have been in terms of story analysis, building on the insights of the formalists in what is now known as "narratology" (e.g., Stephens 1992; Nikolajeva 2002c). But for children's literature, especially, structuralism was also liberating in challenging the sanctity of the canon, showing that the humblest folktale might be structured just like a classic. In the process, the words "text" and "reading" were extended to artifacts other than books (e.g., pictures, films, toys), allowing analysts to read across various forms (Mackey 1998). In short, a way of examining texts was discovered that set aside their pedigree, the continual need to evaluate and rank: literary theory morphed into a more general cultural theory. Furthermore, structuralism not only opened up the textual landscape, it also democratized reading itself, allowing new and innovative interpretations to challenge old orthodoxies. As

Roland Barthes (1977) put it, the death of the author comes with the birth of the reader.

This, more playful, antihierarchical approach led to poststructuralism (although the shift was always implicit). Structuralism ultimately depicted a static world, structured around binary oppositions, whereas language—where structuralism's insights originated—is open-ended and creative. Moreover, structuralism tended to be conservative in other ways, always prioritizing one side of a binary opposition: man over woman and culture over nature (as we saw earlier). Jacques Derrida drew attention to this, and to the fact that each term actually depends on its supposed opposite for meaning. He thus showed not only the interdependence of words and their constituent signifiers, but also their slipperiness, resulting in the notion that readings of texts are always provisional, dependent on systems of thought and concepts that also lack any final grounding (whether in God, King, or country—to name but three ideas, certainly powerful in Victorian England, and in the ascendant for writers such as G. A. Henty).

But if theory was seen as more democratic in this regard, in other ways it was becoming more hieratic ("high theory"), requiring considerable time and energy to master. It became the preserve of the university, leaving behind many of the interest groups that had initially sought it out. Certainly there was a tension here. For some critics of children's literature, theory seemed a way of gaining academic credibility. For others, such as Peter Hunt (1984), adult-oriented approaches betrayed the exceptional status of children's literature; his "childist criticism," therefore, demanded that we, as critics, try to read as might a child—in other words, the child itself became the framer of readings. However, for critics influenced by poststructuralism, the idea of uncovering some special "childness," to use another favored term (Hollindale 1997), was seen as a retrograde step. Rather than a "childist" perspective framing our readings, the child itself needed to be put under the microscope—especially the "Romantic child," which, it was argued, had for too long given theorists an overly simplistic perception of children as innocent and asexual (Rose 1984; Higonnet 1998). Moreover, these and other critics (Kincaid 1992; Honeyman 2005) argued that such a conception actually made children more vulnerable.

For some writers, "reader-response criticism" seemed to provide an answer in its recognition that children read texts in different ways (Benton 2005). A number of critics consequently examined the reading practices of their own progeny, situating these in the children's wider social world (of siblings, television, toys, family life; e.g., Crago and Crago 1983; Wolf and Heath 1992; Lowe 2007). In ethnographic terms, these studies provided excellent "thick description," although the theoretical premises of the movement—for example, Wolfgang Iser's (1974) notion that readers fill preexisting "indeterminacies" in a text—were often neglected. Ironically, the latter readings were mostly conducted by adults in the absence of actual children

(e.g., Chambers 1985b; Steig 1998). It should also be noted that ethnographies of reading don't address the deeper issues of children's literature: why, for example, children are being presented with these particular texts in the first place. What did their writers imagine they were doing? And how do these children's reported readings, themselves usually mediated by their adult observers, begin to capture the pleasures, obsessions, and terrors of texts?

The key theoretical area that has tried to address these issues is, of course, psychoanalysis. Given that childhood experiences are so central to psychoanalysis, it is hardly surprising that Freud's insights have been applied to children's texts (e.g., Phillips 1972; Rollin 1992), with fairy tales being subjected to this form of criticism more than most. Critics, however, are divided. Some argue that the prevalence of stepmothers and abandoned children is a result of contemporary social conditions (high mortality rates for mothers in childbirth, extensive poverty; Darnton 1984), whereas others find more deep-seated concerns revealed by these motifs: a split between good and bad mothers, fears of abandonment, and so on (Bettelheim 1976). Whatever its intrinsic merits, however, psychoanalysis had a particular appeal to marginalized groups precisely because of its lack of respectability and official acceptance; it therefore fed into much feminist theorizing and, perhaps for the same reason, into children's literature criticism (e.g., Wilkie-Stibbs 2002; Coats 2004).

This more strategic approach to theory makes an important point: whereas this entry has attempted to tease out distinct approaches, in practice most critics are more eclectic, using whatever seems apposite. Obviously, for those new to theory it takes a while to come to terms with the different strands, but thereafter one does not apply theory as one might a poultice. Williams, in his original *Keywords*, notes that theory is sometimes seen as opposed to practice, but he points out that this need not be so and suggests a more fruitful way in which we might see the relationship. That approach is to see theory not as separate—as optional, or as off-the-peg—but as something one practices in the course of criticism: speculating, making connections. One might here adopt Gilles Deleuze and Félix Guattari's (1988) notion of a "rhizomatic" form of criticism, one that is antihierarchical, that is not interested in trying to uncover underlying meanings, but, rather, simply wishes to make connections. In this way we can see that children's books are not only illuminated by theory, but that theory is itself informed and enlivened by the literature—as Freud found with Sophocles's *Oedipus*, and as many theorists have found with Carroll's *Alice*, Russell Hoban's *The Mouse and His Child* (1967), or Ursula Le Guin's Earthsea series (1968–2001).

After the end of "grand narratives," as Jean-François Lyotard (1984) famously called them, which morphed into decades of equally high, but more disparate theory (the "theory wars"), some have argued that theory is over (Cunningham 2002; Payne and Schad 2004). It was suggested at the outset that this could never be so. However, theory has undoubtedly become more embedded, more eclectic; for example, those calling themselves New Historicists celebrate a blend of approaches (e.g., Myers 1995; Vallone 1995). Queer theory is particularly interesting in this regard, first growing out of gender studies, then gay and lesbian studies, before emerging as something that not only questions our sexuality but, for many practitioners, is a way of engaging with the continual queering, or querying, of interpretation (Huskey 2002; Bruhm and Hurley 2004; Rabinowitz 2004). This would seem as good a definition as any: theory helps us see how a particular constellation of linkages throws into relief particular elements of a text, and how productive this can be for our understanding of society, its people, and its artifacts. Fantasy, in its seemingly playful way, does much the same, helping us question the everyday and its prejudices, while also letting us speculate on possibilities and alternatives.

47

Tomboy

Michelle Ann Abate

Although the rise of feminism and the advent of queer theory make tomboyism seem like a relatively contemporary phenomenon, the concept originated in the sixteenth century. Interestingly, the term "tomboy" initially referred to rowdy gentlemen courtiers rather than boisterous young women. The first listing in the *Oxford English Dictionary* (*OED*), from 1533, defines "tomboy" as a "rude, boisterous or forward boy." Several decades later, in the 1570s, the term shifted from characterizing a spirited young man to a like-minded young woman. In so doing, it also acquired newfound sexual associations and age coordinates. "Tomboy" lost the innocently playful connotations it had possessed when it referred to an actual boy; it now began to signify a "bold and immodest woman." Finally, in the late 1590s and early 1600s, the term underwent a third transformation, morphing into its current usage: "a girl who behaves like a spirited or boisterous boy; a wild romping girl."

While North Americans commonly see tomboyism as a transnational or cross-cultural concept—as young girls who enjoy climbing trees and playing sports can presumably be found throughout the world—it is distinctly Anglo-American. An array of languages, including Spanish, French, and Dutch, do not have the term, while others, like German with its concepts of *backfisch*

(which literally translates as "baked fish" but idiomatically refers to a rebellious and rambunctious girl) or *trotzkopf* (which means stubborn or pig-headed) have only rough equivalents. The geographic particularity of tomboyism calls attention to the relationship of this code of conduct to issues such as Anglo-European identity, gender roles in the West, and American and British nationalism.

Tomboyism as both a concept and a cultural phenomenon may date back to the Renaissance, but it did not become prevalent in Great Britain until the latter half of the eighteenth century. Both Mary Wollstonecraft and Catherine Macaulay advocate for an approach to raising young girls that can be seen as encouraging tomboyishness. In *Letters on Education* (1790), Macaulay urges new parents: "Let your children be brought up together; let their sports and studies be the same; let them enjoy, in the constant presence of those who are set over them, all that freedom which innocence renders harmless, and in which Nature rejoices." The concept also appears in diaries, journals, and letters from the period. Deborah Simonton (2005) has found instances of young girls explicitly referring to themselves as being a "tom-boy" in documents written as early as 1760.

The appearance of tomboyism in the United States occurred even later, in the nineteenth century. Adolescent girls and adult women who engaged in behavior that could be characterized as tomboyish certainly existed in both the literature and culture of these nations prior to this period; however, these individuals neither considered themselves nor were labeled by others as "tomboys." If such bold and daring female figures were called anything, it was "hoyden," a word which is commonly—although somewhat problematically—seen as a precursor to "tomboy." First appearing in the late sixteenth century, the term shares a similar etymological history: it also initially referred to rambunctious boys and men rather than girls and women. Indeed, the *OED* provides the following definition, from 1593, for "hoyden": "A rude, ignorant, or awkward fellow; a clown, boor." By the late seventeenth century, however, this meaning shifted and the word began referring to like-minded members of the opposite sex: "A rude, or ill-bred girl (or woman): a boisterous noisy girl, a romp." Unlike a tomboy, a hoyden was more closely associated with breaching bourgeois mores than female gender roles. As an entry in the *OED* from 1676 notes, a hoyden "calls people by their surnames," is "ungainly in her Behaviour," and is "slatternly ignorant." When the concept of "tomboy" made its debut during the mid-nineteenth century, it supplanted "hoyden." After 1886, in fact, the *OED* includes no new definitions of, or textual referents to, the latter term.

While "tomboy" may have eclipsed "hoyden," it also expanded on it, for this new code of conduct crystallized around a different set of cultural anxieties and served a vastly different societal purpose. Tomboyism is most commonly associated with the realm of gender, but it is also powerfully raced and classed. Emerging in the mid-nineteenth century as a product of growing concerns over the deplorable state of health among middle- and upper-class white women, tomboyism was created as an alternative and even antidote. Concerned that weak and sickly young girls would become weak and sickly wives who would produce even more weak and sickly children, advice writers during the 1840s and 1850s began to recommend active and unfettered girlhoods. As Sharon O'Brien (1979) has written, "[T]he rowdy tomboy would make a better wife and mother than her prissy, housebound sister . . . for participation in boyish sports and games would develop the health, strength, independence, and competence she would later need as a wife and mother." Calling for sensible clothing, physical exercise, and a wholesome diet, tomboyism would improve the strength and stamina of the nation's future wives and mothers and, by extension, their offspring. In this way, tomboyism was more than simply a new child-rearing practice or gender expression for adolescent girls in the United States; it was also a eugenic practice, a means to help ensure white racial supremacy. In the words of O'Brien (1979) once again, child-rearing manuals asserted that girls who were raised as tomboys "would surely develop the resourcefulness, self-confidence, and, most importantly, the constitutional vibrancy required for motherhood." In this way, while tomboyism is commonly seen as challenging or, at least, standing in opposition to heteronormativity, it was introduced in the 1840s and 1850s as a preparatory stage for it. Young girls embraced this new code of conduct not as a means to transgress their adult roles as wives and mothers, but, on the contrary, to train for them.

The wildly popular central character Capitola Black from E. D. E. N. Southworth's 1859 novel *The Hidden Hand*, who helped launch tomboyism in the nation's literature and culture, offers a powerful example of the original eugenic purpose of this code of conduct. Capitola's tomboyish bravery, daring, and autonomy do not turn her against either men or marriage. Whereas latter-day tomboys frequently proclaim that they dislike boys and will never marry, Southworth's gender-bending character makes repeated reference to her intention of getting married in general and being betrothed to childhood friend Herbert Greyson in particular.

If Cap is eager to get married, many men are eager to wed her. Rather than being repulsed by her physical strength or emotional fortitude, they find these qualities attractive. Impressed by her pluck and amazed by her independence, male characters ranging from the admirable Herbert Greyson and Major Warfield to the villainous Craven Le Noir and Black Donald fall in love with her. Craven swoons at the sight of Cap's "flaming cheeks," Black Donald speaks of her complimentarily as a "brick," and the cantankerous Old Hurricane concedes that the capricious young woman is his favorite.

Given that tomboyism was designed by doctors, parents, and authors of child-rearing manuals to be adopted by youthful girl participants, narratives intended for a largely middle-class female readership used their young female protagonists to present the benefits of tomboyism and persuade young girls to adopt it. From the title character in Mary J. Holmes's *'Lena Rivers* (1856) to the unruly Nancy Vawse in Susan Warner's *The Wide, Wide World* (1850), female figures who displayed the tomboyish traits of athleticism, adventurousness, and autonomy began to emerge in the domestic and sentimental novels written by women and directed at both adult and child audiences.

While it is commonplace to refer to tomboyism as a singular and static classification, it is actually far more fluid and multivalent. As Lynne Yamaguchi and Karen Barber note (1995), the term "tomboy" may connote "a virtually uniform picture of a girl who—by whatever standards society has dictated—acts like a boy," but how one defines a "transgression into boys' territory" differs for every individual because tomboys possess different coordinates of identity: they hail from different historical eras, live in different geographic regions, belong to different racial or ethnic groups or inhabit different socio-economic classes. Gender-bending female characters from the "golden era" of tomboy novels—the period extending from the 1860s through the 1930s—reveal the wide range of possible tomboyish identities. From the wealthy, feminine, and heterosexually alluring Nancy Drew from the mystery series to the poor, plain, and rough-and-tumble title character of Kate Douglas Wiggin's *Rebecca of Sunnybrook Farm* (1903), they demonstrate that tomboys can embody both masculine and feminine gender expressions, possess a diverse array of familial circumstances, and emerge against the backdrop of urban and rural settings.

Although tomboyism was initially conceived as a beneficial code of conduct that girls adopted as adolescents and maintained throughout their adult lives, this attribute quickly changed. Spurred by increased economic opportunities for women along with the emergence of the field of sexology and the accompanying "discovery" of female homosexuality during the *fin-de-siècle*, the phenomenon commonly known as "tomboy taming" (O'Brien 1979) was born. Exemplified most famously perhaps by the character of Jo March in *Little Women* (1868–69), young girls were now expected to slough off their tomboyish traits—ideally by choice but, if necessary, by force—when they reached the beginning of adolescence or the onset of puberty. Indeed, Jo's sister Meg scolds her in one of the opening pages of the novel, "You're old enough to leave off boyish tricks and behave better, Josephine. It didn't matter so much when you were a little girl; but now you are so tall, and turn up your hair, you should remember that you are a young lady."

For tomboys who were unwilling to abandon their tomboyish ways and embrace more feminine gender and sexual roles voluntarily, a popular literary method for compelling them to do so was the onset of life-threatening illness or injury. Susan Coolidge's *What Katy Did* (1872) largely established the paradigm. In the opening chapters of the novel, twelve-year-old Katy Carr "tore her dress every day, hated sewing, and didn't care a button about being 'good.'" But, as Elizabeth Segel (1994) notes, the punishment for her gender disobedience "is an injury to her back that keeps her bedridden and in pain for four years." By the time her injury heals, the young girl has sloughed off her tomboyish independence. By the end of both *What Katy Did* and *Little Women*, these tomboyish characters who had formerly thought about forgoing marriage and pursuing a professional career have abandoned that dream and become model and—in the case of Jo March, who has both biological and adopted children—even multivalent mothers.

This narrative trajectory for tomboy novels remained firmly in place until the second half of the twentieth century, when the advances made by second-wave feminism, the rise of the lesbian, gay, bisexual, transgender, and queer movement, and the emergence of queer theory began offering alternatives. Narratives such as Norma Klein's *Tomboy* (1978), Jerry Spinelli's *Who Put That Hair in My Toothbrush?* (1984), Cynthia Voight's *Jackaroo* (1985), and Pam Muñoz Ryan's *Riding Freedom* (1998) present a tomboy figure who feels pressure to tame her gender-bending ways, but does not completely capitulate to traditional notions of femininity. Some children's narratives have pushed this thinking further by addressing one final taboo—the link between tomboyism and nonheteronormative gender as well as sexual identities. Sharon Dennis Wyeth's illustrated reader *Tomboy Trouble* (1998), for example, resonates with what Judith Butler (1990) famously called "gender trouble." As I have written elsewhere, the book calls similar attention to the way in which gender is artificial and often even performative.

The eight-year-old main character frequently asserts that the outward, public manifestations of her identity—such as her short haircut, blue jeans, and baseball cap—are not accurate predictors of her internal, biological sex. As a result, these iconoclastic and even queer elements are unreliable indices. As such, they become, like the title of Wyeth's text indicates and the storyline repeatedly demonstrate, sites of multiple and multivalent forms of trouble. In doing so, *Tomboy Trouble* ultimately advocates a form of girlhood that transcends the categories of maleness and femaleness. It ultimately places the concept in dialogue with new and emerging categories of queer female identity, namely transgenderism (Abate 2008b).

Tomboyism has broadened from a cultural perspective as well. During the final decades of the twentieth century, both the Anglo-American word "tomboy" and the concept of "tomboyism" began to appear in other countries. In the late 1980s, for instance, anthropologist Ara Wilson (2004) observed that the term "tomboy" was being used by butch lesbians in Southeast Asia. Similarly, around the turn of the millennium, a popular Korean animé figure named Pucca appeared who was explicitly described by the English word "tomboy" on trading cards and merchandise packaging. The presence of these and other elements raises questions about the meaning and purpose of this code of conduct when it assumes an international dimension, and perhaps becomes a force of globalization—that is, when tomboyism is seen as a cultural identity as well as a capitalist "brand" that can be used to sell products around the world. (To name but a few such brands, there are the Colorado-based Tomboy Tools, the TomBoy chain of grocery stores in St. Louis, and the "Tomboy fit" t-shirts at Aeropostale.) In countries where the concept of a tomboy has recently appeared, does this code of conduct constitute a new gender paradigm, or does it simply give name to a behavior that was already extant? What are the societal attitudes about tomboyism, especially in light of the imperialistic nature of Anglo-American culture? Finally, does tomboyism retain its connection to middle- and upper-class women's eugenics and the maintenance of white racial hegemony when it crosses over into other cultures?

The gradual erosion of essentialist views of gender during the late twentieth century and the accompanying expansion of women's gender roles called into question the future relevance of the term "tomboy." In Klein's *Tomboy* (1978), the mother of protagonist Antonia "Toe" Henderson announces that the concept of tomboyism assumes that "there's a certain way girls should act and a certain way boys should act. That's so old-fashioned!'" Given that it is now routine for girls to wear pants, play sports, and have short hair, it would seem that nearly all young women today could be placed on the spectrum of tomboyishness. As tomboyism enters the twenty-first century, the way that it responds to developments in the areas of queer theory, gender identity, and third-wave feminism will reveal whether it will remain a real and relevant social identity or become an increasingly antiquated idea.

48

Voice

Mike Cadden

The first mention of "voice" as metaphor appeared in 1587 when Golding De Mornay wrote that "there is . . . a dubble Speech; the one in the mynd, . . . the other the sounding image thereof, . . . vttered by our mouth" (*Oxford English Dictionary*). Four centuries later, doubleness had become multiplicity. As Charlotte Otten and Gary Schmidt (1989) note, the "word *voice* itself is undergoing changes: it has moved from being a strictly descriptive term into the realm of metaphor that now includes more than point of view and that encompasses all that identity itself connotes." However, "voice" as a narrative metaphor is arguably the defining quality of literature for children and adolescents, and the notion of "dubble speech" marks the inherent tension in determining whether a book is a "children's book." The issue of voice is, then, the critical issue of *how*, between *who*, and *to whom*.

A standard definition of "voice" is "the set of signs characterizing the narrator and, more generally, the narrating instance, and governing the relations between narrating and narrative text as well as between narrating and narrated" (Prince 1987). Children's literature scholars stress the distinction between the narrator's voice in children's books and character dialogue or character narration, noting that it is important whether it is an "anonymous" voice or one with "verbal specificity" (Sircar 1989; Hourihan 1997). Barbara Wall (1991) uses voice as a means of genre definition: "It is not what is said, but the way it is said, and to whom it is said, which makes a book for children."

Uses of the external narrative voice range from the general and imperceptible to the intimate and often didactic. Folk literature set the fashion for an external narrator neither perceptible nor remarkable by voice. As early as the seventeenth century, but more typical of the eighteenth and nineteenth centuries, Western writers for children constructed perceptible external narrators who employed "intimate" voices—"either auntly or avuncular"—in children's books that often talked down to the implied audience; examples include works by Mrs. Molesworth, Lewis Carroll, Charles Kingsley, and George MacDonald (Sircar 1989; Hunt 1991; Wall 1991). These authors influenced the narrative voices of later authors such as Beatrix Potter, Kenneth Grahame, A. A. Milne, and C. S. Lewis. This is not to say that children's books lacked a didactic impulse prior to the eighteenth century; however, *what* was communicated is a different matter than *how*. Earlier, lessons were communicated largely by indifferent external narration and character dialogue. The "overt authorial narrator who flourished in the nineteenth century and spoke as 'I,' 'your author,' 'dear reader,' . . . has been out of fashion with critics in recent years" (Wall 1991), though there are contemporary inheritors who poke fun at this Victorian narrative voice, such as Lemony Snicket in his thirteen-part Series of Unfortunate Events (1999–2006) and Lois Lowry in her recent parody *The Willoughbys* (2008). The avuncular narrator's voice has been otherwise less popular in contemporary children's and young adult fiction, though that fiction often features tale-ending character narration outlining what was learned through the adventure (Trites 2000). Critics continue to argue about the audience reception of narrative voices that may or may not be interpreted as "cute" or condescending (Nodelman 1982; McGillis 1984).

The most important tensions that critics reveal have to do with the use of narration and narrative voice in the definition of children's literature. An extreme position is that children's literature itself is "impossible" because of the distance between the adult author's construction of an implied reader and actual children, and no literary genre has as great a "rupture" between writer, implied reader, and real reader as does children's literature (Rose 1984). While one position is that there is no child addressed but the one constructed by the adult writer, most other critics focus on the nature of the narrative engagement and the presumed ideological and ethical effects it entails. Although the disconnect between the implied and real readers could offer children the opportunity to learn to shift their own subject positions, most critics are concerned that the narrator is in a position to more forcibly prescribe the reader's subject position (Stephens 1992; Zipes 2001). There is the simple matter of power relations to consider—power that comes both with age differentials and narrative authority. Maria Nikolajeva (2002c) summarizes the problem well: "[T]he profound difference in life experience as well as linguistic skills create an inevitable discrepancy between the (adult) narrative voice and both the focalized child character's and the young reader's levels of comprehension" (see also Hunt 1991). This power differential has concerned critics who take a cultural studies approach to the study of children's literature, especially theorists working in feminism and postcolonialism (Nodelman 1992; Romines 1995; Kertzer 1996; McGillis 1999).

Critics see the choice of character narration as potentially more manipulative than more external narration. While for some, the voice in children's literature is a means to gain trust and embrace readers, others worry that first-person/character narration necessarily "invites the reader's acceptance of the narrator's values and judgments" more effectively than external narration (Hourihan 1997). Writers have addressed this concern in different ways. In *Voices in the Park* (1998), Anthony Browne disturbs the conventional authority of the narrator by creating one story composed of four separate "voices," each with its own characteristic typeface and style of illustration. The epistolary form, as seen in Jean Webster's *Daddy-Long-Legs* (1912), is especially compelling in its depiction of the development of the protagonist's voice, as she "moves from feeling 'silenced' in the beginning of the novel . . . [to] ultimately reaching a sense of personal authority and confidence" (Phillips 1999). In contrast, and perhaps ironically, school textbooks tend toward external narration, where the presumption is that the reader is meant to be kept at arm's length by textbook writers and publishers

(McGillis 1991; May 1995; Hourihan 1997). The voice of the character narrator can be made more distant through the time lapse between the events narrated and the telling of them. In Sharon Creech's *Walk Two Moons* (1994), the narrator has gained distance while remaining an engaging, intimate teller of the tale. In contrast, Christopher Paul Curtis's *The Watsons Go to Birmingham, 1963* (1995) is narrated shortly after the events of the novel, and is thus an "immediate" rather than "distant" character narration"; its immediacy is further enhanced by the use of first-person address (Schwenke-Wylie 1999). Some implications are that distance increases the likelihood of irony and decreases reliability. A common but erroneous assumption is that a narrative voice more ironic and unreliable necessarily corresponds to an adult readership.

A healthy critical body of work has been produced that focuses on the ethical implications of narrative voice. John Stephens (1992) has gone so far as to assert that the "most important concept for children to grasp about literary fictions is always that of narrative point of view, since this has the function of constructing subject positions and inscribing ideological assumptions." Arguments that narrative voice can draw in and situate young readers result in a tension between artistic and ethical concerns. While some writers for children who take a rhetorical view have ethical qualms about what one ought to write (Hunter 1976; Paterson 1981; Byars 1982), others take a more aesthetic view and argue that the writer must not censor themselves (Walsh 1973). Some make the case that it is simply right for children's

writers to pay attention to the real and likely audiences to which their books are handed. These arguments center around the notions that children's writers are more willing to focus on ethics than writers for other audiences, that many pursue ethical fiction indirectly by choosing particular genres in which to write, and that children's writers need to be more self-aware than other authors (Rose 1984; Mills 1997; Cadden 2000b). Indeed, Rod McGillis (1999) even wonders whether writers for children "steal the voices of others in the very act of providing a medium for those voices?" As a result, some critics have espoused strategies for defensive or resistant reading, or have celebrated books that employ narrative strategies for presenting multiple voices (McCallum 1999; Cadden 2000a; Trites 2000).

A strand of criticism that hinges on the question of voice concerns "crossover" fiction. In 1989, Otten and Schmidt noted A. A. Milne's narrator's "dual" voice in *Winnie-the-Pooh* (1926). The 1990s saw a marked increase in the study of the phenomenon of crossover work, which often focused on the narrator as the crux for determining when a book works for two audiences and when it doesn't. Barbara Wall's (1991) use of the terms "single address," "double address," and "dual address" was an early taxonomy for the ways narrators in children's fiction speak, respectively, to children, over the heads of children to adults on occasion, or to both children and adults simultaneously. Wall noted that dual address is rare and difficult, "presupposing as it does that a child narratee is addressed and an adult reader simultaneously satisfied"—as is seen, arguably, in works of nonsense especially. Double address—when a writer offers something for both children and adults through the use of irony and side commentary—is much more prevalent in successful children's books; in the special issue of *Children's Literature* on cross-writing, U. C. Knoepflmacher and Mitzi Myers (1997) argue convincingly that "a dialogic mix of older and younger voices occurs in texts too often read as univocal," and that this appeals to both children and adults. Often a text deemed "cross-written" is an accidental occurrence; Sandra Beckett (1999) notes that "many authors now aspire to and engage in the form of crosswriting that consists of addressing the same texts to young and old alike"—either in double or dual address, as Wall would have it—and that most cross-writing is the practice of authors writing for adults and children in separate works. Beckett (2009) has recently extended her inquiry to examine the worldwide trend of cross-writing and how it is changing our notions of separate readerships.

Children's and adolescent literature are genres defined by their audiences, so the voice of the narrator speaking to the implied reader through the narratee is an important consideration in defining them. As we further study narrative voice and the transaction between narrator and narratee, we may come to understand in more significant ways the relationship between adult author and child reader.

49

Young Adult
Lee A. Talley

The phrase "young adult" reflects the history of changing perceptions of childhood, adolescence, and adulthood and how these ideas have shaped parenting, education, libraries, publishing, and marketing (Cart 1996; Eccleshare 1996; Campbell 2009). The Young Adult Library Services Association (YALSA) denotes ages twelve to eighteen as composing "young adult" readers (YALSA 1994). Given the dominant conception that this period of growth is particularly important, understandings of what constitutes "good" young adult literature vary extensively, for there is a great deal at stake.

Readers often imagine young adult (YA) literature as texts that challenge the status quo. They believe that while children's literature finds its roots in a cheerful, Wordsworthian Romanticism, YA literature is heir to the more revolutionary strain of Blakean Romanticism with characters who incisively expose society's ills (Lesnik-Oberstein 1998). An examination of the phrase's history, however, reveals a more complex Romantic inheritance that can illuminate contradictions within the various communities that coalesce around their interest in YA literature, and in their belief in sheltering these readers from or introducing them to a range of texts.

Oddly, "young adult" is not found in most dictionaries even though it is used in thousands of articles in academic, educational, and library journals in addition to the popular press. Patty Campbell (2003) documents the earliest "use of the term young adult for teen books . . . [in] 1937, although it didn't come into general use until 1958." This move followed organizational changes within the American Library Association, dividing the Association of Young People's Librarians into the Children's Library Association and the Young Adult Services Division in 1957 (Starr n.d.), but librarians had already begun creating special spaces and services for their teenaged readers as early as 1926 (Campbell 2003).

"Young adult" is not in the *Oxford English Dictionary*, but *Random House Dictionary* defines it as "a teenager (used especially by publishers and librarians)." Improbably, their editors skip the phrase's adjectival form entirely. Although they gesture toward the textual world—reminding readers that people who work with books use this word—they never remark upon it in the context of YA literature. They also define it as "a person in the early years of adulthood," a definition that only points to the very end of the age continuum, excluding most of the readership addressed by Random House's YA imprint, Delacorte. It does incorporate the more expansive understanding of "young adult" that includes the MTV demographic of readers as old as twenty-five, however (Cart 2001).

The dominant way of imagining and marketing YA literature is shaped primarily by the age of the work's intended reader. Yet "crossover" novels such as Philip Pullman's *His Dark Materials* trilogy (1995–2000) and J. K. Rowling's Harry Potter series (1997–2007)—read by children, adolescents, and adults—challenge the categorization based solely on age. Further complicating the often dualistic category of crossover literature, YA literature comfortably houses award-winning "adult" texts such as Mark Haddon's *The Curious Incident of the Dog in the Night-Time* (2003); children's books like Jon Scieszka and Lane Smith's *The Stinky Cheese Man and Other Fairly Stupid Tales* (1992; see Aronson 2001); texts that have won awards in children's and young adult fiction, such as Nancy Farmer's *The House of the Scorpion* (2002); as well as literature imagined as young adult, such as Sherman Alexie's *The Absolutely True Diary of a Part-Time Indian* (2007).

Importantly, defining "young adult" according to what readers between the ages of twelve and eighteen (or twenty-five) would enjoy or benefit from reveals assumptions about adolescent readers that pre-date the "beginning" of YA literature in the 1960s. Sarah Trimmer appears to be the first to have used the concept of a young adult readership in her periodical, *The Guardian of Education* (1802–6), although she uses the terms "young person" or "young people" (Chambers 1985a; Eccleshare 1996). Trimmer, a deeply religious writer and publisher, loomed large on the intellectual landscape of the late eighteenth and early nineteenth centuries (Ruwe 2001), and upon her death, more than one person publicly urged Britain to memorialize her in Saint Paul's Cathedral (Myers 1990). Trimmer designed *The Guardian* to help adults choose "safe and good" books for children and young persons "from the most respectable sources" (Trimmer 1802). Her primary concern was helping readers avoid books influenced by contemporary philosophy, and promoting those that would shape well-behaved, submissive, and God-fearing youth.

Relying on some of the new theories of child development, Trimmer makes what is likely the first distinction between child and young adult readers, explaining how she

> shall endeavour to separate [texts] into two distinct classes, viz. Books *for Children*, and Books *for Young Persons* . . . [and shall] take the liberty of adopting the idea of our forefathers, by supposing all young gentlemen and ladies to be *Children*, till they are *fourteen* and *young persons* till they are at least *twenty-one*; and shall class books we examine as they shall appear to us to be suitable to these different stages of human life. (Trimmer 1802)

Although Trimmer's understanding of young people is remarkably contemporary in its perception of young adulthood as lasting until "at least twenty-one," and also in how it is conceptualizing young adult readers, *The Guardian*'s recommended reading is literature that might be enjoyed by adolescents but was not necessarily written with them in mind. (See Trites [1996, 2000] on the distinction between adolescent and YA literature; see Immel's index [1990] for the list of texts Trimmer recommended to her adolescent readers.) Undeniably, determining whether or not a work is written expressly for young adults is a significant variable in defining contemporary YA literature.

Contrary to Trimmer's understanding that good literature should fashion young readers into deeply moral people, contemporary YA literature ostensibly shuns that didactic impulse. And while Trimmer's periodical provided children and young people with models of near impossible virtue in order to shape more upright adults, today's YA literature could hardly be said to advance this agenda—indeed, the "adult" in "young adult" is often code for its euphemistic meaning of mature content. Yet, as many have pointed out, the problem novel in the 1970s, a staple genre within YA literature, was freighted with deeply didactic impulses (Cart 1996; Trites 2000). Undeniably, the conventional association between YA literature's beginnings and realism privileges both verisimilitude and a strong sense of moral purpose (see Cart 1996; Tribunella 2007; Campbell 2009; Nilsen and Donelson 2009). For if we take Raymond Williams's (1983a) important articulation of realism as "a description of facing up to things as they really are, and not as we imagine or would like them to be," then we arrive at a dominant theme in much of contemporary YA literature. While Trimmer's understanding of "things as they really are" is grounded in readings that reflect a prerevolutionary world order and a divine transcendental signified, the foundational texts of YA literature, such as S. E. Hinton's *The Outsiders* (1967), Paul Zindel's *The Pigman* (1968), and Robert Cormier's *The Chocolate War* (1974), are anchored in an equally fervent—though more subtly articulated—commitment to "'facing facts'" (Williams 1983a).

S. E. Hinton (1967b) calls for a young adult literature fashioned against romance—those novels about the "horse-and-the-girl-who-loved-it" as well as the "fairyland of proms and double dates." Instead, she insists that texts address the real "violence of teen-agers' lives . . . [such as] the beating-up at a local drive-in" or the "reality" of "the behind-the-scenes politicking that goes on in big schools, [and] the cruel social system" that defines popularity. She demands this realism because of her belief that young people "know their parents aren't superhuman, . . . that justice doesn't always win out, and that sometimes the bad guys win." Her understanding of fiction has an implicit moral imperative: to "face facts," certainly, but also to show that "some people don't sell out, and that everyone can't be bought." Jerry Renault, the protagonist of *The Chocolate War*, could be held up as an example of Hinton's latter claim. (Anita Tarr's [2002] vital rejoinder to this dominant reading extends Hinton's insistence on the importance of exposing the real violence of teenagers' lives. For Tarr reveals that Jerry does not make a conscious choice to "disturb the universe," and asserts that academics' and teachers' attention to his "decision" to resist the chocolate sale shifts critical focus away from the novel's deeply troubling and virulent misogyny—another "fact" readers need to face.)

Many contemporary YA writers, even those not allied with realist works, are also committed to this politics of realism, which often addresses ethical concerns. M. T. Anderson's *Astonishing Life of Octavian Nothing* novels (2006, 2008) present eighteenth-century American society in new and ominous ways, ingeniously illuminating the horrors of slavery, and melding rich historical realism with new imaginary perspectives. *Octavian Nothing* pushes readers to contemplate what it means to be human, and has stirred debate about the nature of youth and what they should be reading. Other significant YA texts also advance a realist agenda ineluctably bound up with a sense of the moral possibilities of literature. Francesca Lia Block's magical realist fiction reminds readers of the transformative potential of love and art in stories that address topics such as sexual abuse and AIDS, all the while challenging heteronormativity by consistently providing readers with gay characters. Other, more realist writers advance similar agendas and illuminate the limits of Block's more utopian yearnings. Jacqueline Woodson makes alarmingly clear that race still clouds how people see other humans in *If You Come Softly* (1998) and reveals the particular challenges facing biracial youth in *The House You Pass on the Way* (1999), as well as presenting a range of sexual identities and experiences for her characters. Walter Dean Myers's *Monster* (1999) scrutinizes flaws in the American judicial system while also trenchantly examining contemporary constructions of masculinity. And Catherine Atkins's *When Jeff Comes Home* (1999) considers sexual violence against boys and men, crucially illuminating effects of trauma as well as the intensely gendered ways we conceptualize victims of sexual violence (Pattee 2004). Other texts that examine rape, such as Laurie Halse Anderson's *Speak* (1999), work to show young readers that adults are not "superhuman," to use Hinton's phrase, but significantly depict them as human and humane—unlike the remote, distasteful, and sometimes sadistic adults presented in *The Chocolate War*. If sex and death are the two primary concepts from which we shelter children (Mills 2000), and then introduce young adults to in texts that reflect their burgeoning maturity, Jenny Downham's *Before I Die* (2007) considers both. Yet her novel and Cynthia Kadohata's *Kira-Kira* (2004) are as much about living fully as they are moving examinations of young people succumbing to terminal illnesses. Aidan Chambers's masterful *Postcards from No Man's Land* (1999) also addresses death, but pushes readers to contemplate the possibility of euthanasia for an aged protagonist, as well as challenging them to think about the Dutch and British legacies of World War II, teenagers' fascination with Anne Frank, and bisexuality.

Novels such as these reflect the breadth of the best of contemporary YA literature, but some would prefer these—and a host of others—to be censored. The disagreements reveal interesting ideas about young adults that recall the phrase's dual Romantic roots: YA readers are innocents in need of further shelter or last-minute instruction, or are readers who need to "face the facts" about the world, ideally becoming more enlightened, democratic world citizens. While contemporary YA writers have largely used literature to advance Western notions of adolescence as a time to question the power structure, rebel, or embrace one's "individuality," scholars should not forget this term's occluded Romantic inheritance of narrower reading practices and antirevolutionary sentiment. The rich field of YA literature is indebted to a number of revolutions, including but not limited to the social movements of the 1960s and the backlash that followed them; it is also heir to the French Revolution and reactions against the Enlightenment philosophies that brought it about. Both legacies reflect people's comprehension of literature's ability to shape, define, expand, and alter experience. Given the considerable changes in mind and body that mark adolescence, and our belief in the significance of this liminal state between childhood and adulthood, it is no wonder that YA literature is viewed—positively or negatively—as potent and transformative.

Works Cited

Abate, Michelle Ann. *Tomboys: A Literary and Cultural History*. Philadelphia: Temple University Press, 2008a.

———. "Trans/Forming Girlhood: Transgenderism, the Tomboy Formula, and Gender Identity Disorder in Sharon Dennis Wyeth's *Tomboy Trouble*." *The Lion and the Unicorn* 32 (2008b): 40–60.

Abdel-Fattah, Randa. *Does My Head Look Big in This?* Sydney: Pan Macmillan, 2005a.

———. "Living in a Material World." *Griffith Review* (Autumn 2005b): 199–209.

———. *Ten Things I Hate about Me*. 2006. New York: Orchard, 2009.

Abley, Mark. "Writing the Book on Intolerance." *Toronto Star*. December 4, 2007: AA8.

Ada, Alma Flor. *A Magical Encounter: Latino Children's Literature in the Classroom*, 2d ed. Boston: Pearson Education, 2003.

Adams, Gillian. "The First Children's Literature? The Case for Sumer." *Children's Literature* 14 (1986): 1–30.

———. "Medieval Children's Literature: Its Possibility and Actuality." *Children's Literature* 26 (1998): 1–24.

Adams, Karen. "Multicultural Representation in Children's Books." 1981. ERIC Document Reproduction Service No. ED219750.

Adams, Richard. *Watership Down*. London: Rex Collings, 1972.

Adamson, Andrew, and Vicky Jenson, directors. *Shrek*. Glendale, CA: DreamWorks Animation, 2001.

Adorno, Theodor. *Aesthetic Theory*. 1970. Translated by Robert Hullot-Kentor. Minneapolis: University of Minnesota Press, 1997.

Ahenakew, Freda. *How the Mouse Got Brown Teeth: A Cree Story for Children*. Illustrated by George Littlechild. Saskatoon, Saskatchewan: Fifth House Publishers, 1988.

Alcott, Louisa May. *Little Women*. 1868–69. Edited by Elaine Showalter. New York: Penguin, 1989.

———. *An Old-Fashioned Girl*. 1870. Online at http://www.gutenberg.org/etext/2787 (accessed July 11, 2008).

Alderson, Brian, and Felix de Marez Oyens. *Be Merry and Wise: Origins of Children's Book Publishing in England, 1650–1850*. New York: Pierpont Morgan Library and Bibliographical Society of America; London: British Library; New Castle, DE: Oak Knoll Press, 2006.

Aldiss, Brian W., and David Hargrove. "Introduction to *Trillion Year Spree*." In *Speculations on Speculation: Theories of Science Fiction*, edited by James Gunn and Matthew Candelaria, 147–61. Lanham, MD: Scarecrow Press, 2005.

Aldrich, Thomas Bailey. *The Story of a Bad Boy*. 1869. Hanover, NH: University Press of New England, 1996.

Alexander, Lloyd. "The Perilous Realms: A Colloquy." Edited by Betty Levin. In *Innocence and Experience: Essays & Conversations on Children's Literature*, edited by Barbara Harrison and Gregory Maguire. New York: Lothrop, Lee and Shepard, 1987.

Alexie, Sherman. *The Absolutely True Diary of a Part-Time Indian*. New York: Little, Brown, 2007.

Alger, Horatio. *Ragged Dick*. 1868. New York, Collier, 1962.

———. *Ragged Dick and Struggling Upward*. 1867/1890. New York: Penguin, 1985.

———. *The Erie Train Boy*. 1890. Peterborough, Ontario: Broadview, 2004.

Allard, Harry. *Miss Nelson Is Missing!* Illustrated by James Marshall. Boston: Houghton, 1977.

"All-Time Best-Selling Children's Books (Hardcover)." *InfoPlease: All the Knowledge You Need*. Online at http://www.infoplease.com/ipea/A0203049.html (accessed July 19, 2006.

Almond, David. *Skellig*. New York: Delacorte, 1997.

Althusser, Louis. *Lenin and Philosophy, and Other Essays*. Translated by Ben Robert Brewster. London: New Left, 1971.

Alvarez, Julia. *How Tía Lola Came to ~~Visit~~ Stay*. New York: Alfred A. Knopf, 2001.

American Library Association. "Attempts to Remove Children's Book on Male Penguin Couple Parenting Chick Continue." Online at http://www.ala.org/ala/newspresscenter/news/pressreleases2009/april2009 (accessed April 16, 2009).

American Library Association. "Frequently Challenged Books." 2009. Online at http://www.ala.org/ala/issuesadvocacy/banned/frequentlychallenged/index.cfm (accessed Sept. 12, 2010).

Ames, Mrs. Ernest [Mary Frances]. *An ABC, for Baby Patriots*. London: Dean and Son, 1899.

Anderson, Laurie Halse. *Speak*. New York: Farrar, Straus and Giroux, 1999.

Anderson, M. T. *Feed*. London: Walker, 2002.

———. *The Astonishing Life of Octavian Nothing, Traitor to the Nation, Volume I: The Pox Party*. Cambridge, MA: Candlewick Press, 2006.

———. *The Astonishing Life of Octavian Nothing, Traitor to the Nation, Volume II: The Kingdom on the Waves*. Cambridge, MA: Candlewick Press, 2008.

Anno, Mitsumasa. *Anno's Alphabet: An Adventure in Imagination*. London: Bodley Head, 1974.

Anzaldúa, Gloria. *Friends from the Other Side / Amigos del Otro Lado*. San Francisco: Aunt Lute, 1993.

Applebee, Arthur. *The Child's Concept of Story*. Chicago: University of Chicago Press, 1978.

Appleyard, J. A. *Becoming a Reader: The Experience of Fiction from Childhood to Adulthood*. New York: Cambridge University Press, 1990.

The Arabian Nights: Tales of 1001 Nights. 1706. Translated by Malcolm C. Lyons with Ursula Lyons. New York: Penguin, 2008.

Arac, Jonathan. *"Huckleberry Finn" as Idol and Target: The Functions of Criticism in Our Time*. Madison: University of Wisconsin Press, 1997.

Ardagh, Philip. "Wrap It Up." *Guardian*, December 20, 2003.

Argueta, Jorge. *Talking with Mother Earth / Hablando con Madre Tierra*. Toronto: Groundwood, 2006.

Ariès, Philippe. *Centuries of Childhood: A Social History of Family Life*. Translated by Robert Baldick. New York: Vintage, 1962.

Aristotle. *Poetics*. In *Classical Literary Criticism*, translated by T. Dorsch. Harmondsworth, UK: Penguin, 1965.

Arizpe, Evelyn, and Morag Styles. "'Love to Learn Your Book': Children's Experiences of Text in the Eighteenth Century," *History of Education* 33 (May 2004): 337–52.

Armstrong, William H. *Sounder*. New York: Harper and Row, 1969.

Arnold, Matthew. "The Study of Poetry." 1880. Reprinted in *The Harvard Classics*, vol. 50, edited by Charles William Eliot, 65–91. New York: P. F. Collier and Son, 1910.

Aronson, Marc. *Exploding the Myths: The Truth about Teenagers and Reading*. Lanham, MD: Scarecrow Press, 2001.

Asante, Molefi Kete. *Race, Rhetoric and Identity: The Architecton of Soul*. Amherst: Humanity, 2005.

Ashcroft, Bill. *Post-Colonial Transformation*. London: Routledge, 2001.

Ashcroft, Bill, Gareth Griffiths, and Helen Tiffin. *The Empire Writes Back: Theory and Practice in Post-Colonial Literatures*. London: Routledge, 1989.

———. *Post-Colonial Studies: The Key Concepts*. New York: Routledge, 2000.

Asheim, Lester. "Not Censorship But Selection." *Wilson Library Bulletin* 28 (1953): 63–67.

Ashford, Daisy. *The Young Visiters*. London: Chatto and Windus, 1919.

Atkins, Catherine. *When Jeff Comes Home*. New York: Puffin, 1999.

Attebery, Brian. *Strategies of Fantasy*. Bloomington: Indiana University Press, 1992.

Augustine, Saint, Bishop of Hippo. *The Confessions of St. Augustine*, Books I–X. A.D. 397–98. Translated by F. J. Sheed. New York: Sheed and Ward, 1942.

Avery, Gillian. *Childhood's Pattern: A Study of Heroes and Heroines of Children's Fiction, 1770–1950*. London: Hodder and Stoughton, 1975.

———. *Behold the Child: American Children and Their Books, 1621–1922*. Baltimore: Johns Hopkins University Press, 1994.

———. "The Beginnings of Children's Reading to c. 1700." In *Children's Literature: An Illustrated History*, edited by Peter Hunt. New York: Oxford University Press, 1995.

Babbitt, Natalie. "The Purposes of Fantasy." In *Innocence and Experience: Essays & Conversations on Children's Literature*, edited by Barbara Harrison and Gregory Maguire. New York: Lothrop, Lee and Shepard, 1987.

Bader, Barbara. *The American Picturebook: From Noah's Ark to the Beast Within*. New York: Macmillan, 1976.

———. "How the Little House Gave Ground: The Beginnings of Multiculturalism in a New, Black Children's Literature." *Horn Book* 78, no. 6 (2002): 657–73.

———. "Multiculturalism Takes Root." *Horn Book* 79, no. 2 (2003a): 143–62.

———. "Multiculturalism in the Mainstream." *Horn Book* 79, no. 3 (2003b): 265–91.

Bakhtin, Mikhail M. *Rabelais and His World*. Cambridge, MA: MIT Press, 1968.

Ball, John Clement. "Max's Colonial Fantasy: Rereading Sendak's *Where the Wild Things Are*." *Ariel* 28, no. 1 (1997): 167–79.

Ballantyne, R. M. *The Coral Island*. 1857. London: Penguin, 1994.

Bank Street School for Children. "History." *About the School*, July 18, 2006. Online at http://www.bankstreet.edu/sfc/history.html.

Banks, Lynne Reid. *The Indian in the Cupboard*. Garden City, NY: Doubleday, 1980.

Bannerman, Helen. *The Story of Little Black Sambo*. Philadelphia: J. B. Lippincott, 1899.

Bannerman, Helen, and Fred Marcellino. *The Story of Little Babaji*. New York: HarperCollins, 1996.

Bansch, Helga. *Odd Bird Out*. Translated by Monika Smith. Wellington: Gecko Press, 2008.

Banyai, Istvan. *Zoom*. New York: Viking, 1995.

Barbauld, Anna. *Lessons for Children from Two to Three Years Old*. London: Printed for J. Johnson, 1778.

Baring-Gould, William Stuart, and R. Hart-Davis, eds. *Lure of the Limerick*. London: Hart-Davis, 1969.

Barnes, Clare, Jr. *Home Sweet Zoo*. Garden City, NY: Doubleday, 1950.

Barrett, Lilly St. Agnan. Childhood Note in the Porter Phelps Huntington Family Papers, Special Collections, Amherst College Library, Amherst, Massachusetts.

Barrie, J. M. *Peter Pan*. 1911. Edited by Jack Zipes. New York: Penguin, 2004.

———. *Peter and Wendy*. New York : Charles Scribner's Sons, 1911.

Barry, Arlene. "Hispanic Representation in Literature for Children and Young Adults." *Journal of Adolescent & Adult Literacy* 41, no. 8 (1998): 630–37.

Barry, P. "Censorship and Children's Literature: Some Post-War Trends." In *Writing and Censorship in Britain*, edited by P. Hyland and N. Sammells. London: Routledge, 1992.

Barthes, Roland. *Image Music Text: Essays*. Translated by Stephen Heath. New York: Hill and Wang, 1977.

Baum, L. Frank. *The Wonderful Wizard of Oz*. 1900. Edited and with an Introduction and Notes by Susan Wolstenholme. New York: Oxford University Press, 1997.

———. *Ozma of Oz*. 1907. New York: Scholastic, 1984.

Baumgarten, Alexander G. *Aesthetica*. 1750–58. Hildesheim: G. Olms, 1986.

Bawden, Nina. *Carrie's War*. Philadelphia: J. B. Lippincott, 1973.

Beaty, Bart. *Fredric Wertham and the Critique of Mass Culture*. Jackson: University Press of Mississippi, 2005.

Bechtel, Louise Seaman. "A Rightful Heritage." 1953. In *Books in Search of Children: Speeches and Essays by Louise Seaman Bechtel*, edited by Virginia Haviland, 21–34. New York: Macmillan, 1969.

———. Untitled memoir. No date. Ms. 136, 4–5. Papers of Louise Seaman Bechtel, Baldwin Library of Historical Children's Literature, University of Florida, Gainesville.

Beckett, Sandra L. "From the Art of Rewriting to the Art of Crosswriting Child and Adult: The Secret of Michel Tournier's Dual Readership." In *Voices from Far Away: Current Trends in International Children's Literature Research*, edited by Maria Nikolajeva, 9–34. Stockholm: Centrum för barnkulturforskning, 1995.

———. *De grands romanciers écrivent pour les enfants*. Montréal: Presses de l'Université de Montréal, 1997.

———. *Transcending Boundaries: Writing for a Dual Audience of Children and Adults*. New York: Garland, 1999.

———. "Crossover Books." In *The Oxford Encyclopedia of Children's Literature*, vol. 1, edited by Jack Zipes, 369–70. New York: Oxford University Press, 2006.

———. *Crossover Fiction: Global and Historical Perspectives*. New York: Routledge, 2009.

Belting, Hans. "Image, Medium, Body: A New Approach to Iconology." *Critical Inquiry* 31 (Winter 2005): 302–19.

Bennett, John. *Letters to a Young Lady on a variety of useful and interesting subjects calculated improve the heart, to form the manners and enlighten the understanding*. London: T. Cadell, 1795.

Bennett, Tony, Lawrence Grossberg, and Meaghan Morris, eds. *New Keywords: A Revised Vocabulary of Culture and Society*. Oxford: Blackwell, 2005.

Benton, Michael. "Readers, Texts, Contexts: Reader-Response Criticism." In *Understanding Children's Literature*, edited by Peter Hunt, 86–102. London: Routledge, 1995; rev. ed., 2005.

Berger, Peter L., and Thomas Luckmann. *The Social Construction of Reality: A Treatise in the Sociology of Knowledge*. 1966. New York: Anchor, 1989.

Berlant, Lauren. *The Queen of America Goes to Washington City: Essays on Sex and Citizenship*. Durham, NC: Duke University Press, 1997.

Beronä, David. *Wordless Books: The Original Graphic Novels*. New York: Abrams, 2008.

"The Best American Books." *The Critic* 19 (June 3, 1893): 589.

Bettelheim, Bruno. *The Uses of Enchantment: The Meaning and Importance of Fairy Tales*. London: Thames and Hudson, 1976.

Bhabha, Homi K. *The Location of Culture*. London: Routledge, 1994.

Billman, Carol. *The Secret of the Stratemeyer Syndicate: Nancy Drew, the Hardy Boys, and the Million Dollar Fiction Factory*. New York: Ungar, 1986.

Birdsall, Jeanne. *The Penderwicks: A Summer Tale of Two Sisters, Two Rabbits, and a Very Interesting Boy*. New York: Random House, 2005.

Birkerts, Sven. *The Gutenberg Elegies: The Fate of Reading in an Electronic Age*. London: Faber, 1994.

Bishop, Gavin. *The House That Jack Built*. Auckland: Scholastic, 1999.

Bishop, Rudine Sims. *Shadow and Substance: Afro-American Experience in Contemporary Children's Fiction*. Urbana, IL: National Council of Teachers of English, 1982.

———. *Free within Ourselves: The Development of African American Children's Literature*. Westport, CT: Greenwood, 2007.

Black, Gavin. *The Golden Cockatrice*. London: Fontana, 1975.

Blair, Lorrie. "Strategies for Dealing with Censorship." *Art Education* (September 1996): 57–61.

Blake, Quentin. *La Vie de la Page*. Paris: Gallimard Jeunesse, 1995.

———. *Tell Me a Picture*. 2001. London: Frances Lincoln, 2002.

Blake, William. *Songs of Innocence*. London, 1789.

———. *Songs of Experience*. London, 1794.

Block, Francesca Lia. *Dangerous Angels: The Weetzie Bat Books*. 1989–2005. New York: HarperCollins, 2007.

Bloor, Edward. *Tangerine*. 1997. New York: Scholastic, 2001.

Blount, Thomas. *Glossographia, or, A dictionary, interpreting all such hard words, whether Hebrew, Greek, Latin, Italian, Spanish, French, Teutonick, Belgick, British or Saxon, as are now used in our refined English tongue also the terms of divinity, law, physick, mathematicks, heraldry, anatomy, war, musick, architecture, and of several other arts and sciences explicated: with etymologies, definitions, and historical observations on the same*. London: Printed by Tho. Newcomb, 1656.

Blue, Rose. *We Are Chicano*. New York: Watts, 1973.

Blum, Virginia. *Hide and Seek: The Child between Psychoanalysis and Fiction*. Urbana: University of Illinois Press, 1995.

Blume, Judy. *Are You There God? It's Me, Margaret*. New York: Bradbury, 1970.

———. *Then Again, Maybe I Won't*. Scarsdale, NY: Bradbury, 1971.

———. Fudge series, comprising *Tales of a Fourth Grade Nothing, Otherwise Known as Sheila the Great, Superfudge, Fudge-a-Mania*, and *Double Fudge*. New York: Dutton, 1972–2002.

———. *Deenie*. Scarsdale, NY: Bradbury, 1973.

———. *Blubber*. Scarsdale, NY: Bradbury, 1974.

———. *Forever*. New York: Bradbury, 1975.

Boas, George. *The Cult of Childhood*. Dallas: Spring, 1966.

Boehmer, Elleke. *Colonial and Postcolonial Literature: Migrant Metaphors*. Oxford and New York: Oxford University Press, 1995.

Boethius, Ulf, ed. *Modernity, Modernism and Children's Literature*. Stockholm: Centrum för barnkulturforskning vid Stockholms universitet, 1998.

Bone, Ian. *Sleep Rough Tonight*. Camberwell, Victoria: Penguin, 2004.

Booker, Christopher. *The Seven Basic Plots: Why We Tell Stories*. London: Continuum, 2004.

"Books Involving Witchcraft, Indian Beliefs Stay in Traditional School," *Vancouver Sun*, December 20, 1994: B7.

Boone, Troy. *Youth of Darkest England: Working-Class Children at the Heart of Victorian Empire*. New York: Routledge, 2005.

Booth, David. *Censorship Goes to School*. Markham, Ontario: Pembroke, 1992.

Borges, Jorge Luis. "The Library of Babel." 1941. In *Collected Fictions*, translated by Andrew Hurley, 112–18. New York: Viking, 1998.

Boswell, James. *The Life of Samuel Johnson*. London: Charles Dilly, 1791.

Bottigheimer, Ruth B. "An Important System of Its Own: Defining Children's Literature." *Library Chronical* 59, no. 2 (1998): 190–210.

Bourdieu, Pierre. "The Forms of Capital." 1982. Reprinted in *Handbook of Theory and Research for the Sociology of Education*, edited by John G. Richardson, 241–58. New York: Greenwood, 1986.

———. *Distinction: A Social Critique of the Judgement of Taste*. 1979. Translated by Richard Nice. Cambridge: Harvard University Press, 1998.

Bracher, Mark. "Identity and Desire in the Classroom." In *Pedagogical Desire: Authority, Seduction, Transference, and the Question of Ethics*, edited by Jan Jagodzinski, 93–121. Westport, CT: Bergin and Garvey, 2002.

Bradbury, Malcolm, and James MacFarlane. *Modernism, 1890–1930*. Harmondsworth: Penguin, 1976.

Bradford, Clare. "Playing with Father: Anthony Browne's Picture Books and the Masculine." *Children's Literature in Education* 29, no. 2 (1998): 79–96.

———. *Reading Race: Aboriginality in Australian Children's Literature*. Carlton: Melbourne University Press, 2001.

———. "Multiculturalism and Children's Books." In *The Oxford Encyclopedia of Children's Literature*, vol. 3, edited by Jack Zipes, 113–18. New York: Oxford University Press, 2006.

———. *Unsettling Narratives: Postcolonial Readings of Children's Literature*. Waterloo, Ontario: Wilfrid Laurier University Press, 2007.

Bratton, J. S. "British Imperialism and the Reproduction of Femininity in Girls' Fiction, 1900–1930." In *Imperialism and Juvenile Literature*, edited by Jeffrey Richards. Manchester: Manchester University, 1989.

Briggs, Jimmie. *Innocents Lost: When Child Soldiers Go to War*. New York: Basic, 2005.

Briggs, Raymond. *The Snowman*. New York: Random House, 1978.

Bristow, Joseph. *Empire Boys: Adventures in a Man's World*. London: HarperCollins Academic, 1991.

Broderick, Dorothy. *Images of the Black in Children's Fiction*. New York: R. R. Bowker, 1973.

Brown, Dan. *The Da Vinci Code*. New York: Doubleday, 2003.

Brown, Gillian. *The Consent of the Governed: The Lockean Legacy in*

Early American Culture. Cambridge, MA: Harvard University Press, 2001.

Brown, Joanne. "Interrogating the 'Real' in Young Adult Realism." *New Advocate* 12, no. 4 (1999): 345–57.

Brown, Margaret Wise. *Goodnight, Moon*. Illustrated by Clement Hurd. New York: Harper and Brothers, 1947.

———. *Buenas Noches, Luna*. Illustrated by Clement Hurd. Translated by Teresa Mlawer. New York: Harper Arco Iris, 1995.

Browne, Anthony. *A Walk in the Park*. London: Hamilton, 1977.

———. *Piggybook*. London: Julia Macrae, 1986.

———. *Bear Hunt*. 1979. London: Puffin, 1994.

———. *Willy the Dreamer*. London: Walker, 1997.

———. *Voices in the Park*. 1998. London: Picture Corgi, 1999.

Bruce, Mary Grant. Billabong series, comprising *A Little Bush Maid, Mates at Billabong, Norah of Billabong, From Billabong to London, Jim and Wally, Captain Jim, Back to Billabong, Billabong's Daughter, Billabong Adventurers, Bill of Billabong, Wings Above Billabong, Billabong Gold, Son of Billabong*, and *Billabong Riders*. London: Ward Lock, 1910–42.

Bruhm, Steven, and Natasha Hurley, eds. *Curiouser: On the Queerness of Children*. Minneapolis: University of Minnesota Press, 2004.

Bruner, Jerome. *Actual Minds, Possible Worlds*. Cambridge, MA: Harvard University Press, 1986.

Bullen, Elizabeth. "Who Is Ryan Atwood? Social Mobility and the Class Chameleon in *The OC*." *The Looking Glass: New Perspectives on Children's Books* 11 no. 1 (2007). Online at http://tlg.ninthwonder.com/rabbit/v11i1/alice1.html.

Bunge, Marcia J., ed. *The Child in Christian Thought*. Grand Rapids, MI: William B. Eerdmans, 2001.

Bunting, Eve. *Fly Away Home*. New York: Clarion, 1991.

———. *A Day's Work*. New York: Clarion, 1994.

Bürger, Peter. *Theory of the Avant-Garde*. Translated by Michael Shaw. Minneapolis: University of Minnesota Press, 1984.

Burgess, Melvin. *Smack*. New York: Holt, 1997.

Burgett, Bruce, and Glenn Hendler, eds. *Keywords for American Cultural Studies*. New York: New York University Press, 2007.

Burke, Kenneth. *The Philosophy of Literary Form*. Berkeley: University of California Press, 1973.

Burnett, Frances Hodgson. *Little Lord Fauntleroy*. London: Frederick Warne, 1886.

———. *A Little Princess: Being the Whole Story of Sara Crewe Now Told for the First Time*. London: Frederick Warne, 1905.

———. *The Secret Garden*. 1911. Harmondsworth, UK: Penguin-Puffin, 1951.

Burroughs, Edgar Rice. *Tarzan of the Apes*. Chicago: McClurg, 1914.

Burton, Robert. *The Anatomy of Melancholy*. 1621. London: Nimmo, 1886.

Busch, Wilhelm. *Max und Moritz*. 1865. Munich: Braun und Schneider, 1925.

Butler, Judith. *Gender Trouble: Feminism and the Subversion of Identity*. New York: Routledge, 1990.

———. *Bodies That Matter: On the Discursive Limits of "Sex."* New York: Routledge, 1993.

Butts, Dennis. "'Tis a Hundred Years Since: G. A. Henty's *With Clive in India* and Philip Pullman's *The Tin Princess*." In *The Presence of the Past in Children's Literature*, edited by Ann Lawson Lucas. Westport, CT: Praeger, 2003.

Byars, Betsy. "Writing for Children." *Signal* 37 (1982): 3–10.

Cabot, Meg. *The Princess Diaries*. New York: Harper Avon, 2000.

Cadden, Mike. "The Irony of Narration in the Young Adult Novel." *Children's Literature Association Quarterly* 25 (2000a): 146–54.

———. "Speaking to Both Children and Genre: Le Guin's Ethics of Audience." *The Lion and the Unicorn* 24, no. 1 (2000b): 128–42.

Cadogan, Mary, and Patricia Craig. *You're a Brick, Angela! A New Look at Girls Fiction from 1839 to 1975*. London: Victor Gollanz, 1976.

Caduto, Michael J., and Joseph Bruchac. *Keepers of the Earth: Native American Stories and Environmental Activities for Children*. 1988. Golden, CO: Fulcrum, 1997.

Calvert, Karin. *Children in the House: The Material Culture of Early Childhood, 1600–1900*. Boston: Northeastern University Press, 1992.

Cameron, Eleanor. *The Wonderful Flight to the Mushroom Planet*. New York: Little, Brown, 1954.

Cammaerts, Emile. *The Poetry of Nonsense*. New York: Dutton, 1926.

Campbell, Eddie. *Alec: How to Be an Artist*. Paddington, Australia: Eddie Campbell Comics, 2001.

Campbell, Joseph. *The Hero with a Thousand Faces*. New York: Pantheon, 1949.

Campbell, Patty. "*The Outsiders*, Fat Freddy, and Me." *The Hornbook* (March/April 2003): 177–83.

———. "Trends in Young Adult Literature." In *Young Adult Literature in the 21st Century*, edited by Pam B. Cole, 66–69. Boston: McGraw-Hill, 2009.

Card, Orson Scott. *Ender's Game*. New York: Tor, 1985.

Carle, Eric. *The Very Hungry Caterpillar*. New York: Philomel, 1969.

Carlson, D. "Who Am I? Gay Identity and a Democratic Politics of the Self." In *Queer Theory in Education,* edited by W. Pinar, 107–19. Hillsdale, NJ: Lawrence Erlbaum Associates, 1998.

Carnegie, Andrew. "Wealth." *North American Review* 148 (June 1889): 653–65.

Carpenter, Carole H. "Enlisting Children's Literature in the Goals of Multiculturalism." *Mosaic: A Journal for the Interdisciplinary Study of Literature* 29, no. 3 (1996): 53–74.

Carpenter, Humphrey. *Secret Gardens: The Golden Age of Children's Literature from Alice's Adventures in Wonderland to Winnie the Pooh*. Boston: Houghton Mifflin, 1985.

Carroll, Lewis. *Alice's Adventures in Wonderland*. 1865. In *The Annotated Alice*, rev. ed., edited by Martin Gardner. Harmondsworth, UK: Penguin, 1970.

———. *The Letters of Lewis Carroll*. Edited by Morton N. Cohen, 2 vols. New York: Oxford University Press, 1979.

———. *Through the Looking-Glass and What Alice Found There*. 1871. Edited by Donald J. Gray. New York: Norton, 1992.

Carruthers, Mary, and Jan M. Ziolkowski, eds. *The Medieval Craft of Memory: An Anthology of Texts and Pictures*. Philadelphia: University of Pennsylvania Press, 2002.

Cart, Michael. *From Romance to Realism: 50 Years of Growth and Change in Young Adult Literature*. New York: HarperCollins, 1996.

———. "From Insider to Outsider: The Evolution of Young Adult Literature." *Voices from the Middle* 9, no.2 (2001): 95–97.

Cary, Stephen. *Going Graphic: Comics at Work in the Multilingual Classroom*. Portsmouth, NH: Heinemann, 2004.

Cech, John. "Touchstones and the Phoenix: New Directions, New Dimensions." *Children's Literature Association Quarterly* 10, no. 4 (1986): 177.

Cervantes, Miguel de. *Don Quixote*. 1606/1615. Translated by Charles Jarvis, with an Introduction and Notes by E. C. Riley, 1742. New York: Oxford University Press, 1992.

Chabram-Dernersesian, Angie. "Latina/o: Another Site of Struggle, Another Site of Accountability." In *Critical Latin American and Latino Studies*, edited by Juan Poblete. Minneapolis: University of Minnesota Press, 2003.

Chakrabarty, Dipesh. "Postcoloniality and the Artifice of History: Who Speaks for 'Indian' Pasts?" *Representations* 32 (1992): 1–26.

Chambers, Aidan. *Break Time*. London: Bodley Head, 1978a.

———. *Dance on My Grave*. London: Bodley Head, 1982.

———. "Three Fallacies about Children's Books." 1978b. In *Signposts to Criticism of Children's Literature*, edited by R. Bator, 54–59. Chicago: American Library Association, 1983.

———. "Alive and Flourishing: A Personal View of Teenage Literature." In *Booktalk: Occasional Writing on Literature and Children*, edited by Aidan Chambers, 84–91. New York: Harper and Row, 1985a.

———. "The Reader in the Book." In *Booktalk: Occasional Writing on Literature and Children*, edited by Aidan Chambers. New York: Harper and Row, 1985b.

———. *Now I Know*. London: Bodley Head, 1987.

———. *The Toll Bridge*. London: Bodley Head, 1992.

———. *Postcards from No Man's Land*. New York: Speak, 1999.

———. *This Is All: The Pillow Book of Cordelia Kenn*. London: Bodley Head, 2005.

Chappell, Sharon, and Christian Faltis. "Spanish, Bilingualism, Culture, and Identity in Latino Children's Literature." *Children's Literature in Education* 38, no. 4 (2007): 253–62.

Character Counts! 2009. Online at http://charactercounts.org/resources/booklist.php.

Charlip, Remy, and Jerry Joyner. *Thirteen*. New York: Parents Magazine Press, 1975.

Chase, Richard. *The American Novel and Its Tradition*. New York: Anchor/Doubleday, 1957.

Chaucer, Geoffrey. *The Prologue to the Canterbury Tales*. 1387. Edited by R. T. Davies. London: Harrap, 1953.

Chaudhuri, Nirad C. *The Autobiography of an Unknown Indian*. Reading, MA: Addison-Wesley, 1951.

Chaudhuri Nupur, and Margaret Strobel. *Western Women and Imperialism: Complicity and Resistance*. Bloomington: Indiana University Press, 1992.

Cherniavsky, Eva. "Body." In *Keywords for American Cultural Studies*, edited by Bruce Burgett and Glenn Hendler, 26–29. New York: New York University Press, 2007.

Cheong Suk-Wai. "Reading into Crossover Trends." *The Straits Times*, March 8, 2004.

Chesworth, Michael. *Alphaboat*. New York: Farrar, Straus and Giroux, 2002.

Child, Lauren. *Hubert Horatio Bartle Bobton-Trent*. London: Hodder, 2004.

Children's Defense Fund. "The State of America's Children 2008." Online at http://www.childrensdefense.org.

"Children's Literature." *The Quarterly Review*, January 13 and 26, 1860: 469–500.

Childress, Alice. *A Hero Ain't Nothin' But a Sandwich*. 1973. New York: Avon, 1982.

Christian-Smith, Linda K. *Becoming a Woman through Romance*. New York: Routledge, 1990.

Christopher, John. *The White Mountains*. London: Hamilton, 1967a.

———. *The City of Gold and Lead*. London: Hamilton, 1967b.

———. *The Pool of Fire*. London: Hamilton, 1968.

Chudacoff, Howard P. *How Old Are You? Age Consciousness in American Culture*. Princeton: Princeton University Press, 1989.

Chukovsky, Kornei. *From Two to Five*. Translated by Miriam Morton. Berkeley: University of California Press, 1963.

Clark, Beverly Lyon. "Thirteen Ways of Thumbing your Nose at Children's Literature." *The Lion and the Unicorn* 16, no. 2 (1992): 240–44.

———. *Regendering the School Story: Sassy Sissies and Tattling Tomboys*. New York: Garland, 1996.

———. *Kiddie Lit: The Cultural Construction of Children's Literature in America*. Baltimore: Johns Hopkins University Press, 2003.

Clark, Gillian. "The Fathers and the Children." In *The Church and Childhood*, edited by Diana Wood, 1–27. Oxford: Blackwell, 1994.

Clarke, John. "Market." In *New Keywords: A Revised Vocabulary of Culture and Society*, edited by Tony Bennett, Lawrence Grossberg, and Meaghan Morris, 205–7. Malden, MA: Blackwell, 2005.

Clements, Andrew. *Frindle*. Illustrated by Brian Selznick. 1996. New York: Aladdin, 1998.

Clute, John, and John Grant, eds. *The Encyclopedia of Fantasy*. London: Orbit, 1997.

Coats, Karen. *Looking Glasses and Neverlands: Lacan, Desire, and Subjectivity in Children's Literature*. Iowa City: University of Iowa Press, 2004.

Coetzee, J. M. "What Is a Classic?" 1993. In *Stranger Shores: Literary Essays*, 1–17. New York: Viking Penguin, 2001.

Cohoon, Lorinda B. *Serialized Citizenships: Periodicals, Books, and American Boys, 1840–1911*. Lanham, MD: Scarecrow, 2006.

Cole, Brock. *The Goats*. New York: Farrar, Straus and Giroux, 1987.

Cole, Henry [Felix Summerly, pseud.]. *Beauty and the Beast with New Pictures by an Eminent Artist*. In *The Home Treasury* series. Edited by Felix Summerly. London: Joseph Cundall, 1843.

Coleridge, Samuel. *Biographia Literaria, or Biographical Sketches of My Literary Life and Opinions*. 1817. Edited by George Watson. London: Dent, 1975.

Collins, Wilkie. "Doctor Dulcamara, M.P." *Household Words* 19 (1858): 49–52. Online, http://www.web40571.clarahost.co.uk/wilkie/etext/DoctorDulcamara.htm.

The Columbia Encyclopedia. 6th ed. New York: Columbia University Press, 2008.

Comenius, Johann Amos. *Orbis Sensulium Pictus*. 1658. Translated by Charles Hoole, 1659. London: Printed for T. R. for S. Mearne, 1672.

Compact Edition of the Oxford English Dictionary. Oxford: Oxford University Press, 1971.

Connell, R. W. "Logic and Politics in Theories of Class." In *Which Way Is Up? Essays on Sex, Class and Culture*, edited by R. W. Connell. Sydney: George Allen and Unwin, 1983.

———. *Masculinities*. 2d ed. Crows Nest: Allen and Unwin, 2005.

Connelly, Mark. *The Hardy Boys Mysteries, 1927–1979: A Cultural and Literary History*. Jefferson, NC: McFarland, 2008.

Constantine, Larry L., and Floyd M. Martinson. *Children and Sex: New Findings, New Perspectives*. Boston: Little, Brown, 1981.

Cooley, Charles H. *Human Nature and the Social Order*. New York: Scribner's, 1902.

Coolidge, Susan. *What Katy Did*. 1872. Boston: Little, Brown, 1938.

Cooper, Susan. *Silver on the Tree*. New York: Atheneum, 1977.

Cormier, Robert. *The Chocolate War: A Novel*. New York: Pantheon, 1974.

———. *Fade*. New York: Delacorte Press, 1988.

Council on Interracial Books for Children. "100 Children's Books about Puerto Ricans: A Study in Racism, Sexism, & Colonialism." *Interracial Books for Children Bulletin* 4 (1972): 1–8.

———. "Chicano Culture in Children's Literature: Stereotypes, Distortions, and Omissions." *Interracial Books for Children Bulletin* 5 (1975): 7–14.

Cox, Cynthia. "'Postmodern Fairy Tales' in Contemporary Literature." *Children's Folklore Review* 16, no. 2 (1994): 13–19.

Crago, Hugh. *The Teller and the Tale: How the Old Brain Shapes the Stories We Live to Tell*. Forthcoming.

Crago, Maureen, and Hugh Crago. *Prelude to Literacy: A Preschool Child's Encounter with Picture and Story*. Carbondale: Southern Illinois University Press, 1983.

Crain, Patricia. *The Story of A: The Alphabetization of America from The New England Primer to The Scarlet Letter*. Stanford: Stanford University Press, 2000.

Crampton, Gertrude. *Tootle*. Illustrated by Tibor Gergely. Racine, WI: Golden Press, 1945.

——. *Scuffy the Tugboat*. Illustrated by Tibor Gergely. 1946. Racine, WI: Golden Press, 1955.

Crawford, Philip, and Stephen Weiner. *Using Graphic Novels with Children and Teens*. New York: Scholastic, 2007.

Creech, Sharon. *Walk Two Moons*. New York: Scholastic, 1994.

Crossoverguide.com. Online at http://www.crossoverguide.com (accessed April 2008).

Cruikshank, George. *George Cruikshank's Magazine*, no 2 (February 1854). Edited by Frank E. Smedley (Frank Fairlegh).

Crutcher, Chris. *Chinese Handcuffs*. New York: Greenwillow, 1989.

Cuffee, Paul. "Memoir of Captain Paul Cuffee, Liverpool *Mercury*, 1811." Online at http://www.pbs.org/wgbh/aia/part3/3h485.html.

Cullen, Countee. *On These I Stand: Anthology of the Best Poems of Countee Cullen*. New York: Harper and Brothers, 1947.

Culler, Jonathan. *Structuralist Poetics: Structuralism, Linguistics, and the Study of Literature*. Ithaca, NY: Cornell University Press, 1975.

——. "Prolegomena to a Theory of Reading," In *The Reader in the Text: Essays on Audience and Interpretation*, edited by Susan R. Suleiman and Inge Crosman. Princeton: Princeton University Press, 1980.

——. *Literary Theory: A Very Short Introduction*. Oxford: Oxford University Press, 2000.

Cunningham, Hugh. *Children & Childhood in Western Society since 1500*. London: Longman, 1995.

——. *The Invention of Childhood*. London: BBC Books, 2006.

Cunningham, Valentine. *Reading after Theory*. Malden, MA: Blackwell, 2002.

Curtis, Christopher Paul. *The Watsons Go to Birmingham, 1963*. New York: Random House, 1995.

Dalgliesh, Alice. *The Courage of Sarah Noble*. Illustrated by Leonard Weisgard. New York: Scribner's, 1954.

Dahl, Roald. *James and the Giant Peach*. New York: Alfre A. Knopf, 1961.

——. *Charlie and the Chocolate Factory*. New York: Alfred A. Knopf, 1964.

——. *The Witches*. New York: Farrar, Straus and Giroux, 1983.

Dana, Richard Henry. *Two Years before the Mast*. New York: Harper, 1840.

Danby, John. F. *Shakespeare's Doctrine of Nature: A Study of King Lear*. London: Faber and Faber, 1961.

Darnton, Robert. *The Great Cat Massacre, and Other Episodes in French Cultural History*. London: Allen Lane, 1984.

Darton, F. J. Harvey. *Children's Books in England: Five Centuries of Social Life*. 1932. 3d ed., revised by Brian Alderson. New York: Cambridge University Press, 1982.

Davis, Will. *My Side of the Story*. London: Bloomsbury, 2007.

Day, Frances. *Latina and Latino Voices in Literature for Children and Teenagers*. Portsmouth, NH: Heinemann, 1997.

Day, Thomas. *The History of Sandford and Merton*. London, 1783–89.

De Anda, Diane. *Kikirikí/Quiquiriquí*. Houston: Piñata, 2004.

Defoe, Daniel. *Robinson Crusoe*. 1719. London: Dent, 1975.

——. *Mere Nature Delineated*. 1726. In *The Works of Daniel Defoe*, edited by W. R. Owens and P. N. Furbank. London: Pickering and Chatto, 2002.

Delacre, Lulu. *Arrorró, mi niño: Latino Lullabies and Gentle Games*. New York: Lee and Low, 2004.

De la Primaudaye, Peter. *The French Academie*. London: Thomas Adams, 1618.

De Lauretis, Teresa. "Queer Theory: Lesbian and Gay Sexualities." *differences: A Journal of Feminist Cultural Studies* 3, no. 2 (1991): iii–xviii.

——. "Habit Changes." *differences: A Journal of Feminist Cultural Studies* 6, nos. 2–3 (1994): 296–313.

Deleuze, Gilles. *Cinema 1: The Movement Image*. 1983. Translated by Hugh Tomlinson and Barbara Habberjam. Minneapolis: University of Minnesota Press, 1986.

Deleuze, Gilles. *Cinema 2: The Time Image*. 1985. Translated by Hugh Tomlinson. Minneapolis: University of Minnesota Press, 1989.

Deleuze, Gilles, and Félix Guattari. *A Thousand Plateaus: Capitalism and Schizophrenia*. Translated by Brian Massumi. London: Athlone, 1988.

Del Vecchio, Gene. *Creating Ever-Cool: A Marketer's Guide to a Kid's Heart*. 1997. Gretna, LA: Pelican Publishing, 1998.

Demers, Patricia. "Classic or Touchstone: Much of a Muchness?" *Children's Literature Association Quarterly* 10, no. 3 (1985): 142–43.

Demers, Patricia, and Gordon Moyles, eds. *From Instruction to Delight: An Anthology of Children's Literature to 1850*. New York: Oxford University Press, 1982.

Denman, Gregory A. *When You've Made It Your Own . . . Teaching Poetry to Young People*. Portsmouth, NH: Heinemann, 1988.

De Palma, Brian. *Carrie*. Written by Lawrence D. Cohen. Based on the novel by Stephen King. United Artists, 1976.

Derrida, Jacques. *Of Grammatology*. 1967. Translated by Gayatri Chakravorty Spivak, 1976. Baltimore: Johns Hopkins University Press, 1997.

——. *Truth and Painting*. 1978. Translated by Ian McLeod and

Geoff Bennington. Chicago: University of Chicago Press, 1987.

Descartes, René. *Discourse on the Method and Meditations on First Philosophy*. 1641. Edited by David Weissman. New Haven: Yale University Press, 1996.

Dewey, John. "My Pedagogic Creed." In *Dewey on Education: Selections*, introduction and notes by Martin S. Dworkin, 19–32. New York: Teachers College Press, 1959.

Dickens, Charles. 1848. *Dombey and Son*. Harmondsworth, UK: Penguin, 1970.

———. "Frauds on the Fairies.' *Household Words*, 1 October 1853. Reprinted in Lance Salway, *A Peculiar Gift. Nineteenth Century Writing on Books for Children*, 111–18. London: Kestrel, 1976.

———. *Hard Times*. London: Bradbury and Evans, 1854.

———. *Great Expectations*. 1861. Edited by Angus Calder. Harmondsworth: Penguin, 1965.

Dickinson, Peter. *Eva*. London: Victor Gollancz, 1988.

Dickson, Gary. "*Rites de Passage*: The Children's Crusade and Medieval Childhood." *Journal of the History of Childhood and Youth* (Fall 2009): 315–32.

Dimock, A. W. *Be Prepared; or, The Boy Scouts in Florida*. New York: Grosset and Dunlap, 1912.

Dirks, Nicholas. "Postcolonialism." In *New Keywords: A Revised Vocabulary of Culture and Society*, edited by Tony Bennett, Lawrence Grossberg, and Meaghan Morris, 267–69. Oxford: Blackwell, 2005.

Dixon, Bob. *Catching Them Young: Sex, Race and Class in Children's Fiction*. London: Pluto Press, 1977.

Dodge, Mary Mapes. *Hans Brinker*. New York: James O'Kane, 1866.

Donovan, John. *I'll Get There. It Better Be Worth the Trip*. New York: Harper and Row, 1969.

Doonan, Jane. *Looking at Pictures in Picture Books*. Stroud, UK: Thimble Press, 1993.

Downham, Jenny. *Before I Die*. London: David Fickling, 2007.

Driscoll, C. "Barbie Culture." In *Girl Culture: An Encyclopedia*, edited by Claudia Mitchell and Jacqueline Reid-Walsh, 39–47. Westport, CT: Greenwood, 2008.

Dudek, Debra. "Dogboys and Lost Things; or Anchoring a Floating Signifier: Race and Critical Multiculturalism." *Ariel* 37, no. 4 (2006a): 1–20.

———. "Of Murmels and Snigs: Detention-Centre Narratives in Australian Literature for Children." *Overland* 185 (2006b): 38–42.

Dudek, Debra, and Wenche Ommundsen. "Building Cultural Citizenship: Multiculturalism and Children's Literature." Editorial. *Papers* 17, no. 2 (2007): 3–6.

Durant, Will. *The Story of Philosophy*. New York: Simon and Schuster, 1926.

Dusinberre, Juliet. *Alice to the Lighthouse: Children's Books and Radical Experiments in Art*. Basingstoke, UK: Macmillan, 1987.

Eagleton, Terry. *The Ideology of the Aesthetic*. Oxford: Blackwell, 1990.

———. *The Illusions of Postmodernism*. Oxford: Blackwell, 1996.

———. *The Idea of Culture*. Oxford: Blackwell, 2000.

Eccleshare, Julia. "Teenage Fiction: Realism, Romances, Contemporary Problem Novels." In *International Companion Encyclopedia of Children's Literature*, edited by Peter Hunt, 386–96. New York: Routledge, 1996.

Eddy, Jacalyn. *Bookwomen: Creating an Empire in Children's Book Publishing, 1919–1939*. Madison: University of Wisconsin Press, 2006.

Edgeworth, Maria. *The Parent's Assistant; or, Stories for Children*. London: J. Johnson in St. Paul's Church-yard, 1796.

Edgeworth, Maria, and Richard Lovell Edgeworth. *Practical Education*. 1798. New York: Harper and Brothers, 1855.

Edgren, Gretchen. *The Playmate Book: Six Decades of Centerfolds*. Introduction by Hugh Hefner. Cologne: Taschen, 2005.

Egan, R. Danielle, and Gail Hawkes. *Theorizing the Sexual Child in Modernity*. New York: Palgrave Macmillan, 2010.

Egoff, Sheila. *Worlds Within: Children's Fantasy from the Middle Ages to Today*. Chicago: American Library Association, 1988.

Eisner, Will. *A Contract with God and Other Tenement Stories*. 1978. New York: DC Comics, 2000.

Eliot, T. S. "What Is a Classic?" 1944. In *Selected Prose of T. S. Eliot*, edited by Frank Kermode, 115–31. New York: Harcourt Brace Jovanovich, 1975.

Elkins, James. *The Domain of Images*. Ithaca, NY: Cornell University Press, 1999.

Ellis, Deborah, and Eric Walters. *Bifocal*. Markham, ON: Fitzhenry and Whiteside, 2007.

Ellis, Sarah. *Odd Man Out*. Toronto: Groundwood, 2006.

Encyclopædia Britannica. Online at http://search.eb.com/eb/article-27201 (accessed February 16, 2009).

Ende, Michael. *Die unendliche Geschichte*. Stuttgart: Thienemann, 1979. Translated by Ralph Manheim as *The Neverending Story*. Garden City, NY: Doubleday, 1983.

Enright, Elizabeth. The Melendy Quartet, comprising *The Saturdays* (1941), *The Four-Story Mistake* (1942), *Then There Were Five* (1944), and *Spiderweb for Two: A Melendy Maze* (1951). New York: Holt, 1941–51.

Erdrich, Louise. *The Birchbark House*. New York: Hyperion, 1999.

Erikson, Erik. "The Legend of Hitler's Childhood." 1951. In *Childhood and Society*, 317–49. Harmondsworth, UK: Penguin, 1975.

Erisman, Fred. "Stratemeyer Boys' Books and the Gernsback Milieu." *Extrapolation* 41, no. 3 (2000): 272–82.

Estes, Eleanor. The Moffats series, comprising *The Moffats, The Middle Moffat, Rufus M.* and *The Moffat Museum*. New York: Harcourt Brace, 1941–83.

———. *The Hundred Dresses*. Illustrated by Louis Slobodkin. 1944. New York: Harcourt, 2004.

Falconer, Rachel. "Crossover Literature." In *International Companion Encyclopedia of Children's Literature*, 2d ed., edited by Peter Hunt, vol. 1, 556–75. London: Routledge, 2004.

———. *The Crossover Novel: Contemporary Children's Fiction and Its Adult Readership*. New York: Routledge, 2009.

Farmer, Nancy. *The House of the Scorpion*. New York: Simon and Schuster, 2002.

Farrar, Frederic. *Eric, or Little by Little*. 1858. New York: Garland, 1977.

Feelings, Muriel. *Jambo Means Hello: Swahili Alphabet Book*. Illustrated by Tom Feelings. 1974. New York: Puffin, 1981.

Feelings, Tom. *The Middle Passage*. New York: Dial, 1995.

Ferguson, Roderick A. "Race." In *Keywords for American Cultural Studies*, edited by Bruce Burgett and Glenn Hendler, 191–96. New York: New York University Press, 2007.

Ferguson, Susan L. Review: *"Plots of Enlightenment: Education and the Novel in Eighteenth-Century England*, by Richard A. Barney." *Philosophy and Literature* 24, no. 2 (2000): 490–93.

Fichtelberg, Susan. *Encountering Enchantment: A Guide to Speculative Fiction for Teens*. Westport, CT: Libraries Unlimited, 2007.

Fielding, Henry. *The History of Tom Jones, a Foundling*. 1749. London: Penguin, 2005.

Fielding, Sarah. *The Governess; or, The Little Female Academy*. 1749. London: Oxford University Press, 1968.

Finazzo, Denise Ann. *All for the Children: Multicultural Essentials of Literature*. Albany, NY: Delmar, 1997.

Fine, Anne. *Bill's New Frock*. London: Methuen, 1989.

Finley, Martha. *Elsie Dinsmore*. New York: Dodd, Mead, 1867.

Fischer, Steven Roger. *A History of Reading*. London: Reaktion, 2003.

Fish, Stanley. *Is There a Text in This Class? The Authority of Interpretive Communities*. Cambridge, MA: Harvard University Press, 1980.

———. "Boutique Multiculturalism, or Why Liberals Are Incapable of Thinking about Hate Speech." *Critical Inquiry* 23 (1997): 378–95.

Fisher, Margery. *The Bright Face of Danger*. Toronto: Hodder and Stoughton, 1986.

Fitzhugh, Louise. *Harriet the Spy: The Most Famous Sleuth of All*. New York: Harper and Row, 1964.

———. *Bang, Bang You're Dead,* New York: Harper and Row, 1986.

Fitzhugh, P. K. *Tom Slade, Boy Scout*. New York: Grosset and Dunlap, 1915.

———. *Roy Blakely, His Story*. New York: Gosset and Dunlap, 1920.

Flanagan, Victoria. *Into the Closet: Cross-Dressing and the Gendered Body in Children's Literature and Film*. New York: Routledge, 2007.

Flax, Jane. "Postmodernism and Gender Relations in Feminist Theory." *Signs* 12, no. 4 (1987): 621–43.

Flesch, Rudolf. *Why Johnny Can't Read: And What You Can Do about It*. New York: Harper and Row, 1955.

Flynn, Richard. "The Intersection of Children's Literature and Childhood Studies." *Children's Literature Association Quarterly* 22, no. 3 (1997): 142–43.

Forbes.com. "The Celebrity 100: #9 J. K. Rowling." *The Celebrity 100*. June 2008. Online at http://www.forbes.com/lists/2008/53/celebrities08_JK-Rowling_CRTT.html.

Forbes, Esther. *Johnny Tremain*. Illustrated by Lynd Ward. Boston: Houghton Mifflin, 1943.

Forman-Brunell, Miriam. *Made to Play House: Dolls and the Commercialization of American Girlhood 1830–1930*. New Haven: Yale University Press, 1993.

Forster, E. M. *Aspects of the Novel*. New York: Harcourt Brace, 1927.

Foucault, Michel. *Power/Knowledge: Selected Interviews and Other Writings, 1972–1977*. Translated by Colin Gordon. New York: Pantheon, 1980.

Fox, Mem, and Helen Oxenbury. *Ten Little Fingers and Ten Little Toes*. Boston: Houghton Mifflin Harcourt, 2008.

Fox, Paula. *One-Eyed Cat*. Scarsdale, NY: Bradbury Press, 1984.

———. *The Eagle Kite*. New York: Dell, 1995.

Freud, Sigmund. 1919. "The Uncanny." In *The Standard Edition of the Complete Psychological Works of Sigmund Freud*, edited by J. Strachey. London: Hogarth, 1955.

Freundlich, Joyce Y. "Fact or Fancy: The Image of the Puerto Rican in Ethnic Literature for Young Adults." Paper presented at the Annual Meeting of the International Reading Association, St. Louis, MO, May 5–9, 1980. ERIC Educational Document Reproduction Service, ED 188 150, 1980.

Fricke, Aaron. *Reflections of a Rock Lobster*: *A Story about Growing Up Gay*. Boston: Alyson, 1981.

Fried, Michael. *Absorption and Theatricality: Painting and Beholder in the Age of Diderot*. Chicago: University of Chicago Press, 1980.

Frith, Simon. "Youth." In *New Keywords: A Revised Vocabulary of Culture and Society*, edited by Tony Bennett, Lawrence Grossberg, and Meaghan Morris, 380–82. Oxford: Blackwell, 2005.

Fullerton, Ronald. "Modern Western Marketing as a Historical Phenomenon: Theory and Illustration." In *Historical Perspectives in Marketing: Essays in Honor of Stanley C. Hollander*, edited by Terence Nevett and Ronald A. Fullerton, 71–89. Lexington, MA: D. C. Heath, 1988.

Gág, Wanda. *Millions of Cats*. New York: Coward-McCann, 1928.

Gaiman, Neil. *Coraline*. London: Bloomsbury, 2002.

Gaines, Kevin. "African." In *Keywords for American Cultural Studies*, edited by Bruce Burgett and Glenn Hendler, 12–16. New York: New York University Press, 2007.

Gangi, Jane. "Inclusive Aesthetics and Social Justice: The Vanguard of Small, Multicultural Presses." *Children's Literature Association Quarterly* 30, no. 3 (2005): 243–64.

Gantos, Jack. *Joey Pigza Swallowed the Key*. 1998. New York: HarperTrophy, 2000.

Garden, Nancy. *Annie on My Mind*. New York: Farrar, Straus and Giroux, 1982.

Garlitz, Barbara. "The Immortality Ode: Its Cultural Progeny." *Studies in English Literature, 1500–1900* 6, no. 4 (1966): 639–49.

George, Rosemary Marangoly. *The Politics of Home: Postcolonial Relocations and Twentieth-Century Fiction*. Cambridge: Cambridge University Press, 1996.

Gergen, M. M., and K. J. Gergen. "The Social Construction of Narrative Accounts." In *Historical Social Psychology*, edited by K. J. Gergen and M. M. Gergen. Hillsdale, NJ: Erlbaum Associates, 1984.

Gikandi, Simon. *Maps of Englishness: Writing Identity in the Culture of Colonialism*. New York: Columbia University Press, 1996.

Gilbert, Dennis. *The American Class Structure in an Age of Growing Inequality*. Belmont, CA: Wadsworth, 2002.

Gillespie, Cindy S., Janet L. Powell, Nancy E. Clements, and Rebecca A. Swearingen. "A Look at the Newbery Medal Books from a Multicultural Perspective." *The Reading Teacher* 48, no. 1 (1994): 40–50.

Gillis, John R. *Youth and Its History: Tradition and Change in European Age Relations, 1770–Present*. New York: Academic Press, 1974.

Gimenez, Martha. "Latinos, Hispanics...What Next!" *Heresies* 7, no. 27 (1993): 38–42.

Giovanni, Nikki. "Poem for Black Boys." *Ego Tripping and Other Poems for Young People*. New York: Lawrence Hill, 1973.

Giroux, Henry A. *Stealing Innocence: Youth, Corporate Power, and the Politics of Culture*. New York: St. Martin's, 2000.

Godwin, William [William Scolfield, pseud.]. Preface to *Bible Stories, Memorable Acts of the Ancient Patriarchs, Judges and Kings, Extracted from Their Original Historians, for the Use of Children*. London: R. Phillips, 1802.

Goldberg, David Theo. *Multiculturalism: A Critical Reader*. Malden, MA: Blackwell, 1994.

Golding, William. *Lord of the Flies*. London: Faber and Faber, 1954.

Gombrich, E. H. "The Mask and the Face: The Perception of Physiognomic Likeness in Life and in Art." In *Art, Perception, and Reality*, 1–46. Baltimore: Johns Hopkins University Press, 1970.

Gomi, Taro. *Everyone Poops*. 1977. La Jolla, CA: Kane Miller, 1993.

Goodwin, M. H. *The Hidden Life of Girls: Games of Stance, Status, and Exclusion*. New York: Wiley-Blackwell, 2006.

Gorman, Michele. *Getting Graphic! Using Graphic Novels to Promote Literacy with Preteens and Teens*. Worthington, OH: Linworth, 2003.

Graetz, Margaret. "From Picture Books to Illustrated Stories: How Children Understand All Those Words." *Children's Libraries Newsletter* (Australia) 12, no. 3 (1976): 79–87.

Grahame, Kenneth. *The Golden Age*. London: John Lane, 1895.

———. *The Wind in the Willows*. 1908. London: Methuen, 1937.

Grauerholz, Elizabeth, and Bernice A. Pescosolido. "Gender Representation in Children's Literature: 1900–1984." *Gender and Society* 3, no. 1 (1989): 113–25.

Gray, Michael, and Rhonda Gray. *The Stew That Grew*. Glebe, Australia: Walter McVitty, 1990.

Gray, William S., and May Hill Arbuthnot. *Fun with Dick and Jane*. Chicago: Scott, Foresman, 1940.

Green, John. *Looking for Alaska*. New York: Dutton, 2005.

———. *An Abundance of Katherines*. 2006. New York: Penguin, 2008.

Green, Martin. *Dreams of Adventure, Deeds of Empire*. New York: Basic, 1979.

Green, Roger Lancelyn. *Tellers of Tales*. New York: Franklin Watts, 1965.

Greene, Graham. *The Graham Greene Film Reader: Reviews, Essays, Interviews, and Film Stories*. New York: Applause, 1993.

Greenwald, Marilyn S. *Secret of the Hardy Boys: Leslie Mcfarlane and the Stratemeyer Syndicate*. Athens: Ohio University Press, 2004.

Grenby, M. O. *Children's Literature*. Edinburgh: Edinburgh University Press, 2008.

Griswold, Jerry. "The Future of the Profession." *The Lion and the Unicorn* 26, no. 2 (2002): 236–42.

Gubar, Marah. *Artful Dodgers: Reconceiving the Golden Age of Children's Literature*. New York: Oxford University Press, 2009.

Guillory, John. *Cultural Capital: The Problem of Literary Canon Formation*. Chicago: University of Chicago Press, 1993.

Gunn, James. "Toward a Definition of Science Fiction." In *Speculations on Speculation: Theories of Science Fiction*, edited by James Gunn and Matthew Candelaria, 5–12. Lanham, MD: Scarecrow Press, 2005.

Gupta, Suman. *Re-Reading Harry Potter*. New York: Palgrave Macmillan, 2003.

Guterson, David. *Snow Falling on Cedars*. New York: Vintage, 1994.

Guy, Rosa. *The Friends*. New York: Holt Rinehart, 1973.

Haddon, Mark. *The Curious Incident of the Dog in the Night-Time*. London: Jonathan Cape, 2003.

Hade, Daniel. "Reading Children's Literature Multiculturally." In *Using Multiethnic Literature in the K–8 Classroom*, edited by V. J. Harris, 233–56. Norwood, MA: Christopher Gordon, 1997.

———. "Storyselling: Are Publishers Changing the Way Children Read?" *Horn Book* 78, no. 5 (2002): 509–17.

Hadjor, Kofi Buenor. *The Penguin Dictionary of Third World Terms*. London: Penguin, 1992.

Hadju, David. *The Ten-Cent Plague: The Great Comic-Book Scare and How It Changed America*. New York: Farrar, Straus and Giroux, 2008.

Hage, Ghassan. *White Nation: Fantasies of White Supremacy in a Multicultural Society*. London: Pluto Press, 1998.

———. *Against Paranoid Nationalism: Searching for Hope in a Shrinking Society*. London: Pluto Press, 2003.

Hale, Shannon. *Princess Academy*. London: Bloomsbury, 2005.

Hall, Donald. *Queer Theories*. New York: Palgrave Macmillan, 2003.

Hall, Stuart. *Race: The Floating Signifier*. Video. Produced and Directed by Sut Jhally. Northampton, MA: The Media Education Foundation, 1996.

Halpern, Richard. *Norman Rockwell: The Underside of Innocence*. Chicago: University of Chicago Press, 2006.

Hamilton, Virginia. *M.C. Higgins, the Great*. New York: Dell–Laurel Leaf, 1974.

———. *Arilla Sun Down*. 1976. New York: Scholastic, 1995.

Harris, Anita. *Future Girl: Young Women in the 21st Century*. London: Routledge, 2004.

Harris, Robie, and Michael Emberley. *It's Perfectly Normal: A Book about Changing Bodies, Growing Up, Sex, and Sexual Health*. Boston: Candlewick, 1994.

Harris, Violet J. "*The Brownies' Book*: Challenge to the Selective Tradition in Children's Literature." Ph.D. dissertation, University of Georgia, 1986.

———. "African American Children's Literature: The First One Hundred Years." *Journal of Negro Education* 59, no. 4 (1990): 540–55.

Hartnett, Sonya. *Sleeping Dogs*. New York: Viking, 1995.

———. *Surrender*. London: Walker, 2005.

Harvey, Robert C. "The Graphic Novel, Will Eisner, and Other Pioneers." *The Comics Journal* 233 (May 2001): 103–6.

Hasegawa, Jack. "What Is Fair? Books That Help Children Understand Diversity." *New England Reading Association Journal* 38, no. 3 (2002): 1–4.

Hatfield, Charles. *Alternative Comics: An Emerging Literature*. Jackson: University Press of Mississippi, 2005.

Haughton, Hugh, ed. "Introduction." In *The Chatto Book of Nonsense*. London: Chatto and Windus, 1988.

Hautzig, Deborah. *Hey Dollface*. New York: Greenwillow, 1978.

Hawkins, Francis. *Youths Behaviour, or, Decencie in Conversation amongst Men*. London: S. G. and B. G. William Lee, 1672.

Hayes, Rosemary. *Mixing It*. London: Frances Lincoln Children's Books, 2007.

Hayes-Bautista, David E., and Jorge Chapa. "Latino Terminology: Conceptual Basis for Standardized Terminology." *American Journal of Public Health* 77, no. 1 (1987): 61–68.

Hearn, Lian. *Across the Nightingale Floor*. Sydney: Hodder, 2002.

Hearne, Betsy. "Booking the Brothers Grimm: Art, Adaptations, and Economics." *Book Research Quarterly* 2, no. 4 (1986–87): 18–32.

Heinlein, Robert A. *Rocket Ship Galileo*. New York: Scribner's, 1947.

———. *Tunnel in the Sky*. New York: Scribner's, 1955.

———. *Citizen of the Galaxy*. New York: Scribner's, 1957.

Heins, Marjorie. *Not in Front of the Children: "Indecency," Censorship, and the Innocence of Youth*. New York: Hill and Wang, 2001.

Heins, Paul. "Children's Classics: Recommended Editions." In *Children's Classics*, edited by Alice Jordan, 10–16. Boston: Horn Book, 1976.

Hentoff, Nat. *The Day They Came to Arrest the Book*. London: Penguin, 1988.

Henty, G. A. *With Clive in India; or, The Beginnings of an Empire*. London: Blackie and Son, 1884.

Hergé. *Tintin au Congo*. Tournai, Belgium: Casterman, 1931.

Heron, Anne. *Two Teenagers in Twenty*. Boston: Alyson, 1993.

Herrera, Juan Felipe. *Featherless/Desplumado*. San Francisco: Children's Book Press, 2004.

Hersey, John. "Why Do Children Bog Down on the First R?" *Life*, May 24, 1954: 136–50.

Hesiod. *Works and Days*. Translated by Hugh G. Evelyn-White. Raleigh, NC: Hayes-Barton, 2007.

Heyman, Michael, with Sumanyu Satpathy and Anushka Ravishankar. *The Tenth Rasa: An Anthology of Indian Nonsense*. New Delhi: Penguin, 2007.

Higginson, Sheila Sweeny. *Mickey Mouse Clubhouse: Are We There Yet?* New York: Disney, 2007.

Higonnet, Anne. *Pictures of Innocence: The History and Crisis of Ideal Childhood*. London: Thames and Hudson, 1998.

Hilkey, Judy. *Character Is Capital: Success Manuals and Manhood in Gilded Age America*. Chapel Hill: University of North Carolina Press, 1997.

Hill, Twyla J. "Multicultural Children's Books: An American Fairy Tale." *Publishing Research Quarterly* 14, no. 1 (1998): 36–44.

Hine, Lewis W. *Men at Work*. New York: Macmillan, 1936.

Hinton, S. E. *The Outsiders*. New York: Viking Press, 1967a.

———. "Teen-agers Are for Real." *New York Times Book Review*, August 27, 1967b.

The History of Little Goody Two-Shoes. London: John Newbery, 1765.

The History of Little Fanny. London: S. and J. Fuller, 1810.

Hoad, T. F. ed. *Concise Oxford Dictionary of Etymology*. Oxford: Clarendon Press, 1986.

Hoban, Russell. *The Mouse and His Child*. 1967. Harmondsworth, UK: Puffin, 1993.

Holland, Isabelle. *Heads You Win, Tails I Lose*. Philadelphia: J. B. Lippincott, 1973.

Holland, Norman. *5 Readers Reading*. New Haven: Yale University Press, 1975.

Hollindale, Peter. *Signs of Childness in Children's Books*. Stroud, UK: Thimble Press, 1997.

———. *Ideology and the Children's Book*. Woodchester, UK: Thimble Press, 1998.

Holmes, Mary J. *'Lena Rivers*. New York: G. W. Dillingham Co., 1856.

Holt, John. *How Children Learn*. 1967. Rev. ed. New York: Dell, 1983.

Homes, A. M. *Jack*. New York: Vintage, 1990.

Honeyman, Susan. *Elusive Childhood: Impossible Representations in Modern Fiction*. London: Routledge, 2005.

Hopkins, Dianne McAfee. "The Library Bill of Rights and School Library Media Programs." *Library Trends* 45, no. 1 (1996): 61–74.

Horn, Pamela. *The Victorian Town Child*. New York: New York University Press, 1997.

Horne, Jackie C. "Punishment as Performance in Catherine Sinclair's *Holiday House*." *Children's Literature Association Quarterly* 26, no. 1 (2001): 22–32.

———. "Empire, Hysteria, and the Healthy Girl: The Deployment of the Body in Juliana Horatia Ewing's *Six to Sixteen*." *Women's Studies* 33 (2004): 249–77.

Horvath, Polly. *Everything on a Waffle*. New York: Farrar, Straus and Giroux, 2001.

Hourihan, Margery. *Deconstructing the Hero: Literary Theory and Children's Literature*. New York: Routledge, 1997.

Howes, Craig. "Afterword." In *The Ethics of Life Writing*, edited by P. J. Eakin, 244–64. Ithaca, NY: Cornell University Press, 2004.

Howker, Janni. *The Nature of the Beast*. London: Julia MacRae, 1985.

Huggan, Graham. *Australian Literature: Postcolonialism, Racism, Transnationalism*. Oxford: Oxford University Press, 2007.

Hughes, Felicity. "Children's Literature: Theory and Practice." *ELH* 45, no. 3 (1978): 542–61.

Hughes, Langston. "Books and the Negro Child." *Children's Library Yearbook* 4 (1932a): 108–10.

———. *The Dream Keeper and Other Poems*. New York: Alfred A. Knopf, 1932b.

Hughes, Monica. *Keeper of the Isis Light*. London: Hamish Hamilton, 1980.

Hughes, Richard. *The Spider's Palace and Other Stories*. 1931. Harmondsworth, UK: Puffin, 1972.

Hughes, Ted. *The Iron Man: A Children's Story in Five Nights*. London: Faber, 1968.

Hughes, Thomas. *Tom Brown's Schooldays*. 1857. New York: Oxford University Press, 1999.

Hulme, Peter. "Including America." *Ariel* 26, no. 1 (1995): 117–20.

Hunt, Caroline. "Young Adult Literature Evades the Theorists." *Children's Literature Association Quarterly* 21, no. 1 (1996): 4–11.

Hunt, Peter. "Childist Criticism: The Subculture of the Child, the Book and the Critic." *Signal* 43 (January 1984): 42–59.

———. *Criticism, Theory, and Children's Literature*. Oxford: Blackwell, 1991.

———. "Passing on the Past: the Problem of Books That Are for Children and That Were for Children." *Children's Literature Association Quarterly* 21, no. 4 (1996): 200–202.

———. "Censorship and Children's Literature in Britain Now, or The Return of Abigail." *Children's Literature in Education* 28, no. 2 (1997): 95–103.

Hunt, Peter, and Karen Sands. "The View from the Center: British Empire and Post-Empire Children's Literature." In *Voices of the Other: Children's Literature and the Postcolonial Context*, edited by Roderick McGillis. New York: Routledge, 2000.

Hunter, J. D. *Culture Wars: The Struggle to Define America*. New York: Basic, 1991.

———. *The Death of Character: Moral Education in an Age without Good or Evil*. New York: Basic, 2000.

Hunter, Mollie. *Talent Is Not Enough*. New York: Harper and Row, 1976.

Huskey, Melynda. "Queering the Picture Book." *The Lion and the Unicorn* 26 (2002): 66–77.

Hutcheon, Linda. *The Politics of Postmodernism*. New York: Routledge, 1989.

Huyssen, Andreas. *After the Great Divide: Modernism, Mass Culture, Postmodernism*. Bloomington: Indiana University Press, 1986.

Hyman, Trina Schart, illustrator. *Little Red Riding Hood*. New York: Holiday House, 1983.

Immel, Andrea. *Revolutionary Reviewing: Sarah Trimmer's "Guardian of Education" and the Cultural Politics of Juvenile Literature: An Index to "The Guardian"*. Los Angeles: Department of Special Collections, University Research Library, UCLA, 1990.

Inglis, Fred. *The Promise of Happiness: Value and Meaning in Children's Literature*. Cambridge: Cambridge University Press, 1981.

Inkamala, Jennifer. *The Rainbow Serpent*. Alice Springs, Australia: Yipirinya (Yeperenye) School Council, 1988.

Ionesco, Eugene. *Story Number 1*. 1967. Illustrated by Joel Naprstek. Translated by Calvin K. Towle. New York: Harlin Quist, 1978a.

———. *Story Number 2*. 1970. Illustrated by Gerard Failly. Translated by Calvin K. Towle. New York: Harlin Quist, 1978b.

———. *Story Number 3*. Illustrated by Philippe Corentin. Translated by Ciba Vaughan. New York: Harlin Quist, 1971.

Iser, Wolfgang. *The Implied Reader*. Baltimore: Johns Hopkins University Press, 1974.

Italiano, Gabriela. "Reading Latin America: Issues in the Evaluation of Latino Children's Books in Spanish and English." *Evaluating Children's Books: A Critical Look: Aesthetic, Social, and Political Aspects of Analyzing and Using Children's Books*. Edited by Betsy Hearne and Roger Sutton. Urbana-Champaign, IL: University of Illinois at Urbana-Champaign, 119–32. Online at http://www.ideals.uiuc.edu/handle/2142/485 (accessed July 29, 2010).

Jackson, Kathryn, and Byron Jackson. *The Saggy Baggy Elephant*. Illustrated by Gustav Tenggren. 1947. Racine, WI: Western, 1974.

Jacobs, Alan. *Original Sin: A Cultural History*. New York: HarperCollins, 2008.

Jacobs, Joseph. *English Fairy Tales*. London: David Nutt, 1890.

James, Henry. "The Future of the Novel." 1899. In Felicity A. Hughes, "Children's Literature: Theory and Practice." *ELH* 45, no. 3 (1978): 542–61.

———. *A Little Tour in France*. 1883–84. Rev. ed. Illustrated by Joseph Pennell. Boston: Houghton Mifflin, 1900a.

———. "The Future of the Novel." 1889. *New York Times,* August 11, 1900b.

———. *The Turn of the Screw*. 1898. Edited by Robert Kimbrough. New York: Norton, 1966.

Jameson, Fredric. *The Political Unconscious: Narrative as a Socially Symbolic Act*. New York: Routledge, 1981.

———. *Postmodernism; or, the Cultural Logic of Late Capitalism*. Durham, NC: Duke University Press, 1991.

Janeway, James. *A Token for Children*. 1671–72. New York: Garland, 1977.

Janiewski, Dolories. "Gendering, Racializing and Classifying: Settler Colonization in the United States, 1590–1990." In *Unsettling Settler Societies: Articulations of Gender, Race, Ethnicity and Class*, edited by Daiva Stasiulis and Nira Yuval-Davis. London: Sage, 1995.

Jansson, Tove. *The Book about Moomin, Mymble and Little My*. 1952. English version by Sophie Hannah. London: Sort of Books, 2004.

Jarrell, Randall. *The Bat-Poet*. Illustrated by Maurice Sendak. New York: Macmillan, 1964.

Jefferies, Richard. *Bevis: The Story of a Boy*. 1882. Edited by Peter Hunt. Oxford: Oxford University Press, 1989.

Jenkins, Elwyn. *National Character in South African English Children's Literature*. New York: Routledge, 2006.

Jenkins, Henry, ed. *The Children's Culture Reader*. New York: New York University Press, 1998.

Jensen, Jeffry. *Sports*. Vero Beach, FL: Rourke Publications, 1995.

Johnson, A. E. *Clarence and Corrine, or God's Way*. Philadelphia: American Baptist Publications Society, 1890.

Johnson, Crockett. *Harold and the Purple Crayon*. New York: Harper and Brothers, 1955.

———. *Harold's ABC*. New York: Harper and Row, 1963.

Johnson, Deidre. *Edward Stratemeyer and the Stratemeyer Syndicate.* New York: Twayne, 1993.

Johnson, Dianne. *Telling Tales: The Pedagogy and Promise of African American Literature for Youth.* New York: Greewood, 1990.

Johnson, Ingrid, Joyce Bainbridge, and Farha Shariff. "Exploring Issues of National Identity, Ideology and Diversity in Contemporary Canadian Picture Books." *Papers* 17, no. 2 (2007): 75–83.

Jonas, Ann. *Round Trip.* 1983. New York: Mulberry, 1990.

Jones, Amelia. "Beauty Discourse and the Logic of Aesthetics." In *Aesthetics in a Multicultural Age*, edited by Emory Elliot, Louis F. Caton, and Jeffry Rhyne, 215–39. New York: Oxford University Press, 2002.

Jones, Diana Wynne. *Howl's Moving Castle.* London: Collins, 1986.

Jones, Gerard. *Killing Monsters: Why Children Need Fantasy, Super Heroes, and Make-Believe Violence.* New York: Basic, 2002.

Joosen, Vanessa. "Realism." In *Oxford Encyclopedia of Children's Literature*, edited by Jack Zipes, 3:328. New York: Oxford University Press, 2006.

Jordan, Alice M. *Children's Classics: With a List of Recommended Editions by Paul Heins.* 1947. Boston: Horn Book, 1976.

Jordan, Anne Devereaux. "ChLA Notes." *Children's Literature* 3 (1974): 249–50.

Jordan, Mary Kate, Abby Levine, and Judith Friedman. *Losing Uncle Tom.* Morton Grove, IL: Albert Whitman, 1989.

Juno, Andrea, ed. *Dangerous Drawings: Interviews with Comix and Graphix Artists.* New York: Juno, 1997.

Juster, Norton. *The Phantom Tollbooth.* 1961. New York: Alfred A. Knopf, 1989.

Kadohata, Cynthia. *Kira-Kira.* New York: Atheneum, 2004.

Kahane, Reuven. *The Origins of Postmodern Youth: Informal Youth Movements in a Comparative Perspective.* Berlin: DeGruyter, 1997.

Kamenetsky, Christa. *The Brothers Grimm and Their Critics: Folktales and the Quest for Meaning.* Athens: Ohio University Press, 1992.

Kamm, Josephine. *Young Mother.* London: Heinemann, 1968.

Kant, Immanuel. *Critique of Judgment.* 1790. Translated by Werner S. Pluhar. Indianapolis, IN: Hackett, 1987.

Kantor, A. "Case against Julie Amero Needs to Be Deleted." *USA Today*, March 16, 2007.

Karolides, Nicholas J. "Political Smoke and Mirrors: The "Hidden Agenda" of Censorship." *Wisconsin English Journal* 41, no. 2 (1999): 16–24.

Kaye, Geraldine. *Comfort Herself.* 1984. London: Methuen, 1986.

Kearney, Mary Celeste. "Coalescing: The Development of Girls' Studies." *NWSA Journal* 21, no. 1 (2009): 1–28.

Keats, Ezra Jack. *The Snowy Day.* 1962. New York: Puffin, 1976.

Keats, John. "To George and Georgiana Keats, 27 September 1819." In *The Letters of John Keats 1814–1821, Volume Two, 1819–1821*, edited by Hyder Edward Rollins, 188. Cambridge, MA: Harvard University Press, 1958.

Keith, Lois. *Take Up Thy Bed and Walk: Death, Disability and Cure in Classic Fiction for Girls.* London: Women's Press, 2001.

Kelly, Eric Philbrook. *The Trumpeter of Krakow.* New York: Macmillan, 1928.

Kemble, E. W. *A Coon Alphabet.* New York: R. H. Russell, 1898.

Kemp, Gene. *The Turbulent Term of Tyke Tiler.* London: Faber, 1977.

Kermode, Frank. *The Classic: Literary Images of Permanence and Change.* New York: Viking, 1975.

Kertes, Joseph. *The Gift.* Illustrated by Peter Perko. Toronto: Groundwood, 1995.

Kertzer, Adrienne. "Reclaiming Her Maternal Pre-Text: Little Red Riding Hood's Mother and Three Young Adult Novels." *Children's Literature Association Quarterly* 21, no. 1 (1996): 20–27.

Keyser, Elizabeth Lennox. *Little Women: A Family Romance.* New York: Twayne, 1999.

Khorana, Meena. *Critical Perspectives on Postcolonial African Children's and Young Adult Literature.* Westport, CT: Greenwood, 1998.

Kidd, Kenneth. "Introduction: Lesbian/Gay Literature for Children and Young Adults." *Children's Literature Association Quarterly* 23, no. 3 (1998): 114–19.

———. "Children's Culture, Children's Studies, and the Ethnographic Imaginary." *Children's Literature Association Quarterly* 27, no. 3 (2002), 146–55.

———. *Making American Boys: Boyology and the Feral Tale.* Minneapolis: University of Minnesota Press, 2004.

———. "How to Make a Children's Classic: The Middlebrow Projects of Louise Seaman Bechtel and Morton Schindel." *Journal of Children's Literature Studies* 3, no. 2 (2006): 51–79.

———. "Prizing Children's Literature: The Case of Newbery Gold." *Children's Literature* 35 (2007): 166–90.

Kincaid, James. *Child-Loving: The Erotic Child and Victorian Culture.* New York: Routledge, 1992.

———. *Erotic Innocence: The Culture of Child Molesting.* Durham, NC: Duke University Press, 1998.

———. "Dickens and the Construction of the Child." In *Dickens and the Children of Empire*, edited by Wendy S. Jacobson, 29–42. New York: Palgrave, 2000.

Kincaid, Paul. "On the Origins of Genre." In *Speculations on Speculation: Theories of Science Fiction*, edited by James Gunn and Matthew Candelaria, 41–53. Lanham, MD: Scarecrow, 2005.

King, Thomas, and William Kent Monkman. *A Coyote Columbus Story*. Toronto: Douglas and McIntyre, 1992.

Kingsley, Charles. *The Heroes; or, Greek Fairy Tales for My Children*. New York: Dutton, 1856.

———. *The Water-Babies: A Fairy-Tale for a Land-Baby*. London: Macmillan, 1863.

Kipling, Rudyard. *The Jungle Book*. 1894. Garden City, NY: Doubleday 1964.

———. *The Second Jungle Book*. Garden City, NY: Doubleday, 1895.

Kivy, Peter. *The Performance of Reading: An Essay in the Philosophy of Literature*. Oxford: Blackwell, 2006.

Klein, Norma. *Mom, the Wolf Man, and Me*. New York: Pantheon, 1972.

———. *It's Not What You Expect*. New York: Pantheon, 1973.

———. *Naomi in the Middle*. New York: Dial, 1974.

———. *It's Okay If You Don't Love Me*. New York: Dial, 1977.

———. *Tomboy*. New York: Simon and Schuster, 1978.

Klingberg, Göte. *Facets of Children's Literature Research: Collected and Revised Writings*. Stockholm: Swedish Institute for Children's Books, 2008.

Knoepflmacher, U. C. "The Hansel and Gretel Syndrome: Survivorship Fantasies and Parental Desertion." *Children's Literature* 33 (2005): 171–84.

Knoepflmacher, U. C., and Mitzi Myers, guest editors. "Cross-Writing Child and Adult." Special issue. *Children's Literature* 25 (1997).

Knowles, Elizabeth. "Cato, Marcus Porcius." In *The Oxford Dictionary of Phrase and Fable*. Oxford: Oxford University Press, 2006.

Knowles, John. *A Separate Peace*. New York: Bantam, 1959.

Knox, Elizabeth. *Dreamhunter*. Toronto: Penguin, 2005.

Konigsburg, E. L. *From the Mixed-Up Files of Mrs. Basil E. Frankweiler*. New York: Atheneum, 1967.

———. *Silent to the Bone*. New York: Atheneum, 2000.

Kostick, Conor. "William of Tyre, Livy, and the Vocabulary of Class." *Journal of the History of Ideas* 65, no. 3 (2005): 353–68.

Kozol, Jonathan. *Savage Inequalities: Children in America's Schools*. New York: Crown, 1991.

Krumgold, Joseph. *. . . and now Miguel*. New York: Crowell, 1953.

Kunzle, David. *Father of the Comic Strip: Rodolphe Töpffer*. Jackson: University Press of Mississippi, 2007.

Kusugak, Michael. *Baseball Bats for Christmas*. Toronto: Annick, 1990.

Kutzer, M. Daphne. *Empire's Children: Empire and Imperialism in Classic British Children's Books*. New York: Routledge, 2000.

Laínez, René Colato. *I Am René, the Boy / Soy René, el Niño*. Houston: Piñata Books, 2005.

Lamont, Charles, director. *War Babies*. Presented by Robert M. Savini. Perf. Shirley Temple. Educational Pictures, 1932. *Shirley Temple: The Early Years Collection* (DVD). American Home Treasures, 2000.

Lancaster, Joseph. *Improvements in Education as it Respects the Industrious Classes of the Community*. 3d ed. 1805. Clifton, NJ: A. M. Kelly, 1973.

Langbauer, Laurie. "The Ethics and Practice of Lemony Snicket: Adolescence and Generation X." *PMLA* 122, no. 2 (2007): 502–21.

Larrick, Nancy. "The All-White World of Children's Books." *Saturday Review of Literature* 48, no. 37 (1965): 63–65, 84–85.

Lavalette, Michael, ed. *A Thing of the Past? Child Labour in Britain in the Nineteenth and Twentieth Centuries*. New York: St. Martin's, 1999.

Lear, Edward. *A Book of Nonsense*. London: McLean, 1846.

———. *Nonsense Songs, Stories, Botany and Alphabets*. London: R. J. Bush, 1871.

———. *More Nonsense, Pictures, Rhymes, Botany, etc*. London: R. J. Bush, 1872.

———. *Laughable Lyrics: A Fourth Book of Nonsense Poems, Songs, Botany, Music, etc*. London: R. J. Bush, 1877.

———. *Nonsense Songs and Stories*. London: Frederick Warne, 1894

Lear, Linda. *Beatrix Potter: A Life in Nature*. New York: Allen Lane, 2007.

Leavitt, Martine. *Tom Finder*. Calgary, AB: Red Deer, 2003.

Le Doux, Joseph. *The Emotional Brain: The Mysterious Underpinnings of Emotional Life*. New York: Simon and Schuster, 1998.

Leeson, Robert. *Reading and Righting: The Past, Present and Future of Fiction for the Young*. London: Collins, 1985.

Le Guin, Ursula K. "From Elfland to Poughkeepsie." 1973. Reprinted in *The Language of the Night: Essays on Fantasy and Science Fiction*, edited by Susan Wood. New York: Putnam, 1979.

———. *The Earthsea Quartet*. 1968–90. London: Penguin, 1993.

Lehr, Susan, ed. *Battling Dragons—Issues and Controversy in Children's Literature*. Portsmouth, NH: Reed Elsevier, 1995.

———. *Beauty, Brains and Brawn: The Construction of Gender in Children's Literature*. Portsmouth, NH: Heinemann, 2001.

Lent, John A., ed. *Pulp Demons: International Dimensions of the Postwar Anti-Comics Campaign*. London: Associated University Presses, 1999.

Lerer, Seth. *Children's Literature: A Reader's History, from Aesop to Harry Potter*. Chicago: University of Chicago Press, 2008.

Lesnik-Oberstein, Karin. "Childhood and Textuality: Culture, History, Literature." In *Children in Culture: Approaches to Childhood*, edited by Karin Lesnik-Oberstein, 1–28. New York: St. Martin's, 1998.

Lester, Julius, and Jerry Pinkney. *Sam and the Tigers*. New York: Dial, 1996.

Levine, Judith. *Harmful to Minors: The Perils of Protecting Children from Sex*. New York: Thunder's Mouth, 2002.

Levine, Lawrence. *Highbrow/Lowbrow: The Emergence of Cultural Hierarchy in America*. Cambridge, MA: Harvard University Press, 1988.

Levithan, David. *Boy Meets Boy*. 2003. New York: Alfred A. Knopf, 2005.

Lewis, C. S. *That Hideous Strength: A Modern Fairy-Tale for Grown-Ups*. London: John Lane, 1945.

———. *The Lion, the Witch, and the Wardrobe*. London: Bles, 1950.

———. *Prince Caspian*. London: Bles, 1951.

———. *The Voyage of the Dawn Treader*. London: Bles, 1952.

———. *The Silver Chair*. London: Bles, 1953.

———. *The Horse and His Boy*. London: Bles, 1954.

———. *The Magician's Nephew*. London: Bles, 1955.

———. *The Last Battle*. London: The Bodley Head, 1956.

———. "On Stories." 1947. In Of Other Worlds: Essays and Stories, edited by W. Hooper, 3–21. London: Bles, 1966.

Lewis, David. *Reading Contemporary Picturebooks: Picturing Text*. New York and London: Routledge/Falmer, 2001.

Lewis, Magda. "Are Indians Nicer Now? What Children Learn from Books about Native North Americans." In *How Much Truth Do We Tell the Children? The Politics of Children's Literature*, edited by Betty Bacon, 135–56. Minneapolis: MEP Publications, 1988.

Lindgrin, Astrid. 1945. *Pippi Longstocking*. Translated by F. Lamborn. New York: Viking, 1950.

Lionni, Leo. *Little Blue and Little Yellow*. 1959. New York: Harper-Collins, 1995.

Lipsyte, Robert. *One Fat Summer*. New York: Harper Trophy, 1977.

Lissitzky, El. *About Two Red Squares: A Suprematist Tale about Two Squares in Six Constructions*. 1922. Berlin: Sythian. Translated for "Modernism in the Picture Book." Online at www.kodomo.go.jp/gallery/modernism.

A Little Pretty Pocket-Book. London: John Newbery, 1744.

Lloyd, Rosemary. "Twenty Thousand Leagues below Modernism." In *Modernity, Modernism and Children's Literature*, edited by Ulf Boethius, 51–74. Stockholm: Stockholm University, 1998.

Lloyd, Saci. *The Carbon Diaries 2015*. London: Hodder, 2008.

Locke, John. *An Essay concerning Human Understanding*. 1690. New York: Meridian, 1964.

———. *Some Thoughts concerning Education*, vol. 37, part 1. 1693. The Harvard Classics. New York: P. F. Collier and Son, 1909–14. Online at http://www.bartleby.com/37/1/22.html.

Lofting, Hugh. *The Story of Dr Dolittle*. 1920. New York: Dell, 1988.

Logan, Mawuena Kossi. *Narrating Africa: George Henty and the Fiction of Empire*. New York: Routledge, 1999.

Lott, Eric. "Class." In *Keywords for American Cultural Studies*, edited by Bruce Burgett and Glenn Hendler, 49–52. New York: New York University Press, 2007.

Lowe, Virginia. *Stories, Pictures and Reality: Two Children Tell*. London: Routledge, 2007.

Lowrey, Janette Sebring. *The Poky Little Puppy*. Illustrated by Gustav Tenggren. 1942. Racine, WI: Western, 1997.

Lowry, Lois. *The Giver*. Boston: Houghton Mifflin, 1993.

———. *The Willoughbys*. New York: Houghton Mifflin, 2008.

Lucashenko, Melissa. "Black on Black." *Meanjin* 59, no. 3 (1999): 112–18.

Lundin, Anne. *Constructing the Canon of Children's Literature: Beyond Library Walls and Ivory Towers*. New York: Routledge, 2004.

Lurie, Alison. *Don't Tell the Grown-Ups: Subversive Children's Literature*. Boston: Little, Brown, 1990.

Lyga, Allison A. W., and Barry Lyga. *Graphic Novels in Your Media Center: A Definitive Guide*. Westport, CT: Libraries Unlimited, 2004.

Lyga, Barry. *Boy Toy*. Boston: Houghton Mifflin, 2007.

Lynch, Chris. *Shadow Boxer*. New York: HarperCollins, 1993.

———. *Inexcusable*. New York: Atheneum Books for Young Readers, 2005.

Lyotard, Jean-François. *The Postmodern Condition: A Report on Knowledge*. Manchester: Manchester University Press, 1984.

Macaulay, Catherine. "Letter IV: Amusement and Instruction of Boys and Girls to Be the Same." In *Letters on Education*. 1790. London: Pickering and Chatto, 1996.

Macaulay, David. *Castle*. Boston: Houghton Mifflin, 1977.

———. *Black and White*. Boston: Houghton Mifflin, 1990.

———. *The Way We Work: Getting to Know the Amazing Human Body*. Boston: Houghton Mifflin, 2008.

MacCann, Donnarae. *White Supremacy in Children's Literature: Characterizations of African Americans, 1830–1900.* New York: Routledge, 1998.

———. "Editor's Introduction: Racism and Antiracism: Forty Years of Theories and Debates." *The Lion and the Unicorn* 25, no. 3 (2001): 337–52.

MacDonald, George. *At the Back of the North Wind.* 1871. With twelve illustrations in color by Maria L. Kirk. Philadelphia: J. B. Lippincott, 1909.

———. "The Fantastic Imagination." In *The Gifts of the Child Christ: Fairy Tales and Stories for the Childlike.* 1882/93. Reprint, edited by Glenn Edward Sadler. Grand Rapids, MI: William B Eerdmans, 1973.

MacDowell, Myles. "Fiction for Children and Adults: Some Essential Differences." *Children's Literature in Education* 10 (1973). Reprinted in *Writers, Critics and Children*, edited by Geoff Fox et al., 140–56. New York: Agathon; London: Heinemann, 1976.

Mackey, Margaret. *The Case of Peter Pan: Changing Conditions of Literature for Children.* New York: Garland, 1998.

MacLean, Paul D. *The Triune Brain in Evolution: Role in Paleocerebral Functions.* New York: Plenum, 1990.

MacLeod, A. "Censorship and Children's Literature." *Library Quarterly* 53, no. 1 (1983): 26–38.

Madsen, Jane M., and Elaine B. Wickersham. "A Look at Young Children's Realistic Fiction." *The Reading Teacher* 34, no. 3 (1980): 273–79.

Malcolm, Noel. *The Origins of English Nonsense.* London: Fontana, 1998.

Mallan, Kerry. *Gender Dilemmas in Children's Fiction.* Houndmills, UK: Palgrave Macmillan, 2009.

Malzberg, Barry. "The Number of the Beast." In *Speculations on Speculation: Theories of Science Fiction*, edited by James Gunn and Matthew Candelaria, 37–40. Lanham, MD: Scarecrow, 2005.

Manguel, Alberto. *The City of Words.* London: Continuum 2008.

Maracle, Lee. *Will's Garden.* Penticton, BC: Theytus, 2002.

Marchetta, Melina. *Looking for Alibrandi.* Ringwood, Australia: Penguin, 1992.

Marcus, Leonard S. *Golden Legacy: How Golden Books Won Children's Hearts, Changed Publishing Forever, and Became an American Icon along the Way.* New York: Golden Books, 2007.

———. *Minders of Make-Believe: Idealists, Entrepreneurs, and the Shaping of American Children's Literature.* New York: Houghton Mifflin, 2008.

Martin, Michelle H. *Brown Gold: Milestones of African-American Children's Picture Books, 1845–2002.* New York: Routledge, 2004.

Martinson, Floyd M. *The Sexual Life of Children.* Westport, CT: Bergin and Garvey, 1994.

Marx, Karl. *Capital: A Critique of Political Economy*, vols 1–3. 1859. Edited by Frederick Engels and translated by Samuel Moore and Edward Aveling. London: Lawrence and Wishart, 1974.

May, Jill P. *Children's Literature and Critical Theory.* New York: Oxford University Press, 1995.

McArthur, Tom. "Bowdlerize." *Concise Oxford Companion to English Language.* Oxford: Oxford University Press, 1998. Online at http://www.encyclopedia.com/doc/1O29-BOWDLERIZE.html (accessed September 19, 2009).

McCallum, Robyn. "Cultural Solipsism, National Identities and the Discourse of Multiculturalism in Australian Picture Books." *Ariel* 28, no. 1 (1997): 101–16.

———. *Ideologies of Identity in Adolescent Fiction.* New York: Garland, 1999.

McCaughrean, Geraldine. *A Pack of Lies: Twelve Stories in One.* 1988. New York: Oxford University Press, 1989.

McCloud, Scott. *Understanding Comics.* Northampton, MA: Kitchensink, 1993.

McDonald, Meme, and Boori Monty Pryor. *Njunjul the Sun.* Crows Nest, NSW: Allen and Unwin, 2002.

McGann, Jerome. *The Romantic Ideology.* Chicago: University of Chicago Press, 1977.

McGillis, Roderick. "Calling a Voice out of Silence: Hearing What We Read." *Children's Literature in Education* 15, no. 1 (1984): 22–29.

———. "The Embrace: Narrative Voice and Children's Books." *Canadian Children's Literature* 63 (1991): 24–40.

———. *A Little Princess: Empire and Gender.* New York: Twayne, 1996.

———. "Keep on Keepin' On: Dialogue on History". *Children's Literature Association Quarterly*, 22, no. 3 (1997): 142–43.

———. "The Delights of Impossibility: No Children, No Books, Only Theory." *Children's Literature Association Quarterly* 23, no. 4 (1998): 202–8.

———. *Voices of the Other: Children's Literature and the Postcolonial Context.* New York: Garland, 1999.

McGuffey, William Holmes. *McGuffey's First [–6] Eclectic Reader* (1836). Eclectic Educational Series. New York: New York American Book Co., 1920–21.

McInally, Kathryn. "Not Quite White (Enough): Intersecting Ethnic and Gendered Identities in *Looking for Alibrandi*." *Papers* 17, no. 2 (2007): 59–66.

———. "Who Wears the Pants? The (Multi) Cultural Politics of *The Sisterhood of the Traveling Pants*." *Children's Literature in Education* 39 (2008): 187–200.

McKibben, Bill. *The End of Nature*. New York: Viking Penguin, 1990.

McMillan, Cheryl. "Playing with Frames: Spatial Images in Children's Fiction." In *Children s Literature and the Fin de Siècle*, edited by Roderick McGillis. Westport, CT: Praeger, 2003.

McNair, Jonda, and Wanda Brooks, eds. *Embracing, Evaluating and Examining African American Children's and Young Adult Literature*. Lanham, MD: Scarecrow, 2008.

Medina, Carmen L., and Patricia Enciso. "'Some Words Are Messengers/Hay Palabras Mensajeras': Interpreting Sociopolitical Themes in Latino/a Children's Literature." *New Advocate* 15, no. 1 (2002): 35–47.

Meek, Margaret [Spencer]. *On Being Literate*. London: Bodley Head, 1991.

Mendlesohn, Farah. "Is There Any Such Thing as Children's Science Fiction? A Position Piece." *The Lion and the Unicorn* 28 (2004): 284–313.

———. *Diana Wynne Jones: Children's Literature and the Fantastic Tradition*. London: Routledge, 2005.

Metzger, George. *Beyond Time and Again*. Huntington Beach, CA: Kyle and Wheary, 1976.

Meyer, Stephenie. *Twilight*. New York: Little, Brown, 2005.

———. *New Moon*. New York: Little, Brown, 2006.

———. *Eclipse*. New York: Little, Brown, 2007.

———. *Breaking Dawn*. New York: Little, Brown, 2008.

Mickenberg, Julia L. *Learning from the Left: Children's Literature, the Cold War, and Radical Politics in the United States*. New York: Oxford University Press, 2006.

Mickenberg, Julia L., and Philip Nel, eds. *Tales for Little Rebels: A Collection of Radical Children's Literature*. New York: New York University Press, 2008.

Midgley, Claire, ed. *Gender and Imperialism*. Manchester: Manchester University Press, 1998.

Miller, J. Hillis. *Illustration*. Cambridge, MA: Harvard University Press, 1992.

Mills, Claudia. "The Ethics of the Author/Audience Relationship in Children's Fiction." *Children's Literature Association Quarterly* 22, no. 4 (1997): 181–87.

Mills, Richard. "Perspectives of Childhood." In *Childhood Studies: A Reader in Perspectives of Childhood*, edited by Jean Mill and Richard Mills, 7–38. New York: Routledge, 2000.

Milne, A. A. *Winnie-the-Pooh*. London: Methuen, 1926.

Milton, John. *Paradise Lost*. 1667. Edited by Alastair Fowler. London: Pearson Longman, 2007.

Minarik, Else Holmelund. *Little Bear*. Illustrated by Maurice Sendak. 1957. New York: HarperCollins, 1985.

Minter, J. *The Insiders*. London: Bloomsbury, 2004.

Mintz, Steven. *Huck's Raft: A History of American Childhood*. Cambridge, MA: Harvard University Press, 2004.

Mitchell, Claudia, and Jacqueline Reid-Walsh. *Researching Children's Popular Culture: The Cultural Spaces of Girlhood*. London: Routledge, 2002.

———. "Girl-Method: Placing Girl-Centered Research Methodologies on the Map of Girlhood Studies." In *Roadblocks to Eequality: Women Challenging Boundaries*, edited by J. Klaehn, 214–33. Montreal: Black Rose, 2009.

Mitchell, Margaret. *Gone with the Wind*. New York: Macmillan, 1936.

Mitchell, Sally. *The New Girl: Girls' Culture in England, 1880–1915*. New York: Columbia University Press, 1995.

Mitchell, Sebastian. "'But Cast Their Eyes on These Little Wretched Beings': The Innocence and Experience of Children in the Late Eighteenth Century." *New Formations* 42 (2000): 115–30.

Mitchell, W. J. T. *Iconology*. Chicago: University of Chicago Press, 1986.

———. *Picture Theory: Essays on Verbal and Visual Representation*. Chicago: University of Chicago Press, 1994.

———. "Visual Literacy or Literary Visualcy?" In *Visual Literacy*, edited by James Elkins, 11–29. New York: Routledge, 2008.

Moebius, William. "Introduction to Picture Book Codes." *Word and Image: A Journal of Verbal/Visual Enquiry* 2, no. 2 (1986): 141–58.

———. "Informing Adult Readers: Symbolic Experience in Children's Literature." In *Reading World Literature: Theory, History, Practice*, edited by Sarah Lawall, 309–27. Austin: University of Texas Press, 1994.

———. "Making the Front Page: Views of Women, Women's Views in the Picturebook." In *Girls, Boys, Books, Toys: Feminist Theory and Children's Culture*, edited by Margaret R. Higonnet and Beverly Lyon Clark, 112–129. Baltimore: Johns Hopkins University Press, 1999.

———. "Introduction: Aura and Prestige: The Literary and the Picture Book." In *Aesthetics and Memory in the Picture Book*. Forthcoming.

Moers, Ellen. *The Dandy: Brummell to Beerbohm*. New York: Viking, 1960.

Mohanty, Chandra Talpade. "Under Western Eyes: Feminist

Scholarship and Colonial Discourses." *Feminist Review* 30 (1988): 61–88.

Mohr, Richard D. "The Pedophilia of Everyday Life." 1996. In *Curiouser: On the Queerness of Children*, edited by Steven Bruhm and Natasha Hurley, 17–30. Minneapolis: University of Minnesota Press, 2004.

Monaghan, Jennifer E. *Learning to Read and Write in Colonial America*. Amherst: University of Massachusetts Press, 2005.

Montgomery, L. M. *Anne of Green Gables*. 1907. Edited by Cecily Devereaux. Peterborough, ON: Broadview, 2004.

——. *Jane of Lantern Hill*. 1937. Online at http://gutenberg.net.au/ebooks02/0200881h.html (accessed July 10, 2008).

Moon, M. "'The Gentle Boy from the Dangerous Classes': Pederasty, Domesticity, and Capitalism in Horatio Alger." In *Curiouser: On the Queerness of Children,* edited by Steven Bruhm and Natasha Hurley, 31–56. Minneapolis: University of Minnesota Press, 2004.

Moore, Anne Carroll. "The Three Owls' Notebook." *Horn Book* 14 (1938): 31–33.

Mora, Pat. *Confetti: Poems for Children*. New York: Lee and Low, 1996.

——. *The Rainbow Tulip*. New York: Puffin, 1999.

More, Sir Thomas. *Utopia*. 1516. Translated by Gilbert Burnet. London: Printed by Richard Chiswell, 1684.

Morgenstern, John. "The Rise of Children's Literature Reconsidered." *Children's Literature Association Quarterly* 26, no. 2 (2001): 64–73.

Mori, Kyoko. *Shizuko's Daughter*. New York: Fawcett, 1994.

Morley, David. *Home Territories: Media, Mobility and Identity*. London: Routledge, 2000.

——. "Audience." In *New Keywords: A Revised Vocabulary of Cultures and Society*, edited by Tony Bennett, Lawrence Grossberg, and Meaghan Morris. Malden, MA: Blackwell, 2005.

Morris, M. "Unresting the Curriculum: Queer Projects, Queer Imaginings." In *Queer Theory in Education,* edited by William F. Pinar, 275–86. Mahwah, NJ: Lawrence Erlbaum Associates, 1998.

Moss, Gemma. "Gender and Literacy." In *Encyclopedia of Language and Education, Vol. 2: Literacy*, 2d ed., edited by B. V. Street and N. H. Hornberger, 95–105. New York: Springer, 2008.

Mott, F. L. *A History of American Magazines, 1850–1865*, vol. 2. Cambridge: Harvard University Press, 1938.

Mullin, Katherine. *James Joyce, Sexuality and Social Purity* New York: Cambridge University Press, 2003.

Müller, Sonja. "Die Gründerjahre der Internationalen Forschungsgesellschaft für Kinder- und Jugendliteratur. Diskussionen und Projekte 1970–1978" [The early years of IRSCL—International Research Society for Children's Literature: Discussions and Projects from 1970 to 1978]. Paper presented at the 19th Biennial Congress of the International Research Society for Children's Literature, Frankfurt, Germany, August 8, 2009.

Mulock, Dinah. *John Halifax, Gentleman*. 1856. Online, July 7, 2008, http://www.gutenberg.org/etext/2351.

Munsch, Robert. *The Paper Bag Princess*. Illustrated by Michale Martchenko. 1980. London: Scholastic, 1993.

Murji, Karim. "Race." In *New Keywords: A Revised Vocabulary of Culture and Society*, edited by Tony Bennett, Lawrence Grossberg, and Meaghan Morris, 290–96. Malden, MA: Blackwell, 2005.

Murray, Gail Schmunk. *American Children's Literature and the Construction of Childhood*. New York: Twayne, 1998.

Myers, Mitzi. "Quixotes, Orphans, and Subjectivity: Maria Edgeworth's Georgian Heroinism and the (En)Gendering of Young Adult Fiction." *The Lion and the Unicorn* 13, no. 1 (1989): 21–40.

——. "Introduction." In *Revolutionary Reviewing: Sarah Trimmer's "Guardian of Education" and the Cultural Politics of Juvenile Literature: An Index to "The Guardian,"* by Andrea Immel. Los Angeles: Department of Special Collections, University Research Library, UCLA, 1990.

——. "De-Romanticizing the Subject: Maria Edgeworth's 'The Bracelets,' Mythologies of Origin, and the Daughter's Coming to Writing." In *Romantic Women Writers: Voices and Countervoices*, edited by P. Feldman and T. M. Kelley. Hanover: University Press of New England, 1995.

——. "Reading Children and Homeopathic Romanticism." In *Literature and the Child: Romantic Continuations, Postmodern Contestations*, edited by James Holt McGavran. Iowa City: University of Iowa Press, 1999.

Myers, Walter Dean. *Monster*. New York: HarperCollins, 1999.

Myracle, Lauren. *ttyl*. New York: Amulet, 2004.

Nabokov, Vladimir. *Lolita*. New York: Putnam, 1955.

Nadelman, Ruth Lynn. *Fantasy Literature for Children and Young Adults: A Comprehensive Guide*. 5th ed. Westport, CT: Libraries Unlimited, 2005.

National Literacy Trust. "Transforming Lives: Policy." Online at http://www.literacytrust.org.uk/policy/index.html (accessed September 17, 2009).

Natov, Roni. "Harry Potter and the Extraordinariness of the Ordinary." *The Lion and the Unicorn* 25 (2001): 310–27.

——. *The Poetics of Childhood*. London: Routledge, 2003.

Naylor, Phyllis Reynolds. *The Grooming of Alice*. New York: Atheneum, 2000.

Neal, Larry. "The Black Arts Movement." In *The Black Aesthetic*, edited by Addison Gayle, Jr., 272–90. Garden City, NY: Doubleday, 1971.

Needle, Jan. *Wild Wood*. London: Deutsch, 1981.

Nel, Philip. "Is There a Text in This Advertising Campaign? Literature, Marketing, and Harry Potter." *The Lion and the Unicorn* 29, no. 2 (2005): 236–67.

Nelson, Blake. *Paranoid Park*. New York: Penguin-Speak, 2006.

Nelson, Claudia. "Selected Bibliography of Multicultural Children's Literature." Unpublished paper, 1994.

———. "Girls' Fiction." In *Girlhood in America: An Encyclopedia*, edited by Miriam Formanek-Brunell, 327–33. Santa Barbara, CA: ABC CLIO, 2001.

———. "That Other Eden: Adult Education and Youthful Sexuality in *The Pearl*, 1879–1880." In *Sexual Pedagogies: Sex Education in Britain, Australia, and America, 1879–2000*, edited by Claudia Nelson and Michelle H. Martin, 15–32. New York: Palgrave, 2004.

Nelson, Katherine, ed. *Narratives from the Crib*. Cambridge, MA: Harvard University Press, 1989.

Nesbit, E. *Nine Unlikely Tales for Children*. London: T. Fisher Unwin, 1901.

———. *The Railway Children*. 1906. London: Ernest Benn, 1957.

New England Primer. 1777. In *Norton Anthology of Children's Literature: Traditions in English*, edited by Jack Zipes et al., 88–128. New York: Norton, 2005.

Newell, Peter. *Topsys & Turvys*. 1902. New York: Dover, 1964.

———. *The Hole Book*. 1908. Boston: Tuttle, 1985.

———. *The Rocket Book*. 1912. Boston: Tuttle, 1969.

Newman, Lesléa. *Heather Has Two Mommies*. Illustrated by Diana Souza. Los Angeles: Alyson Wonderland, 1989.

———. *The Boy Who Cried Fabulous*. Illustrated by Peter Ferguson. Berkeley, CA.: Tricycle, 2004.

Ngũgĩ wa Thiong'o, and Emmanuel Kariũki. *Njamba Nene and the Flying Bus*. Translated by Wangũi wa Goro. Nairobi: Heinemann Kenya, 1982. Translation of *Njamba Nene na Mbaathi i Mathagu*. Nairobi: Heinemann Kenya, 1982.

———. *Njamba Nene's Pistol*. Translated by Wangũi wa Goro. Nairobi: Heinemann Kenya, 1986. Translated of *Bathitoora ya Njamba Nene*. Nairobi: Heinemann Kenya, 1984.

Nikola-Lisa, W. "'Around My Table' Is Not Always Enough: A Response to Jacqueline Woodson." *Horn Book* 74, no. 3 (1998): 315–19.

Nikolajeva, Maria. "Fantasy." In *The Oxford Companion to Fairy Tales: The Western Fairy Tale Tradition from Medieval to Modern*, edited by Jack Zipes, 150–54. Oxford: Oxford University Press, 2000.

———. "'A Dream of Complete Idleness': Depiction of Labour in Children's Fiction." *The Lion and the Unicorn* 26 (2002a): 305–21.

———. "Imprints of the Mind: The Depiction of Consciousness in Children's Fiction. *Children's Literature Association Quarterly* 26, no. 4 (2002b): 173–87.

———. *The Rhetoric of Character in Children's Literature*. Lanham, MD: Scarecrow Press, 2002c.

———. *Aesthetic Approaches to Children's Literature: An Introduction*. Lanham, MD: Scarecrow, 2005.

Nikolajeva, Maria, and Carole Scott. *How Picture Books Work*. New York: Routledge, 2000.

Nilsen, Alleen Pace, and Hamida Bosmajian, eds. "Special Issue: Censorship in Children's Literature." *Para•Doxa: Studies in World Literature* 2, nos. 3–4 (1996).

Nilsen, Alleen Pace, and Kenneth L. Donelson. *Literature for Today's Young Adults*. 8th ed. Boston: Allyn and Bacon, 2009.

Nilsson, Nina L. "How Does Hispanic Portrayal in Children's Books Measure Up after 40 Years? The Answer Is 'It Depends.'" *The Reading Teacher* 58, no. 6 (2005): 534–48.

Noakes, Vivien. "Introduction." In *Edward Lear: The Complete Verse and Other Nonsense*. London: Penguin, 2001.

Nodelman, Perry. "Who's Speaking? The Voices of Dennis Lee's Poems for Children." *Canadian Children's Literature* 25 (1982): 4–17.

———, ed. *Touchstones: Reflections on the Best in Children's Literature*, vols. 1–3. West Lafayette, IN: Children's Literature Association, 1985–89.

———. *Words about Pictures*. Athens: University of Georgia Press, 1988.

———. "The Other: Orientalism, Colonialism, and Children's Literature." *Children's Literature Association Quarterly* 17, no. 1 (1992): 29–35.

———. *The Pleasures of Children's Literature*. 1992. 2d ed. New York: Longman, 1996

———. "Pleasure and Genre: Speculations on the Characteristics of Children's Fiction." *Children's Literature* 28 (2000): 1–14.

———. "Who the Boys Are: Thinking about Masculinity in Children's Fiction." *New Advocate* 15, no. 1 (2002): 9–18.

———. "At Home on Native Land: A Non-Aboriginal Canadian Scholar Discusses Aboriginality and Property in Canadian Double-Focalized Novels for Young Adults." In *Home Words: Discourses of Children's Literature in Canada*, edited by Mavis

Reimer, 107–28. Waterloo, ON: Wilfrid Laurier University Press, 2008a.

———. *The Hidden Adult: Defining Children's Literature*. Baltimore: Johns Hopkins University Press, 2008b.

Nodelman, Perry, and Mavis Reimer. *The Pleasures of Children's Literature*. 3d ed. Boston: Allyn and Bacon, 2003.

Norcia, Megan A. "Angel of the Island: L. T. Meade's New Girl as the Heir of a Nation-Making Robinson Crusoe." *The Lion and the Unicorn* 28 (2004a): 345–62.

———. "Playing Empire: Children's Parlor Games, Home Theatricals, and Improvisational Play." *Children's Literature Association Quarterly* 29, no. 4 (2004b): 294–314.

———. "Puzzling Empire: Early Puzzles and Dissected Maps as Imperial Heuristics." *Children's Literature* 37 (2009): 1–32.

Nyberg, Amy Kiste. *Seal of Approval: The History of the Comics Code*. Jackson: University Press of Mississippi, 1998.

Oboler, Suzanne. *Ethnic Labels, Latino Lives: Identity and the Politics of (Re)Presentation in the United States*. Minneapolis: University of Minnesota Press, 1995.

O'Brien, Sharon. "Tomboyism and Adolescent Conflict: Three Nineteenth-Century Case Studies." In *Woman's Being, Woman's Place: Female Identity and Vocation in American History*, edited by Mary Kelley, 351–72. Boston: G. K. Hall, 1979.

Okami, Paul, Richard Olmstead, and Paul R. Abramson. "Sexual Experiences in Early Childhood: 18-Year Longitudinal Data for the UCLA Family Lifestyles Project." *Journal of Sex Research* 34, no. 4 (1997): 339–47.

Oliver, Narelle. *Dancing the Boom-Cha-Cha Boogie*. Malvern, South Australia: Omnibus, 2005.

O'Malley, Andrew. *The Making of the Modern Child: Children's Literature and Childhood in the Late Eighteenth Century*. New York: Routledge, 2003.

———. "Island Homemaking: Catharine Parr Traill's *Canadian Crusoes* and the Robinsonade Tradition." In *Home Words: Discourses of Children's Literature in Canada*, edited by Mavis Reimer. Waterloo, ON: Wilfrid Laurier University Press, 2008.

O'Neill, Alexis. *Estela's Swap*. New York: Lew and Low, 2002.

Ord, Priscilla, ed. "Special Section on Children's Folklore." *Children's Literature Association Quarterly* 6, no. 2 (1981): 11–34.

Origen, Erich, and Dan Golan. *Goodnight Bush*. Boston: Little, Brown, 2008.

Orwell, George. *Animal Farm*. London: Secker and Warburg, 1945.

Osgood, Samuel. "Books for Our Children." *Atlantic Monthly* 16 (December 1865): 724–36.

Ostry, Ellen. "'Is He Still Human? Are You?' Young Adult Science Fiction in the Posthuman Age." *The Lion and the Unicorn* 28 (2004): 222–46.

O'Sullivan, Emer. *Comparative Children's Literature*. 2001. Translated by Anthea Bell. New York: Routledge, 2005.

Otten, Charlotte F., and Gary D. Schmidt. *The Voice of the Narrator in Children's Literature*. Westport, CT: Greenwood, 1989.

Owens, Robert E. *Queer Kids: The Challenges and Promise for Lesbian, Gay, and Bisexual Youth*. New York: Harrington Park, 1998.

Oxford English Dictionary. 2d ed. Edited by J. A. Simpson and E. S. C. Weiner. Oxford: Clarendon, 1989.

Oxford English Dictionary. 2d ed. Prepared by J. A. Simpson and E. C. S. Weiner, edited by Catherine Soames and Angus Stevenson. Oxford: Oxford University Press, 2005.

Oxford English Dictionary Online. Online at http://dictionary.oed.com (accessed 2001–9).

Padilla, Felix M. *Latino Ethnic Consciousness: The Case of Mexican Americans and Puerto Ricans in Chicago*. Notre Dame, IN: University of Notre Dame Press, 1985.

Pakulski, Jan, and Malcolm Waters. *The Death of Class*. London: Sage, 1996.

Parkes, Christopher. "Treasure Island and the Romance of the British Civil Service." *Children's Literature Association Quarterly* 31, no. 4 (2006): 332–45.

Parkinson, Siobhán. *Breaking the Wishbone*. Dublin: O'Brien, 1999.

Parry, Benita. "Problems in Current Discourse Theory." *Oxford Literary Review* 9 (1987): 27–58.

Parsons, Elizabeth. "The Appeal of the Underdog: Mr. Lunch and Left Politics as Entertainment." *Children's Literature Association Quarterly* 30, no. 4 (2005): 354–67.

Paterson, Katherine. *Bridge to Terabithia*. New York: Crowell, 1977.

———. *The Great Gilly Hopkins*. New York: HarperCollins, 1978

———. *Jacob Have I Loved*. New York: Crowell, 1980.

———. *Gates of Excellence: On Reading and Writing Books for Children*. New York: Elsevier/Nelson Books, 1981.

———. "My Life Is Based on a True Story." *Magpies* 2 (May 1989): 5–10. Revised version of "Story of My Lives." In *The Spying Heart*. New York: Dutton/Lodestar, 1989.

Patron, Susan. *The Higher Power of Lucky*. New York: Atheneum, 2006.

Pattee, Amy S. "Disturbing the Peace: The Function of Young Adult Literature and the Case of Catherine Atkins' *When Jeff Comes Home*." *Children's Literature in Education* 35, no. 3 (2004): 241–55.

Paul, Lissa. "Escape Claws: Cover Stories on Lolly Willowes and Crusoe's Daughter." *Signal* 63 (Sept. 1990): 206–20.

———. "The Naked Truth about Being Literate." *Language Arts* 77, no. 4 (2000): 335–42.

———. "Sex and the Children's Book." *The Lion and the Unicorn* 29 (2005): 222–35.

Paulsen, Gary. *Hatchet*. New York: Bradbury Press, 1987.

———. *Hatchet: The Return*. New York: Bradbury Press, 1991.

———. *Brian's Winter*. New York: Delacorte, 1996.

Pawuk, Michael. *Graphic Novels: A Genre Guide to Comic Books, Manga, and More*. Westport, CT: Libraries Unlimited, 2007.

Payne, Michael, and John Schad. *Life. After. Theory: Jacques Derrida, Frank Kermode, Toril Moi and Christopher Norris*. London: Continuum, 2004.

Pearce, Philippa. *Tom's Midnight Garden*. 1958. Harmondsworth, UK: Penguin-Puffin Books, 1976.

Pearce, Sharyn. "Messages from the Inside? Multiculturalism in Contemporary Australian Children's Literature." *The Lion and the Unicorn* 27, no. 2 (2003): 235–50.

Pearson, Mary. *The Adoration of Jenna Fox*. New York: Henry Holt, 2008.

Peers, Juliette. "Doll Culture." In *Girl Culture: An Encyclopedia*, edited by Claudia Mitchell and Jacqueline Reid-Walsh, 25–38. Westport, CT: Greenwood, 2008.

Pennell, B., and J. Stephens. "Queering Heterotopic Spaces: Shyam Selvadurai's Funny Boy and Peter Wells's Boy Overboard." In *Ways of Being Male: Representing Masculinities in Children's Literature and Film*, edited by John Stephens, 164–84. New York: Routledge, 2002.

Perrot, Jean. *Art Baroque, Art d'Enfance*. Nancy: Presses Universitaires de Nancy, 1991.

Peters, Henk. "Postmodernist Poetics in Children's Literature." In *AUETSA 96, I–II: Southern African Studies*, edited by Hermann Wittenberg and Loes Nas. Bellville, South Africa: University of Western Cape Press, 1996.

Peters, Julie Anne. *Luna*. New York: Little, Brown, 2005.

Pham, Hoa. *Forty-Nine Ghosts*. Illusstrated by Stanley Wong. South Melbourne, Australia: Addison Wesley Longman, 1998a.

———. *No One Like Me*. Illustrated by Stanley Wong. South Melbourne, Australia: Addison Wesley Longman, 1998b.

———. *Quicksilver*. South Melbourne, Australia: Addison Wesley Longman, 1998c.

Phillips, Adam. *The Beast in the Nursery: On Curiosity and Other Appetites*. New York: Pantheon, 1998.

Phillips, Anne K. "'Yours Most Loquaciously': Voice in Jean Webster's *Daddy-Long-Legs*." *Children's Literature* 27 (1999): 64–86.

Phillips, Robert, ed. *Aspects of Alice: Lewis Carroll's Dreamchild as Seen through the Critics' Looking-Glasses, 1865–1971*. London: Gollancz, 1972.

Pilkey, Dav. *The Adventures of Captain Underpants*. New York: Blue Sky, 1997.

———. *Ricky Ricotta's Mighty Robot*. New York: Scholastic, 2000.

Pinchbeck, Ivy, and Margaret Hewitt. *Children in English Society*, Two vols. London: Routledge and Kegan Paul, 1973.

Pinkney, Sandra L. *I Am Latino: The Beauty in Me*. New York: Little, Brown, 2007.

Pitcher, Evelyn Goodenough, and Ernst Prelinger. *Children Tell Stories: An Analysis of Fantasy*. New York: International Universities Press, 1963.

Plotz, Judith. "Secret Garden II; or *Lady Chatterley's Lover* as Palimpsest." *Children's Literature Association Quarterly* 19, no. 1 (1994): 15–19.

———. *Romanticism and the Vocation of Childhood*. New York: Palgrave, 2001.

Plumb, J. H. "The New World of Children in Eighteenth-Century England." *Past and Present* 67 (May 1975): 64–95.

Pointon, Marcia R. *Hanging the Head: Portraiture and Social Formation in Eighteenth-Century England*. New Haven: Yale University Press, 1993.

Porter, Eleanor H. *Pollyanna*. Boston: Page, 1913.

Portman, Frank. *King Dork*. New York: Delacorte, 2006.

Postman, Neil. *The Disappearance of Childhood*. New York: Delacorte, 1982.

———. *The Disappearance of Childhood: Redefining the Value of School*. New York: Vintage, 1994.

Potter, Beatrix. *The Tale of Peter Rabbit*. 1902. London: Frederick Warne, 2002.

———. *The Tailor of Gloucester*. London: Frederick Warne, 1903. Baltimore: Allan Publishers, 1989.

———. *The Tale of Benjamin Bunny*. London: Frederick Warne, 1904.

———. *The Story of a Fierce Bad Rabbit*. London: Frederick Warne, 1906a.

———. *The Story of Miss Moppet*. London: Frederick Warne, 1906b.

———. *The Tale of Tom Kitten*. 1907. New York: Dover, 1995.

Prince, Gerald. *Dictionary of Narratology*. Lincoln: University of Nebraska Press, 1987.

Propp, Vladimir. *The Morphology of the Folktale*. 1928. Austin: University of Texas Press, 1968.

Pullman, Philip. *Northern Lights*. Published in United States as *The Golden Compass*. London: Scholastic; New York: Alfred A. Knopf, 1995.

———. *The Subtle Knife*. London: Scholastic; New York: Alfred A. Knopf, 1997.

———. *The Amber Spyglass*. London: David Fickling Books/Scholastic; New York: Alfred A. Knopf, 2000.

———. *The Scarecrow and His Servant*. London: Doubleday; New York: Alfred A. Knopf, 2004.

Purvis, T., and A. Hunt. "Discourse, Ideology, Discourse, Ideology, Discourse, Ideology . . ." *British Journal of Sociology* 44, no. 3 (1993).

Rabinowitz, Rebecca. "Messy New Freedoms: Queer Theory and Children's Literature." In *New Voices in Children's Literature*, edited by Sebastien Chapleau. Lichfield, UK: Pied Piper, 2004.

———. "Fat-Positive Children's Books, Part One." *Shapely Prose*, September 3, 2008a. Online at http://kateharding.net/2008/09/03/fat-positive-childrens-books-part-one.

———. "Fat-Positive Children's Books, Part Two." *Shapely Prose*, September 4, 2008b. Online at http://kateharding.net/2008/09/04/guest-blogger-rebecca-rabinowitz-fat-positive-childrens-books-part-two.

Radway, Janice. *A Feeling for Books: The Book-of-the-Month Club, Literary Taste, and Middle-Class Desire*. Chapel Hill: University of North Carolina Press, 1997.

Rand, E. *Barbie's Queer Accessories*. Durham, NC: Duke University Press, 1995.

Random House Complete Unabridged Dictionary. 2d ed. New York: Random House, 1996.

Ransome, Arthur. *Swallows and Amazons*. 1931. London: Cape, 1958.

Rasula, Jed. *American Poetry Wax Museum: Reality Effects, 1940–1990*. Urbana, IL: National Council of Teachers of English, 1995.

Rassuli, Kathleen M. "Evidence of Marketing Strategy in the Early Printed Book Trade: An Application of Hollander's Historical Approach." In *Historical Perspectives in Marketing: Essays in Honor of Stanley C. Hollander*, edited by Terence Nevett and Ronald A. Fullerton, 91–107. Lexington, MA: D.C. Heath, 1988.

Rehak, Melanie. *Girl Sleuth: Nancy Drew and the Women Who Created Her*. Orlando, FL: Harcourt, 2005.

Reid-Walsh, Jacqueline. "Harlequin Meets the Sims: A History of Interactive Narrative Media for Children and Youth from Early Flap Books to Contemporary Multimedia." In *International Handbook of Children, Media and Culture*, edited by Sonia Livingstone and Kirsten Drotner, 71–86. London: Sage, 2008.

Reimer, Mavis, ed. *Home Words: Discourses of Children's Literature in Canada*. Waterloo, ON: Wilfrid Laurier University Press, 2008.

Renaud, Catherine. *Les <<incroyabilicieux>> mondes de Ponti: Une etude du double lectorat dans l'oeuvre de Claude Ponti*. Uppsala: Uppsala University Press, 2007.

Renold, E. "Tomboy." In *Girl Culture: An Encyclopedia*, edited by Claudia Mitchell and Jacqueline Reid-Walsh , 578–80. Westport, CT: Greenwood, 2008.

Rey, H. A. *Curious George*. Boston: Houghton Mifflin, 1941.

Reynolds, Kimberley. *Girls Only? Gender and Popular Children's Fiction in Britain, 1889–1910*. Philadelphia: Temple University Press, 1990.

———. *Radical Children's Literature: Future Visions and Aesthetic Transformations in Juvenile Fiction*. Basingstoke, UK: Palgrave Macmillan, 2007.

———. "Families Forever? Changing Families in Children's Fiction." In *The Cambridge Companion to Children's Literature*, edited by M. O. Grenby and Andrea Immel. Cambridge: Cambridge University Press, 2008.

Reynolds, Kimberley, and Nicholas Tucker. "Preface." In *Children's Book Publishing in England Since 1945*, edited by Kimberley Reynolds and Nicholas Tucker, xi–xiv. Aldershot, UK: Scolar Press, 1998.

Rich, Motoko. "Scholastic Accused of Misusing Book Clubs." *New York Times*, February 9, 2009.

Richards, Jeffrey, ed. *Imperialism and Juvenile Literature*. Manchester: Manchester University Press, 1989.

Richardson, Alan. *Literature, Education, and Romanticism: Reading as Social Practice 1780–1832*. New York: Cambridge University Press, 1994.

Richardson, Samuel. *Clarissa*. 1747–48. London: J. M. Dent, 1932.

Ricoeur, Paul. *Memory, History, Forgetting*. Translated by Kathleen Blamey and David Pellauer. Chicago: University of Chicago Press, 2004.

Ringgold, Faith. *Tar Beach*. New York: Crown, 1991.

Rivera, Tomás. *. . . y no se lo tragó la tierra / And the Earth Did Not Devour Him*. Berkeley, CA: Quinto Sol, 1971.

Rivers, Christopher. *Face Value: Phyisognomical Thought and the Legible Body in Marivaux, Lavater, Balzac, Gautier, and Zola*. Madison: University of Wisconsin Press, 1994.

Robinson, F. C. "European Clothing Names and the Etymology of Girl." In *Studies in Historical Linguistics in Honor of George Sherman Lane*, edited by Walter W. Arndt, 233–37. Chapel Hill: University of North Carolina Press, 1967.

Robson, Catherine. *Men in Wonderland: The Lost Girlhood of the*

Victorian Gentleman. Princeton: Princeton University Press, 2001.

Rochman, Hazel. "And Yet . . . Beyond Political Correctness." In *Evaluating Children's Books: A Critical Look: Aesthetic, Social, and Political Aspects of Analyzing and Using Children's Books,* edited by Betsy Hearne and Roger Sutton, 133–48. Urbana-Champaign: University of Illinois at Urbana-Champaign, 1993.

Rodríguez, Luis J. *It Doesn't Have to Be This Way: A Barrio Story / No tiene que ser así: Una historia del barrio.* San Francisco: Children's Book Press, 1999.

Rollin, Lucy. *Cradle and All: A Cultural and Psychoanalytic Reading of Nursery Rhymes.* Jackson: University Press of Mississippi, 1992.

Rollins, Charlemae. *We Build Together.* Chicago: National Council of Teachers of English, 1941.

Romines, Ann. "Preempting the Patriarch: The Problem of Pa's Stories in *Little House in the Big Woods.*" *Children's Literature Association Quarterly* 20, no. 1 (1995): 15–18.

Rose, Jacqueline. *The Case of Peter Pan, or The Impossibility of Children's Fiction.* London: Macmillan, 1984.

Rose, Jonathan. "John Newbery." In *The British Literary Book Trade, 1700–1820,* edited by James Bracken and Joel Silver, 216–28. Detroit: Gale, 1995.

Rosen, Judith. "Breaking the Age Barrier." *Publishers Weekly,* September 8, 1997: 28–31.

Rosenberg, Teya. "Transforming the Quotidian: Borges, Nesbit, and Threads of Influence." Paper presented at the Children's Literature Association Annual Conference, Illinois State University, Normal, June 14, 2008.

Rosenblatt, Louise. *The Reader, the Text, the Poem: The Transactional Theory of the Literary Work.* Carbondale: Southern Illinois University Press, 1978.

Rosman, Mark, director. *A Cinderella Story.* Written by Leigh Dunlap. Perf. Hilary Duff, Jennifer Coolidge, Chad Michael Murray. Warner Brothers, 2004.

Rosoff, Meg. *How I Live Now.* 2004. New York: Wendy Lamb Books (Random House), 2006.

Rousseau, Jean Jacques. *Émile.* 1762. Translated by Barbara Foxley. London: Dent, 1911.

———. *Émile, or On Education.* 1762. Translated by Allan Bloom. New York: Basic, 1979.

Rowbotham, Judith. *Good Girls Make Good Wives: Guidance for Girls in Victorian Fiction.* Oxford: Blackwell, 1989.

Rowling, J. K. *Harry Potter and the Philosopher's Stone.* London: Bloomsbury, 1997; New York: Scholastic, 1998.

———. *Harry Potter and the Chamber of Secrets.* London: Bloomsbury, 1998; New York: Scholastic, 1999.

———. *Harry Potter and the Goblet of Fire.* London: Bloomsbury; New York: Scholastic, 2000.

———. *Harry Potter and the Deathly Hallows.* London: Bloomsbury; New York: Scholastic, 2007.

Rubin, Joan Shelley. *The Making of Middlebrow Culture.* Chapel Hill: University of North Carolina Press, 1992.

Rudd, David. *Enid Blyton and the Mystery of Children's Literature.* London: Macmillan, 2000.

———. "Theorising and Theories. The Conditions of Possibility of Children's Literature." In *International Companion Encyclopedia of Children's Literature.* 2d ed., edited by Peter Hunt, 30–43. London: Routledge, 2005.

Rudman, Masha Kabakow. "Multiculturalism." In *The Oxford Encyclopedia of Children's Literature,* volume 3, edited by Jack Zipes, 111–13. New York: Oxford University Press, 2006.

Ruskin, John. *The King of the Golden River or The Black Brothers: A Legend of Stiria.* 1841. Edited by Katharine Lee Bates. Chicago: Rand, McNally, 1903.

Ruwe, Donelle. "Guarding the British Bible from Rousseau: Sarah Trimmer, William Godwin, and the Pedagogical Periodical." *Children's Literature* 29 (2001): 1–17.

Ryan, Pam Muñoz. *Riding Freedom.* New York: Scholastic, 1998.

Rybczynski, Witold. *Home: A Short History of an Idea.* London: Heinemann, 1986.

Sachar, Louis. *Marvin Redpost: Is He a Girl?* New York: Random House, 1993a.

———. *Marvin Redpost: Why Pick on Me?* New York: Random House, 1993b.

———. *Holes.* New York: Dell Laurel-Leaf, 1998.

Said, Edward. *Orientalism.* New York: Pantheon, 1978.

———. *Culture and Imperialism.* New York: Alfred A. Knopf, 1993.

Sainte-Beuve, Henri. "Qu'est qu'um classique." *Causeries du Lundi.* 3d ed., vol. 3. Paris: Garnier Freres, n.d.

Saldanha, Louise. "White Picket Fences: At Home with Multicultural Children's Literature in Canada?" In *Home Words: Discourses of Children's Literature in Canada,* edited by Mavis Reimer, 129–43. Waterloo, ON: Wilfrid Laurier University Press, 2008.

Salinger, J. D. *Catcher in the Rye.* 1951. New York: Bantam, 1964.

Salmon, Edward. *Juvenile Literature as It Is.* London: Henry J. Drane, 1888.

Sanchez, Sonia. "Rashada Receives a Gift, Part I." *Muhammad Speaks* 25 (September 1975).

Sánchez-Eppler, Karen. *Dependent States: The Child's Part in*

Nineteenth-Century American Culture. Chicago: University of Chicago Press, 2005.

Sanders, Dori. *Clover*. New York: Random House, 1990.

Sands-O'Connor, Karen. "Smashing Birds in the Wilderness: British Racial and Cultural Integration from Insider and Outsider Perspectives." *Papers* 13, no. 3 (2003): 43–50.

Sarland, Charles. "The Impossibility of Innocence: Ideology, Politics, and Children's Literature." In *Understanding Children's Literature, Key Essays from the International Companion Encyclopedia of Children's Literature*, edited by Peter Hunt, 39–55. London: Routledge, 1999.

Saxton, Ruth O., ed. *The Girl: Constructions of the Girl in Contemporary Fiction by Women*. New York: St. Martin's, 1998.

Say, Allen. *Grandfather's Journey*. Boston: Houghton Mifflin, 1993.

Sayers, Frances Clarke, and C. M. Weisenberg. "Walt Disney Accused." *Horn Book* (December 1965). Online at http://www.hbook.com/magazine/articles/1960s/dec65_sayers.asp.

Schorsch, Anita. *Images of Childhood: An Illustrated Social History*. New York: Main Street, 1979.

Schwarcz, Joseph H. *Ways of the Illustrator: Visual Communication in Children's Literature*. New York: American Library Association, 1982.

Schwartz, Albert W. "*Sounder*: A Black or a White Tale?" *Interracial Books for Children Bulletin* 3, no. 1 (1970). Reprinted in *The Black American in Books for Children: Readings in Racism*, edited by Donnarae MacCann and Gloria Woodard, 147–50. Metuchen, NJ: Scarecrow Press, 1985.

Schwartz, Elaine G. "Crossing Borders/Shifting Paradigms: Multiculturalism and Children's Literature." *Harvard Educational Review* 65, no. 4 (1995).

Schwenke-Wylie, Andrea. "Expanding the View of First-Person Narration." *Children's Literature in Education* 30, no. 3 (1999): 185–202.

———. "The Value of Singularity in First- and Restricted Third-Person Engaging Narration." *Children's Literature* 31 (2003), 116–41.

Scieszka, Jon, and Lane Smith. *The Stinky Cheese Man and Other Fairly Stupid Tales*. New York: Viking Penguin, 1992.

———. *Baloney (Henry P.)*. New York: Viking, 2001.

Scott, Sir Walter. *Ivanhoe*. 1819–20. New York: Dodd, Mead, 1941.

Scudder, Horace E. *Childhood in Literature and Art*. Boston: Houghton, Mifflin, 1894.

Sealander, Judith. *The Failed Century of the Child: Governing America's Young in the Twentieth Century*. New York: Cambridge University Press, 2003.

Sedgwick, Eve K. *Tendencies*. Durham, NC: Duke University Press, 1993.

Seed, Patricia. *American Pentimento: The Invention of Indians and the Pursuit of Riches*. Minneapolis: University of Minnesota Press, 2001.

Segel, Elizabeth. "Tomboy Taming and Gender Role Socialization: The Evidence of Children's Books." In *Gender Roles through the Life Span: A Multidisciplinary Perspective*, edited by Michael R. Stevenson, 47–61. Muncie, IN: Ball State University Press, 1994.

Seidel, Michael. *Robinson Crusoe: Island Myths and the Novel*. Boston: Twayne, 1991.

Seiter, Ellen. *Sold Separately: Children and Parents in Consumer Culture*. New Brunswick, NJ: Rutgers University Press, 1993.

Sekeres, Diane. "Renewed But Not Redeemed: Revising Elsie Dinsmore." *Children's Literature in Education* 36, no. 1 (2005): 15–39.

Sen, Satadru. "A Juvenile Periphery: The Geographies of Literary Childhood in Colonial Bengal." *Journal of Colonialism and Colonial History* 5, no. 1 (2004).

Sendak, Maurice. *Where the Wild Things Are*. New York: Harper and Row, 1963.

———. *In the Night Kitchen*. New York: Harper and Row, 1970.

———. *Outside over There*. New York: Harper and Row, 1981.

———. *We Are All in the Dumps with Jack and Guy*. New York: HarperCollins, 1993.

Seuss, Dr. *And to Think That I Saw It on Mulberry Street*. New York: Vanguard, 1937.

———. *The Cat in the Hat*. New York: Random House, 1957.

———. *Fox in Socks*. New York: Random House, 1965.

———. *The Lorax*. New York: Random House, 1971.

———. *The Butter Battle Book*. New York: Random House, 1984.

Sewell, Elizabeth. *The Field of Nonsense*. London: Chatto and Windus, 1952.

Shakespeare, William. *King Lear*. 1608/1623. In *William Shakespeare: The Complete Works, Compact Edition*, edited by Stanley Wells, Gary Taylor, John Jowett, and William Montgomery. Oxford: Clarendon, 1988.

Shariff, S., and Manley-Casimir, M. "Censorship in Schools: Orthodoxy, Diversity, and Cultural Coherence." In *Interpreting Censorship in Canada*, edited by Allan C. Hutchinson and Klaus Petersen, 157–81. Toronto: University of Toronto Press, 1999.

Shaull, Richard. "Foreword." In *Pedagogy of the Oppressed* by Paolo Freire, translated by Myra Bergman Ramos. New York: Continuum, 2000.

Shavit, Zohar. *The Poetics of Children's Literature*. Athens: University of Georgia Press, 1986.

Shelley, Mary. *Frankenstein, or the Modern Prometheus*. 1818, revised 1831. Edited by M. K. Joseph. New York: Oxford University Press, 1969.

Shorter Oxford English Dictionary. Edited by C. T. Onions. Oxford: Clarendon Press, 1970.

Shorter Oxford English Dictionary. Edited by C. T. Onions. Oxford: Clarendon Press, 1987.

Shortsleeve, Kevin. "The Politics of Nonsense: Civil Unrest, Otherness and National Mythology in Nonsense Literature." Doctoral dissertation, University of Oxford, 2007.

Silverstein, Shel. *Uncle Shelby's ABZ Book: A Primer for Adults Only*. New York: Simon and Schuster, 1985. (Originally published 1961 with the subtitle *A Primer for Tender Young Minds*.)

Silvey, Anita. *Children's Books and Their Creators*. Boston: Houghton, 1995.

Simonton, Deborah. "Women and Education." In *Women's History: Britain, 1700–1850: An Introduction*, edited by Hannah Barker and Elaine Chalus, 33–56. New York: Taylor and Francis, 2005.

Sims, Rudine. *Shadow and Substance: Afro-American Experience in Contemporary Children's Fiction*. Urbana, IL: National Council of Teachers of English, 1982.

Sinclair, Catherine. *Holiday House: A Book for the Young*. 1839. New York: Garland, 1976.

Singer, Dorothy G. "Piglet, Pooh, and Piaget." *Psychology Today*, 6 (1972): 70–74.

Singer, Isaac Bashevis. Acceptance speech for National Book Award, 1970. Re-used as Nobel speech, 1978. *Nobel Lecture*, 3–10. New York: Farrar, Straus and Giroux, 1979.

Sipe, Lawrence R. "How Picture Books Work: A Semiotically Framed Theory of Text-Picture Relationships." *Children's Literature in Education* 29, no. 2 (1998): 97–108.

Sircar, Sanjay. "The Victorian Auntly Narrative Voice and Mrs. Molesworth's *Cuckoo Clock*." *Children's Literature* 17 (1989): 1–24.

The Slave's Friend. New York: R. G. Williams for the American Anti-Slavery Society, 1836–38.

Sleator, William. *Test*. New York: Amulet, 2008.

Slemon, Stephen. "Monuments of Empire: Allegory/Counter-Discourse/Post-Colonial Writing." *Kunapipi* 9, no. 3 (1987): 1–16.

Slemon, Stephen, and Jo-Ann Wallace. "Into the Heart of Darkness?: Teaching Children's Literature as a Problem in Theory." *Canadian Children's Literature* 63 (1991): 6–23.

Slobodkina, Esphyr. *Se Venden Gorras*. Translated by Teresa Mlawer. New York: Harper Arco Iris, 1995.

Smith, Katharine Capshaw. *Children's Literature of the Harlem Renaissance*. Bloomington: Indiana University Press, 2004.

Smith, Michelle. "Adventurous Girls of the British Empire: The Pre-War Novels of Bessie Marchant." *The Lion and the Unicorn* 33 (2009): 1–25.

Smith, William Jay. *Laughing Time: Collected Nonsense*. New York: Farrar, Straus and Giroux, 1990.

Snicket, Lemony. *The Grim Grotto*. New York: HarperCollins, 2004.

Sontag, Susan. *On Photography*. New York: Farrar, Straus and Giroux, 1977.

Sorby, A. *Schoolroom Poets: Childhood, Performance, and the Place of American Poetry, 1865–1917*. Hanover: University of New England Press, 2005.

Soto, Gary. *Chato's Kitchen*. Illustrated by Susan Guevara. New York: Putnam and Grosset, 1995.

———. *Chato and the Party Animals*. Illustrated by Susan Guevara. New York: Puffin, 2000.

Southworth, E.D.E.N. *The Hidden Hand*. Published serially 1859. Published as novel 1888. New Brunswick: Rutgers University Press, 1988.

Spinelli, Jerry. *Who Put That Hair in My Toothbrush?* New York: Scholastic, 1984.

Spivak, Gayatri. "Can the Subaltern Speak? Speculations on Widow Sacrifice." In *Colonial Discourse and Postcolonial Theory: A Reader*, edited by Patrick Williams and Laura Chrisman. Hemel Hempstead, UK: Harvester Wheatsheaf, 1985.

Spyri, Johanna. *Heidi*. 1880. Translated by Louise Brooks. New York: Platt and Peck, 1884.

Starke, Ruth. "What Is a Multicultural Book?" *Viewpoint* 3, no. 1 (1995): 22–24.

Starr, Carol. "Brief History of the Young Adult Services Division." *YALSA: Young Adult Library Services Association*. Online at http://www.ala.org/ala/mgrps/divs/yalsa/aboutyalsa/brief-history.cfm.

Stearns, F. P. *Sketches from Concord and Appledore*. New York: Putnam's, 1895.

Stearns, Peter N. *Childhood in World History*. New York: Routledge, 2009.

Stedman, Jane W. *W. S. Gilbert: A Classic Victorian and His Theatre*. Oxford: Oxford University Press, 1996.

Steedman, Carolyn. *Strange Dislocations: Childhood and the Idea of Human Interiority, 1780–1930*. Cambridge, MA: Harvard University Press, 1995.

Steig, Michael. "Response and Evasion in Reading *The Wind in the Willows*." In *Stories of Reading: Subjectivity and Literary Understanding*. Baltimore: Johns Hopkins University Press, 1998.

Stein, Gertrude. *The World Is Round*. 1939. New York: Barefoot, 1993.

Steinbeck, John. *Of Mice and Men*. New York: Penguin, 1937.

Stephens, John. "Advocating Multiculturalism: Migrants in Australian Children's Literature after 1972." *Children's Literature Association Quarterly* 15, no. 4 (1990): 180–85.

———. *Language and Ideology in Children's Fiction*. New York: Longman, 1992.

———. "Gender, Genre and Children's Literature." *Signal* 79 (1996): 17–30.

———. "Multiculturalism in Recent Australian Children's Fiction: (Re-)constructing Selves through Personal and National Histories." In *Other Worlds, Other Lives*, vol. 3, edited by Myrna Machet, Sandra Olen, and Thomas van der Walt, 1–19. Pretoria: University of South Africa, 1996.

———. "Continuity, Fissure, or Dysfunction? From Settler Society to Multicultural Society in Australian Fiction." In *Voices of the Other: Children's Literature and the Postcolonial Context*, edited by Roderick McGillis, 55–70. New York: Garland, 2000.

———, ed. *Ways of Being Male: Representing Masculinities in Children's Literature and Film*. London: Routledge, 2002.

Stern, Daniel. *The Present Moment, in Psychotherapy and Everyday Life*. New York: Norton, 2004.

Stevens, Paul. "Milton and the Icastic Imagination." *Milton Studies* 20 (1984): 43–71.

Stevenson, Deborah. "'If You Read This Last Sentence, It Won't Tell You Anything': Postmodernism, Self-Referentiality, and *The Stinky Cheese Man*." *Children's Literature Association Quarterly* 19, no. 1 (1994): 32–34.

———. "Sentiment and Significance: The Impossibility of Recovery in the Children's Literature Canon, or, The Drowning of *The Water-Babies*." *The Lion and the Unicorn* 21, no. 1 (1997): 112–30.

Stevenson, Robert Louis. *Treasure Island*. 1883. Oxford: Oxford University Press, 1998.

Steward, James Christen. *The New Child: British Art and the Origins of Modern Childhood, 1780–1830*. Berkeley: University Art Museum and Pacific Film Archive, University of California, Berkeley; Seattle: University of Washington Press, 1995.

Stimpson, Catharine R. "Reading for Love: Canons, Paracanons, and Whistling Jo March." *New Literary History* 21, no. 4 (1990): 957–76.

Stine, R. L. *Challenge of the Wolf Knight*. Wizards, Warriors and You Series, no. 1. New York: Avon, 1985.

Stoehr, Shelley. *Crosses*. New York: Bantam Doubleday, 1991.

Storey, John. "Postmodernism." In *New Keywords: A Revised Vocabulary of Culture and Society*, edited by Tony Bennett, Lawrence Grossberg, and Meaghan Morris. Malden, MA: Blackwell, 2005.

Strachey, Edward. "Nonsense as a Fine Art." *Quarterly Review* 167 (July–October 1888): 335–65.

Streeby, Shelley. "Empire." In *Keywords for American Studies*, edited by Bruce Burgett and Glenn Hendler. New York: New York University Press, 2007.

Summerfield, Geoffrey. *Fantasy and Reason: Children's Literature in the Eighteenth Century*. London: Methuen, 1984.

Sunderland, Jane. "Gendered Discourses in Children's Literature." In *Gendered Discourses*, 141–64. New York: Palgrave Macmillan, 2004.

Sutherland, Robert D. "Hidden Persuaders: Political Ideologies in Literature for Children." *Children's Literature in Education* 16, no. 3 (1985): 143–57.

Susman, Warren. *Culture as History: The Transformation of American Society in the Twentieth Century*. New York: Pantheon, 1984.

Sutton-Smith, Brian, et al. *The Folkstories of Children*. Philadelphia: University of Pennsylvania Press, 1981.

Suvin, Darko. "On the Poetics of the Science Fiction Genre." *College English* 34, no. 3 (1972): 372–82.

Svendsen, Kester. *Milton and Science*. Cambridge, MA: Harvard University Press, 1956.

Swift, Jonathan. *Gulliver's Travels*. 1726. Oxford: Oxford University Press, 2008.

Tabart, Benjamin. *Fairy Tales, or the Lilliputian Cabinet: Containing Twenty-four Choice Pieces of Fancy and Fiction*. London: Tabart and Co., 1818.

Tabbert, Reinbert. Personal communication with William Moebius, Paris, 1999.

Tan, Shaun. *The Arrival*. Sydney: Lothian, 2006.

Tarr, Anita C. "The Absence of Moral Agency in Robert Cormier's *The Chocolate War*." *Children's Literature* 30 (2002): 96–124.

Taylor, Ann, and Jane Taylor. *Signor Topsy-Turvy's Wonderful Magic Lantern*. London: Tabart, 1810.

The Ten Little Niggers. New York: McLoughlin Brothers, 1875.

Thacker, Deborah. "Disdain or Ignorance? Literary Theory and the Absence of Children's Literature." *The Lion and the Unicorn* 26, no. 1 (2000): 1–17.

Thacker, Deborah Cogan, and Jean Webb. *Introducing Children's Literature*. London, Routledge, 2002.

Thiel, Elizabeth. *The Fantasy of Family: Nineteenth-Century Children's Literature and the Myth of the Domestic Ideal*. New York: Routledge, 2008.

Thompson, E. P. *The Making of the English Working Class*. 1963. Harmondsworth, UK: Penguin, 1980.

Thompson, J. M. "Post-Modernism." *Hibbert Journal* 12 (1914): 733–45.

Thompson, Terry. *Adventures in Graphica: Using Comics and Graphic Novels to Teach Comprehension, 2–6*. Portland, ME: Stenhouse, 2008.

Thompson, Vetta L. Sanders, and Maysa Akbar. "The Understanding of Race and the Construction of African-American Identity." *Western Journal of Black Studies* 27, no. 2 (2003): 80–88.

Thompson, William, and Joseph Hickey. *Society in Focus*. Boston: Pearson, Allyn and Bacon, 2005.

Thurber, James. *The Wonderful O*. Illustrated by Marc Simont. New York: Simon and Schuster, 1957.

Thwaite, Ann. *A. A. Milne, His Life*. London: Faber and Faber, 1990.

Tigges, Wim. *An Anatomy of Literary Nonsense*. Amsterdam: Rodopi, 1988.

Todd, Dennis. *Imagining Monsters: Miscreations of the Self in Eighteenth-Century England*. Chicago: University of Chicago Press, 1995.

Tolkien, J. R. R. *The Hobbit*. London: Allen and Unwin, 1937.

———. "On Fairy-Stories." In *Essays Presented to Charles Williams*, edited by C. S. Lewis, 38–89. London: Oxford University Press, 1947.

———. *The Fellowship of the Ring: Being the First Part of The Lord of the Rings*. London: Allen and Unwin, 1954a.

———. *The Two Towers: Being the Second Part of The Lord of the Rings*. London: Allen and Unwin, 1954b.

———. *The Return of the King: Being the Third Part of The Lord of the Rings*. London: Allen and Unwin, 1955.

Townsend, John Rowe. *A Sense of Story: Essays on Contemporary Writers for Children*. London: Longman, 1971a.

———. "Standards of Criticism for Children's Literature." 1971b. Reprinted in *Children's Literature: Critical Concepts in Literary and Cultural Studies*, edited by Peter Hunt, 86–97. London: Routledge, 1990.

Travers, P. L. *Mary Poppins*. 1934. New York: Harcourt, Brace and World, 1962.

Trelease, Jim. "Censors and Children's Literature: Are They Watch Dogs or Mad Dogs?" *Trelease-on-Reading Website*, 2007. Online at http://www.trelease-on-reading.com/censor%20_entry.html (accessed 2007).

Tribunella, Eric. "Institutionalizing *The Outsiders*: YA Literature, Social Class, and the American Faith in Education." *Children's Literature in Education* 38 (2007): 87–101.

Trimmer, Sarah. *Fabulous Histories. Designed for the Instruction of Children, Respecting Their Treatment of Animals*. London: T. Longman, G. G. J. and J. Robinson, and J. Johnson, 1786.

———. "Observations on the Changes Which Have Taken Place in Books for Children and Young Persons." 1802. In *A Peculiar Gift: Nineteenth Century Writings on Books for Children*, edited by Lance Salway. Harmondsworth, UK: Kestrel, 1976.

———. *The Guardian of Education*, vols. 1–3. London: J. Hatchard, 1802–5.

Trites, Roberta Seelinger. "Manifold Narratives: Metafiction and Ideology in Picture Books." *Children's Literature in Education* 25, no. 4 (1994): 225–42.

———. "Theories and Possibilities of Adolescent Literature." *Children's Literature Association Quarterly* 21, no. 1 (1996): 2–3.

———. *Disturbing the Universe: Power and Repression in Adolescent Literature*. Iowa City: University of Iowa Press, 2000.

Tucker, Nicholas. *The Child and the Book: A Psychological and Literary Exploration*. 1981. Cambridge: Cambridge University Press, 1990.

Tudge, Colin. *The Secret Life of Trees: How They Live and Why They Matter*. London: Allen Lane, 2005.

Turner, Edith. "The Literary Roots of Victor Turner's Anthropology." In *Victor Turner and the Construction of Cultural Criticism*, edited by Kathleen Ashley, 163–69. Bloomington: Indiana University Press, 1990.

Turner, Ethel. *Seven Little Australians*. 1884. Montville, Australia: Walter McVitty, 1994. Series continued with *The Family at Misrule*, *Little Mother Meg*, and *Judy and Punch*. Ringwood, Australia: Puffin, 1994.

Turner, Victor. *The Ritual Process*. Chicago: Aldine, 1969.

Turner-Bowker, Diane M. "Gender Stereotyped Descriptors in Children's Picture Books: Does 'Curious Jane' Exist in the Literature?" *Sex Roles* 35, nos. 7–8 (1996): 461–88.

Tuttle, Carolyn. *Hard at Work in Factories and Mines: The Economics of Child Labor during the British Industrial Revolution*. Oxford: Westview, 1999.

Twain, Mark. *The Adventures of Tom Sawyer*. 1876. In *The Unabridged Mark Twain*, volume 1, edited by Lawrence Teacher, 436–85. Philadelphia: Running Press, 1976.

————. *The Adventures of Huckleberry Finn.* 1884. New York, Heritage Press, 1940.

Twist, L., I. Schagen, and C. Hodgson. *Readers and Reading: The National Report for England.* PIRLS: Progress in International Reading Literacy Study. Slough: National Foundation for Educational Research, 2006.

UNESCO. "Education: Why Literacy Is Important." Online at http://www.unesco.org/en/literacy/literacy-important/.

UNICEF. "Why We Do It." Online at http://www.unicef.org/why/why_preventable_causes.html (accessed March 2009).

U.S. Department of Education. "Reading First." Online at http://www.ed.gov/programs/readingfirst/index.html (accessed September 17, 2009).

The Universal Declaration of Human Rights. 1948. Online at http://www.un.org/Overview/rights.html (accessed February 2009).

Vaizey, Mrs. George de Horne. *A Houseful of Girls.* London: Religious Tract Society, 1902.

Vallone, Lynne. *Disciplines of Virtue: Girls' Culture in the Eighteenth and Nineteenth Centuries.* New Haven: Yale University Press, 1995.

Van Allsburg, Chris. *The Mysteries of Harris Burdick.* Boston: Houghton Mifflin, 1984.

Van der Linden, Sophie. *Claude Ponti.* Paris: Éditions Être, 2000.

Van Gennep, Arnold. *Rites of Passage.* 1909. Translated by M. Vizedom and G. Caffe. 1960. London: Routledge, 2004.

Van Loon, Hendrik Willem. *The Story of Mankind.* New York: Boni and Liveright, 1921.

Van Sant, Gus, director. *Paranoid Park.* Perf. Gabe Nevins, Daniel Liu, Taylor Momsen, and Scott Patrick Green. IFC Films, 2007.

Voight, Cynthia. *Jackaroo.* New York: Scholastic, 1985.

Von Ziegesar, Cecily. *Gossip Girl.* New York: Little, Brown, 2002.

Waboose, Jan Bourdeau. *Morning on the Lake.* Toronto: Kids Can Press, 1997.

Wadsworth, Eliza. Marginalia in the Hewins Collection of the Connecticut Historical Society Library copy of T. H. Galludet and Horace Hooker. *The Practical Spelling-Book.* Hartford: Hamersley, 1861.

Walkerdine, Valerie. "Developmental Psychology and the Child-Centred Pedagogy: The Insertion of Piaget into Early Education." In *Changing the Subject: Psychology, Social Regulation and Subjectivity,* edited by Julian Henriques et al., 153–202. London: Methuen, 1984.

————. *Daddy's Girl: Young Girls and Popular Culture.* Cambridge, MA: Harvard University Press, 1997.

Wall, Barbara. *The Narrator's Voice: The Dilemma of Children's Fiction.* 1991. Houndmills, UK: Macmillan, 1994.

Walsh, Jill Paton. "The Writer's Responsibility." *Children's Literature in Education* 10 (1973): 30–36.

Wannamaker, Annette. *Boys in Children's Literature and Popular Culture: Masculinity, Abjection, and the Fictional Child.* New York: Routledge, 2008.

Ward, Lynd. *Gods' Man.* 1929. New York: St. Martin's, 1978.

Warner, Michael. *Fear of a Queer Plant: Queer Politics and Social Theory.* Minneapolis: University of Minnesota Press, 1993.

Warner, Susan. *The Wide, Wide World.* 1850. New York: Feminist Press, 1987.

Warner, Sylvia Townsend. *Lolly Willowes.* New York: Viking, 1926.

Watson, Victor, ed. *The Cambridge Guide to Children's Books in English.* Cambridge: Cambridge University Press, 2001.

Watts, Isaac. "Praise to God for Learning to Read." *Divine Songs Attempted in Easy Language for the Use of Children.* 1715. Facsimile edition. Oxford: Oxford University Press, 1971.

Weber, Max. *Economy and Society.* Berkeley: University of California Press, 1922.

Webster, Jean. *Daddy-Long-Legs.* New York: The Century Co., 1912.

Weiner, Stephen. *The 101 Best Graphic Novels.* Rev ed. New York: NBM, 2005.

Wells, Carolyn, ed. *A Nonsense Anthology.* New York: Scribner's, 1902.

Wells, Rosemary. *Yoko.* New York: Hyperion, 1998.

Wertham, Fredric. *Seduction of the Innocent—The Influence of Comic Books on Today's Youth.* New York: Rinehart, 1954.

Wesley, John. "Sermon 96: On Obedience to Parents." 1784. In *The Works of John Wesley,* edited by Albert C. Outler et al., 3:361–72. Nashville: Abingdon, 1986.

Westman, Karin E. "Spectres of Thatcherism: Contemporary British Culture in J. K. Rowling's Harry Potter Series." In *The Ivory Tower and Harry Potter: Perspectives on a Literary Phenomeon,* edited by Lana Whited, 305–28. Columbia: University of Missouri Press, 2002.

————. "Children's Literature and Modernism: The Space Between." *Children's Literature Association Quarterly* 32, no. 4 (2007a): 283–86.

————. "Perspective, Memory, and Moral Authority: The Legacy of Jane Austen in J. K. Rowling's *Harry Potter.*" *Children's Literature* 35 (2007b): 145–65.

Whelan, Debra Lau. "SLJ Self-Censorship Survey." *School Library*

Journal, February 1, 2009. Online at http://www.schoolli-braryjournal.com.

White, Dorothy Neal. *Books before Five*. 1954. Portsmouth, NH: Heinemann, 1984.

White, E. B. *Charlotte's Web*. Illustrated by Garth Williams. New York: Harper and Row, 1952.

White, Michael. *Maps of Narrative Therapy*. New York: Norton, 2007.

White, Richard Grant. "Old New York and Its Houses." *Century Illustrated Monthly Magazine* 26, no. 2 (1883): 845–59.

Wiesner, David. *The Three Pigs*. New York: Clarion, 2001.

Wiggin, Kate Douglas. *Marm Lisa*. 1896. Online at http://www.gutenberg.org/etext/3149 (accessed July 10, 2008).

———. *Rebecca of Sunnybrook Farm*. 1903. New York: Penguin, 1985.

Wilbur, Richard. *Loudmouse*. New York: Crowell-Collier, 1963.

———. Personal communication to Lissa Paul, April 18, 2008.

Wilk, Christopher, ed. *Modernism 1914–1939: Designing a New World*. London: V&A Publications, 2006.

Wilkie-Stibbs, Christine. *The Feminine Subject in Children's Literature*. New York: Routledge, 2002.

Willard, Nancy. *A Visit to William Blake's Inn: Poems for Innocent and Experienced Travelers*. New York: Harcourt Brace, 1982.

Willhoite, Michael. *Daddy's Roommate*. Boston: Alyson, 1990.

———. *Uncle What-Is-It Is Coming to Visit!!*. Boston: Alyson Wonderland, 1993.

Williams, Raymond. *Border Country*. London: Chatto and Windus, 1960.

———. *Keywords: A Vocabulary of Culture and Society*. 1976. New York: Oxford University Press, 1983a.

———. *Writing in Society*. London: Verso, 1983b.

Wilson, Ara. *The Intimate Economies of Bangkok: Tomboys, Tycoons and Avon Ladies in the Global City*. Berkeley: University of California Press, 2004.

Wimsatt, William K., and Monroe C. Beardsley. "The Intentional Fallacy." Sewanee Review 54 (1946). Revised and republished in The Verbal Icon: Studies in the Meaning of Poetry. Lexington: University of Kentucky Press, 1954.

Winch, Christopher, and John Gingell. *Key Concepts in the Philosophy of Education*. London: Routledge, 1999.

Winnubst, Shannon. *Queering Freedom*. Bloomington: Indiana University Press, 2006.

Wittlinger, Ellen. *Parrotfish*. New York: Simon and Schuster, 2007.

Wojcik-Andrews, Ian. "Editor's Introduction: Notes towards a Theory of Class in Children's Literature." *The Lion and the Unicorn* 17, no. 2 (1993): 113–23.

Wolf, Doris, and Paul DePasquale. "Home and Native Land: A Study of Canadian Aboriginal Picture Books by Aboriginal Authors." In *Home Words: Discourses of Children's Literature in Canada*, edited by Mavis Reimer, 87–105. Waterloo, ON: Wilfrid Laurier University Press, 2008.

Wolf, Maryanne. *Proust and the Squid: The Story and Science of the Reading Brain*. Illustrated by Catherine Stoodley. Cambridge: Icon, 2008.

Wolf, Shelby Anne, and Shirley Brice Heath. *The Braid of Literature: Children's Worlds of Reading*. Cambridge, MA: Harvard University Press, 1992.

Wolfreys, Julian, Ruth Robbins, and Kenneth Womack. *Key Concepts in Literary Theory*. 2d ed. Edinburgh: Edinburgh University Press, 2006.

Wollman-Bonilla J. E. "Outrageous Viewpoints: Teachers' Criteria for Rejecting Works of Children's Literature." *Language Arts* 75 (1998): 287–95.

Wollstoneraft, Mary. *Original Stories, from Real Life; with Conversations, Calculated to Regulate the Affections, and Form the Mind to Truth and Goodness*. London: J. Johnson, 1788.

———. *A Vindication of the Rights of Woman*. 1793. Excerpted in *The Feminist Papers: From Adams to Beauvoir*, edited by Alice S. Rossi. Boston: Northeastern University Press, 1973.

Wood, Samuel. *Cries of New York*. New York: Samuel Wood, 1808.

Woodson, Jacqueline. *If You Come Softly*. New York: Puffin, 1998.

———. *The House You Pass on the Way*. New York: Laurel Leaf, 1999.

Woolf, Virginia. "A Sketch of the Past." In *Moments of Being*, edited by Jeanne Schulkind. New York: Harcourt Brace Jovanovich, 1976. Originally published in 1939.

Woolson, Constance Fenimore. "Felipa." *Harpers Magazine* (June 1876). Reprinted in *The Signet Classic Book of Southern Short Stories*, edited by D. Abbott and S. Koppelman. London: Penguin, 2005.

Wordsworth, William. "Ode: Intimations of Immortality from Recollections of Early Childhood." 1807. Reprinted in *The Norton Anthology of Poetry*, 3d ed., edited by Alexander W. Allison et al. New York: Norton, 1983.

———. "Preface." *Poems by William Wordsworth: Including Lyrical Ballads, and the Miscellaneous Pieces of the Author. With Additional Poems, a New Preface, and a Supplementary Essay*, 1:vii–xlii. London: Printed for Longman, Hurst, Rees, Orme, and Brown, Paternoster-Row, 1815.

———. *The Prelude 1799, 1805, 1850*. New York: Norton, 1979.

Wright, Erik Olin. *Classes*. London: Verso, 1985.

Wyeth, Sharon Dennis. *Tomboy Trouble*. New York: Random House, 1998.

Yamaguchi, Lynne, and Karen Barber. "Introduction." In *Tomboys! Tales of Dyke Derring-Do*, edited by Lynne Yamaguchi and Karen Barber, 9–14. Los Angeles: Alyson, 1995.

Yang, Gene Luen. *American Born Chinese*. New York: First Second (Roaring Brook Press), 2006.

Yee, Paul. *Tales from Gold Mountain*. Toronto: Groundwood, 1989.

Yolen, Jane. *Owl Moon*. Illustrated by John Schoenherr. New York: Philomel, 1987.

Yonge, Charlotte. *The Heir of Redclyffe*. 1853. Oxford World's Classics. Oxford: Oxford University Press, 1997.

Young Adult Library Services Association. "YALSA Vision Statement." 1994. Online at http://www.ala.org/ala/mgrps/divs/yalsa/aboutyalsab/yalsavision.cfm.

Younger, Beth. "Pleasure, Pain, and the Power of Being Thin: Female Sexuality in Young Adult Literature." *NWSA Journal* 15, no. 2 (2003): 45–56.

Zimmerman, Michael E. "Possible Political Problems with Earth-Based Religiosity." In *Beneath the Surface: Critical Essays in the Philosophy of Deep Ecology*, edited by Eric Katz, Andrew Light, and David Rothenberg, 169–94. Cambridge, MA: MIT Press, 2000.

Zindel, Paul. *The Pigman*. 1968. New York: Starfire, 1983.

Zipes, Jack. "Marx and Engels without the Frills." *The Lion and the Unicorn* 4, no. 1 (1980): 83–89.

———. *Fairy Tales and the Art of Subversion*. London: Heinemann, 1983.

———. *Sticks and Stones: The Troublesome Success of Children's Literature from Slovenly Peter to Harry Potter*. New York: Routledge, 2001.

Zipes, Jack, et al., eds. *The Norton Anthology of Children's Literature: The Traditions in English*. New York: Norton, 2005.

Zuidervaart, Lambert. *Adorno's Aesthetic Theory: The Redemption of Illusion*. Cambridge, MA: MIT Press, 1991.

Zusak, Markus. *Fighting Ruben Wolfe*. 2000. Gosford: Scholastic Australia, 2005.

About the Contributors

Michelle Ann Abate is a faculty member in the English Department at Hollins University in Roanoke, Virginia, where she teaches graduate and undergraduate courses in children's and adolescent literature. She is the author of *Tomboys: A Literary and Cultural History*.

Deirdre Baker is Assistant Professor of English at the University of Toronto. Her books include *Becca at Sea* and *A Guide to Canadian Children's Books*. She is children's book reviewer for the *Toronto Star* and a frequent contributor to *The Horn Book Magazine*.

Sandra L. Beckett is Professor of French at Brock University in St. Catharines, Ontario. She is a former president of the International Research Society for Children's Literature. Her books include *Crossover Fiction: Global and Historical Perspectives*; *Red Riding Hood for All Ages: A Fairy-Tale Icon in Cross-Cultural Contexts*; *Recycling Red Riding Hood*; *De grands romanciers écrivent pour les enfants*; *Transcending Boundaries*; and *Reflections of Change: Children's Literature since 1945*.

David Booth is Chair of Literacy at Nipissing University in North Bay, Ontario, and Professor Emeritus and Scholar in Residence at the Ontario Institute for Studies in Education at the University of Toronto. His latest books include *In Graphic Detail*; *Whatever Happened to Language Arts*; and the series *BoldPrint Kids*.

Clare Bradford is Professor of Literary Studies at Deakin University in Melbourne, Australia. Her books include *Reading Race: Aboriginality in Australian Children's Literature*; *Unsettling Narratives: Postcolonial Readings of Children's Literature*; and (with Kerry Mallan, John Stephens and Robyn McCallum) *New World Orders in Contemporary Children's Literature: Utopian Transformations*.

Elizabeth Bullen is Senior Lecturer in Literary Studies at Deakin University in Victoria, Australia, where she teaches in the children's literature masters program. She is co-author of *Consuming Children: Education, Entertainment, Advertising*.

Mike Cadden is Professor of English, Director of Childhood Studies, and Chair of the Department of English, Foreign Languages, and Journalism at Missouri Western State University. He is author of *Ursula K. Le Guin beyond Genre* and editor of *Telling Children's Stories: Narrative Theory and Children's Literature*.

Julie A. S. Cassidy is Assistant Professor of English at Borough of Manhattan Community College, City University of New York. Her articles include "Transporting Nostalgia: Little Golden Books as Souvenirs of Childhood" and "Fairy Tale Women in 1990s Film." She was also a writer for *Recess!* on National Public Radio.

Beverly Lyon Clark is Professor of English at Wheaton College in Norton, Massachusetts. Her recent work includes *Kiddie Lit: The Cultural Construction of Children's Literature in America* and the Norton Critical Edition of *The Adventures of Tom Sawyer*.

Karen Coats is Professor of English at Illinois State University. She is author of *Looking Glasses and Neverlands: Lacan, Desire, and Subjectivity in Children's Literature*, and co-editor of *The Gothic in Children's Literature: Haunting the Borders* and *Handbook of Research on Children's and Young Adult Literature* (forthcoming).

Hugh Crago is senior lecturer in counseling, University of Western Sydney, Australia. He is co-author (with Maureen Crago) of *Prelude to Literacy*, a landmark study of a preschool child's early encounters with stories, and author of *The Teller and the Tale: How the Old Brain Shapes the Stories We Live to Tell* (forthcoming).

June Cummins is Associate Professor of English and Comparative Literature at San Diego State University. Her published articles range in subject from Beatrix Potter to Harry Potter and are concerned with topics such as ethnicity, feminism, consumerism, and national identities. She is writing a biography of Sydney Taylor.

Debra Dudek is Lecturer in English Literatures and Deputy Director of the Centre for Canadian-Australian Studies at the University of Wollongong in New South Wales, Australia. She has published internationally on Australian, Canadian, and children's literature. In her current research, she analyses discourses and representations of social justice in children's literature.

Richard Flynn is Professor of Literature at Georgia Southern University. He edited the *Children's Literature Association Quarterly* from 2004 to 2009.

Elisabeth Rose Gruner is Associate Professor of English and Women, Gender and Sexuality Studies at the University of Richmond, where she also coordinates the first-year seminar program. Her essays on children's literature have appeared in *The Lion and the Unicorn* and *Children's Literature*; her current research is on education, fantasy, and intertextuality in children's and young adult literature

Marah Gubar is Associate Professor of English and Director of the Children's Literature Program at the University of Pittsburgh. Her book *Artful Dodgers: Reconceiving the Golden Age of Children's Literature* was chosen as a *Times Higher Education* "Book of the Week" in 2009.

Kelly Hager is Associate Professor of English and Women's and Gender Studies at Simmons College in Boston. She is the author of *Dickens and the Rise of Divorce* and a contributor to *The Oxford Handbook of Children's Literature*; *The American Child: A Cultural Studies Reader*; and *The Oxford Encyclopedia of Children's Literature*.

A. Waller Hastings is Associate Professor and Chair of the Department of Humanities at West Liberty University in West Virginia. He has previously written on Disney animation, the writings of L. Frank Baum, and other children's books.

Erica Hateley teaches children's and adolescent literature at Queensland University of Technology in Brisbane, Australia. She is the author of *Shakespeare in Children's Literature: Gender and Cultural Capital*.

Charles Hatfield is Associate Professor of English at California State University, Northridge. He is the author of *Alternative Comics: An Emerging Literature*, the forthcoming *The Burning Hand: The Comic Art of Jack Kirby*, and numerous articles on comics and children's culture.

Michael Heyman is Associate Professor of English at the Berklee College of Music in Boston. He is the lead editor of *The Tenth Rasa: An Anthology of Indian Nonsense* and is currently working on the *Anthology of World Nonsense* with Kevin Shortsleeve.

Peter Hollindale was Reader in English and Educational Studies at the University of York. His publications include *Ideology and the Children's Book*; *Signs of Childness in Children's Books*; and editions of both the prose and dramatic texts of *Peter Pan*.

Peter Hunt is Professor Emeritus in Children's Literature at Cardiff University. He has published 23 books and 130 articles and is currently editing *Alice's Adventures in Wonderland*; *The Wind in the Willows*; *The Secret Garden*; and *Treasure Island* for Oxford University Press's World's Classics series.

Michael Joseph is Rare Books Librarian at Rutgers University in New Brunswick, New Jersey, and author of *The True History of Puss in Boots*; *A Teaching Guide to The Norton Anthology of Children's Literature*; and *Lynd Ward's Last, Unfinished, Graphic Novel*.

Kenneth Kidd is Associate Professor of English at the University of Florida. He is associate editor of *The Children's Literature Association Quarterly*, author of *Making American Boys*, and co-editor of *Wild Things: Children's Literature and Ecocriticism*.

Kerry Mallan is Professor at Queensland University of Technology, Australia. Her books include *Gender Dilemmas in Children's Fiction* and *New World Orders in Contemporary Children's Literature: Utopian Transformations* (with C. Bradford, J. Stephens, and R. McCallum). She is co-editor of *Papers: Explorations into Children's Literature*.

Michelle Martin, Associate Professor of English at Clemson University in South Carolina, teaches children's and young adult literature. The author of *Brown Gold: Milestones of African-American Children's Picture Books, 1845–2002*, she is working on a book titled *Dream Keepers for Children of the Sun: The Children's Literature of Arna Bontemps and Langston Hughes*.

Jay Mechling is Professor Emeritus of American Studies at the University of California, Davis. His book *On My Honor: Boy Scouts and the Making of American Youth* reflects his ongoing interest in the folk cultures of children and adolescents.

Cathryn M. Mercier is Professor of Children's Literature and English and directs The Center for the Study of Children's Literature and its MA and MFA degree programs at Simmons College in Boston. She chaired the 2009 Laura Ingalls Wilder Committee and recently published *Russell Freedman*, her third co-authored biocritical study.

William Moebius is Professor and Program Director of Comparative Literature at the University of Massachusetts Amherst. His publications include poetry in *Elegies and Odes* and elsewhere, translations of Philodemus (*Greek Anthology*), of Sophocles' *Oedipus at Colonus*, and book chapters in French and English on the picture book.

Philip Nel is Professor of English and Director of Kansas State University's Program in Children's Literature. His most recent books are *Tales for Little Rebels* (co-edited with Julia Mickenberg); *The Annotated Cat*; and *Dr. Seuss: American Icon*. His critical biography of Crockett Johnson and Ruth Krauss is forthcoming.

Claudia Nelson is Professor of English at Texas A&M University. Her books include *Boys Will Be Girls: The Feminine Ethic and British Children s Fiction, 1857–1917*; *Invisible Men: Fatherhood in Victorian Periodicals, 1850–1910*; *Little Strangers: Portrayals of Adoption in America, 1850–1929*; and *Family Ties in Victorian England*.

Nathalie op de Beeck is Associate Professor of English and Director of Children's Literature coursework at Pacific Lutheran University in Tacoma, Washington. Her books include *Little Machinery: A Critical Facsimile Edition* and a forthcoming volume on American picture books and modernity.

Elizabeth Parsons is Senior Lecturer in Literary Studies at Deakin University, Melbourne, Australia, where she coordinates the undergraduate children's literature program. She has published widely on contemporary picture books, junior and young adult fiction, and children's film from a cultural politics perspective.

Lissa Paul is Professor of Education at Brock University. She is the author of *Reading Otherways* and *The Children's Book Business*, associate general editor of the *Norton Anthology of Children's Literature*, and was an editor of the journal *The Lion and the Unicorn*.

Philip Pullman lives in Oxford, England. He was once a teacher and has always been a writer. He is the author of the *His Dark Materials* trilogy and the fairy tales *Clockwork*, *I was a Rat!*, and *The Scarecrow and His Servant*.

Jacqueline Reid-Walsh is Associate Professor in Education and Women's Studies at The Pennsylvania State University, where she specializes in children's literature and girlhood studies. She is co-editor of *Girl Culture: An Encyclopedia* and founding editor of *Girlhood Studies: An Interdisciplinary Journal*.

Mavis Reimer is Canada Research Chair in the Culture of Childhood at the University of Winnipeg, coauthor of the third edition of *The Pleasures of Children's Literature*, editor of the scholarly collection *Home Words: Discourses of Children's Literature in Canada*, and senior editor of the journal *Jeunesse: Young People, Texts, Cultures*.

Kimberley Reynolds is Professor of Children's Literature in the School of English Literature, Language and Linguistics at Newcastle University. She was President of the International Research Society for Children's Literature (2003–7). Recent publications include *Radical Children's Literature: Future Visions and Aesthetic Transformations* and *Children's Literature Studies: A Handbook to Research* (co-editor).

David Rudd is Professor of Children's Literature at the University of Bolton (UK), where he administers the master's program in Children's Literature and Culture. He is best known for his monograph *Enid Blyton and the Mystery of Children's Literature* . Most recently he edited the *Routledge Companion to Children's Literature*.

Karen Sánchez-Eppler is Professor of American Studies and English at Amherst College. The author of *Touching Liberty: Abolition, Feminism and the Politics of the Body* and *Dependent States: The Child's Part in Nineteenth-Century American Culture*, she is also one of the founding co-editors of the *Journal of the History of Childhood and Youth*.

Phillip Serrato is Assistant Professor of English and Comparative Literature at San Diego State University. His areas of interest include Chicano/a children's and adolescent literature.

Kevin Shortsleeve is Assistant Professor of English at Christopher Newport University in Virginia. He is the author of several children's books, including *13 Monsters Who Should Be Avoided*. He has published academic studies on Edward Gorey, Walt Disney, and Dr. Seuss (forthcoming).

Stephen Slemon teaches postcolonial studies at the University of Alberta. He writes on postcolonial theory and culture in the age of the corporate academy. His current research project pertains to mountaineeering literature in the context of globalization, race, and gender.

Katharine Capshaw Smith is Associate Professor of African American Literature and Children's Literature at the University of Connecticut. She is the author of *Children's Literature of the Harlem Renaissance*, which won the 2006 Book Award from the Children's Literature Association. She is editor of the *Children's Literature Association Quarterly*.

Angela Sorby is Associate Professor of English at Marquette University in Milwaukee. Her books include *Bird Skin Coat: Poems*; *Schoolroom Poets: Childhood, Performance, and the Place of American Poetry 1865–1917*; and *Distance Learning*.

Margaret Meek Spencer is Reader Emeritus in the University of London Institute of Education. Her publications as author, editor, and contributor include *The Cool Web*; *Learning to Read*; *On Being Literate*; *How Texts Teach What Readers Learn*; and *Information and Book Learning*. Her research affiliations are with the Department of Education at the University of Cambridge and The Centre for Language in Primary Education.

Lee A. Talley is Associate Professor of English at Rowan University in Glassboro, New Jersey. She is the editor of Broadview's edition of Anne Brontë's *The Tenant of Wildfell Hall* and has published essays on the Brontës, Jamaica Kincaid, and Jeanette Winterson.

Joseph T. Thomas, Jr., is Associate Professor of English and Comparative Literature at San Diego State University. He is the author of *Strong Measures* and *Poetry's Playground: The Culture of Contemporary American Children's Poetry*, which was named a 2007 Honor Book by the Children's Literature Association.

Eric L. Tribunella is Assistant Professor of English at the University of Southern Mississippi. He is the author of *Melancholia and Maturation: The Use of Trauma in American Children's Literature*.

Jo-Ann Wallace is Chair of the Women's Studies Program and Professor of English and Film Studies at the University of Alberta. A commitment to feminist literary history informs her research across the fields of late-nineteenth and early-twentieth-century literatures.

Index